Majdanek

Koszary SS

Koszary SS

wjazd do Komendy

Komenda obozu

Politische Abteilung

poczta

Thuman Abteilung III

I
e Krematorium
II
III
IV
chonfeld reglowe
V

VI

Kamienio Zong

Lagergut

Jerzy Kwiatkowski
sporządził więzień Nr 8830

Legenda

xxxx Grosse Postenkette warty stojące w dzien
ooo Kleine Postenkette warty stojące w nocy

barak Nr 1 Effektenkammer Nr 2 stajnia
Nr 3 Ławce Nr 4 SS Küche Nr 5 garaże

□ wieże strażnicze ⇑ Blockführerstube

rowy z trupami

nowe Krematorium

485 DAYS AT MAJDANEK

485
DAYS AT
MAJDANEK

JERZY KWIATKOWSKI

INTRODUCTION BY
Norman M. Naimark

TRANSLATION BY
Nicholas Siekierski and Witold Wojtaszko

HOOVER INSTITUTION PRESS

STANFORD UNIVERSITY | STANFORD, CALIFORNIA

With its eminent scholars and world-renowned library and archives, the Hoover Institution seeks to improve the human condition by advancing ideas that promote economic opportunity and prosperity, while securing and safeguarding peace for America and all mankind. The views expressed in its publications are entirely those of the authors and do not necessarily reflect the views of the staff, officers, or Board of Overseers of the Hoover Institution.

hoover.org

Hoover Institution Press Publication No. 715

Hoover Institution at Leland Stanford Junior University, Stanford, California 94305-6003

First printing 2020

27 26 25 24 23 22 21 20   7 6 5 4 3 2 1

Manufactured in the United States of America
Printed on acid-free, archival-quality paper

Library of Congress Cataloging-in-Publication Data

Names: Kwiatkowski, Jerzy, 1894–1980, author. | Naimark, Norman M., writer of introduction. | Siekierski, Nicholas, translator. | Wojtaszko, Witold, translator.
Title: 485 days at Majdanek / Jerzy Kwiatkowski ; introduction by Norman M. Naimark ; translation by Nicholas Siekierski and Witold Wojtaszko.
Other titles: 485 dni na Majdanku. English | Four hundred eighty-five days at Majdanek | Hoover Institution Press publication ; 715.
Description: Stanford, California : Hoover Institution Press, 2021. | Series: Hoover Institution Press publication ; No. 715 | Translation of: 485 dni na Majdanku. Originally published: Lublin : Wydawnictwo Lubelskie, 1966. | Includes bibliographical references and index. | Summary: "In its first English translation, Jerzy Kwiatkowski's memoir of surviving a sixteen-month internment at Majdanek concentration camp forms a rich documentary record of one of the Third Reich's most horrific camps"— Provided by publisher.
Identifiers: LCCN 2020039199 (print) | LCCN 2020039200 (ebook) | ISBN 9780817924140 (cloth) | ISBN 9780817924164 (epub) | ISBN 9780817924171 (mobi) | ISBN 9780817924188 (pdf)
Subjects: LCSH: Kwiatkowski, Jerzy, 1894-1980. | Majdanek (Concentration camp) | Concentration camps—Poland—Lublin. | Concentration camp inmates—Poland—Lublin—Biography. | Holocaust, Jewish (1939-1945)—Poland—Personal narratives.
Classification: LCC D805.5.M35 K94 2021 (print) | LCC D805.5.M35 (ebook) | DDC 940.53/18092 [B]—dc23
LC record available at https://lccn.loc.gov/2020039199
LC ebook record available at https://lccn.loc.gov/2020039200

Contents

II

III

Foreword

It is with great pleasure that the Hoover Institution Library & Archives has collaborated with the State Museum at Majdanek (Państwowe Muzeum na Majdanku) and Hoover Institution Press to publish *485 Days at Majdanek*. Drawn from an original typescript held in the Jerzy Kwiatkowski papers at Hoover, this World War II memoir recounts the experience of a prisoner at one of Nazi Germany's largest and most notorious concentration camps in Poland: *Konzentrationslager* (KL) Lublin, known informally to locals as Majdanek.

Kwiatkowski's memoir of his incarceration at Majdanek, rich in details documenting the infrastructure and routines of daily life, provides one of the most historically significant accounts of the realities of hard labor, violence, war crimes, and mass extermination in a Nazi war camp. The volume was called into evidence in the trials of Nazi guards from KL Lublin; has been discussed in the United States Congress; and has been used in classes and educational programs to teach students about the history of the Second World War, the excesses of authoritarian rule, and the precedents for current laws and policies concerning crimes against humanity. With this, the first English-language edition of *485 Days at Majdanek*, Kwiatkowski's account of life at KL Lublin is poised to reach a global audience. The book serves as a sober and timely reminder of the importance of maintaining free and open societies where all individuals, despite differences in race, nationality, religion, sexual orientation, or political persuasion, are treated with respect and protected from persecution.

The successful publication of the English-language edition of *485 Days at Majdanek* is due in large part to the dedication and vision of Dr. Maciej

Siekierski, who for nearly three decades has held the position of curator for European collections at Hoover Institution Library & Archives and who recently took the title senior curator emeritus. An expert on Polish history and politics, Dr. Siekierski has vastly expanded Polish holdings at Hoover, making our archives a research hub and a necessary destination for scholars from all over the world.

The Jerzy Kwiatkowski papers, acquired by Hoover in 1975, join the ranks of the collections of such notable Polish historical figures as Jan Karski, one of the most important resistance fighters of World War II; Polish Army General Władysław Anders; and August Zaleski, president of the Polish government in exile during the war. Across a long and storied career, Siekierski has transformed the Hoover Archives into perhaps the world's most important center of scholarship concerning the experiences of Poland and Poles during the war. This publication, as well as hundreds of Polish collections now accessible in the Hoover Archives reading room, is a manifestation of Siekierski's unwavering dedication to preserving the record of history. We thank Siekierski wholeheartedly for his years of service and his expertise as a scholar, curator, colleague, and friend.

Many additional colleagues dedicated time, knowledge, and tireless effort to the undertaking of producing this volume. Our colleagues at Hoover Press guided the process of transforming a nearly seventy-five-year-old manuscript from archival treasure to beautiful bound book: we thank them for their patience and powers of organization. Dorota Niedziałkowska, our colleague at the State Museum at Majdanek, has been an indispensable editor and promoter of the project, and an endless resource of knowledge about Kwiatkowski's life and the history of Majdanek. She guided the creation of this manuscript to reflect its author's original intent, supplementing the contents of the previous published edition, which was heavily censored, with the text from Kwiatkowski's original typescripts, stored on-site at the Hoover Archives. Wojciech Lenarczyk further provided a historian's perspective, creating a biographical and historical introduction that has been an indispensable resource for readers of the Polish edition, including the author of the introduction to this English-language edition, Norman M. Naimark, and contributing footnotes for Kwiatkowski's text that provide important context.

Hoover Archives curatorial assistant and expert on Polish collections Gerardina Małgorzata Szudelski spent countless hours poring over the manuscript of the memoir and also the accompanying letters, photographs, and drawings in the Jerzy Kwiatkowski collection. Finally, Nicholas Siekierski provided his valuable skills for the translation, editing, and development of the overall presentation of the volume.

Our thanks also go to every Hoover Library & Archives staff member who works indefatigably to collect, preserve, and make available the world's most significant materials related to war, revolution, and peace movements across the globe, and to the many donors and supporters who make scholarly projects such as the publication of *485 Days at Majdanek* possible. Collections and memoirs such as those of Jerzy Kwiatkowski continue to teach, warn, and inform. This volume stands testament to our founding mission to provide unfettered access to the record of history, that we may learn its valuable lessons for the present and future.

Eric Wakin
Deputy Director
Research Fellow
Director of Library & Archives
Hoover Institution, Stanford University

A Note from the
State Museum at Majdanek

"One of the most important accounts about Majdanek"; "a mine of information about the camp"—with these and similar statements made about *485 Days at Majdanek*, we encourage you to read this book if you are interested in learning the history of the German concentration camp that functioned in Lublin from 1941 to 1944. For newly hired employees of the State Museum at Majdanek (Państwowe Muzeum na Majdanku), which has been taking care of the remnants of the camp and documenting its history since 1944, this is required reading, regardless of position. The memoir of former prisoner Jerzy Kwiatkowski (1894–1980), a representative of the Polish intelligentsia from the Eastern Borderlands of the Second Polish Republic, contains valuable information for historians and museum guides as well as archivists and art historians documenting artifacts from the camp.

This text holds a special place in the collections of the State Museum at Majdanek, whose holdings total more than 1,100 accounts and memoirs, first of all because of its content, but also due to the history of its creation, its form, and the biography of the author himself. Many historians and scholars recognize it as one of the most important autobiographical sources describing the tragic fate of Poles under German occupation in the years of the Second World War.

So what makes this such a unique account? Let's start with the observation that the testimonies of Holocaust survivors and former prisoners of Nazi concentration camps not only record and reconstruct past events but also reveal profiles of the authors—the ways in which they perceived and experienced the situations described. In their memoirs they generally appear in a dual role: as both eyewitness and narrator. It happens that these perspectives can blur into each other, which can reduce the documentary value of their text, particularly when it is written many years after the end of the war.

Kwiatkowski's book, however, is different. His account has the character of a diary. He started writing it shortly after regaining his freedom, in 1945, with the facts, dates, names, and multiplicity of details concerning daily life of the camp—and the enormity of crimes committed by the Germans—fresh in his memory. He precisely memorized them over the course of his entire stay in Majdanek, for 485 days.

The intention of his memoir was to serve as an indictment. That's why he wanted to commit all of the "facts and names" to paper, aiming for "photographic precision of not only facts, but also [his] feelings and mental reactions at the time." He accomplished this intention in full. Thanks to this he constructed a narrative in which, on the one hand, he appears as the meticulous chronicler of KL Lublin, endowed with a phenomenal memory and exceptional observational ability; while on the other he is a tremendously erudite commentator, critical in his judgments, who, despite the dramatic circumstances and experiences, maintains his distance from the reality described. In this, he doesn't concentrate solely on his own situation and experiences but renders the overall reality of the camp, recalls the most important events, analyzes the mutual relations between prisoners, shows the fates of his fellow prisoners, and piercingly profiles the cruelest members of the SS camp. He dedicates much attention to presenting the tragedy of the Jews, whom the SS men treated with absolute brutality and murdered in great numbers in the gas chambers. In effect, we get a broad and at the same time detailed panorama of the camp, as well as a study of it as a total institution and a space of extreme experiences.

We owe these unquestionable cognitive merits of 485 Days at Majdanek to the origin, education, and personality of Jerzy Kwiatkowski. He spent his childhood and school years in multicultural Czernowitz (Chernivtsi), the hometown of Paul Celan, author of "Death Fugue," a poem iconic to the memory of the Holocaust. Out of the family home, Kwiatkowski carried with him a patriotic upbringing and engagement in social matters. He was splendidly educated (becoming a doctor of law), and he fluently commanded several languages. His knowledge of German led to him being moved by the SS to work in the camp office in November 1943. There, his military experiences from the First World War turned out to be useful: completing a cipher course and serving as a liaison officer responsible for gathering numerical data. As a consequence, his memoir of Majdanek contains precise descriptions of the functioning of the camp administration, the documents it used, and its method of keeping files, as well as a lot of information concerning various prisoner categories and statistics, which could only be accessed by members of the headquarters staff.

The reliability of the source and the profusion of details about KL Lublin are highly valued by historians today. Testifying to this are the very positive reviews of the first edition of *485 Days at Majdanek* and the numerous references in academic publications to Kwiatkowski as a witness to history. It suffices to mention that the authors of *Majdanek 1941–1944*, the comprehensive monograph fundamental to learning the history of the camp, published in 1991, refer to him as many as 173 times.

In my research I have also often reached for the memoir of prisoner 8830—the number under which Jerzy Kwiatkowski was registered into the camp in March 1943. I most utilized his information in an article analyzing the mortality of those deported to Majdanek, the abbreviated version of which appeared in *Yad Vashem Studies* in 2007.

Kwiatkowski's memoir came into being in Germany. The author was liberated there on May 3, 1945, by American soldiers during an evacuation march of prisoners from KL Sachsenhausen, where he had ended up via Auschwitz in August 1944. By the end of 1949, he had emigrated to the United States. He had long strived for the publication of his memoir, first in Great Britain and in the United States (unfortunately without success) and then in Poland. It didn't happen in his homeland for various reasons—mainly resulting from the realities of the then Communist-controlled state—until 1966.

Exactly three years later, Kwiatkowski's account was presented in the forum of the House of Representatives of the US Congress. The author had desired for it to be published in English, but the lack of funds for its translation thwarted these plans.

The book enjoyed great popularity among Polish readers and was eagerly purchased by visitors to the State Museum at Majdanek. In 1988, already after Kwiatkowski's death, a second edition came out from the Wydawnictwo Lubelskie (Lublin Publisher) in a large print run of thirty thousand copies.

Three decades later, a new edition of the memoir of the "gardener from field 3" (as Kwiatkowski was called in the camp due to the function he performed in his first months there) was prepared and published by the State Museum at Majdanek. We utilized our own archival material as well as the documentary legacy deposited by the author in the Hoover Institution Library & Archives at Stanford University. Thanks to the cooperation between both institutions, we were able to publish the version closest to the original manuscript from 1945—free from the intervention, censorship, and content changes that the text was subject to at different stages of the editorial process in the 1960s. And precisely this edition from 2018, prepared for print through scholarship and editing by employees of the State Museum, Wojciech Lenarczyk, and Dorota Niedziałkowska, constitutes the basis for the American edition.

I feel great happiness that together we are fulfilling the will of Jerzy Kwiatkowski and are placing his work in the hands of readers in the United States. There is a symbolic dimension to the fact that this is occurring eighty years after the establishment of *Konzentrationslager* Lublin— one of the largest concentration camps erected in Europe by the Third Reich, about which *New York Times* correspondent William H. Lawrence wrote on August 30, 1944: "I have just seen the most terrible place on the face of the earth."

I sincerely thank all of the individuals and institutions who contributed to the creation of this publication. Special thanks is directed to the Hoover Institution, our organization's main partner in the realization of this publication project, so important to us all.

Tomasz Kranz
Director of the State Museum at Majdanek

A Note from the
Hoover Library & Archives

How unique and valuable collections find their way into the Hoover Institution Library & Archives is often a compelling story in itself. In the case of Jerzy Kwiatkowski's papers, the link to Hoover was a connection to the family of Witold Sworakowski, the curator of the Polish and Eastern European collections and later the associate director of the Hoover Institution (1947–68). Compatriots raised in Bukovina, Sworakowski in Suceava (born in 1903) and Kwiatkowski in Czernowitz (born in 1894 in Vienna), their fathers undoubtedly knew each other well, both as high-ranking civil servants in the administration of the easternmost crown land of the Austro-Hungarian empire and as Polish community activists. For a time, Sworakowski attended the university in Czernowitz (Chernivtsi); their nine-year age difference rather ruled out childhood acquaintance, but they undoubtedly knew each other very well before the Second World War.

As far as their postwar contacts, it cannot be ruled out that Sworakowski, who settled in California in 1947, played some role in Kwiatkowski's emigration to the United States, where he settled in Chicago in 1950. They may have shared a mutual acquaintance with Melchior Wańkowicz, the war correspondent for the Polish Armed Forces in the West, who visited both the Hoover Institution and Kwiatkowski in Chicago in 1956.

Unfortunately, archivists seldom think about their own personal archives. I was able to track down just two letters from Kwiatkowski to Sworakowski from 1971 (they surely were friends; Kwiatkowski used the familiar "Dear Witold"), which included correspondence between

Kwiatkowski's father and Archbishop of Lwów (L'viv) Józef Bilczewski, who was canonized as a saint in 2005. Kwiatkowski also sent Sworakowski his Majdanek memoir, copies of reviews, and a large map of the camp (the same one in the book). This was a fascinating snapshot from the Polish émigré world of New York, where Kwiatkowski spent the last years of his life.

The rest of Kwiatkowski's archive ultimately arrived at Stanford in 1975–76—ten large cartons—but was regrettably not repacked in accordance with the accompanying inventory of its contents, which made it practically impossible to make immediate use of the collection. By this time, Sworakowski was already retired and served only as a consultant to the director.

The collection was received and partially unpacked but not organized. It wasn't a priority, as the first edition of Kwiatkowski's book was already an accomplished fact (it was published in Poland in 1966), and it did not seem like there would be a second. Polish and Jewish suffering at the hands of the Third Reich was not a totally neglected subject in the People's Republic of Poland—for the Polish diaspora, matters of the country's enslavement by Soviet Russia and the Gehenna of Poles in the east were more relevant—but these were blank spots as seen by the Polish emigrant community and Witold Sworakowski.

It was not until 2018, when I was contacted by Dr. Dorota Niedziałkowska, from the Exhibition Department of the State Museum at Majdanek, that the proper importance was assigned to Jerzy Kwiatkowski. The organization of the collection was accelerated, and access to it was made possible at last. The Kwiatkowski papers were an invaluable resource for the museum, as they include the original typescript of Kwiatkowski's memoir from 1945, upon which the new Polish edition (2018) and this translation are based. Two other typescripts and more than thirty boxes of archival material allowed the museum to achieve its goal of reproducing the author's original text, free from postwar communist censorship and unfounded editorial interference. Far from being simply a reprint of the memoir, the extensive editing and scholarly research undertaken to prepare this work make it the definitive edition of what was already described as not just an astoundingly detailed memoir but a veritable encyclopedia of knowledge about the Majdanek concentration camp. It is a prime example of the particular richness of the Polish collections of the Hoover Institution.

The Polish collections form a significant portion of the Hoover Library & Archives (6,500 total collections, of which around 400 are Polish or mainly concern Poland). The collections relating to the Second World War period are being continuously expanded. Two days before my last visit to Europe, I obtained a very unique album and set of photographs of Hitler's 1938 visit to Italy, along with special glasses for their three-dimensional viewing—a fantastic war trophy of a recently deceased American officer and Second World War veteran. Polish materials from this era are rarer and chiefly concern Polish emigrants in the United States, such as the interesting collection of Jan Jasiewicz (from the POW camp for Polish officers in Murnau, Bavaria) and the large collection of General Wacław Stachiewicz, chief of the General Staff of the Polish Army during the September Campaign of 1939 (from his recently deceased son in Colorado).

The General Władysław Anders Collection, a valuable trove of information for generations of researchers, includes 35,000 testimonies and 14,000 release certificates of former prisoners held in gulag camps. In 2017 the Hoover Library & Archives signed a cooperation agreement with the Witold Pilecki Center for Totalitarian Studies for the transcription, translation, and indexing of these materials, which will paint the full picture of the martyrdom of tens of thousands of the inhabitants of Poland's Eastern Borderlands. Records from the Polish Ministry of Information and Documentation, and the partial records of the Ministry of Justice, served as the basis for the publication of *The Black Book of Poland* (1942), documenting Nazi crimes during the occupation. The first investigation of the Katyń massacre was also based in part on Hoover's collections. The famed courier for the Polish underground, Jan Karski, author of his own wartime memoir, *Story of a Secret State* (1944), not only left his own archive to Hoover but helped secure the Anders Collection (then known as the "Documents Bureau" records) when he worked for the Hoover Library for a year after the war, at the urging of Herbert Hoover himself.

This, the first English translation of *485 Days at Majdanek*, coupled with the new edition in Polish, the first published in free Poland, finally bring the recognition due to the work by Jerzy Kwiatkowski in preserving for history the story of life in Majdanek, and pay tribute to his sense of justice to his friends and other victims. Keeping in line with the mission of the Hoover Library & Archives to provide access to our holdings collected over more than a century, we are proud to make this valuable historical record available to a wider audience than ever before.

Maciej Siekierski
Senior Curator Emeritus of the European Collections
Hoover Institution Library & Archives

Introduction

Norman M. Naimark

The Nazi camp at Majdanek in occupied Poland was a monstrous byproduct of the Germans' ambitions in what they believed was their colonial "East." Reich Leader of the SS (*Schutzstaffel*) Heinrich Himmler and his plenipotentiary in Lublin, Odilo Globocnik, met in the city July 20–21, 1941, and designated an expanse of land five kilometers southeast of the center of Lublin on the road to Zamość and Lwów (today L'viv) as a future camp for twenty-five thousand to fifty thousand prisoners.[1] During the planning stages, the SS envisioned a camp containing 150,000 prisoners, but it never approached anywhere near that size, averaging roughly ten to fifteen thousand inmates at a time.[2] The 567 acres of land they chose bordered a suburb called Majdan Tatarski, and the camp quickly became known as Majdanek ("little Majdan") to the locals and eventually to the prisoners and German administration alike.[3] It was initially named the Waffen-SS Prisoner of War Camp, Lublin, as a way to protect the camp administratively from the

My thanks to Katherine Jolluck, Tomasz Kranz, Dorota Niedziałkowska, Nicholas Siekierski, and Beata Szymkow for their comments on the introduction. Kranz, director of the State Museum at Majdanek, helped in particular with the still difficult issues involving numbers. Thanks, too, to Dorota Niedziałkowska for sending me relevant materials in electronic form from the State Museum at Majdanek.

1. Himmler, "Vermerk," Lublin, July 21, 1941. In *Majdanek w dokumentach*, ed. Wojciech Lenarczyk (Lublin: Państwowe Muzeum na Majdanku, 2016), 37.

2. For the fluctuation in camp size, see Tomasz Kranz, "Lublin-Majdanek," in *Der Ort des Terrors: Geschichte der nationalsozialistischen Konzentrationslager*, eds. Wolfgang Benz and Barbara Distel (Munich: Beck, 2008), 33–84.

3. On the name, see Tomasz Kranz, "Majdanek—Erinnerungsort, Gedenkstätte, Museum," in *Forschendes Lernen in Majdanek: Erfahrungen aus der Projektarbeit* (Schwalbach, Germany: Wochenschau-Verlag, n.d.), 13–14.

local German civilian authorities, but after April 9, 1943, it was designated the KL (*Konzentrationslager*) Lublin, as it was called in official German documents.[4] The camp was in continuous use from October 1941 until its liberation by the Red Army on July 22, 1944. One hundred and fifty thousand people passed through Majdanek's gates, mostly Jews, Poles, and Belarusians, but also representatives of dozens of other European nations.[5] Approximately sixty thousand Jews died there as well as twenty thousand prisoners of other nationalities, mostly Poles.[6]

First and foremost, Majdanek served the shifting purposes of the SS organization headquartered in Lublin. Just as Himmler and Globocnik

4. The change in name was ordered by Himmler on February 16, 1943, and implemented in an order of April 9, 1943. For all practical purposes, the camp can be considered a concentration camp from the beginning until the end.

5. *Więźniowie Majdanka/The Prisoners of Majdanek: Katalog Wystawy/Exhibition Catalogue* (Lublin: Państwowe Muzeum na Majdanku, 2015), 7. Significantly larger numbers were used earlier in the historiography. It is extremely difficult to know the numbers of those who were in Majdanek, given the fact, also described in Kwiatkowski's memoir, that prisoners were given numbers 1 to 20,000. When prisoners died, their names were struck from the books and replaced by another with that number. The records of those who died were incomplete and in many cases were destroyed at the end by the SS. The Jews who were selected for elimination were not registered. For a variety of other reasons, a number of other Majdanek arrivals were also not registered. Transfers from the camp and those who were released were also irregularly registered.

6. Immediately after the liberation of the camp, Soviet commentators estimated that more than a million prisoners were killed at Majdanek. The first scholarly estimate by Zdzisław Łukaszkiewicz in 1948 used the number 360,000, which was considered standard in Poland, Israel, and the West almost until the fall of communism. See Józef Marszałek, *Majdanek: Konzentrationslager Lublin* (Warsaw: Verlag Interpress, 1984), 6. The online *Holocaust Encyclopedia* of the United States Holocaust Memorial Museum states that between October 1943 and January 1945 between 95,000 and 130,000 prisoners died in the Majdanek system, which included several subcamps. Of these prisoners, between 89,000 and 110,000 were Jews. "Lublin/Majdanek Concentration Camp," https://encyclopedia.ushmm.org. The recent standard text by David Engel, *The Holocaust: The Third Reich and the Jews*, 2nd ed. (New York: Pearson, 2013), 66, states that 150,000 Jews were killed in the gas chambers at Majdanek. The newest and most reliable number, which is the one cited in the text, was researched in a foundational article by Tomasz Kranz and is used in most of the contemporary historiography. Tomasz Kranz, "Ewidencja zgonów i śmiertelność więźniów KL Lublin," *Zeszyty Majdanka* 23 (2005): 48–51. An updated English version of the discussion of numbers is in Tomasz Kranz, *Extermination of Jews at Majdanek Concentration Camp* (Lublin: State Museum at Majdanek, 2010), 70–75. See also Czesław Rajca and Anna Wiśniewska, *Majdanek: Concentration Camp*, trans. Anna Zagórska (Lublin: State Museum at Majdanek, 1983), 29.

viewed the city of Lublin and the district surrounding it as the future forward base of the SS empire in the western part of the Soviet Union, Majdanek was to hold a reservoir of slave labor—especially Soviet POWs, Poles, and Jews—that would build the housing, roads, and infrastructure of that empire. The Hitlerian *Generalplan Ost* ("General Plan for the East") called for the vast movement and destruction of peoples (Jews, Slavs, and others) and the implementation of far-reaching plans to construct strategically located German colonies throughout the western periphery of the Soviet Union.[7] Lublin itself would be completely transformed into an SS bastion from which Himmler and his cronies would oversee the "ethno-political" reordering of the east.[8] The city center would be rebuilt, the town would be cleared of its Polish and Jewish inhabitants, and large settlements for SS members and their families would be developed. Moreover, industries would be constructed in and moved to Lublin that would support the transplanted German population and the Waffen-SS fighting men keeping order in the east. Lublin would become the center of SS-run munitions factories, textile production, and food-processing plants, all served by the slave labor from KL Lublin.

One of the most important aspects of the memoir of Jerzy Kwiatkowski is its attention to the Polish story central to the history of the concentration camps, Majdanek in particular.[9] The initial Nazi attack and occupation of Poland included SS plans to eliminate the Polish intelligentsia, in order to decapitate the nation of its leadership: politicians, professors, lawyers, industrialists, clerics, and cultural figures. Tens of thousands of members of the Polish intelligentsia were murdered as a consequence in the

7. For the various formulations of *Generalplan Ost* and their follow-up, the General Settlement Plan, see "Der Generalplan Ost: Dokumentation," *Vierteljahrshefte für Zeitgeschichte* 6, no. 3 (1958): 525; *Vom Generalplan Ost zum Generalsiedlungsplan*, ed. Czesław Madajczyk (Munich: K. G. Saur, 1994), and *Der "Generalplan Ost": Hauptlinien der national-sozialistischen Planungs- und Vernichtungspolitik*, eds. Mechtild Rössler and Sabine Schleiermachter (Berlin: Akad. Verlag, 1993).

8. Peter Longerich, *Heinrich Himmler* (Oxford: Oxford University Press, 2012), 526.

9. This story sometimes gets buried in the enormous and impressive American and West European historiography of the Holocaust, with its inevitable attention to the horrific murder of the Jews. In this connection, Majdanek attracts much less scholarly attention than Auschwitz, which has become the centerpiece of the public memory of the Holocaust.

first months of the war.[10] The idea was to transform the Poles themselves
into a denationalized class of helots, who would serve the Nazi cause as
minimally educated, dutiful laborers. Eventually, according to *Generalplan
Ost*, tens of millions of Poles would be deported east of the Urals to make
room for German colonists. Once Hitler invaded the Soviet Union in June
1941, it became clear to Hans Frank, the leader of the administration in
the *Generalgouvernement* (the central territorial unit of German-occupied
Poland), that as long as the war went on with the Allies, various compro-
mises short of autonomy would have to be made with the Polish people to
assure their passivity under German rule. The growing underground resistance of the Poles to Nazi rule and the concomitant need for Polish labor
in the camps prompted the widespread arrest of Poles suspected of hostility to the Nazis and indiscriminate police roundups of innocent Poles on
city streets. The sharpening armed struggle between the underground and
the Nazis led to the designation of the *Generalgouvernement* as a "bandit
control area," which meant that the security police could deal with alleged
opponents under a martial-law regime. Poles accused of committing any
offense against "the work of German reconstruction" could be shot on
the spot.[11] Tens of thousands of Poles ended up in Majdanek, including
those Poles who were randomly arrested as hostages to be held in repri-
sals for underground actions.[12] Many of the hostages were released, but
some two-thirds of them died in the camp, primarily from disease and
overwork.[13]

Himmler and Globocnik's ideas of turning the Zamość region in the
Lublin district into a model area for German colonialization and "the rec-
lamation of German blood" precipitated the brutal expulsion of 120,000
Poles from their villages and farms. The Nazi strategy was to encircle the
Polish population and "crush [it] to death economically and biologically."[14]

10. Alexander Rossino, *Hitler Strikes Poland: Blitzkrieg, Ideology, and Atrocity* (Lawrence, KS: University of Kansas Press, 2003), 9.

11. Longerich, *Himmler*, 659.

12. According to Marszałek, *Majdanek*, 62, in the first four months of 1942, some twenty thousand Poles were arrested as political prisoners or in street raids and sent to Majdanek.

13. Elizabeth B. White, "Majdanek: Cornerstone of Himmler's SS Empire in the East," in *Simon Wiesenthal Center Annual* 7 (1990): 8.

14. Cited in White, "Majdanek: Cornerstone," 5.

As many as twenty-five thousand Poles fled on their own rather than be deported.[15] Roughly nine thousand Zamość expellees—men, women, and children—were transferred to Majdanek as a way station before being transported to work camps in Germany itself.[16] Many of them died of exhaustion and disease in the camp, including large numbers of children, before the transports could be arranged.[17] Those too old or infirm to work were sometimes released to underprovisioned "retirement" villages elsewhere in the *Generalgouvernement*. The chaos that resulted from the expulsions, the paucity of German colonists interested in moving to the region, and the confrontation with the Polish resistance produced by the Zamość experiment led Josef Goebbels, Hitler's propaganda chief, to denounce it as "massive political idiocy," and to Globocnik losing his position in Lublin and being transferred to Trieste in September 1943.[18]

Majdanek

Like the course of World War II itself, Majdanek was in constant flux. One of the camp's leading historians, Tomasz Kranz, has aptly called Majdanek a "multifunctional Provisorium," changing its character and size depending on the needs of the Nazis and the fortunes of battle.[19] The camp was constantly under construction and was never really finished. At different times and with different constellations of prisoners, Majdanek was a Soviet POW camp, a camp for Jewish laborers, a camp for Polish political prisoners, a camp for Polish hostages, a camp for the elimination of the

15. Halik Kochanski, *The Eagle Unbowed: Poland and the Poles in the Second World War* (Cambridge, MA: Harvard University Press, 2012), 269–70.

16. Dawid Barczyk, "Germanisierungsprozesse in Generalgouvernement am Beispiel 'Aktion Zamość' in der Zamoyszczyzna," in *Forschendes Lernen*, 90.

17. White, "Majdanek: Cornerstone," 8. One-third of them died in Majdanek according to Rajca and Wiśniewska, *Majdanek Concentration Camp*, 15. See also Janina Kiełboń, *Wysiedleńcy z Zamojszczyzny w obozie koncentracyjnym na Majdanku 1943* (Lublin: Państwowe Muzeum na Majdanku, 2006), 29–30. The author states that 1,000 of the 9,000 perished in Majdanek.

18. Mark Mazower, *Hitler's Empire: How the Nazis Ruled Europe* (New York: Penguin, 2008), 214.

19. Tomasz Kranz, "Das KL Lublin—zwischen Planung und Realisierung," in *Die nationalsozialistischen Konzentrationslager: Entwicklung und Struktur*, eds. Ulrich Herbert, Karin Orth, and Christoph Dieckmann (Göttingen, Germany: Wallstein, 1998), 363–89. See also Barbara Schwindt, *Das Konzentrations- und Vernichtungslager Majdanek: Funktionswandel im Kontext der "Endlösung"* (Würzberg, Germany: Königshausen & Neumann, 2005), 17.

Jews, a transit camp for Polish labor to the old Reich, a camp for families of alleged Belarusian and Ukrainian partisans, a camp for the sick and dying from other German concentration camps, and a camp for Soviet invalids. Himmler also set up a women's camp of some five thousand prisoners in October 1942, famous in Polish camp lore for its evening performances of *Radio Majdanek*, an improvised show put on between February and May 1943 by mostly Polish women to announce recent news, sing songs, and host cultural events in a make-believe "world free of beatings and hunger."[20] Himmler planned for a children's camp at Majdanek in March 1943, but it never came to fruition. Instead, children were interspersed throughout the camp, sometimes in the women's camp, sometimes in their own barracks. Unlike most concentration camps, Majdanek did not have an elaborate network of sub-camps. There were only five or six altogether, and these came and went during Majdanek's history.

With the outbreak of the war against the USSR on June 22, 1941, and the alacritous advance of Hitler's armies into the Soviet Union during the summer and fall, Himmler and Globocnik's plans for building the camp were put in motion. It was to comprise five rectilinear "fields," each with two parallel rows of barracks, with extra barracks for washing and kitchens, as well as separate areas for the SS quarters and workshops.[21] There would be twenty-two barracks in all, each of which was to hold in the neighborhood of up to one thousand prisoners. The work began in earnest with the transfer in October 1941 of a construction crew of some two thousand Russian POWs. With a number of Jewish prisoners from the Polish Army and a few Polish prisoners, the POWs were to clear and level the land and build the first barracks. Yet the contingent of Soviet POWs arrived in such bad shape that not only were they unable to do much work, but they also began dying in huge numbers. They had already been terribly mistreated by their *Wehrmacht* captors, who in the first months of the war

20. Marszałek, *Majdanek*, 151. For memoirs of the radio, see Stefania Blonski, "Radio Majdanek Calling," in Rajca and Wiśniewska, *Majdanek: Concentration Camp*, 91–92, and Eugenia Piwińska (1967), in *Majdanek: Obóz koncentracyjny w relacjach więźniów i świadków*, ed. Marta Grudzińska (Lublin: Państwowe Muzeum na Majdanku, 2001), 85. *Więźniowie Majdanka*, p. 48.

21. Kranz, "Majdanek—Erinnerungsort," 14.

purposely left their prisoners in huge outdoor detention camps to expire without food, medicines, or protection from the elements. Oswald Pohl, one of Himmler's chief deputies, wrote that the POW laborers arriving in Majdanek "were in such catastrophic bodily shape that it is impossible to imagine that they can be employed successfully in work tasks."[22] One camp survivor reported that even after coming to the camp the prisoners were fed so poorly they could barely walk and helplessly died in agony and in their own filth.[23] By mid-January 1942, hardly any of the two thousand Soviet POWs initially brought to Majdanek were still alive.[24] Although there were periodic small transports of Soviet POWs to Majdanek throughout the war, the much larger numbers anticipated by the SS were never sent to the camp. The German General Staff used Soviet POWs for their own purposes, and in the spring of 1942, Hitler and his labor officials began to realize that they needed them to replace German industrial workers in the Reich who were bound for the front.[25]

In a propaganda gesture in 1943, the Germans did transfer several thousand Soviet invalids to Majdanek, most without one or more limbs, to spend the rest of the war in a special infirmary barracks and be treated by Soviet medical personnel.[26] These individuals were never formally part of the camp's internal system and were not registered as camp prisoners. When the Soviets liberated the camp on July 22, 1944, they found almost one thousand disabled Soviet POWs (some had been marched away earlier). More than one thousand Polish peasants who had been drafted by the *Wehrmacht* into forced labor fled the camp before the entry of the Soviet troops.[27] Only a few days before the liberation, nine hundred

22. Pohl to Himmler, December 19, 1941, in *Majdanek w dokumentach*, 55.

23. Edward Karabanik (1966), in *Majdanek: Obóz koncentracyjny*, 12.

24. Nikolaus Wachsmann, *KL: A History of the Nazi Concentration Camps* (New York: Farrar, Straus and Giroux, 2015), 283.

25. Omer Bartov, *Hitler's Army: Soldiers, Nazis, and War in the Third Reich* (Oxford: Oxford University Press), 91.

26. Himmler order of January 6, 1943, in *Majdanek w dokumentach*, 99. Here Himmler states that the POWs were to get the same food and accommodations as the other prisoners, but that they should not have access to German prostheses, rather they should be satisfied with the more primitive Russian sorts.

27. Elizabeth White, "Lublin Main Camp (aka Majdanek)," in *Encyclopedia of Camps and Ghettos, 1933–1945*, general ed. Geoffrey P. Megargee, vol. 1, part B (Bloomington and

people were shot near the crematorium, mostly Poles from the Lublin Castle prison and a number of highly skilled Jewish craftsmen who had worked with the *Wehrmacht*.[28]

In the beginning of 1942, Himmler and Globocnik started pressing into service workers from the huge number of Jewish internees in ghettos and camps in the *Generalgouvernement*.[29] They intended to select those Jewish men capable of work to build the new camp and fill the industries and workshops the SS had planned for Lublin. From the very outset, however, there was a fundamental contradiction in Nazi thinking between murdering all the Jews and using them profitably for labor. During the late summer and fall of 1941, the Nazis began to implement what we know of as the Final Solution (*Endlösung*) of the Jewish question, meaning the Jews' complete destruction (*Vernichtung*). The Wannsee Conference of January 1942 drew up interagency plans that would see to it that Europe's Jews would be eliminated from the continent. Already in March 1942, Himmler set out the goals of Operation Reinhard, named after the SS paragon Reinhard Heydrich.[30] With the goal of eliminating the Jews in the *Generalgouvernement* supposedly incapable of hard labor—meaning primarily the elderly, women, and children—Himmler authorized the building of three death camps: Bełżec, Sobibór, and Treblinka. These camps were outfitted with gas chambers to murder the Jews, and this they did with ghastly efficiency.[31] There was no pretense of "selection" in these camps; the Jews in the transports were almost immediately eliminated.

Indianapolis: Indiana University Press, in association with the United States Holocaust Memorial Museum, 2009), 877. Available at https://www.ushmm.org/research/publications/encyclopedia-camps-ghettos/download.

28. Kranz, *Extermination of Jews*, 69.

29. Himmler's telegram of January 25, 1942, in *Majdanek w dokumentach*, 88. Here he orders in typically grandiose fashion that 150,000 Jewish men and women were to be transported in the following weeks to Majdanek.

30. The operation is also variously referred to in the literature as Operation Reinhardt. Heydrich was assassinated by Czech commandos in Prague on May 29, 1942.

31. Altogether in Operation Reinhard, 1,274,666 Jews were killed. Of the two million Jews who lived in the territory of what became the *Generalgouvernement* in 1939, only 297,914 remained. Dariusz Libionka, *Zagłada Żydów w Generalnym Gubernatorstwie: zarys problematyki* (Lublin: Państwowe Muzeum na Majdanku, 2017), 179. White, "Lublin Main Camp," 877.

More than 400,000 Jews were killed in Bełżec, 180,000 in Sobibór, and at least 700,000 in Treblinka.[32]

Majdanek and Auschwitz-Birkenau served as mixed-purpose camps, both as labor camps and as death camps outfitted with gas chambers and crematoria, though Majdanek, with a death toll of some sixty thousand Jews and twenty thousand Poles and prisoners of other nationalities, never came close to the killing function of Auschwitz-Birkenau, whose dead numbered almost one million Jews and some seventy-five thousand Poles.[33] Even for those Jews who remained alive to work in camps like Majdanek, the end was near. As Himmler noted to the armed forces (October 9, 1942): "Our goal will be to replace the Jewish work force with Poles and, when possible, collect a large number of those Jewish shops in concentration camps/factories in the east of the *Generalgouvernement*. Yet, even there, one day the Jew shall disappear, in accordance with the wishes of the *Führer*."[34]

The idea of forced labor as applied to the allegedly inferior nations (Jews, Poles, and others), but in practice to all prisoners, was to work the inmates to death, *Vernichtung durch Arbeit*. This meant that workers would labor under the harsh conditions of living with minimal sustenance until they dropped dead and would be replaced by new ones.[35] With so many Jews and Slavs under their control, the SS leaders calculated that they had access to unlimited reserves of labor. As a result, the work in Majdanek and elsewhere in the vast concentration-camp system could never be performed efficiently and well, since the prisoners themselves were undernourished and weak, struggling to stay alive from day to day, given meager diets, and exposed to the incessant cold in winter and heat in summer. The prisoners had to survive in frightful hygienic conditions, which promoted widespread disease, especially typhus and dysentery, not to mention all kinds of skin, bone, and organ maladies. The SS intentionally designed the

32. Timothy Snyder, *Bloodlands: Europe between Hitler and Stalin* (New York: Basic Books, 2010), 275. Updated figures from Tomasz Kranz. Communication of July 16, 2020.

33. The numbers for Auschwitz are those used by the United States Holocaust Memorial Museum. "Auschwitz," https://encyclopedia.ushmm.org.

34. Cited in Kranz, *Extermination of Jews*, 19.

35. See Longerich, *Himmler*, 560.

camp system to punish, dehumanize, and brutalize the prisoners to such an extent that their spirit was sapped and their will to live was demolished. This was much worse than modern slavery, as a number of scholars have noted.[36] Slave owners would keep their workers reasonably healthy and fed, so that they could effectively perform their duties. The regime of work in the concentration camp never lived up to that standard, even when the SS, through a series of orders, formally tried to improve conditions from mid-1943 on as a way to build labor reserves.

Majdanek was particularly primitive in this connection. It was one of the last camps established and one of those located furthest to the east.[37] It had been built from scratch with cast-off materials, slave labor, and insufficient attention. Even though Himmler had grand designs for its future, the camp never assumed either the key labor functions of many other camps or the major role in the Final Solution played by the purely death camps (or the mixed-function Auschwitz-Birkenau). On the outskirts of Lublin, Majdanek was off the main rail lines, so that trucks and buses had to be used for transporting materials (and sometimes prisoners) in and out. The local German civilian administration in Lublin was more concerned with its own needs than those of the SS and was a constant source of problems for Globocnik and the camp's commandants, especially when it came to controlling the assignments of Polish and Jewish labor.[38] Prisoners who arrived from other camps routinely noted how backward the conditions at Majdanek were.[39]

Once the fortunes of war turned against the *Wehrmacht* in the fall and winter of 1942–43 and the Soviets were able to not only stabilize the front but engage in counterattacks, the expected boom in construction and industrial production that the SS had counted on for the Lublin

36. See, for example, Wolfgang Sofsky, *The Order of Terror: The Concentration Camp* (Princeton: Princeton University Press, 1997), 22.

37. Koslov believes that the particularly harsh conditions in Majdanek can be seen as an explanation for the exceptionally brutal behavior of both the male and female overseers. Elissa Mailänder Koslov, "'Going East': Colonial Experiences and Practices of Violence among Female and Male Majdanek Camp Guards (1941–44)," *Journal of Genocide Research* 10, no. 4 (December 2008): 563.

38. Libionka, *Zagłada Żydów*, 95.

39. See *Majdanek w dokumentach*, 120.

region, including Majdanek, was delayed because of pressing military priorities. The railways would not be able to deliver materials for new installations, and labor, with the exception of that directly available in the camps, would be used for military purposes, not for those of the SS. The result was that the barracks in Majdanek were substandard, even for the SS-run concentration camps; medical supplies were limited to a few easily available remedies; and local camp construction projects predominated, meaning physically exhausted prisoners were outside all day exposed to the elements, instead of having factory or workshop jobs, which would have allowed them to be usually indoors with some heat in the frigid winters. Frequently, there was not enough "real" work to be done, so the overseers forced prisoners to move stones from one location to another, dig and re-dig ditches, and break up boulders into gravel for no reason.

Majdanek suffered in particular from problems with the water supply. The original wells on the site were polluted, and the water was undrinkable. Those prisoners who drank the water because they could no longer stand being parched with thirst came down with fierce bouts of typhoid fever and dysentery and often died. Baths were unthinkable in the first year of the camp's existence and it was even impossible for the prisoners to wash their faces, not to mention launder the rags that served as their clothes. The situation changed only when Majdanek was hooked up to the Lublin water system in mid-1943, though the water did not begin to flow until the fall.[40] Even then, the water connections with the city frequently broke down, leaving the camp to deal with the impossible sanitary conditions and the acrid smell of buildings and barracks. For a month in midsummer 1943, the camp commander shut down the water pumps to the barracks because of water shortages in the city of Lublin.

Given the fact that the prisoners were unable to wash their bodies and clean their clothes, and with Majdanek's disgusting hygienic conditions regarding human waste, typhus—one of the biggest killers in the camp—spread with alacrity, frightening even the SS bosses, who sometimes refused to venture onto the grounds. It was almost impossible to be

40. White, "Majdanek: Cornerstone," 14.

rid of the contagion of typhus-bearing lice under these conditions. The barracks where typhus prisoners were isolated—there was no need to guard them, since the prisoners could barely crawl—were simply way stations to the gas chambers. The same applied to the typhus section of the Revier (hospital), where the German overseers periodically selected out the most pathetic-looking patients for elimination. Early on in the camp's history, typhus-infected prisoners were simply shot as a way to control the spread of the disease. So many corpses accumulated that not all could be burned in the crematorium. Many of the typhus victims were burned on open pyres or buried in mass graves in the Krępiecki Forest, just outside the camp. Only at the end of 1943 were the authorities able to run a sewer line to the barracks and build halfway decent bathrooms and sanitary facilities, which quickly reduced the danger of another typhus epidemic.[41] According to figures that Otto Pohl presented to Himmler in August of 1943, Majdanek was the most deadly concentration camp in the system, with ten times the likelihood of prisoner death than in Buchenwald.[42] The figures are somewhat distorted by the fact that sick prisoners from other camps were sent to Majdanek at this time to die.

The system of camp administration, designed already in the mid-1930s in Dachau and introduced into Majdanek by SS veterans, was diabolical in the extreme; one could find no match in Dante's hell itself with the consummate brutality of the KL Lublin.[43] The SS leadership of the camp and the soldiers who guarded and operated it were big parts of the problem. Sadistic SS overseers like Anton Thumann, who roamed the camp with a vicious German shepherd looking for victims (and was hanged by the British in 1946 for his near-daily crimes), and Hildegard Lächert, "bloody Brigitta," who was tried for torturing and brutalizing her female charges in

41. *Majdanek w dokumentach*, 120.

42. Wachsmann, *KL: A History*, 426. In 1943, writes Elizabeth White, Majdanek's official mortality rate—excluding the Jews who were selected for gassing on their arrival—was 4.41, with the next-highest concentration-camp mortality rate being 3.61 among women prisoners at Auschwitz. White, "Majdanek: Cornerstone," 14. Marszałek suggests that the relatively high mortality rate at Majdanek was partially due to the high percentage of peasants who were incarcerated there and who had fewer resources to survive. Marszałek, *Majdanek*, 61.

43. The explicit comparison is made by Sofsky, *The Order of Terror*, 279.

the long Majdanek Process in Dusseldorf, 1975–81, took a fierce toll on the prisoners, both men and women.[44]

As camp memoirists like Jerzy Kwiatkowski frequently note, the most consistent and frightful violence in the camps came from fellow prisoners who were delegated authority at various levels to oversee the camp inmates. At the highest level, this started with the kapos, usually Germans, Austrians, and *Volksdeutsche* from various regions of Nazi-dominated Europe. These men (and sometimes women), frequently with criminal pasts, terrorized the prisoners, including their own underlings in the camp hierarchy who held a variety of supervisory jobs: commanding the sections and barracks in the camp; leading work expeditions; and working in the prisoner administration and functional institutions such as the Revier, bathhouses, crematoria, and kitchens. Beatings, whippings, killings, punishment, torture, graft, and bribery inhabited every relationship in the camp between various levels of power and even within the same branches, whether in the SS itself or, especially, among the ranks below it. Most of the time, there was no rhyme or reason to the brutality—it was purely gratuitous, could come at any time and from any quarter, even from fellow prisoners. The atmosphere of incessant violence was permeated by unremitting hunger and exhaustion, which forced prisoners to submit to every humiliation, verbal and physical, in order to survive.

Jerzy Kwiatkowski

Jerzy Kwiatkowski was born on June 8, 1894, in Vienna, the oldest of three sons of a respected Polish doctor and surgeon who settled his family in Czernowitz a year later (Chernivtsi in Ukrainian, Cernăuți in Romanian,

---

44. On the Majdanek Trial, see Schwindt, *Das Konzentrations- und Vernichtungslager Majdanek*, 11. The trial is documented in the three-part German documentary film by Eberhard Fechner, *Der Prozess: Eine Darstellung des Majdanek Verfahrens in Düsseldorf* (Nordwestdeutschen Rundfunk, 1984), three videotapes, 270 min. On Thumann, see Marszałek, *Majdanek*, 44–45. Also see Kwiatkowski's memoir, p. 114, where he writes that "the word 'Thumann' means terror in the camp." Regina Pinczewska (1989) says of "Brigitta" that she never could have imagined "that a woman could also be such a sadist; murder was in her eyes the moment she got close." *Majdanek: Obóz koncentracyjny*, 96.

Czerniowce in Polish), capital of the Austrian crown land of Bukovina.[45] He received his "matura" (diploma) at the Imperial First Gymnasium in Czernowitz and studied at both the universities of Czernowitz and Vienna, receiving his doctorate in law in 1919. Kwiatkowski came from a distinguished Polish Catholic upper-class family, loyal to the Austro-Hungarian Empire, with ties to local Czernowitz Polish patriotic and social organizations dedicated to Polish language, culture, and education in the region. Polishness (*polskość*), Catholicism, education, and duty were the cornerstones of young Jerzy's upbringing.

Jerzy's father, Stanisław, participated in World War I on the Austrian side as an army doctor but moved his family to the newly independent Poland in 1923, where he died in Warsaw in 1925. As his memoir tells us, Jerzy served with distinction as a cadet in the Imperial Third Dragoons, part of Franz Ferdinand's Fourth Army, where he was decorated with a silver medal for bravery and was eventually promoted to first lieutenant. He then served as the recruitment officer with the Fourth Rifle Division, under the renowned general Lucjan Żeligowski, which fought against the newly established Soviet government, until retreating from Odessa back to newly independent Poland, where his unit was absorbed into the army of the Second Republic. In mid-1919, Kwiatkowski served with the Romanian army as a liaison officer, a role that helped meet the needs of Żeligowski's Fourth Rifle Division, earning him another well-deserved medal and promotion to cavalry captain. Before his own demobilization

45. Wojciech Lenarczyk, "Jerzy Kwiatkowski i jego dzieło," in Jerzy Kwiatkowski, *485 dni na Majdanku* (Lublin: Muzeum na Majdanku, 2018), 5. Much of the biographical information on Kwiatkowski's early life in this section comes from Lenarczyk's introduction to the 2018 Polish edition of Kwiatkowski's memoir. See also the valuable study of the editorial and publishing history of the memoir by Dorota Niedziałkowska, "Problemy edytorskie w *485 dniach na Majdanku* Jerzy Kwiatkowskiego," *Sztuka Edycji*, 2 (2019): 49–66. Niedziałkowska from the State Museum at Majdanek conducted research in Kwiatkowski's archives, deposited in the mid-1970s in the Hoover Institution Archives. Thanks to the help of Sarah Patton, I was able to check some documents from the Jerzy Kwiatkowski Papers, via scans from the Hoover Institution Archives (they were closed to researchers during the production of this volume in 2020 as a result of the COVID-19 pandemic). HIA, Jerzy Kwiatkowski Papers, Box 1, "Korespondencja moja w sprawie wydania pamiętnika o Majdanku," no. 7, 1966–67, and Box 6, "Anti-Jewish Agitation in Poland," no. 20. Nothing in this material altered my reading of Lenarczyk and Niedziałkowska.

after the Polish-Soviet war (1919–21), Kwiatkowski suffered the battlefield loss of his youngest brother, Stanisław, in August 1920.

After entering the army reserves in October 1921, Jerzy joined the Polish Trade Bank in Warsaw, advancing as far as the position of director of the Warsaw branch and vice director of the bank. He sat on boards of various companies and ran a publishing business in the 1930s before becoming co-owner and director of administration for the Warsaw factory Pioneer, which manufactured machinery, ammunition, and airplane parts for the military. He married Maria Horodyńska in April 1924, and in 1925 they had a daughter, Julinka, who unfortunately died after only two days. In his memoir, he writes about the deep sadness he felt at having lost both his father and daughter, but also his wife, who died in February 1939, and his mother, who perished, he notes, in the last German bombardment of Warsaw on September 25, 1939, just one day before the surrender. He was little involved in Polish politics, but he made it clear in his memoir that he followed "a nationalist course" (p. 394).

Grieving for his family, Kwiatkowski threw himself into his work in the factory, which was under German supervision during the occupation. He quickly became attached to the resistance, helping to finance and organize arms transfers to the underground. But the Gestapo arrested him on February 18, 1943, and transferred him to the Pawiak Prison in Warsaw, which had famously served as a jail for generations of Polish fighters against Russian imperial rule in the nineteenth century. Along with a number of other Polish political prisoners, he was transferred to Majdanek on March 25, 1943, where he was subjected to the degrading and dehumanizing experience of being initiated into the concentration camp: kicked and struck, forced to disrobe, humiliated by guards, robbed of his clothes and possessions, and treated like a number, in his case 8830, rather than a human being. Like other prisoners, he was given tatters for clothing, a metal dog tag to wear with his number on it, and a red triangle that marked him as a political prisoner, with a *P* for Pole, to sew on his camp "uniform" front and back. He later was forced to wear a patch of white with a red "point" the size of a coin in the middle that designated him as a potential escapee. This marker caused him much grief, though he noted that it was also useful in that he was not allowed to leave camp on hard work details.

Kwiatkowski held a number of jobs in the camp, first as a gardener, then as a clerk in the camp administrative office (November 1943 until spring 1944), and, at the end, as a regular heavy laborer doing various mindless tasks. As the Red Army approached Lublin, Kwiatkowski was a member of the last transfer from Majdanek on July 22, 1944, after which he ended up in Auschwitz for a month; from there, he was moved to Sachsenhausen, where he worked as a translator. On being evacuated with other prisoners from Sachsenhausen because of the approaching Red Army, he was picked up by the US Army near Schwerin in Mecklenburg on the morning of May 3, 1945. He was "dizzy with joy," he wrote, when a Polish-American soldier informed him and his friend in Polish that they were free. He felt a huge thrill witnessing the surrender of the German troops to the Allies and assisting in disarming the formerly feared *Wehrmacht* soldiers.[46]

Kwiatkowski joined a group of Polish officers in Schleswig-Holstein, Germany, and was assigned to the staff of General Stanisław Maczek's much-acclaimed First Polish Armored Division, which had assumed occupation duties in the British zone of Germany neighboring the Netherlands. He took on a number of tasks related to the care of Polish DPs (displaced persons) in the British zone, as well as to the development of Polish organizations for war veterans and victims of German repression. It was during his time living in Haren an der Ems (temporarily renamed Maczków, after the Polish hero) in the British occupation zone in 1945 that he finished his memoir in its present diary form. Many survivors of the concentration camps wanted nothing to do with revisiting the pain of the past so soon after liberation. But others, Primo Levi, Tadeusz Borowski, and Viktor Frankl among them, seemed intent on relating their experiences and naming their persecutors as soon as they could. Kwiatkowski belonged to this latter group. Despite the problems of getting both decent paper—he had to use the back sides of billing sheets from a local shipping company—and a typewriter, which was pro-

---

46. He writes about his liberation in the afterword to the first Polish edition of his book, Jerzy Kwiatkowski, *485 dni na Majdanku* (Lublin: Wydawnictwo Lubelskie, 1966), 489.

vided to him by the Polish Scouting organization, and wearing a coat and hat in the freezing cold and dark of his quarters, Kwiatkowski wrote in a frenzy. He committed from memory all that he had observed and mentally recorded in the hellhole of Majdanek. He told an interviewer later in 1967: "During the whole time in Majdanek, I systematically recorded facts in my memory, impressions of the camp, the names of the hangmen, their habits, crimes, orders."[47] One of his major goals was to hold accountable those people who had caused himself and others such misery and pain in the camp.[48] The memoir was not a "photographic reportage," he wrote; instead, the purpose was "to give the atmosphere and psychological reaction of the prisoners."[49] The manuscript was finished as early as Christmas 1945.[50] He had to seek treatment for his fingers, which had nearly frozen on the typewriter keys.

The Polish occupation strip in the British zone came to an end in 1948; Maczków was again named Haren an der Ems; and Kwiatkowski, never a friend of the communists, chose not to return to Poland, and instead to emigrate to the United States in 1949. He lived first in Chicago, where he worked for an air-conditioning company, and then, in 1958, he moved to New York, where he found a job as an administrator and eventually as director of the Pekao Trading Corporation and Linen Trading Co., which gave him a chance to return to Poland periodically for business reasons. Always the Polish patriot, he involved himself in the affairs of Polonia in New York, especially in connection with issues of Polish compensation for Nazi war crimes. It must have also given him some satisfaction to be able to testify at the 1964–70 Düsseldorf trials of the brutal Nazi criminals whom he had witnessed at work in Majdanek. He was described by Erich Schiele, the son of his longtime partner, Henrietta Schiele, as a dapper,

47. Lenarczyk, "Jerzy Kwiatkowski," 12.

48. Kwiatkowski recorded names and crimes of his camp persecutors in a letter to the Polish minister of foreign affairs in London (June 10, 1945), in his testimony before the Polish Liaison Group at British army headquarters (April 8, 1946), and later at the Düsseldorf Trials of Nazi perpetrators (1975–81).

49. Cited in Niedziałkowska, "Problemy edytorskie," 56.

50. Kwiatkowski also wrote a tract on German war crimes for the British, entitled "Oskarżam," in Jesteśmy świadkami: wspomnienia byłych więźniów Majdanka, ed. C. Rajca, E. Rosiak, A. Wiśniewska (Lublin: Wydawnictwo. Lubelskie, 1969), 407–48.

cultivated, and meticulous gentleman, kind to all and well organized, a regular reader of the *New York Times* and frequent visitor to New York art museums, a portrait that fits the camp personality reflected in the memoir.[51]

Kwiatkowski's manuscript remained unpublished for twenty years. If he was burning up to get the message about the camps that he related in his memoir to the world, there was little interest in the West in the sufferings of the war, which most people, even the Poles and Jews, wanted to forget. The publication history of *485 Days at Majdanek* reflects the relative indifference of publishers and readers alike to the history of Nazi genocide in the early postwar years. Holocaust "consciousness" is a relatively new phenomenon, beginning only in the early 1960s with the Eichmann Trial and the first authoritative history of the Holocaust by Raoul Hilberg. The television series *The Holocaust*, first broadcast in 1978, was a signpost of the broader interest of society in the travails of the Jews. During the late 1970s and 1980s, German, Anglo-American, and Israeli scholarly efforts to explore the dynamics of the Final Solution refined the West's historical understanding of the Shoah. Poles, too, became increasingly interested in relating their own suffering during the Second World War, though they were constrained by government censorship and societal limitations on how to present that history.

When the State Museum at Majdanek expressed a desire to publish Kwiatkowski's hard-hitting, detailed, and candid memoir in 1964, a number of objections were raised from different quarters. Particularly difficult for the authorities were Kwiatkowski's praise of the anti-communist resistance forces; his indifference to the communists at Majdanek; his negative portrayal of Jewish, Ukrainian, and Russian prisoners; his uncompromising, condemnatory language about the hated Nazi accomplices, Poles, Jews, and others; and his portrayal of some SS officers as relatively lenient in comparison. Even some of his camp mates, including Stanisław Zelent, raised objections to his critical characterizations of some of his

51. See email communications of Erich Schiele to Dorota Niedziałkowska, especially of November 13 and November 17, 2019. My thanks to Niedziałkowska for sending me copies of these communications.

fellow prisoners. (Zelent also objected to what he felt was the excessive praise of his own person.)[52] It took two years, until 1966, for the book to be finally published, with numerous modifications—with Kwiatkowski's agreement—of the original text. Many of the changes were quite petty. For example, mentions of excessive drinking and sexual matters at the camp were stricken from the original manuscript. Objecting to his religiosity, the authorities changed his description of "my silver medallion of Our Lady of Częstochowa" to "my silver medallion."[53] A second edition of the book followed in 1988, which was exactly the same as the 1966 original. After the publication of the first edition, Kwiatkowski, with the State Museum at Majdanek, planned an expansion of the book, including a variety of documents and materials that would illustrate some of the major arguments he made about the camp. But this never came to fruition. He died in Brooklyn on February 3, 1980. The museum returned to the original unexpurgated text of the memoir for the 2018 edition, which has been translated for this volume.

Kwiatkowski's memoir provides extraordinary insights into both the functioning of KL Lublin and into the man himself, who represents in important ways a generation of Polish leaders who had fought as young men in World War I; battled the Nazis in World War II in Allied armies, usually under British command, and in the resistance and camps; and desperately tried to keep their country from falling into the hands of the communists. In his struggle to maintain his humanity in Majdanek and resist the temptations of ubiquitous evil, Kwiatkowski is a model of dignity and perseverance that characterized the best of his generation. He was not perfect; who could be in a situation of constant pummeling, humiliation, and mistreatment, severe hunger ("hunger . . . absorbs my mind completely," p. 144), disease (including a severe case of typhus), exhaustion, and repeated disappointments about release? But the acuity and trustworthiness of his observations about the character and purpose of the camp and about his fellow prisoners at Majdanek are hard to match.

52. See the excellent discussions of the complicated publication history in Lenarczyk, "Jerzy Kwiatkowski," 13–26, and in Niedziałkowska, "Problemy edytorskie," 57–61.

53. See Niedziałkowska, "Problemy edytorskie," 61.

The Man and the Camp

The regime of power and torture that underlay the SS administration of the camp made an immediate impression on Kwiatkowski. He understood the system perfectly: the Germans had developed an "entire system of tormenting people," the implementation of which "was saddled onto the prisoners themselves, who, as loyal *Lageraltester*, kapos, *Vorarbeiter*, block overseers, physicians, or orderlies, are made personally responsible for carrying out elements of this diabolical regime" (p. 87). The violence did not derive from emotion or anger, but, as he writes in the case of an SS man knocking down prisoners with a single blow from his fist, it was routine. "Calm practice, without any emotion" (p. 59). One after another, prisoners were knocked down by the SS man until the aggressor grew tired of the game. The same was true of the regular lashings of prisoners for a variety of alleged offenses, sometimes as innocuous as forgetting to take off one's hat properly in front of an SS man, offending a barracks boss by turning up late for one of the incessant roll calls in the camp, or simply looking the wrong way at a kapo. This was punishment for the alleged offender, but it was also about humiliating him (and sometimes her) while other prisoners were forced to watch, just as they helplessly witnessed countless hangings, beatings, and murders.

Kwiatkowski notes the absurdity of the elaborate rules about dress, etiquette, eating, and lining up at roll call given the stark contrast to the filth, dishevelment, and infestation of the camp with lice and fleas. He writes about the fact that their beds had to be made perfectly, despite the lumpy, straw-filled, lice-ridden mattresses. "The black stripes on the gray blankets must all be aligned. When you stand next to the first bed and look down the entire row of beds, all the stripes must form a perfectly straight line" (p. 67). Woe be to the person whose blanket was out of line. (Blankets were a relatively late arrival at camp; for the first year or so, bedclothes were made up more of assorted rags.) More often than not, the entire barracks would suffer some punishment or another if the inspection was not successful. Kwiatkowski captures insightfully the deeper meaning of the violence when he states that "there is the same tendency everywhere to ruin and break our spirits (p. 451).

Kwiatkowski's cohort at Majdanek, many of whom he knew or had heard of prior to his arrest or while he was in Pawiak Prison, were, like him, political prisoners and self-aware members of the Polish intelligentsia. His first bunkmate, an important source of heat at night and mutual help in the camp, was the son of one of his brother's colleagues. Almost all were Catholics, and many, like himself, were devoted to the rituals, holidays, songs, and literature associated with traditional Polish Catholicism. As best they could within the camp, the Poles celebrated holidays together and supported one another in sharing meager food and clothing resources. They helped one another get out from under the tyranny of particularly brutal camp bosses and find work details that were less threatening to their lives and not quite so exhausting. Kwiatkowski was devoted to his intelligentsia friends, whom he considered "the most biologically valuable part of the society," and was able, in his jobs as head gardener or in the administration, to help them avoid potentially dangerous transfers to other camps. Commenting on a major transport of Poles from Majdanek to Auschwitz, he writes, "The real 'Majdanek' is leaving now, Poland's best sons, those who suffered for their convictions in the camp, who are proud of their stripes, the elite of Majdanek" (p. 368). He estimated that the political prisoners made up roughly 10 percent of the Polish prisoners altogether, and therefore about 5 percent of the camp population before the mass murder of the Jews in the fall of 1943. At the same time, he complained about the majority of common Poles in the camp, many of whom he considered petty criminals. He was especially critical of those who cooperated with the Germans in the camp. The Nazis had come to the conclusion that the Polish resistance was infused by lower-class elements and ordered at the beginning of 1943 the arrest and incarceration in Majdanek and Auschwitz of unemployed and "proletarian" Poles.[54]

Kwiatkowski was fully cognizant of the incessant chicanery, corruption, and bribery practiced at all levels of the camp administration. He was deeply offended by those camp guards and kapos who amassed

---

54. Himmler to Heinrich Müller, head of the Gestapo, January 11, 1943, in *Majdanek w dokumentach*, 102.

small fortunes at the cost of the lowliest prisoners. He bridled at the lack of restraint of camp authorities and privileged prisoners when rifling through the piles of clothes of the dead and gassed, looking incessantly for fabled "Jewish gold," jewelry, money, and precious possessions of one sort or another.[55] SS men, Poles, and Jews were involved in the ongoing smuggling and bartering of goods, something noted by the SS chiefs as well.[56] Each level of the camp hierarchy extracted its "percentage" from the one below, and the graft went all the way to the top. Two of Majdanek's SS commanders, Karl Otto Koch (September 1941–August 1942) and Hermann Florstedt (November 1942–September 1943) were tried and sentenced to be executed by the SS for stealing and corruption.[57] In one set of investigations, the SS arrested hundreds of its officers and men for various camp crimes and replaced one-third of the camp commanders.[58]

During the first year of his confinement, Kwiatkowski was able to avoid the worst of the labor details by becoming the chief gardener in Field 3, the section of the camp where he and most of his compatriots were barracked. He planted trees, did odd gardening jobs for the kapos and SS, and grew flowers and vegetables. The SS men even came to him for bouquets for their wives and girlfriends. His horticultural skills had accumulated from working on his property in Komorów, as well as from attending classes at the Warsaw Institute of Life Sciences over a two-year period. His growing stature as a camp gardener allowed him to protect weaker compatriots by arranging for them to be transferred to his crew.

None of this prevented him and others from being berated, beaten, and mistreated, yelled at as "*Scheisspolacken*" (shitty Poles), the common epithet for his countrymen (which he hated), and humiliated in various other ways. The abuse, combined with the incessant hunger—he lost some forty-five pounds in the first six weeks in camp—made his life miserable. Added to this were the many diseases and afflictions he suffered

---

55. On the mythologies surrounding Jewish gold, see Jan Grabowski, *Hunt for the Jews: Betrayal and Murder in German-Occupied Poland* (Bloomington: Indiana University Press, 2013), 109.

56. Order of the *kommandant*, May 3, 1943, in *Majdanek w dokumentach*, 196.

57. White, "Majdanek: Cornerstone," 14.

58. Mazower, *Hitler's Empire*, 310.

from (scabies, cramps, mycotic infection, eczema, swollen legs, blistered feet, dysentery, typhus, etc.). Especially early on, Kwiatkowski worried that he might share the fate of a *musselman* or *gamel*, as a certain type of enfeebled inmate was called in Majdanek. These were prisoners who had been robbed of their strength, will, and character by the incessant hunger and mistreatment, were little more than walking skeletons, half alive and half dead, who eventually perished in place or were carried to the "*gamel-blocks*," where they expired in the same barracks with others in their filth and misery.[59]

Fortunately for Kwiatkowski and the other Poles, conditions improved in early 1943 when the Polish prisoners were able to receive packages from their relatives through the Polish Red Cross and the Polish Central Welfare Council (*Rada Główna Opiekuńcza*, or RGO) in Lublin. Both organizations also contributed to improving the diets and medical conditions of the prisoners through modest, though crucial, contributions of bread, soup, medicines, and immunizations. These and other upgrades in the camp had a lot to do with Himmler's realization that he needed to make some concessions to keeping his camp labor force alive and healthy enough to work. Otherwise the supply of workers would dry up, given the expanding needs of the Reich for industrial and agricultural labor and the decision to eliminate all the Jews in the *Generalgouvernement* in Operation Reinhard.

The presence of civilian workers in the camp helped in manifold ways to improve conditions for the Polish prisoners, as these laborers brought communications in and out of the camp and regularly managed to smuggle in provisions and medicines. Polish inmates also could get packages from relatives and friends through the regular mail. Kwiatkowski's spirits were buoyed up by crucial communications with loved ones, though the constant assurances of his brother, family members, and a woman friend, Mary, that he would soon be released brought repeated disappointments.

---

59. The most famous description of "*musselmänner*" is in Primo Levi, *If This Is Man* (London: Abacus, 1987), 103. The word is used throughout the camp system. See Captain Witold Pilecki, *The Auschwitz Volunteer: Beyond Bravery*, trans. Jarek Garliński (Los Angeles: Aquila Polonica, 2012), 120. The name *gamel* apparently comes from the Silesian German indicating a mentally handicapped person "with uncontrolled motions." Marszałek, *Majdanek*, 96.

Appropriate bribes and careful planning made it possible for him to meet with his brother across the fence of the grounds of the nursery. The food that was sent, despite the constant thievery of the SS, the kapos, and the overseers, clearly made a huge difference to Kwiatkowski's survival. By the end, he talked about having enough to eat (three thousand calories a day); at the outset, when he was afraid of dying of starvation, he was taking in barely eight hundred calories. There was even enough food among the Poles who received packages (Jews and Soviet POWs received none) that they could help the traumatized Zamość expellees and sometimes other non-Polish friends in the camp supplement their meager diets. But these improvements were not complemented by a commensurate cessation of the brutality of the camp overseers. Especially in early 1944, the regular transports of Polish political prisoners from the Lublin Castle to be executed and incinerated in the camp crematorium reminded the prisoners, if they needed any reminding, that there was always the danger of being eliminated.

It is not too much to assert that Kwiatkowski's involvement with his Polish milieu at the camp helped keep him alive, spiritually as well as physically. When he was sick with typhus, a compatriot gave him *The Anthology of Religious Poetry*, edited by Stanisław and Wanda Miłoszewscy and endorsed by Archbishop Józef Teodorowicz, a friend of his family. He writes, "Every poem read with feeling—at least as much as I can muster—is a prayer, and I am so thirsty for it" (p. 389). The immunizations he received against typhus via his cousin Stefan on the outside also helped; although they did not prevent the onset of the disease, they may well have lessened its virulence in his case. The RGO also managed to deliver immunizations against typhus to the Revier.

The Polish underground exerted a strong presence on the camp, and Kwiatkowski sought out and maintained contacts with its leaders, especially with Stanisław Zelent ("Stach"), sometimes known as "the engineer," who was the dominant Home Army (Armia Krajowa, or AK) representative in the camp and the informal leader of the Polish political prisoners. Kwiatkowski was also close to the leader of the National Armed Forces (NSZ) group in the camp, Emil Lipiński. (The communist People's Army, the AL, is barely mentioned.) Virtually every Polish political party and its underground affiliates were present in the camp. The Poles managed to smuggle a raft of underground literature into Majdanek, including the major weekly the *Information Bulletin*, and to keep up with the news of the war through their contact with relatives and friends. Some Polish prisoners also surreptitiously listened to Polish broadcasts from London on the camp commandant's car radio in the auto shop, where a number of them worked. The underground in Majdanek tried to uphold the values of the "Secret State," even to the point of committing to memory the names of those Poles who collaborated with the SS bosses and who mistreated their compatriots and the Jews.

The Home Army and NSZ groups exchanged ideas and drew up plans about a joint uprising inside the camp coordinated with an assault from underground fighters from outside. But nothing came of these schemes in the end, due to "massive SS pressure around Lublin."[60] Security measures taken within the camp made an uprising unlikely in the absence of an attack from outside, and disagreements between the Home Army and the NSZ in the underground, which sometimes even led to fighting between them, made it impossible for the resistance on the outside to forge a cohesive plan for the liberation of Majdanek. There were periodic breakouts from the camp of Soviet POWs, Jews, and Poles, but most of the attempts failed and ended in shootings, hangings, torture, and the punishment of the respective barracks. However, according to Rajca and Wiśniewska, specialists on Majdanek, there were more than fifty escapes from the main camp and its subcamps, involving some three hundred persons.[61] But a heavy proportion of these escapes were from the subsidiary camps and during work details away from Majdanek itself. Kwiatkowski tried to arrange an escape to contact the underground in Lublin, but the plan came to naught.

Although Kwiatkowski was not a resistance leader, he was thrilled to be considered an important figure among the Polish intelligentsia. He was proud of his friendships with leading Poles. This included his relationship with the sculptor Albin Maria Boniecki, who was allowed by the SS to make sculptures for Kwiatkowski's gardens, including one of three eagles

---

60. White, "Lublin Main Camp," 878.
61. Rajca and Wiśniewska, *Majdanek Concentration Camp*, 36.

and a second of a turtle.[62] The artist secretly turned the *Column of Three Eagles* into a memorial for Poles who had died in the camp by planting a box of ashes of deceased Polish prisoners in the column of the monument, while the turtle symbolized for the prisoners the slowing down of work to hinder the Nazi war effort. Kwiatkowski's description of Christmas 1943 in the camp is especially poignant. The RGO had provided traditional Christmas Eve specialties and even a decorated Christmas tree for a gathering of the leading Poles. Kwiatkowski writes about the evening: "The ideological elite of the prisoners have put me in the honorary place today [next to Zelent], and it's the most valuable gift that they could have given me. It's my most beautiful day in the camp" (p. 291). He even compared the evening to the emotional and spiritual joy of receiving Holy Communion in 1927 on Calvary in Jerusalem.

The Jews were the primary victims at Majdanek and the people who suffered its worst violence and degradation at the hands of the camp leaders and administrators, as Kwiatkowski readily acknowledges. Still, Kwiatkowski's views of the Jews are ambivalent. On the one hand, he is decidedly friendly with many Jews. He loves talking to one of his favorite sleeping partners, Krongold, a former Jewish factory owner from Łódź, who exchanged nightly stories with him about life in France. He says prayers for Jews who were hanged at Majdanek, and he finds a delightful young friend in a Jewish thirteen-year-old boy named Eli Szydlower, who managed, he admiringly writes, to stay immune to the ugliness of the camp. (He identifies another thirteen-year-old Jewish boy, "Bubi," the youngest of the kapos, as one of the worst sadists in the camp.) He befriends a Slovak Jewish administrator by the name of Horowitz, a former bank manager, and notes that "he is an exceptionally modest, quiet, and tactful person, treating not just me but every prisoner very decently" (p. 56). Kwiatkowski was particularly helpful to the intellectuals among the thousands of survivors of the Warsaw Ghetto Uprising who were transported to Majdanek in April and May 1943, most of whom eventually died there.[63]

---

62. See Albin Maria Boniecki (1959), in *Majdanek: Obóz koncentracyjny*, 188–90.

63. Timothy Snyder notes that 56,065 Jews were captured during the Warsaw Ghetto Uprising; 7,000 were shot, 6,924 were sent to Treblinka, and "most of the rest" were transported to Majdanek and its subcamps in the Lublin district. Snyder, *Bloodlands*, 292.

At the same time, Kwiatkowski shared many of the prejudices of his Polish milieu of the 1930s. He was sharply critical of Russians (often "Bolsheviks") and Ukrainians. But it was especially the Jews who drew his ire. He was distrustful of a Dr. Goldberg from Lublin, who "can't speak Polish correctly" and whom he accuses of being reluctant to serve the medical needs of Polish prisoners in the Revier (pp. 81–82).[64] About a Jewish journalist who tries to buy his way into working in his garden crew, Kwiatkowski writes that he was worried about further extortion, "knowing the speculative sense of the Jews" (p. 167). Poles know better than the Germans who is of "Semitic blood" (p. 274). He disparages the Jews for screaming more than the stoic Poles when being lashed and for being too flighty to be counted on in a camp uprising. He is particularly disdainful of the brutal Jewish kapos and the exploitative Jewish overseers and their helpmates in the camp. Kwiatkowski is not the only one who bridles under the fierce rule of some Jewish kapos. Despite his friendship with Horowitz, Kwiatkowski is disgusted by the surviving large contingent of "dressed to the nines" and "exquisitely fed" Slovak Jews who managed to insinuate themselves into important positions in the camp administration. They act "with arrogance, exclusion, and condescension toward all foreigners" (p. 135). There were definitely lapses in his overall fair-mindedness and Christian spirit when it came to the Jews. He really did not like the fact that the Jews, especially the Slovak Jews, controlled so much of prisoner life during his first year in the camp.[65]

The block overseers, clerks, and office workers are almost 99 percent Jewish. Slovak Jews occupy all the positions in the offices, the political department, the *Arbeitseinsatz*, kitchens, washroom, laundry, and post

---

64. Zelent disagreed with Kwiatkowski's critical characterization of Dr. Goldberg, which became an issue in the publication of his memoir. Lenarczyk, "Jerzy Kwiatkowski," 17–18.

65. Kwiatkowski was not alone in his resentment of the Slovak Jews in Majdanek. See, for example, the contemporaneous notes and letters of Witold Sopocki and Henryk Wieliczański in *Majdanek w dokumentach*, 428, 433. Still, Kwiatkowski exaggerates the influence of the Jews; even his own account contradicts this quote. Reports back to the underground resistance from Polish prisoners also note Jewish mistreatment of Polish inmates. See Joshua D. Zimmerman, *The Polish Underground and the Jews, 1939–1945* (Cambridge, England: Cambridge University Press, 2015), 357.

office, and serve as doctors, nurses, and orderlies in the hospital. When
there is no Slovak Jew for a position, then a Polish Jew might get it. On
the outside, the Germans lock Jews into ghettos, force them to take off
their hats in their presence and portray the Jews as social rejects, who have
to be eradicated. Here in the concentration camp, Jews rule over Aryans,
Jews carry whips, and the Aryans must stand at attention and take off their
hats before them. Here, Jews address Aryans as "you" while the Aryans say
"sir" to the Jew! Jews and SS men work hand in glove, Jews beat Christians
bloody. Everything the opposite of *Mein Kampf*. Where do these Jewish
privileges come from? (pp. 134–35)

In attempting to assess Kwiatkowski's relationship to the coming of the
Holocaust to Majdanek, it is useful to remember that very few Jews or
non-Jews could grasp what was going on around them, in Yehuda Bauer's
words, "before their shocked eyes and paralyzed minds."[66] All they really
could recognize until the mass murder began was the ghettoization of the
Jews under German occupation; occasional killing, poverty, and want
among the Jews; and the harsh exploitation of working Jews.[67] Meanwhile,
Jews themselves frequently complained about the exploitative behavior of
their own Jewish compatriots who held positions of power in the ghettos
and in the camps.[68]

Kwiatkowski shared his sense of shock and his sympathy with the Jewish victims and their fate as the Holocaust unfolded in the camp. Like
many of his intelligentsia compatriots, he was horrified at the selection
of the Jews to be either killed or sent off to work details, which began in
the fall of 1942 and became a common occurrence from the spring of 1943
onward in the camp.[69] Arriving victims were disrobed and separated into
groups of those capable of strenuous labor and those designated for elimi-

66. Cited in Engel, *The Holocaust*, 71.

67. Engel, *The Holocaust*, 71–72

68. See Evgeny Finkel, *Ordinary Jews: Choice and Survival during the Holocaust* (Princeton:
Princeton University Press, 2017), 70–74.

69. Most of the selections went on near a rail siding in Lublin, two kilometers from the
camp. Still, there were enough selections occurring in the camp itself to shock the prisoners
who witnessed them. See Kranz, *Extermination of Jews*, 21, 40–47.

nation. Terrified and naked, men, women, and children were driven to the gas chambers, sometimes forced to wait outside for days before their "turn" came. Many were bludgeoned to death with iron pipes before being incinerated in the crematorium or buried in the forest. Two gas chambers were in use in Majdanek between September 1942 and September 1943. Like others in the system, they employed both the poison fertilizer Zyklon-B and carbon monoxide poisoning (in this case from steel bottles in liquid form) to kill their victims.[70] As best we know, about twenty thousand Jews were gassed in the camp.[71] Kwiatkowski was haunted, he writes, by the "crying, sobbing, and wails of mothers whose children were taken from them by force" and sent to the gas chambers (p. 157).

In response to the Warsaw and Białystok Ghetto Uprisings, and the insurrections in the camps at Treblinka and especially Sobibór (October 14, 1943), Himmler decided to put an end to the lives of the Jews in the Lublin region, no matter their value to SS production.[72] On November 3, 1943, as part of the obscenely named Operation *Erntefest* (Harvest Festival), the SS and auxiliary German police stationed in Lublin marched some ten thousand Jewish males from various SS subcamps and workshops in thick "clouds of dust" from Lublin to Majdanek, bringing an additional two to three thousand Jewish women from the Old Airport Camp, where most had sorted mounds of Jewish clothes for shipment to the Reich (p. 260). Meanwhile, the SS assembled six thousand Jewish men and women among the prisoners in Majdanek itself to join the throng that had come to the camp. In a clearing beyond Field 5, roughly 18,000 Jews were murdered in less than twenty-four hours. The Jews were forced to disrobe and stand astride the unusually deep and wide trenches that had already been dug earlier by Jewish prisoners in crisscross patterns just outside the barbed wire. Supposedly these trenches were dug for the

70. Marszałek, *Majdanek*, 130.

71. White, "Majdanek: Cornerstone," 10.

72. Tomasz Kranz thinks that a more important factor was Himmler's rivalry with other parts of the German government that wanted to control Jewish labor. Himmler may have thought that it was better to kill those in the Lublin region than to let them fall into the hands of his rivals. Kranz, *Extermination of Jews*, 64. The evidence is inconclusive.

purpose of taking shelter during air attacks. "Naked, arms raised," the crying and trembling Jews were marched through the barbed wire to the
trenches and murdered by German security police. They were killed by
machine-gunners, whose weapons were reloaded by other executioners
while they continued to shoot the next batch of Jews, forced to lie down in
the trenches on top of their murdered compatriots.[73]

Kwiatkowski quickly understood what was happening.

> Suddenly, I hear music, some woeful milonga tango, then a waltz by Strauss,
> it's music played from records through a loudspeaker. The sounds carry
> from the direction of the crematorium. Where did this loudspeaker come
> from, we never heard it before. The music plays continuously. Record after
> record. A plane is circling low around the camp, so that sometimes you
> can't hear your own voice. There are short breaks between the records and
> then I hear a muffled "ta ta ta—ta ta ta," just like the sound of a machine
> gun" (p. 260).

When told that all the Jews will be killed, he writes: "We are overwhelmed
by an indescribable tension and depression." His intimate Krongold was
gone, and "so many other personal acquaintances" (pp. 260, 261). Operation *Erntefest* cost the lives of some forty-two thousand Jews in the Lublin
District, including those machine-gunned at Majdanek, which was the
single largest massacre to take place in the concentration-camp system.[74]

Jerzy Kwiatkowski's *485 Days at Majdanek* is a sad and depressing book,
one that documents the horrors of the Third Reich and Nazism, the deep
perverseness of the concentration-camp system, the sadistic policies of
the SS against the Jews and Poles, and the devastation of the Holocaust.
It also explores the proposition, as Kwiatkowski titles one of the chapters of his memoir, that *Homo homini lupus*, "Man is wolf to man." Under

---

73. The massacre is described in detail in Christopher Browning, *Ordinary Men: Reserve
Battalion 101 and the Final Solution in Poland* (New York: Harper Perennial, 1998), reissued,
135, 138–39.

74. Roughly three hundred Jewish women from the Lublin *"Flugplatz"* camp and another
three hundred men from the Lipowa Street camp were selected to survive the massacre. Some
Jews were able to hide but were eventually found and shot. See Kranz, *Extermination of Jews*, 30.

the conditions of a concentration camp like Majdanek, the bestial cruelty that men (and women) inflict on one another is hard to absorb and even harder to explain. Kwiatkowski does as well as anyone in identifying those aspects of Nazi ideology, human psychology, and the exercise of power in the camp that make this kind of brutality in part explicable. Kwiatkowski himself emerges in the book as a welcome antidote for the reader to the dark revelations of his account of the camp. He is humane and dignified; his proud Polish patriotism is elitist yet also natural and unassuming; his religiosity in face of the torments of hell is admirable. The camp survivor Viktor Frankl wrote, also in 1945, "The prisoners were only average men, but some, at least, by choosing to be 'worthy of their suffering' proved man's capacity to rise above outward fate."[75] Kwiatkowski was such a man.

---

75. Viktor Frankl, *Man's Search for Meaning*, trans. Ilse Lasch (Boston: Beacon Press, 2006), 9.

Welcomed by Crows

"Alles aussteigen!"[1]

The words alert us to the fact that our eighteen-hour journey on the cargo car is finally over. We hear keys turning inside padlocks and suddenly, the door slides open. We see a crowd of SS men in front of the train. We hear their urging *"Los, los!"*[2] and moments later, the butts of their rifles start aiming for any older or weaker prisoner unable to make the meter-and-a-half jump down onto the track nimbly enough. Rolling out from my rail car are: the rector of the Warsaw Polytechnic, Engineer Kazimierz Drewnowski; Professor Mieczysław Michałowicz, MD; Doctors Jastrzębski and Zembrzuski; Engineer Witold Sopoćko, and many others. The head of the Warsaw Seminary, Father Roman Archutowski, PhD, is hit on the back of his neck so hard that he staggers down under the train's wheels. Finally, all fifty of us are out of the car. They line us up in fives and tell each group to march arm in arm. Overall, some seven hundred men and four hundred women arrive on the transport.

I look around—we are at the Lublin cargo station, which means we are headed for Majdanek—despite what the "initiated" SS men at the 5th transport division of Pawiak Prison told us yesterday, it is not Auschwitz. I feel relieved; over the last six months Auschwitz has already made quite a name for itself,[3] while the former POW and Jewish camp at Majdanek was

---

Footnotes providing historical and biographical context for Jerzy Kwiatkowski's memoirs were written by Wojciech Lenarczyk for the 2018 Polish edition and have been translated here by Witold Wojtaszko and Nicholas Siekierski. Further notes, including translations of foreign words and terms into English and clarification of certain points for US readers, were contributed by Siekierski and Norman M. Naimark.

1. "Everyone out!" (literally, "Everything get out!"). All foreign terms retained in this text are in German unless otherwise noted.

2. "Forward, forward!"

3. The first large group of prisoners arrived at KL (*Konzentrationslager,* or "concentration camp") Auschwitz on a transport from Tarnów on June 14, 1940.

only converted into a concentration camp three months ago, so its slate was still relatively clean.[4]

Dawn. The cold, gray morning of March 26, 1943, looms overhead. Above our column, still being lined up and slowly prepared for the march, cawing crows circle. My neighbor quips:

"They welcome new victims!"

We march through the sleeping city, from time to time an odd passerby stops to acknowledge us with a sad glance and a silent nod. We walk slowly, burdened by our bundles, surrounded by a thick throng of SS men with *Empis*[5] ready to fire—not to mention the several dozen German shepherds, Great Danes, and Dobermans they keep on leashes. About half an hour later, we reach the camp—we can see the wooden barracks lined up along the road leading to Chełm. This is Majdanek!

They tell us to stop in front of a barracks, and so we wait while the women continue on. We can see prisoners in gray uniforms with blue stripes, terribly emaciated, stooped down and barely able to shoulder the weight of a single straw mattress. Someone in our group reassuringly suggests they are probably typhus convalescents. Another voice advises us to eat all of our food before they take it all away, but no one believes it. Several SS men (I can't tell who outranks whom among them) approach our group and tell us to enter the empty barracks. Once inside, we are told to quickly undress and hold all our valuables, as well as belts and suspenders, in our hands. So we stand there, naked, and wait. The gates of the stable barracks are ajar; we quickly get goose bumps. We wait like that for maybe an hour. Finally, they start reading out the transport manifest and every man whose name is called out has to walk to the other end of the barracks. It takes a while to read out seven hundred names. Once called, we have to

4. The concentration camp at Majdanek was originally named the Waffen-SS Camp for Prisoners of War in Lublin, and it was not until February 1943 that it officially became the *Konzentrationslager* Lublin, sometimes referred to in this text as KL. In 1941–42, most of its prisoners were Soviet POWs, Jews, and imprisoned peasants from the Lublin region. In January 1943, Majdanek started to receive large transports of political prisoners, and that is the change that Kwiatkowski refers to here.

5. Slang term for the German machine pistol EMP (Erma Maschinenpistole), produced by the Erma factory.

part with our clothes and food, none of which are marked with a name or even a number. I can't help but wonder how I'm going to find my beautiful ferret-skin coat with otter-fur collar later. Regrouped, we wait again. They set up a table and we walk up to it to be registered—each of us receives a number pressed into a piece of sheet metal from cut up tin cans.

I get "8830." As instructed, I surrender my gold cuff links to the deposit. A prisoner speaking with a markedly Jewish accent asks, somewhat surprised, possibly even with a certain avarice in his tone of voice, if it is in fact real gold; he keeps them in his grasp and calls for the next prisoner to approach, telling me over his shoulder that the cuff links will be deposited under my number, but he never even writes it down. My silver medallion of Our Lady of Częstochowa, which I was given when heading out to the First World War front lines, is thrown to the ground by another prisoner of the Jewish kind as a worthless thing. The registration process, or more accurately, the collection of deposits, takes a long time again. I am trembling all over, my muscles contracting, relaxing, and quivering. Finally, they order us to form groups of one hundred and proceed to the baths. We run, naked and barefoot on frozen ground, toward the adjacent building some one hundred meters away. Several barbers are sitting in the cold changing room, Slovak Jews, who cut hair from your head, moustaches, armpits, and the entire body. During this procedure, we ask about the living conditions at Majdanek. They all reply that the only way out of Majdanek is through the chimney. I listen with only half an ear, since, shortly before leaving Pawiak Prison, I received a letter from my brother in which he informed me that Puc (my playful family nickname) "would recover within three weeks." After the haircutting, which lasts quite a while, they drive us out in haste and with shouting toward the baths. It's two to three people to each shower nozzle. Our soap and towels stayed with our things. The hot water warms us, despite the fact that all the windows of the bathhouse are wide open. We are given some sulfur ointment to rub on our head and groin against lice. Then we are issued clothing. From one pile they dispense shirts, long underwear from a second, then socks, pants, jackets, wooden-soled clogs, and hats. But, dear Lord—how does it look—where did they get the hundreds and thousands of such raggedy clothes? We put the shirts and underpants on our wet bodies. The shirts are mostly child-sized, too narrow around the neck, all are buttonless; many of us receive women's leotards or swim trunks instead of long underwear. You have to take the clothing you get, without trying it on. The clogs are mismatched and often too small to wear. I get such big clogs that they fall off my feet. I am issued cocoa-colored cotton pants patched on both knees and the seat—but they are so tight that I can't button them up. Since the barber had eyed my nice suspenders and advised me to give them to him because they would take them at the baths anyway, now I have to hold my unbuttoned pants up with my hands. They reach the middle of my calves and have oil-painted red stripes on both legs. I have no way to button up the shirt on my chest but at least the jacket I get is fairly new; unfortunately it's a summer style with a silk lining and a single button. The hat will not fit on my head so I have to simply perch it on top.

Half-dressed, with clothes still draped on our arms, we are driven outside where our one hundred finishes dressing and struggles to attach the shoes to our feet. We stand bare-breasted and cool down in the frostiness. I notice that all the jackets have the same oil-painted, thick red line down the back with the roughly fifteen-centimeter-tall letters K and L on either side. Naturally, the bathhouse is surrounded by SS men. Around noon, they rush us under armed escort to Camp Field 1 nearby. They tell us to march in even fives. Before the barbed-wire gate leading to Field 1, there is a small *Blockführerstube* gatehouse for the *Blockführer*[6] guards. They come out and start counting the fives going through. Anyone unable to hold the line, maybe because of the clogs constantly falling off his feet, gets whipped on the head and back by the SS men. The gate of the concentration camp closes behind us . . .

They take us to Block 17. There we wait again. They point out the latrines in the open square and inform us that running along the barbed-wire fence surrounding Field 1 is the death zone, i.e., a strip of land approximately five meters wide and separated from the rest of the field by only a single eighty-centimeter-high barbed wire. Any prisoners crossing that barrier

---

6. An SS supervisor of a prisoner barracks or group of barracks. The block overseer (or barracks leader), who is a prisoner, reports to him.

and approaching the perimeter fence will be shot by the guards posted on the towers positioned outside the four corners of the field. The entanglements consist of two barbed-wire fences, approximately three meters tall and two and a half meters apart. The space between the two fences is filled with a braiding of barbed wires pulled diagonally, so from the base of one fence to the top row of wires on the other. This braiding is called *Stolperdraht*.[7] On the inner fence, spaced twenty centimeters apart, porcelain isolators attach to conductors carrying high-voltage electricity. If any of the wires are cut, an alarm will go off at the *Blockführer* gatehouse. Every ten meters, posts with powerful 500-candela lamps with shades focus the beams of light on the fence. The guard towers also have directional spotlights. The death zone and the space between the two fences is graveled with white limestone so that every human silhouette is more visible at night against the white background.

They finally let us into Block 17. It is an empty living space—one large room, new bunk beds stand there—three-tiered without mattresses. Doors and windows are like those found in homes. After a moment, the temperature of the space rises from our own body heat and we finally start feeling warm. A number of prisoners working in the *Lagerschreibstube*[8] sit behind a table and begin filling out quite comprehensive questionnaires, including our: profession, education, parents' names, mother's maiden name, home address, contact person in the event of death, languages known, physical appearance, number of rotten teeth, date of arrest, political affiliations, and so on. The work is arduous and requires a number of interpreters who can communicate with the crowd of prisoners of the most various nationalities. Of those tasked with preparing these so-called *Aufnahme* is the well-known writer Pomirowski, who shares a few hushed suggestions, like not to declare your profession as a military officer or lawyer—they are persecuted the most. We also learn from him about the basics of camp life. Those who have finished registering are to line up outside the barracks—and it is freezing there. So we get creative by lining up again for other tables—once we get close, we back away.

---

7. Literally, trip wire.
8. The camp administrative office.

After shaking off the initial shock of it all, we stand with Rector Drewnowski and Professor Michałowicz between the beds, we look at our outfits which can be described as a *Lumpenball*[9] gone too far. Nodding my head I say to them:

"Don't we look dandy."

They stare in silence. Suddenly, the lights go off. An SS man asks if there are any electricians. A scruffy magnificence steps forward, obtains a ladder from somewhere, and ten minutes later the lights come on again. The theoretician who had been lecturing at the faculty of electrical engineering has just passed his practical exam! During the registration process, the *Lagerältester*[10] from Field 1, a German, comes over several times brandishing a whip and cursing at us for no apparent reason, hurling abuse in his hoarse voice, calling us *"Scheisspolacken."*[11] We are overcome with helpless fury.

The registration is over by the evening—they lead us out of the block and we learn that we must proceed to Field 3, where it is supposedly worse than Field 1. Lining up in fives again, we are counted on the square, and walk through the gate of Field 1 where the *Blockführer* counts us; then, upon entering Field 3, we are counted once more by another *Blockführer* at an identical gate.

We stand in front of Block 5. The night is dark. There, we are handed over to our new ruler, the Block 5 overseer,[12] Feder, with a long whip in his hand, a Jew from Małopolska who counts us again and orders us inside. He refers to us as "you" but we have to call him "Mister Block Overseer." We enter the barracks through squeaky double doors, wide enough for us to enter five abreast. As I pass through, I spot an enameled plate with an inscription in German, saying that horses suffering from scabies should not be led in, and that in stables where horses have already been sick with scabies, any further horse transports can only be led in with the approval

---

9. A rag ball held after Karneval festivities.
10. The seniormost prisoner.
11. "Shitty Poles."
12. Translation from *Blockältester*; a prisoner functionary, the senior prisoner responsible for maintaining order in the barracks.

of an army veterinarian. I look around the stable which is to serve as our living space. The block is dimly lit with only three light bulbs. It is completely empty, one large hall without a single partition. The floor is covered in a layer of heavily trampled mud. There are no windows to be seen. The block overseer instructs us that in the evening, we are allowed to use the outdoor latrine only as long as the red light bulb on top of the tall post in the middle of the assembly square is on; once it turns off, the guard posts have orders to shoot anyone passing through the square. At night, you must relieve yourself into containers. These are large crates that can hold around two hundred gallons each, with long carrying poles nailed to either side. They are not sealed, which means urine and liquid excrement will seep out of them all night onto the floor.

There are no beds in the barracks, not to mention any benches or tables. There is no food for us. The block overseer tells us to go to sleep. It's moist and stuffy inside. We sit on the floor with disgust, even though we are already wearing rags; we huddle against one another to share some of our body heat. The floor is ice-cold and freezing wind rushes in through the cracks from below. Exhausted by the events of the day and the previous night, the sleepless journey on the freight car, I try my best to lay on the floor—but it proves impossible as my head keeps dropping backward with nothing to put underneath it. I'm not sure when I manage to fall into a heavy sleep, only to be woken shortly by the nagging cold. My legs are totally stiff and I can barely feel them. I doze off and wake up a number of times.

At 3:15 a.m., the block overseer wakes us up. I get up eagerly, so I can stretch my legs and warm up. The block has no washroom or even a water source so we are all ready for roll call in no time. They don't serve breakfast. We have to carry the toilet crates, filled to the brim, out of the building. Every leaking crate leaves traces across the floor of the entire block and all the way across the yard to the latrine. We wait and wait for the roll call to start. At 4:30 a.m., under the full moon light and in the biting cold, the block overseer leads us onto the square and lines us up in five rows. We stand there and wait some more. It is damn cold, we haven't had anything to eat since the day before yesterday, and the threadbare rags we are wearing, buttoned neither at the waist nor at the neck, do nothing to protect us against the steady wind blowing across the square.

At 5:00 a.m., the SS *Blockführer* arrive, and each one takes the roll call of their respective blocks, noting down the head counts in the barracks register, which they take with them. As the SS man approaches, the block overseer commands: "*Stillgestanden, Mützen ab, Augen links,*"[13] while he, hat in hand, runs to the *Blockführer* and reports the number of prisoners.

During the long roll call, I have enough time to take in the place that is to become my permanent residence. The field is rectangular with eleven barracks on the left and on the right, lined up along its longer sides, with their gables (with large entrances) facing the roll call square, occupying the entire center of the field. Behind the row of barracks stands a kitchen on one side, and a washroom barracks on the other. After the roll call, which lasts around an hour and a half, the longtime prisoners, dressed in concentration camp stripes, march out of the camp in various groups. We remain on the square.

During the roll call I noticed a number of men walking about the square, dressed like Austrian cavalry officers in red horse-riding breeches and dark blue, military-style shirts. The cut and condition of the uniforms is first-rate, but these "cavalrymen" are wearing ordinary civilian cycling caps on their heads, and the letters KL are discretely located and carefully painted on their backs. On their left arm is a black armband with the word KAPO in white. So these are the kapos,[14] whom we've already heard about on the outside.

So we stand, freezing and waiting again. After a while, one of the kapos approaches and addresses us in German. This is *Lagerältester* Rockinger, the most senior prisoner on Field 3. A young man, about thirty years old, with a fairly elegant appearance. The block overseer translates the speech into Polish—but very carelessly, leaving out half of it. Nonetheless we do learn that in the presence of every SS man and kapo we must take off our hats and run toward them if called. Sitting down or standing around dur-

---

13. "At attention, hats off, eyes to the left."
14. Slang term for the prisoner functionaries who are responsible for a prisoner work squad.

ing work is not allowed. We should always move quickly. Going to the latrine during work is not allowed. We cannot raise our collars or tuck our jackets into our pants (to insulate ourselves). We are not allowed to wear two shirts or sets of long underwear. Sweaters are not allowed. It is prohibited to carry: pencils, handkerchiefs, pocketknives, tobacco, or paper; we cannot enter the barracks during the day; or talk to civilian prisoners coming in to work at the camp. Tearing up blankets to wrap yourself is considered an act of sabotage and will be punished by death. Keeping your hands in your pockets is a major offense. In short, everything is forbidden, except dying.

Once the briefing is over, the block overseer orders us to proceed to a building where unfilled paper mattresses are stored. We each take one, line up in fives, are counted by the overseer, and led out the gate where he reports the number of prisoners leaving. The *Blockführer* notes it down and double-checks, and anyone that doesn't keep step with their row gets hit in the head with a cane. The overseer leads us in between the agricultural buildings with various warehouses and into the camp's vast vegetable gardens across several hundred acres called the *Gärtnerei*. There, we find the remains of two straw piles, now completely rotten and crushed into chaff. He orders us to stuff our mattresses with the foul chaff and carry them back to the camp. Near the straw, some fifty meters away, are mounds. Some prisoners run up to them and dig through the dirt to retrieve fodder beets which they wipe against their sleeves and start eating. We warn them not to do that as they could get diarrhea, but they don't listen to us, hunger triumphs over reason. The SS men accompanying our group notice the prisoners eating the beets; they stop them, order them to bend over and press their arms against their knees, and whip their behinds with all their might. Inhuman screams of pain cry out from the mouths of the beaten. With stuffed mattresses, we head back to the camp, the block overseer reports the number of prisoners returning to the *Blockführer*. He checks in his register the number of people that left against the number returning. We throw down the stuffed mattresses in the barracks, again take empty ones, line up in fives again, are counted by the overseer on the square and the *Blockführer* at the gate, again.

While stuffing the mattresses, I scan the terrain and notice an extended line of SS guard posts in roughly an eight-hundred-to-one-thousand-meter radius surrounding the camp structures, spaced out maybe one hundred meters from each other. This is called *Postenkette*.[15] This chain surrounds the areas where prisoners work during the day.

Leaving for the third time with the mattresses, we pass a column of women in concentration camp stripes and white head scarves. They ask:

"Where from, boys?"

We say we came from Pawiak Prison, to which the women reply:

"Hang tight, don't give up!"

At a distance they immediately recognized us as new *Zugang*,[16] the same way you can spot a conscript from afar. The encounter does a lot to buck up our spirits. As they passed us, the women sang *"O mój rozmarynie."*[17]

The carrying of mattresses lasts until noon, the work has warmed us up. At a quarter to twelve, a bell rings—lunch break. We get no meal as we have not yet been formally admitted into the camp. We spend the break in front of our barracks and we see that all the prisoners eat their meal outdoors. The break lasts fifty minutes. Then the bell again and the command: *"Arbeitskommando formieren."*[18] In the afternoon we continue carrying the mattresses while some stay at the camp and carry three-level bunk beds from one barracks to another. It is standard procedure that one prisoner must carry the headboard, and sideboards must be carried four at a time. Anyone carrying less is whipped.

At 6:00 p.m., the bell rings out signaling the end of work. We line up for the roll call which officially begins at 6:30 p.m. The work details, called *Kommando*, return from beyond the wire. The roll call can begin when the *Blockführer* gatehouse affirms that the last group has returned. Before the SS men arrive, the block overseer instructs us on how to properly take off our caps. At the word *"Mützen"* we must grab the visor with our right

---

15. Literally, chain of guard posts. There are actually two of these at Majdanek as Kwiatkowski explains below: the *grosse* (large) *Postenkette* and the *kleine* (small) *Postenkette*.

16. Here, a transport of newly arrived prisoners.

17. Polish: "Oh My Rosemary"—a popular Polish soldier's song.

18. "Form work details."

hand, at the word "*ab*" we must slap the caps against our thighs in unison. The roll call lasts over an hour and a half.

It has gotten completely dark. Finally the order "*Blockweise abrücken*"[19] is given. We proceed in military formation toward the barracks with the block overseers chanting rhythm to the left leg, calling out: "*Links . . . links . . . links . . . eins, zwei, drei, vier.*"[20]

We return to Block 5. Out front are metal cauldrons of fifty liters each with hermetic lids. The block overseer orders us to line up, next to him there is a pile of gray, enameled tin bowls. Most of them are badly damaged, the enamel is chipped, the metal is all rusty and partially twisted. At the bottom is a red label, marked at the factory: "Waffen-SS Lublin." The overseer ladles out half-liter portions of some greenish-yellow, hazy liquid. There are no spoons. I try it—it's some kind of herbal concoction, I taste mint. It's called tea, which is unsweetened of course. There is no bread, since we are still not yet admitted—and the tea is given to us unofficially. After this supper, we return the bowls and the overseer points us toward a pile of blankets lying in the corner of the barracks and instructs us to take one blanket each. Everyone hurls themselves onto the blankets, a tangled throng forms instantly. They start to push me back, I make room for others, convinced that a blanket has been allotted for each person. As the crowd settles, I near the pile of blankets—but all that remains are incomplete halves, with pieces already torn off. I show the scraps, useless as a covering, to the overseer standing nearby. He just shrugs his shoulders and walks away. So I take a torn blanket and start looking for my companion from the night before, with whom I huddled to stay warm.

It is Struczowski, the son of my brother's colleague from the Ministry of Education. A former officer cadet, tall, lean, dark-haired, calm, with a charming manner. He tells me that he was arrested for his work in the underground intelligence, he spent eight months in solitary confinement at Pawiak. He tells me about his deceased father and all his concern focuses on his lonely mother, deprived of the care of her only child. He

19. "March off by blocks."
20. "Left . . . left . . . left . . . one, two, three, four."

lives in Warsaw in the Żoliborz district. We spread the torn blanket on the floor and cover ourselves with the other one. It's awful that there's nothing to put under your head. We both lie down on our right side, huddle up and agree that if one of us needs to turn over, the other will of course turn as well.

In the evening, the thermometer drops below zero again. This night is better than last—only our feet are cold since the blanket was short. The block overseer orders us to return the blankets, I hear suspicious sounds, as if fabric is being ripped. Some tear off narrow strips to make scarves or to wrap them around their stomach. I go look outside—the moon is shining—the night is frosty. I go back in, shivering. I find half a flannel blanket, so very thin, and in a dark corner, I fold it three times and wrap it around my stomach and kidneys. It becomes delightfully warm. For breakfast, we get half a liter of unsweetened coffee. Before we go out to the square—again without any chance to wash, obviously—the block overseer tells us that he will search everyone for any blankets on their person. Blankets start flying in the air, I also quickly pull out my flannel and toss it onto the general pile.

We stand and wait for the roll call. I gaze at the moon whose soft light I used to enjoy so much, but it has lost much of its romantic appeal here.

It is piercingly cold. My neighbor, Doctor Jastrzębski, about sixty years old, is trembling all over. I start rubbing his back for warmth and he returns the favor. He changed the moment he stepped off the train, his cheeks have sunken and since his small beard was shaved off, his face is even more diminutive than before. Some of us move our arms around energetically to warm up a little—but that is only an option for those standing in the middle rows. Everyone tries to position themselves in the second, third, or fourth row, as the first and fifth are visible, besides being exposed to the wind. The sun has risen, the moon has paled, the roll call ends. "*Arbeitskommando formieren*"—we go with mattresses for straw again and line up the beds in Block 9.

For lunch—our first memorable meal—we get rutabaga soup mixed with fodder beets covered with rye flour. The food is so disgusting that despite my hunger, I leave some beets. We don't get spoons so we have to drink the soup from the bowl, and our mouths and chins are smeared with soup which we wipe with our sleeves. Some have already picked up sticks and splinters from the ground, none of them washed or whittled down of course, and use them like forks or Japanese chopsticks. We all eat outside. Our legs hurt like crazy, we sit down on the damp ground, which the sun has thawed by noon. Some Russians walk among us, asking for any left-overs, they are not picky when it comes to food! After lunch we continue organizing Block 9.

After the evening roll call, we are split up. Some of us (myself included) go over to empty Block 9, others to the partially inhabited Block 10. The prisoners living there are from Warsaw and were brought in with the first transport from Pawiak on January 17, 1943; some of them were caught during that famous three-day street roundup. Our new block overseer is Zygmunt Stauber, a former Polish Army corporal from Lwów.[21] He divides us into eight sections. The beds are lined up next to each other in twos, with narrow spaces in between other beds. They stand with the headboards to the longer walls of the barracks, forming a wide corridor along the middle length of the block.

I get a promotion, because Zygmunt designates me the section supervisor. I have about forty people. The beds are numbered as they are occupied so I have to assign a bed to every prisoner in my section and return the bed list to the block overseer. This seems like a simple matter, but the overseer says that he can't give me a pencil or paper. I have to "organize it" for myself. I had to think about it, since I didn't understand the word. I know about organizing a ball committee, I took academic courses in work organization, but how should I "organize" pencils—at that moment I couldn't comprehend it.

Each of us gets a bed with a straw mattress, but without any headrest, and two blankets. What luxury compared to the last three nights. For the first time, besides coffee, we also get some bread today. One loaf for eight people. The block overseer issues each section supervisor the appropriate number of loaves, which need to be cut and distributed. Another predicament, what should I cut the bread with: a knife needs to be organized!

21. Today L'viv, Ukraine. Most place names in this memoir appear in the form commonly used in interwar Poland and by Jerzy Kwiatkowski.

After supper, the overseer doesn't allow us to go to sleep, because he begins to issue numbers: they are two small linen cloths, roughly twelve by four centimeters, with our numbers printed on them. We are also given two red cloth triangles about four centimeters long with a printed letter P. We are supposed to sew the numbers onto the left breast and the left pant leg above the knee, and under the numbers, a red triangle. The red triangle marks us as political prisoners, and the letter P, that we are Polish. The overseer hands out ten needles plus an adequate amount of thread and now we must sew—and first of all, wait our turn. One person sews quickly and skillfully, the other learns to do the first stitches of their lives. Long past the 8:45 p.m. bell to return to barracks and 9:00 p.m., for lights-out and sleep, life is still bustling in our block. Late at night, I think it's past 11:00 p.m., the block overseer finally turns off the lights, announcing that the rest have to sew their numbers on before roll call in the morning. He wakes us before the bell, so at 3:00 a.m., and the sewing starts. Not everyone is able to finish by the morning roll call, some go out without their numbers, it turns out that the rest can sew them on in the evening.

We spend the day cleaning up empty barracks, sweeping, flipping over straw mattresses, our faces getting caked with a thick layer of dust. We are all extremely drowsy, having slept four hours at most today, and not more than six hours each of the previous nights. During the day, news reaches us that the entire Pawiak transport is soon to leave for Buchenwald. Naturally, it's a name that we hear for the first time. In Warsaw, you heard of Dachau, Auschwitz, Oranienburg, and Mauthausen. But Buchenwald is unknown and nobody, even roughly, knows where it is. Supposedly, it is in Bavaria. During the day, they list us by profession and arrange us in groups. The smart alecks claim to be farmers, thinking that they will be sent to work with peasants on the outside. About fifty from our transport are chosen for the *Kommando Unterkunft* and just as many for *Standortverwaltung*,[22] and they already know that they'll stay in the camp. I am assigned to the group meant to leave. When we return to the barracks after the evening roll call,

22. These are both tasks performed by the *Kommando*; see the chapters "A Hand through the Barbed Wire" for a description of *Unterkunft* (accommodation), and "The Camp Administration" for a description of *Standortverwaltung* (here, the camp administration and supply department).

the overseer commands us to take off our shoes by the doors so as to not dirty the floor. Since it was only just scrubbed in the afternoon, the floor is totally damp, and water is still standing in wood notches. The temperature inside is 5 degrees at best and while walking in socks, which are soaked through in moments, many of us catch cold, which is exactly the point![23]

I thought that today we would go to sleep earlier, since sewing the rest of the numbers on won't take much time. It turns out that nearly all the needles that the overseer issued yesterday have "evaporated" and no one will admit to having them. Instead, we have a different job today. One of our companions from the transport, Ludwig Knips, who had been transferred the day before departure to Pawiak from the Mokotów Prison[24] and immediately declared himself a *Volksdeutsch*,[25] has now been appointed as the *Blockschreiber*, the block secretary. He has already been issued leather shoes, a good jacket, and a hat. He sleeps next to the overseer, does not have to get up at 3:00 a.m. with the others, and is already distancing himself from us. He says that he is from Cieszyn Silesia, that he took part in the Silesian Uprisings, and he is supposedly doing time for this, and that the Germans found his application to the Polish authorities for him to be awarded the Upper Silesian Cross. Whereas he had bragged to me in the transport that he collaborated with the Germans in October 1939 in taking the documents of our Ministry of Foreign Affairs, and that later he was a powerbroker in the *Treuhandaussenstelle*,[26] located in the building of the Ministry of Internal Affairs on Nowy Świat Street. He oversaw all the mills in the Warsaw district. He wore a uniform with an official dagger. He belonged to the *Selbstschutz*,[27] his son serves as a volunteer in the

23. This would be 41° Fahrenheit. Temperature references throughout the memoir are in Celsius.

24. The prison on Rakowiecka Street in Warsaw, managed by the German criminal police (*Kripo*) during the occupation, was used to hold criminal prisoners.

25. A person of German descent living outside the Reich who declared themselves a member of the German nation.

26. A branch of the trust office responsible for the receivership of seized property in Warsaw.

27. Specifically: *Volksdeutscher Selbstschutz*, a paramilitary organization composed of citizens of the Second Polish Republic of the German national minority. During the early stages of the occupation, members of the *Selbstschutz* were actively involved in various extermination operations.

German air force, his wife is Polish. And so, Herr Knips starts to prepare the block register, he does it very clumsily and sluggardly, stopping work, getting involved in some private chats, while the poor *Häftlinge*[28] have to stand and wait. One of them already got it "in the face" on the first day in the office of Mr. "Schreiber." He keeps us on our feet for several hours after the bell again. There is no clock in the barracks, or on the field, so we don't know the time.

Last night I froze, despite the "luxurious" sleeping conditions. The very dirty mattresses of course have no sheets. I leave one blanket on the mattress, I undress down to my long underwear and shirt, and cover myself with the other, heavily frayed blanket. Naturally, we are not allowed to sleep in our clothes. I rolled up my clothes and used them as a headrest. I hid my shoes beneath the mattress under my head, as I had been warned that footwear gets stolen at night. Having frozen under the single blanket, I arrange to sleep together with Struczowski tonight. This way, we will have three whole blankets to cover ourselves with. Once again, we sleep a maximum of four hours.

28. Prisoners.

I Become a Gardener

In the morning, they start selecting for the Buchenwald transport again. The *Lagerältester* approaches and asks who of us is a gardener. Three of us step out. He starts questioning us and since I am fluent in German, he keeps me. He tells me I will remain for another fourteen days, until the spring gardening work on Field 3 is complete, and I won't leave until the next transport. He tells me to pick four professional helpers, who will also be excluded from the transport. I ask Father Archutowski, Engineer Sopoćko, Struczowski, and Captain Macieliński if they would like to stay on as my helpers. All four agree and by the glint in their eyes I see their satisfaction, but they all also warn me that they have no clue about gardening. I reassure them that I will show them exactly what to do.

The *Lagerältester* takes us away and shows us the work that needs to be done. I can immediately see that this is a project for longer than two weeks, and besides, I realize that once the spring work is finished, the garden will require constant, uninterrupted maintenance. There is not a single tree or bush on Field 3; there is a patch of grass with several flower beds in front of the first barracks from the road, Block 12, housing the Field 3 infirmary. But other than that, it is all hard, bare soil, trampled down by thousands of feet and various vehicles.

We start digging up the flower beds, Father Archutowski gets the rake, so the lightest work, and I show him how to hold and use it. I get several farmers from outside the Pawiak transport who know how to use a spade, so my pupils are easily lost in the crowd and do not draw particular attention with their dilettantism. Besides, the field commandant and the *Lagerältester* are busy putting together the transport. People are changing into camp stripes, they get striped coats, and once again have to sew on numbers and *Winkel*,[29] transport lists are prepared.

29. Literally, angle; refers to the triangles the prisoners are to sew onto their uniforms, like the red one Kwiatkowski has to sew on his that denotes him as a political prisoner.

A medical examination is scheduled for 2:00 p.m. On the square, several hundred people undress and parade naked in front of an SS doctor, the commandant of the camp hospital. Anyone with severe ulceration, scabies, or other glaring defects, is segregated—the doctor deems the rest healthy. In two hours maybe six hundred people are "examined" this way. The SS men keep watch to make sure that the healthy don't move over to the group rejected from the transport. Next, again, the writing down of who was rejected from the transport.

In the evening, as we are about to fall sleep, the doors open and I hear the block overseer talking to someone, who rushes us out of bed in our underwear. There is an order for a *Läusekontrolle*.[30] We have to take off our shirts and turn them inside out to show the doctor. It lasts over an hour. Lice are found on a dozen or so people. We'll have less than five hours of sleep again.

The following day, after the evening roll call, Blocks 9 and 10 are eliminated. Everyone designated for transport is separated, counted, and taken to the two empty blocks, 15 and 16. The rest of us return to overseer Feder in Block 5, also empty, without beds or blankets. Blocks 9 and 10 are left unoccupied. Around a hundred people gather into Block 5. To think that there are two empty barracks—9 and 10—with beds and blankets, while hundreds of people are told to sleep on the muddy, disgusting floor without blankets!

We sit around one of the posts, concentrically—in ever larger circles, so that everyone can lean against their neighbor's knees. In a moment it gets warm, but after half an hour our legs start to go numb and we don't know where to stretch them in the crowd. Among us are the first ones already suffering diarrhea (enteritis). These are the effects of eating raw beets and potato peels and drinking unboiled water. Their pants are soaked past their knees from frequent discharges, and you can smell the characteristic sickly sweet, vomit-inducing odor from far away. Unfortunately, we have to ask the sick to sit separately since we can't bear being near them. Another tor-

---

30. A lice-infestation check.

turous night. Dr. Jastrzębski sits next to me, sunk into himself. Professor Michałowicz was already moved to the hospital as a doctor—he won the lottery. Rector Drewnowski, through the intervention of friends from the first Pawiak transport, also got a good assignment—peeling potatoes. The work is in a damp room, but it has two colossal benefits: first, that he is sitting down and does not have to stand continuously from 3:30 a.m. to 9:00 p.m., and that the room is stuffy but warm, it also gets him an extra bowl of soup.

Roll call in the morning, as usual, but we see that it is dragging out. There is counting again, an officer arrives by motorcycle, then two, then a few more still. We learn that a prisoner is missing. The search begins, most likely someone meant for the transport made a run for it or hid somewhere. Apart from the SS men, a larger unit is recalled from the neighboring field where an even larger unit of Russian POWs in uniforms are held, and they start to turn the field upside down. They even get down on the ground to look inside gutters and under the footbridges thrown over the ditches in front of every barracks. Result negative!

The SS officers talk with the block overseers, Polish Jews, in whose barracks the prisoners slated for transport to Buchenwald had spent the night. I can see that the overseers are gesticulating too much. Suddenly, from the group of SS men comes the shout *"Ein Dolmetscher."*[31] I run up to them, taking my hat off on the way. Then, one of the officers, short and chestnut-haired in a leather coat, orders me to ask both the overseers if their barrack's doors were boarded up for the night. One replies affirmatively, the other, negatively. The officer orders the entire transport to enter the barracks one by one and instructs the SS men to count them as they go in. Since the number matches that on the transport list, they assume the SS men made a mistake while counting, because one prisoner is indeed still missing from the field. So they keep the whole transport inside the barracks, they bring over a table, and they start reading out the names on the list. When your name is read out, you have to line up on the square.

31. "An interpreter."

And the entire field is standing at roll call . . . A chilly wind is blowing, it's maybe 4 or 5 degrees below freezing. I've gotten so numb I don't even feel the cold anymore. And under the eyes of the SS officers you can't rub your back or move like a horse-cart driver waiting for a fare and rubbing his torso with his arms. The reading goes on until 11:00 p.m. With only a handful of people still waiting, an unexpected order comes: *"Blockweise abrücken."* Just hearing the words warms me up.

The rest of those from the transport whose names were unread leave the barracks and join the others on the square. Everyone is commanded to take off their clogs, and they give them sabots (Dutch slippers made entirely from wood)—to hamper escape from the train. Everyone is also issued a loaf of bread and a piece of sausage. They trudge and shuffle in their sabots, marching to the train, surrounded by SS men armed with automatic rifles ready to fire and dogs on leashes.

What happened that they ordered us to leave before they finished read-ing the transport list? It turns out the *Schreibstube*[32] made a mistake while preparing the roll call plan. Due to the disbanding of a number of blocks, only the block overseers remain in their empty barracks. Since one of them, Neumeister, a Polish Jew, spent the night in a different, occupied barracks and was given food there, he was listed twice during the roll call: in his own barracks and in the one where he slept. Whenever there is a dis-crepancy in the roll call, the *Schutzhaftlagerführer*,[33] *SS-Untersturmführer*[34] Anton Thumann, is immediately notified. During his inspection of Field 3 due to the alleged missing prisoner, he happens to note that one of the "transport" barracks had not been boarded up for the night, against regu-lations. Thus I met Thumann, the one before whom the entire camp trem-bles, whom all of the SS men (not to mention the prisoners) fear and hate.

After the departure of the Buchenwald transport, the remainders from the emptied barracks are again gathered into Blocks 9 and 10. I return to Block 9. The overseer informs us that we must always take off our shoes when coming back from work in the evening. So we walk with only socks

32. The clerks' office on each field.
33. Here, the SS officer who is the chief of the prisoner department.
34. SS Second Lieutenant.

on, our dirty toes already peeking out, across the wet floor. I contract a strange inflammation of my mucous membranes in my nose from being outside constantly, and freezing. It's not the common cold that we all get several times a year, which has its peak and then passes. It is just more of an excess of moisture in my nose, making my nostrils constantly wet, now and again it drips. In the breeze, my nose gets dry, then some mucus oozes out again and the skin gets chapped, crust keeps forming on the tip of my nose. I'm not the only one suffering from this affliction, I see that many of us are forced to constantly wipe our noses with our sleeves and hats. We get beds in a different place—but Struczowski sleeps above me again—in fact we are sleeping in one bed.

I don't know exactly how long I've been at Majdanek, but I have yet to wash myself. The next day I join up with the group carrying water for scrubbing the floor before roll call. I use this opportunity to wash myself for the first time—without soap or a brush—but what a delight it was that the sticky filth came off my hands and face. I feel so refreshed after this wash under the tap. I wipe myself with my hat. I can feel that I've grown quite a beard, after all I can see the same on the faces of my friends. They were supposed to shave us on Sunday, but since we've been working until the evening every day, we've lost track of the day of the week. But there was no shaving.

We have the first days of April, the temperature hasn't risen at all, we get strong winds and night freezes. I comfort myself that, according to the calendar, spring starts on March 21. What can I do to protect myself from the cold? I have an idea. In the morning, I take a handful of straw from my mattress, I hide behind the bed and stuff it in my shirt, on my back, on my chest and spread it around evenly. The straw itches somewhat. During the morning roll call, I can feel it warming me a bit. I shake it out in the evening, it all crumbled, all that's left is chaff. After supper, there is a lice check. When Dr. Jastrzębski examines me, he spends a long time checking my shirt, he looks me over again, puts me to the side, and tells me to wait. I notice that my entire body is covered in what looks like a rash, it's from the straw pricking my chest and stomach. Privately, Dr. Jastrzębski tells me that lice have bitten me terribly, although to his surprise he couldn't find a single one. I tell him that I don't have lice and that I'm scratched from the straw. He shakes his head doubtfully and insists it looks like irritation from lice bites.

Two days after the transport's departure, I am called to the office of the *Feldführer*,[35] Groffmann, who points to a large sack and says it's park grass to sow. I open the sack and I see it's not grass but some sort of clover seed. It gives off a moldy smell, the seed is rotten. I explain to him that this isn't park grass and give it to him to smell—I tell him that I'll carry out a germination test but I will need some cotton or lignin and a place with a stable, warm temperature. He is visibly impressed, and takes me to the infirmary and orders lignin issued. I count out one hundred seeds, place them on the moist lignin, and set a dish in the *Schreibstube*—the Field 3 office. I bless the man for it because the office is blissfully warm, the stove is roaring. Every couple of hours I drop in for five minutes to check if the grass has already started sprouting. The clerks employed at the office, all Slovak Jews—knowing I am acting on orders from the *Feldführer*—gaze at my bowl with great respect and tolerate my presence. This gives me the opportunity to meet the head of the office, a Slovak Jew, Dr. Horowitz—a bank manager. He is an exceptionally modest, quiet, and tactful person, treating not just me but every prisoner very decently.

---

35. The field commandant, or the SS officer who is in charge of a prisoner field.

Camp Life

As I work near the gate and two barracks, the first housing the infirmary and the other the field commandant's office and the *Schreibstube*, I can see what's happening on the field. As a newcomer, my attention is particularly drawn to the *Wagenkolonnen*.[36] These are old army wagons on heavy, chest-height wheels, with the seat two meters above the ground, pulled by four heavy artillery horses. Here, the wagons are currently without horses, they are drawn by the prisoners. There are "harnesses" made of wire, which cuts deep into your chest and shoulders; also, additional wires are attached to the sides of the wagon (four on each side) with a piece of wood wrapped in as a grip. Twenty people form up like this: two lead the wagon tongue, four pull the leader bars in front, eight on the sides, and six pushing from behind. They transport mainly potatoes to the kitchen. Each wagon can hold at least two tons. There are several of them, going all day on the grounds of the vegetable farm, loading up at the potato mounds and unloading at the kitchens. There are no hardened roads in the vegetable gardens, the soil is sandy and heavy vehicles have left ruts full of water, mud, and potholes. The worst place is in front of the camp gate, where there are massive pools of mud and huge pits. When a loaded wagon gets stuck, the kapos and SS men start shouting, then both start lashing with their whips across straining backs.

It's a spectacle that repeats every couple of minutes. It makes a huge impression on me, calling to mind Egyptian slaves under the whips of the Pharaoh's guards transporting boulders across the sands to build the pyramids. So this is *Der Mythus des 20. Jahrhunderts*[37] in practice! Other columns with human-yoked wagons deliver bread, others use buckets, constantly slipping off the poles, to scoop up excrement from latrine cesspits and remove it to the compost heaps in the gardens. Others take away

36. Columns of carriages.
37. *The Myth of the Twentieth Century*, a book by the apostle of National Socialism Alfred Rosenberg.

garbage, also for composting. Whips start whistling in the air whenever a wagon gets stuck in the road. The most gruesome sight, however, is the wagons pulling up every morning in front of the infirmary. Prisoners carry out totally naked corpses and throw them onto the wagon—like butchers toss slabs of pork fat. The bodies are so thin and emaciated, all that's left is literally skin and bones. Chests jut out—and their abdomens are totally caved in. The outline of the spine is almost visible through the stomach. Arms and legs are just bones draped in skin, none have buttocks, you can clearly see the pelvis. Only the nose and cheekbones protrude on the face, the rest is collapsed. Hands and feet black with dirt, bodies coated in feces. Most of the bodies are totally stiff, with bluish bedsores. The *Feldführer*, watching this "funeral" from the window of his office next door, leans out and starts shouting about why the loading of bodies is taking so long. Prisoners grab the corpses by the arms and legs, swing and heave them onto the tall wagon, one body on top of another. A tangled mass of arms and legs forms sticking out in all directions. What a nightmare! *Ecce homo*!

Before long, I too am harnessed to a wagon. Outside the camp gate stood a three-ton car trailer loaded with earth. The *Lagerältester* led twenty of us to the trailer and ordered that we drag it somewhere else since they are leveling the road running along all the fields. We push the trailer but it won't budge. The *Lagerältester* assumes that we don't feel like pushing and starts yelling at us. I see that one of the wheels is stuck in a pothole and that's why it will be hard to move. When he sees that his shouts aren't effective, he starts blindly whipping us across our backs and heads, circling around the trailer. Despite the whips we can't do it. So the *Lagerältester* stops another group of thirty prisoners marching by, but even the fifty of us, backed by whips, can't move it. So the *Lagerältester* gives up and takes us back to the camp. Later, through the wires, I see a tractor jerking the trailer a few times and it also can't move it. Only after the wheel has been dug out with spades does it move. I see that at the camp they demand impossible things—that which even an engine can't move, a starved and sleep-deprived prisoner is expected to achieve. It's no surprise, because there is nothing cheaper here than human life. So it is of no consequence if such strain causes several people to have hernias or even to die right on the spot.

The most pleasant prisoner-driven vehicle is the bread wagon. It rides onto the field every day and the crew calls out several times in unison: "*Brot holen*,"[38] which is the sign for the *Stubendienst*[39] from individual barracks to run out with their ration containers.

Every morning during the roll call, an SS man riding a bicycle supervises the cooks. A big fellow, over two meters tall. Since the road leads uphill, he usually calls the nearest prisoner, and orders him to run behind and push the bicycle, so that the SS man does not have to strain too hard. It's a distance of about four hundred meters.

I see how SS men on bicycles escort prisoners to the *Politische Abteilung*[40] for interrogation. An SS man rides, while the prisoner must run in front of the bike. During the evening roll call, I notice field commandant Groffmann beating one of the prisoners. You can't really call it a beating though. It's practicing to strike a man down with a single blow. He seeks out his victim—any pretext is easy to find—pulls him out of line, positions him diagonally in front of himself, moves toward the prisoner, feels where the liver is, steps back, practices a semicircular swing of his arm to check if his distance is right, spreads his legs in a boxer's stance, and then with one swift blow punches the chosen spot. Calm practice, without any emotion. Woe to the felled if he stays on the ground too long, then he gets kicked or whipped. Once he's up, the punch is repeated, with the same touching and sizing-up. The field commandant selects a second person to practice hooks or strikes to the heart.

The daily lice check affirms an infestation increasing by the day. After the morning roll call the following day, the afflicted are sent for delousing. At first, there are only a few, but then the numbers begin to mount. The delousing process entails a shower and issue of "fresh" shirts and other clothing. But what of it when lice remain on the blankets and beds. Prisoners find lice on the "fresh" clothes before even leaving the bathhouse, and it's the norm to have nits that hatch swarms of young lice within six

---

38. "Collect the bread."
39. A member of the barracks maintenance crew, a prisoner functionary.
40. Political Department.

days. Underwear is not boiled, but gassed in the *Gaskammer*[41] and then washed in tepid water, and that's why there's no way to eradicate the lice. Although the gas chamber works without complaint when used against people, its effectiveness against lice leaves a lot to be desired. The only positive aspect of the delousing is the shower, the negative part is getting different clothes, which are always much worse than what you had before. Everyone knows that at night, new lice will come from your neighbor or your own blanket.

Some of us managed to change part of our wardrobe by swapping with those who left for Buchenwald. They knew that they were going to get striped uniforms, so whoever had a warmer jacket or pants exchanged them with us and we gave them the worst rags.

The morning roll call normally lasts an hour and a half, since 6:00 a.m. is set for the march out for work. The overall population of the field and each individual barracks is noted by the office in the *Appelplan*,[42] handed to the *Rapportführer*.[43] The *Blockführer* checks whether the number reported to him squares with reality. The sick and the dead do not need to be reported—since they are carried out to the roll call and laid in the mud or snow at the left wing of each barracks and they are counted with the living, after which they are carried back in front of the barracks. The *Blockführer* reports the actual state of the barracks to the *Rapportführer*. If the office makes a mistake in the roll call plan—or an SS man miscounts—then the "roll call is incorrect" and has to be received again. This means adding at least another half an hour for a recount. Either way, we have to keep standing there until the roll call adds up. Zygmunt, the block overseer, says that if the office makes a mistake, the head clerk is called to the *Rapportführer* and gets a dozen lashes right away. And if the discrepancy cannot be rectified, the list of names from all the blocks is read out until the missing person is identified, unless fellow prisoners themselves notice who ran away or is otherwise missing. In that case, the entire field stays standing on the square while the *Blockführer* and the SS men that arrive start search-

41. Gas chamber.
42. Roll call plan.
43. Here, the SS officer responsible for the prisoner count.

ing the barracks, looking under mattresses, in warehouses, sheds, workshops, latrines, pipes under walkways, as long as it takes until the lost one is found. Everyone prays for it to end quickly as standing motionless in flimsy rags, freezing at attention, leads to a heavy cold.

Once the roll call is correct, the *Rapportführer* submits the report of the roll call for the entire field to the *Feldführer* and then the entire field gets the order: "*Mützen ab.*" The slap with our caps in unison has to be hard enough to be heard (like the block overseer taught us) at the Lublin railway station, some two or three kilometers away as the crow flies. If the slap isn't simultaneous, the hats come off again and it is repeated several times, until it's done right.

Immediately afterward, we hear the command: "*Arbeitskommando formieren.*" Prisoners assigned to different work columns form up at designated places and march out, mainly to jobs outside the wires. The groups that remain to work on the field are called the *Innenkommando*.

Since nobody but the block overseer and the so-called *Stubendienst* is allowed inside the barracks during work, the sick sit or lie outside the barracks during the day. The dead lie naked on the ground in front of the barracks and they are only struck off the list after the morning roll call, and then carried to the crematorium. So if someone dies at 9:00 a.m., his corpse is brought to the evening's and following morning's roll call. They tell me that in February 1943, there regularly used to be a third roll call at noon, so the deceased could actually "stand" for three more roll calls after dying. During roll call the *Blockführer* and kapos often walk up to the motionless bodies of the dying, and with the tip of their boot deliver a sharp strike to the temple, checking if the man will still move after the kick, whether he will raise his closed eyelids for the roll call, or if his cheeks maintain their frozen grimace.

The evening roll call is more complicated than in the morning because new transports arrive during the day, the dead are subtracted from the rolls, the sick are transferred to Field 1 (at the center of which is the camp hospital, called "the Revier"), prisoners are moved from one block to another or to other fields, etc. There are incidents when the roll call doesn't add up because a new prisoner loses their way and returns from work with another group to a different field. So there is a surplus there and a prisoner missing on another field. In the evening, the *Blockführer* gate-houses from all the fields communicate by telephone to make sure the roll call is correct—only then can the *grosse Postenkette* (chain of guard posts) surrounding the camp be called in. And since the prisoners don't need to punctually march out for work after the evening roll call, the SS men take their time with the counting and the whole thing drags on endlessly. The field commandant summons the block overseers, kapos, and *Vorarbeiter*,[44] issues instructions, identifies faults, metes out whippings, and so on.

The *grosse Postenkette*, surrounding the area of the camp where prisoners work during the day, is manned in the morning, before the prisoners march out to work, and its guards stay in position until the end of the evening roll call. At night, the so-called *kleine Postenkette* is stationed just outside the wires on the field side and in the area of the utility buildings so that the guards can still stop a prisoner who manages to make it through the barbed-wire entanglements. But if the roll call does not add up and someone disappears, the whole field stands, so all the prisoners on the square and the *grosse Postenkette*. They tell me that once the *Postenkette* stood for two days straight because the search for an escapee lasted that long.

I find out that in March there was a great increase in people coming down with typhus fever and Block 10 was the seedbed where new cases are still being reported. The lice infestation cannot be underestimated. Meanwhile in our barracks, the lice checks have stopped. They probably gave up. I also find lice from time to time. It's terrible that such a beast can crawl up and down your body all night with impunity, you can feel it but you're defenseless because there is no light at night in the barracks and you have to wait until morning to squash it. So far, the ones I find on myself have migrated from other beds. I still feel completely helpless in my battle against lice.

As a section supervisor, both before work in the morning and after the roll call in the evening, I have to deal with a lot of headaches. I distributed the bread by taking a group of eight people and gave them an entire loaf to

44. Foremen.

divide among themselves. By the way, one-eighth of a loaf is the ration for twenty-four hours. I wanted to speed up the distribution. But soon people start coming over with complaints. One brought his "slice" and grumbles that the bread wasn't cut into eight equal pieces, another claims he never got his slice. The block overseer obliges me to distribute each person's portion of bread separately, directly into their hands. There are two or three knives in the barracks. So we have to wait until the coveted knife reaches our section. Forty people stand and gaze at the five loaves laid out on my bed. I finally get the knife and start dividing the bread. In the middle of this, they call me to the overseer to collect the "ration" of side dishes: margarine, sausages, marmalade, or dry cottage cheese. These extras are not given every day, margarine is twice a week, and the same with sausage. I leave the undistributed bread under the care of my people, and when I come back with the extras and finish dividing the bread, it turns out that one or two pieces are missing. This happens even when I'm not distracted away from my work, they steal it right out from under my nose. Some take it for their "friends," but when the friend shows up a moment later he says he knows nothing about it. Some try and come forward twice for bread. The easiest thing would be to have a table of names, types of extras, and days of the week—but that would only require . . . a pencil and paper. Several times I'm left without bread myself—because I can't explain that my bread was stolen. Some people show up for bread an hour after it was handed out because they loiter around other barracks. There's no other way out, so I announce that I will only give out bread when the entire section in full gathers 'round. I have forty portions and only thirty-nine people are there—so we wait. Finally, it turns out that one person went to the hospital but the overseer, not knowing which section he came from, gave me bread according to the previous day's list. Bread is issued to the blocks based on the morning roll call numbers—and when someone departs from the barracks by dying or transferring to the Revier—the remainder belongs to the block overseer. When portioning out bread loaves, the overseer doesn't want to check which sections have lost people, but during the evening, he calls the supervisors over and demands any surplus. Whoever doesn't return bread gets one portion less the next day. Bread is hard currency in the camp, for which anything can be bought—not just for a single slice, of course. It would seem like such a simple thing to divide five loaves of bread, but despite my knowledge of algebra and logarithms, I run into colossal difficulties.

What am I to do with one or two unclaimed portions of bread? There is no cupboard to lock it in; if it's under the blanket or mattress, the universal hiding place in the camp, they'll take it out from under me; I won't stow it in my pocket, so I have to sit next to the portions and watch over them until—just before the bell rings that the red light in the field is about to go out—their owners return to the barracks. The division of marmalade or hard cottage cheese, made from a powder mixed with water, poses the same problem. I usually get it after distributing the bread. So there is nothing to put it on for people, since it's rare for someone to have bread, which is devoured in moments. And divide a bowl of marmalade into thirty-nine even portions! Usually this works out to one tablespoon per head. But if the marmalade happens to be good—the overseer keeps more for himself, and if too much water is added to the cheese, the normal measure fails. The first serving is a skimpy spoonful on bread, paper, or an outstretched palm (unwashed since the day of arrival), and again you have to visually remember so that no one takes seconds. Then whatever is left is divided again, using just the tip of the spoon. Thirty-eight pairs of eyes look suspiciously upon each spoon, to see if their neighbor didn't get a fuller spoonful or if his wasn't shaken off too much. Primal instincts come out with this hunger and all masks come off. Again, one or two unclaimed portions of marmalade remain.

Supper begins with black coffee, which we have to line up for by section—and the section supervisors have to stand by the cauldron and count the number of portions given for his section. There are still controversies, because either someone from another section stands in line or someone from your section gets their portion, sets down their bowl and goes to the back of the line again. Next to the cauldron stands either the block overseer, or one of five or six *Stubendienst*, the personnel that takes care of the barracks, keeps it clean, and doesn't go out to work. It's understood that such a thief, who wants to deprive his fellow prisoner of their half a liter of coffee or soup, deserves to be punished—they are slapped in the face, hit in the head and the back with a ladle, and in tougher cases, the overseer pulls out the whip and starts thrashing them. Naturally, more than one portion of coffee or soup gets spilled on the floor in the struggle. If anything is left in the cauldron, they serve out a *Nachschlag*,[45] a *repeta* in Polish. This second helping is served in turns to a different section every day. But there is never enough for the whole section to get even a quarter of a liter each, so there is constant shoving to stand first in line for the *repeta*. The overseer only issues bread after the coffee is served. In sum, distributing half a liter of unsweetened coffee, about 187 grams of bread, and a spoon of marmalade or dry cottage cheese, lasts at least an hour and a half. A portion of margarine is the size of a matchbox. It's divided in such a way so that there's enough for the overseer, the *Stubendienst*, and the barracks clerk to fry potatoes. The horsemeat sausage, a normal size, is given in pieces of around five centimeters, with a very high water content (so the weight adds up). It spoils so quickly that the following morning it already smells bad. There are so few bowls in the barracks, that there are at most enough for three sections. So you have to eat quickly because the next sections yank the bowls out of your hands. They are not rinsed of course, since there is no water in the barracks. There are no spoons. Three mouths drink coffee or soup from one bowl, what a hive of tuberculosis, syphilis, and typhoid fever bacteria on the edge of that bowl!

Sometimes, instead of the side dishes, they serve unpeeled, steamed potatoes. But there are days of the week when you get only the coffee and 187 grams of bread. The potatoes are rotten, eaten by fungus, with straw mixed in. Each of us receives eight to ten tiny potatoes, of course without salt. They give us potatoes into our hats or cradled into the front of our jackets. The potatoes for pigs are in much better condition and carefully rinsed. That they're steamed and not boiled is another reason they are disgusting. There is a crate in the barracks where we throw the potato peels. Soon enough I see that some people are digging through this crate, pulling out the peels and eating them.

Each day a different section has duty hours, their responsibilities are to bring in the cauldrons with breakfast and take away the empty ones to the kitchen, take out the full containers (excrement crates) in the morning,

---

45. Second helping.

bring the cauldrons with supper in the evening and take them back to the kitchen after they've been rinsed, and bring the empty containers back from the latrine. The section supervisor assigns people from his section to these tasks. The chosen ones often don't show up for these functions, they just vanish or if they are called (among three hundred people) they don't reply. The block overseer is immediately informed about this delay by the *Stubendienst*, and, lying in bed, curses out the section supervisor about why the section isn't getting its work done. So the supervisor grabs the first good person from his section, like when a fourth person is needed to carry out the crates. People often refuse to obey, saying it's not their turn—but the rush is necessary since so much work needs to be done before the roll call. There's nothing left to do but grab the resister by the sleeve and take him by force to work. This kind of insubordination and avoidance of work by those on duty leads to the first animosities and scuffles. The one shirking their responsibilities only harms his fellow prisoners, not the section supervisor, but the animosity is directed toward the supervisor, and not at the one who ducked out of the main duty to keep the barracks clean.

Even though the *Stubendienst* is supposed to keep the barracks clean, most of the heavy lifting falls on the prisoners. And so, the section on duty has to go to the *Waschbaracke*[46] (where the water supply system and the washroom are under construction) and bring around twenty or thirty buckets of water, as well as large vats of approximately thirty or forty liters each. The water is poured onto the floor, the mud gets soaked, and then the floor is scrubbed with brushes and a squeegee (of the kind used to clean asphalt surfaces), which clears the water. The water drains under the barracks through gaps in the floor or under boards lifted for this purpose. Every day, hundreds of liters of water run down under the floor of the block like this and soak into the foundation and soil. As the work progresses, prisoners become crammed against the very entrance, and in the end have to leave the barracks, even though there was no bell to form up for roll call. Some overseers hustle people out by serving coffee at the door and you have to leave the block with your bowl, and aren't able to return until evening. Our overseer is decent enough that he doesn't do this.

---

46. Washroom barracks.

Naturally, the beds must be made before leaving in the morning. This takes a lot of time. A narrow passage of no more than fifty centimeters provides access to six bunks. So no more than two people at a time can make beds in this narrow space. Above all, the straw in the mattresses has to be evened out so there are no lumps. Blankets must be tucked in between the mattress and the bed frame and stretched, and the crease of the blanket along the edge of the bed must be sharp enough to form an exact 90-degree angle. Next, we have to take a special plank and use it to press and smooth the blanket to create an ideally flat surface. And not only that: the black stripes on the gray blankets must all be aligned. When you stand next to the first bed and look down the entire row of beds, all the stripes must form a perfectly straight line. We make it easier on ourselves by discretely marking the place on each bed frame where the first black stripe must go. But not all the blankets have the same number of stripes, and some people have colored blankets. So we gather the uniform blankets on the first and second levels of the bunks—and the mixed lot on the third, since they can't be seen from the ground. We have to take straw out of mattresses on the third level to stuff those in the bottom rows so that the beds can be nicely made. So on top, mattresses are left with only chaff and people sleep on a totally hard surface. Keeping anything under the mattresses is prohibited. For now we don't have anything to hide, but more than one person conceals at least a fragment of bread until the morning, to have a bite to eat with their bitter coffee. The beds are made starting at the top, then the middle row, and finally the bottom. The top row has the least to do—the mattresses are so anemic that there is not much to fix, and with a mishmash of blankets, you don't have to mind the stripes. It's the compensation for sleeping hard, and it has already sorted itself out that the careless and sloppy rush to sleep on the top row. After making the bed, you have to stand next to it until you leave the barracks, since, if your neighbor from a higher row forgot something and climbs up the sideboards—especially in shoes—you have to brush off the blanket, smooth the surface, and crease the edges all over again. Sometimes the indifference of your "friends" brings you nearly to tears—the bed has been stomped on and they're already coming, scrubbing the floor, telling you to move. Meanwhile, during the day the block overseer will walk around and write down the numbers of improperly made beds, and in the evening, before bed, he rations out three to five, or even eight, lashes to the buttocks, while a "friend" holds the delinquent by the head to make sure he is bending over properly.

It is much worse if during the daily inspection of his barracks (sometimes he has two or three), a *Blockführer* determines that the beds are not made properly, then the overseer himself has to bend over and get whipped, and besides this the *Blockführer* writes down that he noticed problems in the barracks in the block inspection book. It's already customary during his inspection for the *Blockführer* to walk up to the beds to see if the blanket stripes are properly aligned, to check whether there is garbage in front of the barracks, if there is anyone sleeping inside, or if anyone besides the barracks personnel is inside. But, the fact that lice are crawling over the blankets, or that someone heavily sick or dying is lying in front of the barracks, or that the block overseer beat someone so badly that they are incapable of going to work—he doesn't see it and he's not interested. "*Bettenbau*"[47] is the watchword issued by the field commandant to his subordinates, "*Bettenbau*" is repeated by the SS men to the block overseers, "*Bettenbau*" is yelled at the prisoners by the overseers. "Building" a good bed takes at least ten or fifteen minutes.

Because the doors to the barracks where prisoners leaving for Buchenwald spent the night were not boarded shut, field commandant Groffmann is demoted to a regular *Blockführer*. A new field commandant takes his place, bringing with him a new *Rapportführer*, SS-*Unterscharführer*[48] Kaps. The new field commandant is not particularly interested in the field, so all the power is taken over by Kaps. Life fundamentally changes, after the evening roll call he introduces an extra two hours of work under the slogan "*Schmücke dein Heim*,"[49] and so, we are beautifying the camp. This way he robs us of two hours of rest.

The work is varied. For several evenings we carry an assortment of beams, planks, and scraps left over from some dismantled barracks from

47. Making (literally building) beds.
48. SS corporal.
49. "Decorate your home."

Field 3 to a storehouse outside the wires. The lengths vary and nails stick out. While carrying these uneven pieces it's very hard to march in even fives through the gate and more than once someone gets scraped or wounded by a protruding nail. On our way back, each person has to carry six bricks to the camp. The SS men speed us along, nearly running, we carry our bricks through the slippery mud and swampy puddles. We make four trips in one evening, carrying wood there and bricks back. Next, we spend a series of evenings digging up the squares in front of the barracks to make vegetable gardens. The soil is so hard that we need to break it up with pickaxes before we can start digging. Sometimes trucks bring trailers filled with earth, which needs to be carried in handbarrows to certain places and formed into flower beds. The locations are only pointed out to me, as the person responsible for gardening work, after the evening roll call, so when the earth is already being carried over and heaped up. Instead of supervising this work, I have to immediately prepare some stakes to mark out where the beds should be made. It's rare that you can ask for someone's help and send them to bring stakes. They take the opportunity and disappear for the entire evening, knowing that I won't report them; meanwhile I get cursed out because half an hour has passed without any stakes being driven in. Full handbarrows have to be carried at a quick step, and you need to run with empty ones. Those with a half-full handbarrow, one where the soil isn't in a heap, or those moving at a regular pace with an empty handbarrow, are whipped. SS men and kapos line up along the path tread by the columns of prisoners going one way and another, cracking their whips and shouting, constantly driving everyone to speed up. Hundreds of starving people being chased, bending under the weight of the filled barrows, looking around with vacant stares at where the whip will hit them, the clacking strike of the whip, wails of pain, the swearing of the kapos and SS men, it all makes a nightmarish, crushing impression on me. In part, the SS men and kapos are unloading their fury upon these innocent souls because they can't sit down in comfortable slippers in their heated rooms after roll call. Of course Kaps doesn't stay to the end of the work, but shows the *Lagerältester* what needs to be done and goes to the canteen for a beer. The amount of work is measured out so that the entire field can barely finish it before dusk.

My First Whipping

While digging up the hard, trampled square, my clog slips off when I press my foot on the spade and I hit my shin against the edge. I don't attach much significance to the relatively light hit. The next day, I feel pain in my leg, the spot turns red. In the evening, I can feel that my leg has swollen. On the third day, it makes it hard to walk and I sign up with the block clerk, Knips, to go to the clinic after the evening roll call. The doctor checks both legs and is pleased to verify that only one leg is swollen, since a common affliction among all the newcomers is swelling of both legs due to the total lifestyle change, namely, standing for sixteen to eighteen hours every day, the related heart conditions, and an almost entirely liquid diet. After swollen legs come swollen arms and the patient rarely returns from the Revier. I get bandages and a compress for my leg. I have the chance to see that the clinic has practically no medicines. There is no aspirin, pyramidon, or iodine. All they have is Ichthyol and zinc ointment, as well as "white powder" against diarrhea, which is very common around here. So the doctors are not really able to provide effective medical care. Some prisoners only come to the clinic to avoid the two extra hours of work. As for myself, though, the *Lagerältester* refuses to release me, tells the doctors to put me first in line, and comes over twice for the changing of the bandages, to be sure that I am not faking it.

And just now, when every step causes me pain, during the morning roll call I hear that I have to go with two other prisoners to the villa of the new *Feldführer* in Lublin to do gardening work. We go with *Lagerkapo*[50] Wyderka and two SS men. I am limping, and using the spade for support, so I lag behind, and the SS man walking in front has to stop and wait for me to catch up with the others.

50. The kapo that is the deputy/assistant to the *Lagerältester*.

The three of us work in the vegetable garden, digging up the soil all day without a lunch break. The SS men and Wyderka are called to the house of the *Feldführer* for food and drinks—meanwhile, his wife and children watch us working all day. Then, one of the SS men leaves to go to a restaurant; he comes back, sits down on a bench in the garden without a backrest, and then the other SS man and Wyderka also go to the bar. I can see that our caretaker is terribly red in the face. A moment later, I hear a swoosh, I look over and see the SS man's feet flying in the air. What happened? The rifle is on the ground, and the SS man, resting on the bench after consuming a *"setka"* or a *"czterdziestka,"*[51] lost his balance and fell off the bench onto his back, but he picks himself up in a flash.

Once we had dug up all of the patches and are getting ready to leave, the former field commandant, Groffmann, approaches and tells us to also dismantle the outhouse in the garden. Appetizing work . . . Luckily, the current field commandant comes over and stops the demolition, saying the outhouse will be needed for prisoners working in the garden. I barely drag myself back to the camp, the pain in my leg is excruciating. The SS men pay no attention, since this is a common symptom among prisoners, the first stage of finishing them off. I ponder whether there will also be work after roll call.

As I enter the field, I notice ten large ash trees, maybe twenty years old, brought from who knows where. The roots have been terribly mutilated; it is evident that not only did amateurs dig them up, but that there wasn't even any professional supervision of the digging. It's a shame to waste these trees. The field lines up for the roll call. The *Lagerältester* calls me over and says I have to get a group of people together after roll call and plant the trees.

I tell him that holes haven't been dug, and they would need to be at least one meter deep and two meters wide in soil that's as hard as a rock, that the roots are lacerated and smashed, so they need to be trimmed,

---

51. Polish: *setka* is one hundred, *czterdziestka* is forty; refers to 100 milliliters and 40 milliliters of alcohol, respectively.

otherwise the trees will not take. He shrugs his shoulders and says this is an order from the *Rapportführer* and that's that. He shows me where the trees have to be planted: four along the entry road in the shape of a square, three in front of the infirmary, two in front of the auto shops, and one in front of the office. Each spot is at least 150 meters away from the next, so that just walking between these four places with my hurting leg consumes lots of time. I am told that unless all the trees are planted today, I will get my "*Arsch voll.*"[52] During the roll call, my friends tell me that in the late afternoon, a dozen or so guys were suddenly taken with pickaxes and told to dig out the trees from a nearby peasant farmstead. No surprise that using pickaxes to dig crushed practically all of the roots . . .

After the roll call we start digging—but no more than two people can work on a single hole at a time, otherwise they just get in each other's way. Every step demonstrates incompetence and cluelessness about the task at hand. The SS men think that if a lot of people are assigned to a job, it should be done that much sooner. In this case a mass of people have been assigned, but only some of them are working, the rest just watch. Trimming the roots is out of the question, since we don't have pruning shears or a gardening knife, and there isn't enough time to walk around the barracks and ask to borrow a kitchen knife. On the other hand, I know that such old trees with such mangled roots simply won't take. It's getting dark, so the trees have to be "planted" or, more accurately, "buried" in their current condition. Of course, the full brunt of responsibility for the failure of the trees to take root will fall on me, not the one who ordered them dug up this way. During the planting I have to make sure that the trees are placed in a straight line, and each step hurts so much that I have to strain with all my might to force myself to walk. It is already so dark that it's hard to gauge. My friends are working full steam, because they know that all our hides are on the line. The last trees are buried in complete darkness, to where we can barely see the contours of the next tree. The nervous tension passes.

I drag myself back to the barracks, remembering that I haven't eaten since morning. I get my eighth of bread. All the coffee is gone, obviously.

52. To get one's *Arsch voll* is to get one's ass kicked.

I undress. The leg is inflamed and pulsing. The doctor told me yesterday that it is periostitis. I am extremely weary. I lie down to bed with a quiet groan, and groan as I fall asleep. I am troubled by nightmares where everyone is sleeping while I have to do additional work. As I'm dreaming I realize it's just a dream, I fall into an even deeper sleep and again the same nightmare about urgent work, while others are at ease. I wake up in the morning totally exhausted. Unfortunately, this psychological complex has plagued me constantly for a week and deprives me of much rest.

In the morning, after counting off roll call, while all the blocks are still formed up, the *Lagerältester* comes to our block and calls out:

"*Gärtner.*"[53]

I step forward. Indignant, he says to me:

"You discredited me nicely in front of the *Feldführer*, why didn't you choose four trees of the same crown size for the entry gate? *Bück dich.*"[54]

I try to explain. "*Bück dich,*" he repeats, and in front of my block I get fifteen lashes in the buttocks. After "collecting" my portion, I tell the *Lagerältester* that today I need garden shears and a saw.

"What for?" he asks.

"To trim the crowns, since every newly planted tree needs its crown heavily trimmed!"

Tableau[55]—that was my entire revenge, but my fifteen lashes can't be taken back now. The incident circulates throughout the field. My friends tell me with respect that I held up strongly. Before noon I receive the necessary tools, borrowed from Field 1, and the embarrassed *Lagerältester*, now striking a friendly tone, asks me to explain why the crowns need to be trimmed, whether it's just a superstition or if there is a biological reason behind it. He listens to my answers with incredulity.

While working, I scratch the skin on the joint of my left pinkie finger but pay it no mind. Instead of scabbing over, the finger goes red—I think it

---

53. Gardener.
54. "Bend over."
55. French: an event that puts someone in an embarrassing situation.

will pass but the spot becomes very painful. During the next changing of the dressing on my leg, I show the finger to the doctor, he presses on it, pus spurts out. He puts on a dressing.

The next day, after the evening roll call, we get another order, to secure the newly planted trees against the wind by anchoring them on four sides with wire. There are no posts to which we could tie them so we need to fashion stakes to be hammered into the ground, small strips of wood to which wire will be attached from around the trunk, and the appropriate length of wire. To do this work we have one ax and one pair of pincers. The stakes still have to be hewn. What does it matter that thirty people are assigned to this job when they don't have tools to do it with? As befits a concentration camp, we only have barbed wire at our disposal, which obviously makes our work harder.

Our hands are lacerated during the work and most of the men, lacking for tools, watch as several of us take turns manipulating the pincers and ax, pulling the wire toward the trees. We work for maybe an hour in the dark, practically doing the job blindfolded. And when any part of a task in these work conditions is inadequately carried out, the reprimand will first and foremost emphasize that, after all, so many people were assigned to the job. When we return to the barracks, everyone is already asleep . . . This time bowls of coffee, already cold, are set aside for us.

The next day it is raining, a fine drizzle all day long, the wind is cutting. We try to work so that the barracks shields us from the wind. But on our hill it is blowing so strongly, it doesn't really matter where we stand, the wind still gets to us. My jacket is soaked, my shirt is wet. Kapo Wyderka puts on a raincoat and tells us to clear the ditches alongside the barracks to improve the flow of water dripping down from the eaves. He himself is full, well-rested after a good night's sleep, dressed warmly, and snacking on candy.

In the course of my work I meet the director of the primary school for girls in Kuty, his last name is Horodyski, and he is about sixty years old. He is a tall, broad-shouldered man. His assignment is to keep the entire roll call square clean. The area is around ten *mórg*.[56] Just walking around it takes a lot of time. Horodyski goes around all day with wheelbarrows, a broom, and a shovel, and cleans up. But he is helpless against the constant gales that keep tearing off shreds of tar paper from the roofs. The barracks have been standing for less than two years,[57] but the roofing is already cracked and rolling up, with bare boards exposed. He scarcely manages to collect the roofing from one end of the field when the wind starts blowing pieces onto the ground at the other end, which he has to chase after and grab. We are not allowed to talk to prisoners from another *Kommando* on the square; up close I can see how much Horodyski has changed. Hunched over, bent down, bloody bruises under his eyes, a bloody welt across his head, ear, and cheek, cut skin all over. I approach with my tools, pretending to work nearby, I ask him what happened. He tells me the *Lagerältester* whipped him badly and beat him with his fists because of the tar paper fluttering across the square. He lamented that he had also kicked him repeatedly.

I have gone completely stiff with cold in this rain, my fingers are bluish, numb. One of the "gardeners" working for me is a villager by the name of Krzyżanowski. For the last two weeks he has had three huge carbuncles on his chin, so-called sycosis. He goes for dressings every day but his condition is not serious enough to admit him to the Revier. The paper bandages quickly get soggy in the rain and pieces start flapping around his head, revealing more and more of the ulcers, each of which is the size of a plum. Pus is dripping from each of them onto his clothes, the spade handle, and the ground. Tomorrow, someone else will be given that spade and will get infected. The infirmary is closed during the day, so Krzyżanowski has to walk around like that until the evening roll call.

We eat our lunch outside, even though it's raining. There's no place to even squat down and rest our legs for even fifteen minutes. It rains like this until the evening. I can't wait to get back to the barracks to warm up a little under my blanket and take off my wet jacket and pants that are stuck to my

---

56. Polish: a unit of measurement equal to approximately two-thirds of an acre.
57. The barracks in Field 3 were erected in 1942.

thighs. After supper, there is movement in the barracks. The clerk received new work assignments from the *Arbeitseinsatz*[58] for numerous prisoners and is now calling individuals by name to inform them about their assignment and the gathering points of various *Kommando* after the morning roll call.

Meanwhile, a new misfortune presents itself. The roof of our barracks is damaged like all the others. Water is dripping in countless spots, forming large puddles on the floor. That's not even so terrible—but there are also many places where water drips directly onto the top bunks. You can't patch the holes in the roof and you can't move the beds. Many of the upper bunks are unusable for sleeping and in some cases, water is dripping through the mattress of the top bed into the middle bunk. At this point there is nothing more to be done, you have to try and sleep in this dripping water. At night you can hear water dripping onto the floor throughout the entire barracks. There is a raging wind and the rain whips against the walls, like pelting peas. Fearful and anxious I think about going out to work in the morning in my wet clothes and toiling in the rain again.

I get terrible cramps in my legs during the night. I do my best to stretch and massage the muscles. The pain is so severe I could scream. Instinctively, I jump off the bed onto the wet floor and take a few steps, the cramp finally passes and I lie back down next to Struczowski. Unfortunately, cramps become my constant companions during sleep, and even in the morning while putting on my pants, affecting me when I move my leg a certain way, plaguing me like my nightmarish dreams about extra work. The doctor explains that many prisoners suffer this, it's caused by straining the leg muscles which are unaccustomed to standing all day, from 3:00 a.m. until 9:00 p.m., as well as walking in clogs, which stiffen our feet, forcing the entire foot to tread inflexibly.

It's still raining in the morning. They order us to work in the garden. Naturally, our clothes haven't dried overnight. I see them taking Horodyski, who was beaten last night, to the hospital in the morning. Two people are supporting him, he is barely able to drag his feet. It's pouring mercilessly. The *Lagerältester* comes over to us. I lie to him that we need more stakes

58. Literally, labor section; a group of SS men responsible for organizing prisoner work.

for the garden and that we will have to hew them ourselves. He agrees. So I take my gardeners to the warehouse at Block 21. There, I tell them to remove nails from slats lying on a pile, straighten nails, carve stakes, and pretend to be very busy. Father Archutowski is trembling all over. Even though his shoes have wooden soles, his feet are completely soaked since water dripped down his pants into his shoes. I sit him down behind a pile of wooden beams and bring him sawdust to submerge his feet into to dry them. There isn't a piece of cloth or sack to wipe his feet. After drying his feet, he sits on the beams for a while and rests. He complains about pain in his legs and light swelling, which we all suffer. The effect of a weakening heart and poor circulation, which lead to edema. He is shivering with a fever.

Suddenly, Bubi, the *Lagerjüngster*,[59] appears before us. A thirteen-year-old Jew, the bane of Field 3, a sadist about whom I heard things when I was still in Warsaw. In all the clatter and noise, we never heard the squeaky double doors of the barracks opening. Seeing a prisoner sitting down, Bubi leaps toward him and beats him on the face with his hand; next, he orders the tall man to bend over and whips him in the behind. The painful lashes last a long time. His whip is reinforced with wire. The priest emits a quiet groan. An old, gray-haired Polish Jew, block overseer Bass, standing near me, mumbles curses at Bubi under his breath. But what can we do, we are helpless.

It starts snowing in the afternoon. During the roll call, large snowflakes fall so densely that they form a thick layer on the lapels of my jacket. The wind blows the snow from the lapels onto my shirt where it melts. There is no extra work after the roll call today. In the barracks, of course, we have to take off our shoes and walk barefoot on the wet floor. We get in touch with friends who have been at Majdanek longer than us, to organize a different job assignment for Father Archutowski, allowing him to work with a roof over his head. For my part, there is nothing more I can do other than excuse him to the infirmary after roll call where he can sit through the

---

59. The most junior prisoner functionary, a prisoner joke: the opposite of the "seniormost" prisoner.

two extra hours of work in front of the doors. It turns out that among the *Leichenträger* (corpse carriers) someone is sick and they need a replacement. So Father Archutowski is transferred to that *Kommando*. Admittedly, it is unpleasant work, because you have to collect bodies from our field, load them up on a wagon, and take them to the crematorium, but there is one benefit: the work only lasts several hours in the morning, and then you can cut loose for the rest of the day, in any case you can shelter under a roof.

Sickness and Disease

Dr. Jastrzębski passed away as well, even though he spent two to three days each week working indoors at the infirmary; of course he still had to stand for the roll calls. He was taken to the Revier with a high fever. I find out that Pomirowski, who had registered us when we arrived, contracted typhus right after and died.[60] Varsovians from the January transport tell me that in those days the editor of the *Wieczór Warszawski*,[61] Hieronim Wierzyński, brother of Kazimierz, died of phlegmon in a barracks on Field 3. And in the infirmary on Field 3, Steinhagen,[62] the co-owner of the Steinhagen-Stránský machine tool factory, also died recently. I knew them both. The latter fell ill with enteritis. A lot of prisoners get sick with this disease due to the constant rutabaga diet, which leaves the body without various chemical elements. There is no special diet in the infirmary. The sick get the same cabbage or rutabaga soup. When diarrhea lasts more than fourteen days, you develop intestinal tuberculosis and then you're beyond saving. Although Steinhagen's friends were able to establish contact with someone in town through civilian workers and get rice and medicines for him (gruel was made for him by Captain Antoni Wolf, administrator of the Ujazdów Hospital), it was evidently too late and Steinhagen himself realized that his fate was sealed. Around the same time, Jałowiecki also died in the same way, he was a department head at the Central Welfare Council,[63] arrested in connection with the so-called Swedish scandal, i.e., the uncovering of contacts between Warsaw and London via the personnel of the Swedish legation.

---

60. Leon Pomirowski died on March 31, 1943.

61. Polish: "Warsaw Evening."

62. Artur Steinhagen died on March 29, 1943.

63. *Rada Główna Opiekuńcza* (RGO)—a Polish charity organization founded during the First World War and reactivated in 1940, one of the few allowed to operate in the General Government.

Prisoners are afraid to go to the Revier, because it is not synonymous with getting medical assistance, rest, and treatment. The infirmary on Field 3 is in Block 12, which isn't any different from the other barracks. There are just two small rooms separated from the hall by partitions. One serves as the living space for the doctors and male nurses, the other as the outpatient treatment room. In the one main hall, on regular three-level bunk beds, lie patients suffering from various types of diseases: typhus, enteritis, phlegmon, etc. But mostly, everyone gets infected there, in the hospital, with typhus, and that's what finishes them off. People complain that the orderlies take away the excrement-soaked mattresses from diarrhea sufferers, as there are no rubber mats or oilcloth sheets to put under the sick, so they have to lie on bare wood. Furthermore, every two weeks committees come through to conduct "selections," meaning that they pick out the heavily sick and send them to be gassed. Getting admitted into the hospital also isn't easy, it is not enough to have a fever of 39 degrees [102°F] in the evening, it needs to be over 38 degrees [100°F] in the morning, when the Revier commandant's assistant, an SS man with the title of SDG (*Sanitätsdienstgehilfe*),[64] decides about admissions into the Revier. There are often people in agony, but they don't meet the official SS criteria for hospitalization.

A great amount of dying happens here. From the Warsaw transport that arrived on January 18, 1943, numbering 1,600 men, six hundred people were quartered in Block 10. Three months later, only half remain and new typhus cases continue. The majority died of typhus and pneumonia, some met a worse fate . . . Namely, in mid-February 1943, the "Varsovians" were asked who among them felt sick and unfit for work. Eighty-six Poles came forward, mostly members of the intelligentsia, who, after their four-week stay in the camp, had descended into useless "freeloaders." They met with no difficulties, and every frail one was assiduously noted down. They were then transferred to Block 15 to block overseer Janusz Olczyk, where they were to recuperate; after a brief stay they were all taken to the gas chamber. Among them was Michał Sobański, from the management of the *Kurier Warszawski*.[65]

64. Technically *Sanitätsdienstgrad*: an SS paramedic.
65. Polish: "Warsaw Courier."

Fearing these various deceits and selections, many decide to "walk it off" literally, by going on as usual, while suffering through typhus fever. It's an unbelievable strain on the body, and also a walking plague for others, since lice are plentiful. As for the death rate, I have the best grasp of it, working near the infirmary on Field 3. There are about 150 people, sick with different things, and they carry about fifteen or twenty corpses out each day; thus a minimum of 10 percent daily, so over the course of ten days, the entire infirmary completely dies out! It's only thanks to the influx of new sick people that the infirmary keeps all of its beds full.

In the first half of April 1943, the infirmary in Field 3 is liquidated and moved to Field 1. The process is very simple. The sick are driven out of their beds, and everyone, as they stand, in a shirt, throws a blanket on their back and with bare legs and bare feet they are moved to Field 1. The bedridden who can't walk are driven out just the same, naked, covered in a blanket, to a wagon standing by the entrance to the barracks. It's the same wagon that moments earlier carried dead bodies to the crematorium. Those completely unable to stand are carried out by the orderlies and placed on the wagon. The rest clamber up on their own. The dying are of course on the wagon too. It is a bleak, cold day. The temperature is about 5 or 6 degrees [41–42°F]. The seriously ill are like sardines stuffed into the wagon. A nurse climbs onto the driver's seat and starts counting the sick to know how many to report at the gate. He is counting heads. There are more than twenty people on the wagon. Some of those sick with typhus with temperatures over 39 degrees are unconscious and writhing in the wagon. The nurse counts several times, and each total is different. Finally, he starts to write the sick down by name and again he has problems with the typhus-ridden with fever. He starts swearing in Slovak and German at the sick and assures them that they're all goners anyway. He keeps the sick on the wagon for over an hour, not being able to count twenty-something people.

I consider the bad fortune of the sick, will their chances improve at the "real" Revier? Will they, fevered and yearning for a drink, have to continue giving the orderlies their daily portion of bread for a bowl of coffee? Will there be a more serious manager of the hospital than the "manager" of the infirmary—Doctor Goldberg, who is from the Lublin region but can't speak Polish correctly? Goldberg disappears whenever *Revierkapo*[66] Benden, one of the *Sanitätsdienstgrad*,[67] or even *Lagerältester* Schmuck, Rockinger's predecessor, comes to the infirmary, leaving the sick in the hands of his deputy, a Polish doctor. The reasons for Goldberg's disappearances are not known.

Together with my people, I've prepared the strips of land between the barracks for planting vegetables, above all, potatoes. For the last two weeks, the contents of the latrines have not been taken to the *Gärtnerei*, but poured out on these strips between the blocks. I comment to the *Lagerältester* that human excrement is too harsh, that the amounts are too great, and that you can't fertilize immediately before planting. Both he and Wyderka nod their heads in assent but say that's what the *Rapportführer* ordered.

One day, the *Lagerältester* sends me and ten other people with a heavy wagon, normally operated by twenty prisoners, to the *Gärtnerei* to fetch potatoes for planting. The empty wagon quickly gets driven into the ground in the sandier sections. At last, we arrive at the mounds where they are loading wagons with potatoes for the kitchens. There is a line, since they are taking potatoes for five fields and the SS kitchen from one mound. So the prisoner in charge of distribution tells me to wait. I stand there and look around. Maybe two hundred steps away, you can see the houses of the Dziesiąta village, only recently incorporated into the city of Lublin. The road leading near the houses is lined with guard posts. Hundreds upon hundreds of prisoners are working in the vast fields of the vegetable gardens. Nearby, I can also see huge, wide, and flat compost heaps, there is also a large, wide manure pit with a dozen or so prisoners standing knee-deep in it and working. I can see people bustling about in front of their houses and in their yards, going about their normal way of life, and here, a loosely arranged cordon of SS men separates two different worlds

---

66. German: prisoner functionary serving the role of kapo at the camp hospital.
67. An SS paramedic.

from one another. There are ruins of several houses in the gardens where prisoners are working. I ask what they are, and they tell me the houses were expropriated and the area was incorporated into the gardens and that's why they are being torn down. Dozens of such houses have already been dismantled.

It's still a long way until my turn for potatoes. Other prisoners are sitting—the regular *Wagenkolonne* crews—so I sit down next to them. Some kapo comes over, a German, with a thick bat in his hand, he slaps me in the face and asks me what I'm doing there. I explain my purpose for being there. He then asks why I am sitting idly instead of digging up another mound. I reply that the distribution supervisor told me to wait, not to dig a new mound. Then the stereotypical words come out, "*Bück dich*," and I get several strong blows to my buttocks with a stick as thick as a shovel handle. After the beating, the kapo informs me that I am getting off easy because I didn't talk back to him. So, lessons in savoir vivre at the concentration camp as well.

I walk over to the distribution supervisor to ask which mound I should dig up. He doesn't want to, but having witnessed what happened to me, he agrees for us to immediately begin loading potatoes without waiting in line. We have a full wagon. The *Lagerältester* told us to fill it to the brim, since any surplus potatoes are meant for the private use of the *Feldführer*, *Rapportführer*, and kapos. We pull the wagon uphill. On a turn, we get stuck in the sand. Despite all our efforts, we can't move any further. At a distance of fifty meters, women prisoners are working, planting something. We are so weary and exhausted that flirting is far from our minds and we're not even looking in that direction. Some tall, stout German woman comes flying over in calf-high boots, a whip in her hand and in a dress of a military style and color. She screams that we've stopped here on purpose to talk to the women. When I explain to her that our wagon got stuck in the sand and that there are too few of us, she smacks me on the face, asking why I haven't taken off my cap when addressing her. She writes down my number and warns that she will report us to Thumann, and orders us to move immediately. With the force of desperation we manage to push the wagon another fifteen meters before we stop again, but the fire-breathing dragon has left by then. That was an *Aufseherin*,[68] a guard of the female camp. We get stuck with the wagon a few more times, finally we arrive before the gate of our field, we report in and enter through the wires.

I sigh with relief, it feels like coming back home, because the whole expedition for potatoes beyond the wires was unpleasant and I don't know if that battle-ax will actually report me to Thumann. If she does, woe unto me. We start sorting the potatoes, the larger ones for the *Feld-führer* and kapos, the smaller ones for planting. Lots of block overseers and *Stubendienst* show up to each get a bowl of potatoes, everyone is a friend now. But if he gets caught with the potatoes, I'll be the one getting it in the hide.

We carry the potatoes in sacks to the warehouse located in the *Schreib-stube* barracks. I have the right to enter as I continue to watch over the bowls with germinating grass seeds, which, by the way, absolutely refuse to grow. I keep the potatoes intended for planting separate from the others. The next day, we mark out the fields and I go to the warehouse to get the sacks, and we start to plant the potatoes.

Suddenly, Bubi rushes over to me and asks:

"Did you take the potato sacks?"

I confirm. In reply he smacks me in the face, standing up on his toes, and says:

"It was you who stole my potato sack."

"Mister Bubi," I reply, "the potatoes for planting were placed separately, besides, you can go ahead and check the sacks, we haven't planted half of them yet."

We go over there together and he recognizes one of the sacks as his own. Calmed down that he found his potatoes, he admits that he intentionally put "his" sack with our planting potatoes so that none of the other kapos would take them. The little whelp only forgot about one thing, to tell the gardeners that's where he hid "his" potatoes.

My closest companions are leaving me. Engineer Sopoćko already managed to get in touch with the outside world. His wife arrived in Lublin

68. Female prisoners' supervisor.

and managed to send him food and money through some worker, thanks to this he is able to buy his way into the kitchens to peel potatoes. He is already sitting in a warm room and won't have to look for jobs on the side of the barracks that is best protected from the wind. Captain Macieliński had such swollen legs that he couldn't walk and had to sit during roll call, the doctors tell him that if he lies down for a couple of days and rests his heart, the swelling will subside. Struczowski is leaving as well. He has been complaining of a fever and chills for a few days now and apparently has the flu.

I also find out that Father Archutowski has been transferred to Field 1 with a fever: apparently they suspect pneumonia. As he leaves, Struczowski gives me his warm jacket of thick cloth, a sort of loden, which can be buttoned to the neck, with a linen lining, quilted with hemp. A first-rate present, moreover, the jacket has two diagonal pockets in front. So you can sometimes "accidentally" slide your hands in and warm them up. I give him my own jacket from which I hastily take my number and sew it onto my new acquisition.

Struczowski was a rich man, because he gives me two carrots and hands me his spoon, mirror, and pocketknife, for safekeeping, with the right to use them. We warmly say our goodbyes, but with the conviction that we'll see each other back on the field in a week. Of my four original helpers wrangled out of the Buchenwald transport several weeks ago, none are with me anymore.

From day to day the number of people unable to stand upright through morning roll call increases, and they sit through it, and then there are some who you lay down in the mud. There's room for them with the corpses on the left-hand side. Sometimes they carry out a corpse who had just yesterday been denied admittance to the Revier. More than one died so quietly in the night that their neighbors didn't notice until after the morning bell when they yanked him by the leg to get up. But he's already standing at assembly before the Lord Almighty.

The attachment to warm clothes is understandable, but it can go so far that some prisoners would rather die than give them up. When someone is taken to the Revier, their clothes are taken away from them in the hospital, and returned to the general warehouse, the *Bekleidungskammer*.[69] Once recovered, the patient receives raggedy clothing in the Revier, which has been taken from the warehouse.

One of the men in my section, Ruszkowski, a carpenter from Radomsko, had a wadded *kitajka*[70] and wadded trousers formerly belonging to Russian POWs. His legs started swelling and he could no longer walk, he spent a few days sitting in front of the barracks and had to be carried out for the roll calls. Despite my repeated urgings to go to the hospital, he refused and said that he would regret losing his warm clothes. The next day, he was already lying down for roll call, and the day after, he died during roll call, still wearing his warm clothes.

During the lunch break, you can identify those who are on their last legs. After eating their soup, they will drop like a log to the ground and will lie motionless—and when the bell sounds, friends have to help them get back up. We are powerless to help those dying at night, you can't even give them a bowl of water, and are equally helpless when faced with the sick, whose faces are already marked with death—and help would be so easy: a few bowls of nourishing food, a kilo of sugar, and a good night's sleep.

We are all so sleepy all the time that if I stand motionless for several minutes during work, my eyes start closing and I begin to drift off. In other barracks, where prisoners from earlier transports live, I can see greater losses during roll call than in our block. After two or three weeks, we still have some remnants of fat left on and in our bodies. But our last grams of fat will also be exhausted before long.

The sick who passed the exam in the infirmary before the morning roll call and had a fever of over 38 degrees are not taken directly to the hospital—they have to go through delousing. The process involves a hot shower at the camp baths, where we washed after arrival, and then a new shirt, most with lice nits—and then they are sent to the Revier. There, they have to wait in front of the office, until admitting, examination, and registration begins. In the cold months, most of them get pneumonia in the process, but that is exactly the point. Delousing before admittance to

---

69. Clothing warehouse.
70. Term used in Poland and other places that here refers to a jacket.

the Revier is just a pretext, since the lice infestation in the hospital is worse than on any of the other fields.

Examination of new arrivals is very strict if conducted by the SS physician on that day. The Polish doctors let all of the sick through. So it happens often that up to half of the sick who have gone through delousing and waiting in front of the office are sent back to the field as the SS physician refused to qualify them for the Revier. After consecutive larger returns like this, the prisoner-physician in the infirmary of a given field gets a message that he is sending "the healthy" to the Revier and he is forced to use stricter standards when qualifying the sick for the Revier.

This is the perfidy of the entire SS camp structure, that the entire system of tormenting people was created by them, but its implementation was saddled onto the prisoners themselves, who, as loyal *Lagerältester*, kapos, *Vorarbeiter*, block overseers, physicians, or orderlies, are made personally responsible for carrying out elements of this diabolical regime of torturing people.

In isolation, the individual aspects aren't that terrible, such as the sleep deprivation, walking barefoot on a wet floor, the impossibility of sitting down all day, working in the rain without any cover, water dripping through the roof onto our beds, the insufficient and homogenous diet, the inability to wash, lice infestation, lack of medicines, etc. We all had sleepless nights on the outside and at the same time were on our feet for twelve hours straight, dancing or traveling, each of us has been soaked to the bone and sometimes caught a cold. But the sum of these factors, cumulatively and perpetually, reaps a harvest of death among the weak, and for the more resilient, it sets the stage for tuberculosis, diarrhea, phlegmons, etc. No one can defend against typhus and typhoid fever, indeed, the mightiest and best-fed men can't handle a fever any better than the sickly can. The system itself runs people down, you can't say that it's the block overseer's fault that he wakes the prisoners up every day at 3:15 a.m. for example. And what remains for those who stubbornly refuse to get sick and die, is the iron bar, the rope, the revolver, or the gas chamber.

Our meals are monotonous, still rutabaga soup for lunch, sometimes you can find half a potato in it. The only real sustenance we get is the eighth of bread. In camp trade it costs ten zlotys, so an entire loaf is eighty zlotys, but there was a time when a loaf cost up to 120 zlotys and a single cigarette was seventeen zlotys, even in January 1943.

One day, we learn from the block overseer that there is a collection, to which we all have to chip in, for the *Feldführer*, and everyone must give five zlotys. I laugh on the inside at this announcement, seeing as prisoners are not allowed to have any money, and if someone is caught with it, they are reported and whipped. But I've discovered that the SS has a way around that as well. The block overseer issues bread to the section supervisors with the order not to distribute it to those unable to pay. Here and there somehow people have money and pay the squeeze. But most of us don't get any bread, which sweetens the deal. A slice of bread is kept, priced at five zlotys apiece, but it will lead to a gain of ten zlotys. Right in front of us, several dozen loaves are taken to the Slovak barracks where they are monetized for eighty zlotys each. The surplus of forty zlotys per loaf is pocketed by the block overseer, the rest goes to the powers that be. A week later we have a collection for the *Lagerältester*, I sell a slice loaned to me on my word for ten zlotys, I pay back five zlotys, and I have five zlotys left for the next collection, but I go to sleep hungry.

I am constantly going around hungry, but even these starvation rations have to be handled with economy. When they give us steamed pota-toes besides coffee for supper, I hide them to have a "second breakfast" the next day. Cold potatoes, unsalted, partially rotten or fungal, are not a tasty thing, but it always fills your stomach up a bit. Once a week, on Thursday morning, instead of coffee we get soup made from powder, it tastes like barley flour and smells like mushrooms. It's called *"berlaj."* I haven't researched the etymology of this term. Supposedly it refers to shoemaker's glue. I save my piece of bread, which is largely composed of chestnuts and sawdust, for the next morning. Twice a week, we get twenty to thirty grams of margarine. I would like to save it to get two spreads out of it, but I don't have a dish to store it in. Finally I find an empty tin powder box, unfortunately without the lid, I clean it and hide it under my mattress. I was really delighted with this find. The next day we get margarine, I reach under my mattress confidently, and someone has already stolen my box.

I've rarely felt such pain at losing a material possession as with the theft of that box. How the scale of value and needs changes!

Kapo Wyderka has a female fox terrier that has just had pups. Keeping dogs in the camp is forbidden for prisoners. Just this fact testifies to how important a role a kapo like this plays in the camp. I jealously look at the food that this dog gets. She has her own doghouse in the warehouse barracks. Muszka gets milk, groats, pearl barley, and never any rutabaga. They really treat us worse than dogs here.

A Hand through the Barbed Wire

We only know it is Sunday because the second roll call is not in the evening but at noon, so the SS men can have their day off in town. But it doesn't bother the *Rapportführer* to have us working in the field until evening. Through the wires, we can see prisoners in Fields 2 and 4 taking strolls, but we have to beautify Field 3. Even so, we have to be shaved for Monday morning. The barracks barbers shave and cut hair on Sunday afternoons. There are two or three of them per block, so one per one hundred people on average. Several people at a time sneak away from work and go to the barracks for shaving. There is a soap dish and a shaving brush, one brush to lather up the entire block. Prisoners stand in line waiting for a more or less painful procedure, since the razors are totally dull. If someone hands over a cigarette, though, the barber will pull a different razor out of his pocket. But where can I get a cigarette? So I am shaved with the dull blade. My skin stripped, nonetheless I feel totally different with a smooth face.

We have a little more freedom on Sunday afternoon because the SS men no longer walk the field. At night, there are never any SS men on the field and they are not even allowed to be there. If, however, in some special case, an SS man has to come onto the field at night, the *Blockführer* gate-house will turn on the red light on the pole in the middle of the square to let the guards in the towers know that there is an SS man on the field and not to shoot at anyone walking around there.

There is no supper on Sundays, instead they give us bread with sausage, so there is a little more time. We spend it on our beds and under our blankets, reading the rag *Kurier Lubelski*[71] smuggled in by some worker. You can always glean something from the press. This is when we begin to write the first secret messages back home.

71. It should be *Nowy Głos Lubelski* ("New Lublin Voice"), a German propaganda newspaper published in Polish in the Lublin district between January 1940 and July 1944.

Officially, we are totally prohibited from writing or receiving any letters. But I know that during the lunch break, in the unfinished washroom
barracks, people meet with civilian workers who bring letters, money,
and medicines. The *Lagerältester*, Kapo Wyderka, and Bubi are always
on the prowl there, frisking the prisoners coming out. I know that they
took money and medicines away from some prosecutor, and that they also
poked around this barracks, since more than one person has stashed the
money they received there, afraid to bring it back to their block. Willingly
giving up their lunch break is obviously worth it for our kapos. After all,
they can catch up on their rest after the lunch break. They linger around
for fifteen minutes after work begins and then each of them disappears
into some barracks for a longer nap, putting a guard out front. The SS men
also lie down for a snooze in the afternoon, so for the most part, a sleepy
atmosphere pervades the field until 3:00 p.m.

My friends point out the prisoner who is the alleged walking mailbox,
who takes letters to be sent by the civilian workers. I write a short note on
a piece of paper to my brother in Warsaw telling him I am at Majdanek,
healthy, and asking him to make contact and send some money and cigarettes. I go to the washroom with the letter but the man is not there, I go
back several times but I cannot find him. I stash my note in the gap of a
handbarrow and once work starts I stick it in the ground. That evening I
meet up with Engineer Sopoćko and tell him that I wanted to send a letter
to my brother and that I can't find the prisoner from the washroom. He
wrings his hands and says:

"For the love of God, he's a snitch. You're lucky you didn't meet him.
Your letter would have ended up in Wyderka's hands."

Witold suggests that he can send the letter for me through the worker
his wife used to establish contact with him. Delivery of the letter normally
costs one hundred zlotys, sometimes more. The predetermined amount
is to be paid to the delivery person by the recipient in Lublin. It gets
more complicated when a letter has to be sent beyond Lublin. My friend
arranges it for me so that it's free, possibly asking his wife to cover the
price for me. Sending letters outside of Lublin is made more difficult by
the special censorship department active in the Lublin post office, due to

the concentration camp being here. A letter written in pencil, on a piece of packing paper, folded a dozen or more times, crumpled from being hidden under a sock in a shoe, with an envelope addressed in someone else's handwriting, already draws attention to itself on the surface. The same with the content of the letters, which, besides information about health, are mainly requests to send food and money. A large portion of these messages never arrive, we don't know whether it's due to unconscientious messengers or if they are destroyed by the censors. I haven't heard of anyone, be it the sender or the recipient, getting in trouble based on a report from the postal censorship.

Sending that letter to my brother excited me. My imagination started working; even the act of arranging the letter, trying to smuggle through as much content as possible using guarded language, was a profound experience. I am in an extremely good mental state compared to other prisoners, since just before my transfer from Pawiak, my brother assured me that my release was only a matter of two or three weeks. I counted the days—as a hopeless optimist—from the date of my arrest, naively beguiling myself that maybe before the train left from the Warsaw East railway station, a breathless Gestapo agent would come running and release me from the transport. After all, things like this have happened! I reason that my transfer to Majdanek delayed my release of course, since various letters had already been sent, but it's just a matter of days. I experience the same feelings as an audience member at the Grand Guignol[72] in Paris, who knows that he will see four macabre, single-act plays, full of blood, crime, and mystery, and after 11:00 p.m. he will go for a delicious supper to *La Coupole* . . . Despite this, more than one woman in the audience will scream loudly, moved by the danger, more than one *étranger*[73] will quickly leave the theater after the first act. This conviction of my imminent release makes me approach my fate with a completely different mindset. I see myself as a spectator, and at worst—an extra, but not as an actor in this tragedy taking place here. I look with interest, sympathy, disgust, and a sense of peril at the individual fragments, but I have the conviction that

72. A theater in Paris specializing in staging naturalist horrors.
73. French: a foreigner.

all of it doesn't apply to me, I am just "passing through." This is what gives me the strength to survive even the worst moments without collapsing into despair. Other friends are faced with the prospect of indeterminate imprisonment in the camp. In the best case, staying alive in the camp until the end of the war. The intelligentsia lose hope and fold easily after being slapped and beaten. For me, getting hit is an unconditionally nasty experience, but I am able to brush it off, since I believe that in a few days, surrounded by my family, I will be able to tell them about all of this.

Together with a young student from Warsaw, Kleniewski, who works for me, we even make plans for the first things we will do after our release. We are in accord that first we will go to the baths, then we'll go to his sister living in Lublin and will sleep for twenty-four hours, and only then will we eat something substantial.

Sometimes I find myself in a state of such physical exhaustion that there are moments when I actually wish for a serious illness, just to be able to lie down and sleep. Aside from all the rest, the sick have those two things at will, and they don't get drenched in the rain or freeze in the wind. Pawiak now seems almost like a luxurious sanatorium compared to my current living conditions. I alluded to my "previous accommodations" in my message to my brother.

I learn that the following day we are going to a gardener to purchase various shrubs that will need to be dug up and brought back. Therefore, I was to select several gardeners with spades and wait at the ready. We work near the gate and wait. I see a group of Jewish block overseers pulling a light hay wagon through the gate and I wonder where they are going. In that moment I hear them calling me from beyond the gate, I run over and find out that I'm supposed to go get the shrubs. I want to call my gardeners but the overseers tell me that they are going as gardeners. Since I am a "real" gardener, they tell me to pull the tongue while they push. We are accompanied by Kapo Wyderka with the inseparable Bubi, *Rapportführer* Kaps, and two SS men. The three are carrying *Empi* machine pistols, which they load with high-capacity magazines at the gate.

We "drive" through the village-suburb of Dziesiąta. The houses stand empty, yards deserted. I find out that some of the villagers have been resettled to prevent contact with the camp. After going two kilometers down the road we reach a solitary farmstead standing in the field. Here is the alleged gardener. After a long haggle, Kaps buys four white cedars, which I have to dig up. Then we go another two or three kilometers to the forest. Once there, Kaps warns us that if we try to escape the guards will shoot us. Kaps entertains himself by shooting crows with his rifle and hits a couple; he has a reputation as the best shot among the SS men in the camp. He carefully stashes the crows and promises himself to make a tasty dish out of them. That's the first time I hear of Germans eating crows. Are things so bad already in the *Vaterland*?[74]

The kapo tells us to dig up juniper bushes. I choose the smallest ones, knowing that they don't take root very well and the ones a meter tall will almost never take. The block overseers spin their spades around, pretending to work, but in reality they leave all the work to me, bantering that I am the gardener after all.

It is the first day of spring—the sky is clear, the sun is shining, the forest is quiet. They get warm quickly, they take off their jackets, then sweaters, working finally in just their shirts, and even then, they're still pouring out sweat. Wyderka also strips down to almost half-naked. No wonder: all of them are fattened and in splendid physical shape. Meanwhile, I am still wearing my warm jacket and even though I have to dig nonstop, and am doing three times as much as any of them, I am not sweating whatsoever. I gather from this that my body is very emaciated and depleted from a lack of calories.

I ask everyone to dig out shrubs with large bodies. The wagon starts to fill up with bushes. From a distance, we can see through the tall, bright forest that a peasant wagon is approaching. Kaps orders us to stop working immediately and drive off, he must have gotten scared that the owner of the forest was coming. We travel a kilometer. Kaps stops us and tells us to start digging again. Once the wagon is filled past the edges, Kaps orders us to head back. But along the way, whenever he spots a "lovely," old, two-meter-tall juniper, he orders us to dig it up as well. I report to him that

74. Fatherland.

these shrubs will not take root, but he pays no mind, and at every juniper we encounter he orders us to stop and dig.

Our load shifts and slides off the wagon one way or the other. I estimate we are carrying at least a ton of earth alone. Finally we reach the local road, it leads uphill. We have to stop and rest every twenty minutes. A peasant passes us by with a pair of harnessed horses, returning from work. After getting permission from the SS man, I ask him to hitch up his horses and pull the wagon up the hill for us. He sees that we are from the camp, the locals know our outfits well. He looks at me, shrugs his shoulders, and drives his horses with a whip and trots away. We hauled over to the camp in the sweltering sun. The block overseers left me alone in the square with the wagon, I have to unload the bushes myself. The *Lagerältester* comes over and observes the shrubs. He asks Wyderka how much they cost. Without missing a beat, he answers: "One thousand." I remember how in the forest we had to run away from some peasant wagon. Evidently, Kaps was reluctant to part with the money he was given to buy the shrubs with, and Wyderka is obviously covering for the *Rapportführer*.

Kaps enjoyed our expedition so much that he says we will be going again the next day. I am not looking forward to this picnic. I don't eat my bread that evening to save a meal for myself during work in the forest. When I wake up in the morning, I establish that my bread has been stolen. Luckily, today Kaps hires one of the civilian wagon drivers, who constantly service the camp and are paid one hundred zlotys daily, so three thousand zlotys a month (as they also work half a day on Sundays). Additionally, they get feed for their horses at discount rates. They are doing very well for themselves. The Jewish block overseers, with fat Jacob at the forefront (a porter from the Warsaw Main Railway Station), organize a picnic for themselves and Kaps. They brought hard-boiled eggs, sausage, a liter bottle of vodka, and bread of course. I ask one of them for a piece of bread, since mine was stolen, and I get one. As I sit on the side of the road during the break, Wyderka patronizingly tosses me one egg. Once the feast is over, Wyderka dumps out the rest of the salt on the ground. What a waste! After a little while, unnoticed, I go to that place and scrape up the salt from the moss. What bliss for a body deprived of salt for so long.

We are back in the same forest, digging up juniper again. On the way back, Kaps stops us next to some abandoned houses in the village of Dziesiąta and tells us to dig up lilacs, irises, lilies, and other perennials from the peasant gardens. Once again, the block overseers dump all the work on me. On the way back, we go to Lublin to a gardener on Bychawska Street to buy plants, 150 pansies and two hundred carnations. Jacob pays for everything. The gardener starts digging up the pansies, but since he is picking smaller plants, Wyderka orders me to choose them myself. Bubi takes a spade to start digging and ends up mangling several plants. When the gardener sees me choosing the pansies, he stops digging and leaves the work to me. He points out that I don't know how to dig because I ruined some plants. I told him that it was the little Jew; he doesn't believe it and sits down to chat with the block overseers and SS men.

An elegant man comes over and watches me work. It turns out he is the gardener's son. I tell him that I'm terribly exhausted and starved, that my vision is blurred, and I ask if he could give me an onion. He replies:

"But you look relatively well, there are no onions in April."

I implore him:

"But you must have one, I'm sure you still have a few onions for cooking."

On the same lot stands a modern, multistory villa, yet to be plastered, where the gardener resides. He replies that he will try and walks away. I dig and collect the plants into flat boxes and load them on the wagon. The gentleman-gardener collects five hundred zlotys from Jacob, but doesn't give me an onion, I look relatively too healthy . . .

My first encounters with the local populace left a negative impression on me. Do they not realize what our lives are like and how we suffer, or is it selfishness to the highest degree?

Kaps tells me to plant the junipers along both sides of the new road being built, with the shortest ones by the gate and taller ones further on. I don't have a gardening rope to mark out a straight line. I fashion such a "rope" from pieces of wire. The planting lasts two days. Others dig holes and I do the planting myself to make sure the junipers are placed properly, and are in the best conditions to take root. The junipers had been sitting in the ground for barely a week when the field commandant came over and said that because the future entry gate will be located on the other side of the square, so between the kitchen and washroom barracks, the junipers should actually be planted in reverse order. The tallest ones by the current gate, which will be eliminated someday, and the smallest ones in the direction of the roll call square and the future gate. And so, we have to dig everything up, prepare new holes, and replant again. The sun is scorching and the roots are starting to wither. Wherever there was a clump of soil around the roots, everything has crumbled away. The chances of the junipers actually taking root are getting smaller and smaller. The SS men think that you can transfer junipers every couple of days just like fives of prisoners at roll call.

The *Arbeitseinsatz* formed two official *Kommando* for work on the field: the *Gärtner*, with thirty full-time positions, and *Kommando* Zelent, with fifty.

Zelent is an assistant professor and a lecturer from the Warsaw Polytechnic and I start to have closer contact with him as our work is connected and there are many things we have to coordinate. He is taciturn, very diligent, and a model boss for his subordinates. They give him the title "engineer." Since I am in charge of an analogous section of gardening works and also have thirty people under me, my men, and other prisoners after them, start calling me "engineer" as well. I keep correcting them that I am not, and admitting to my intelligentsia friends that I have a different academic title, but apparently even in a concentration camp titles can't be eradicated and for Majdanek I became an "engineer." After a while, I give up on correcting people and many prisoners are convinced that I really am one; even those in the know say:

"We know you are a PhD, but we've already gotten used to calling you engineer."

Engineer Zelent is grading the roll call square, regulating the ditches and gutters, laying paths alongside the barracks with rubble, and building a wide entry road onto the roll call square. Meanwhile, the gardeners dig up every piece of earth between the barracks for vegetable gardens, form up rows for flowers along the entire square, and dig up parts of the square near the office for flower beds. The same goes on in other fields, but at a far smaller scale, since the other commandants are not as zealous and they only order the work during the day, i.e., only until the evening roll call. The main camp road is all dug up since it is being leveled, the surplus soil is formed into berms along its sides. There are deep trenches everywhere as a sewage system is being created. Several hundred acres of land in the *Gärtnerei* are plowed for vegetables.

Everywhere you look, there is bare, freshly turned earth. Once it dries after the rain and the cold, the winds start picking up billowing clouds of dust. Sometimes it takes on the character of a desert sandstorm. The gale carries dirt and sand with such a speed that it stings our faces like needles. It gets so dark that on several occasions the *Kommando* working beyond the wires, within the *Postenkette*, are ordered to return inside the camp as the guards cannot see anything even five paces away. Anyway, you can't open your eyes at all then because they immediately start tearing up due to sand getting under your eyelids. One of my friends from Lublin tells me that these storms are a known phenomenon in the area, and arise due to the light composition of the region's humus (loess I believe), and are called a*kurzawica*[75] or similar names. Now imagine Majdanek, with hundreds of acres of soil turned up without any winter crops to bind it. After such a storm sand dunes with wavy surfaces form in certain places, some up to fifteen centimeters tall. We have to remove them later, of course. A Polish king supposedly lost his way while traveling near Lublin during such a storm.

Kaps got a new sack of clover seeds for the lawns and orders us to sow it everywhere. There is a large wedge-shaped area between a diagonal path leading from the gate to the office and the wide entry road currently under construction. Wagons ride and squads march there. After the roll call, I am told that we are to spread soil and sow grass on the square that evening. It is more than a quarter of an acre. There is so little soil available, it will barely be enough for a layer two or three centimeters deep, which will be washed off the sloping ground by the first rain. I recommend that the earth should first be loosened with pickaxes, dug up, and then covered with humus, otherwise the grass will not root. The commandant agrees but on the condition that all of it has to be done this evening. Any

75. Polish slang for "dust storm."

layperson would realize that work like that cannot be done all at once: loosening the earth with pickaxes, digging, leveling with rakes, and covering it with a fresh layer of soil. But Kaps orders everything done at once, because it must be done *"schnell, schnell."*[76] You can force a prisoner to eat lunch in five minutes, force two or three people under a single shower to "bathe" in two minutes, force someone being escorted to an interrogation to run in front of a bicycle, rushing him as if a train were about to leave, but you cannot cheat nature, she requires normal, diligent work and returns as much as the work you put in.

Even though we rush, the work drags out across two evenings. Naturally, it is done shoddily after the roll call, by prisoners who spent the whole day toiling somewhere else and what do they care how some part was dug up. Let "the gardener," as they call me in the camp, worry, but the gardener cannot just go to Wyderka and say, "These and those are not digging right, they are just lightly scratching the soil's surface." Of course, the responsibility for the results of the work will be shouldered by the gardener.

When on the second day, in the dark twilight, the soil is finally spread out everywhere and raked, Kaps comes over and says to also sow the grass. I tell him the wind is too strong and will carry away the seeds, they should be mixed with the soil, besides you cannot see footprints at night and bald spots will appear, while elsewhere there will be double the seed. Very reluctantly, he agrees to put off the sowing but stresses that it must be done first thing in the morning. Once again the *"schnell, schnell"* principle, not caring in the slightest for the adage "Haste makes waste."

Almost without exception the SS men show such a cardinal lack of all practical experience, the most straightforward concepts of farming, that I have to wonder what these SS men did before the war. Did not a single one of them grow up in the country or even have a garden? If I, as a prisoner, of my own initiative, had dug up ash trees like that, planted them at night, planted and dug up junipers, wanted to plant grass like this at night, I would be quite rightfully accused of sabotage at every step and the deliberate destruction of property. No one would believe in such an absence of general knowledge.

76. "Quick, quick."

There is a man in my block, a trainee attorney, Zagórski, who claims to be the nephew of a general who met a tragic end after 1926.[77] He goes to work with the *Unterkunft*[78] *Kommando*. They prepare the grounds for the construction of administrative barracks located near the main road, with normal civilian traffic. My friends from this *Kommando* tell me that there are many people from Warsaw who take walks along the road, looking for their loved ones among the prisoners, and some have spotted their wives and fiancées from a hundred meters away. The *Unterkunft Kommando* works alongside outside laborers. These have white armbands stamped by the camp command; they also have identity cards. Upon entering the camp, they receive a token with a number. These tokens are kept on a numbered board. When leaving, the token has to be returned. That way they can control whether all the outside workers have left the camp in the evening, and a missing number indicates which worker is still on the camp grounds. One might think that one of the prisoners could dress up as a worker and leave using his token, and the worker could then lie that he lost his token or something like that. Well, so far this hasn't happened once.

While working with the "civilians," as the prisoners call the outside workers, they get to know each other. This obviously makes it much easier to ask someone you are familiar with to contact your family—easier than it is for a family to ask a worker to look for a stranger imprisoned among many thousands of men scattered across five isolated fields. Every civilian has their designated work area, for example within the *Postenkette* and around the administrative buildings, but they have no right to enter the fields. Another, who might work on the sewage system, might have the right to enter Field 3 but not Field 4. Among the civilians, a certain Zieliński has made a name for himself by his resourcefulness. He even collects secret messages and personally delivers them to families in Warsaw. His associate approaches me to suggest that I could use this opportunity to write a letter to my family. Naturally, I take advantage of the offer and tell my brother in the letter to pay Zieliński the agreed amount. Zieliński

---

77. Referring to the May Coup carried out by Marshal Józef Piłsudski.
78. Accommodations.

leaves the following day and promises to deliver the letter to his associate's father, who will get in touch with my brother by telephone.

Three days later, during our traditional rutabaga soup dinner, Zagórski asks me:

"Do you know Miss Mary X? She was on the road today, asking about you."

It took my breath away, my heart skips a beat, I feel hot blood in my veins, my brain goes cold. I nod in assent.

"I have a letter for you, sit down on the ground next to me. Place your palm next to mine, I'll put it there unnoticed."

He starts to adjust his shoe, pretending to fix his sock. A moment later I feel his hand and a wad of paper. At the same time he says:

"I have soap for you, a handkerchief, cigarettes, money, and some kind of medicine. It's back at my workplace, I'll bring it to you in the evening."

The note is burning in my hand. I can't just unfold it here, in front of everyone, they won't let me into the barracks, I won't be able to read it while working in front of the office, and Wyderka is lurking around the washroom barracks. What to do? I will go to the warehouse under the pretext of needing some tool for the afternoon. The store man is there, Eugeniusz Malanowski, a friend from the first transport from Warsaw, no one else is in sight. I stand at the back of the warehouse behind a stack of boards and unfold the paper. Her handwriting. I fly through the sentences, my breathing stops, I want to absorb the words as quickly as possible, then no one will be able to take them away from me. The letter is written in her style, like a man, without sentimentality, it contains an appeal to my reason for living and a promise of regular contact. At the end, several tender words, that she had never told me before. The letter doesn't mention anything specific about my release but for me, it is a revelation. I have known her for a long time. She was always cold and distant toward me. After my return from the "hike" initiated by Colonel Umiastowski (who ordered all troops to leave Warsaw on September 6, 1939), I took no interest in what happened to her. We telephoned one another from time to time. And now the veil of Isis is lifted. She opened up her helmet shield before me and my immediate surroundings, and had the courage to stand by me in my hour of need and was the first to extend a hand through the barbed wire. Admittedly, I was also by her side when over the course of fourteen days she lost her brother, a promising writer, to tuberculosis; her father, a judge, to a heart aneurysm; and her mother to cancer. It's an opening to new prospects for me. It brought warmth into my emptiness and solitude. I saw the first firm point on the horizon, a support for my inner being. It is a life-giving shot of energy, a mental antidote to the moral toxins of camp life behind barbed wire.

I hear a bell, what is it? *"Arbeitskommando formieren!"*—I snap back to reality—oh right, I am in a concentration camp, and with the loud clunk of my wooden shoes I run out of the barracks. I see the square and the wires surrounding me in more cheerful colors, with inner joy and a flippant smile I perform the *"Mützen ab"* ritual in front of the first cutthroat in an SS uniform that I encounter. I cannot wait until the evening roll call. We are already lined up on the square when the *Unterkunft Kommando* with Zagórski returns from work. Once we are back in the barracks after the roll call, he hands me a large blue silk handkerchief smelling of her Normandie perfumes, a piece of soap, one hundred hand-rolled cigarettes, five hundred zlotys, and a bottle of coramine heart drops. From now on, I use the handkerchief as a towel. I hand the cigarettes over to be kept in the warehouse. The store man lifts one of the floorboards and stashes my cigarettes, money, and medicine. Zagórski promised Zieliński 20 percent, so one hundred zlotys, for the delivery. I pay it gladly. Having permission to clean myself at the washhouse barracks, I go there right after the extra two hours of work and soap myself up from head to toe. Before I fall asleep, I read the letter from Mary a few more times, trying to analyze every word and fall blissfully asleep. I always carry the soap in my pocket, since everywhere else they'll steal it. Unfortunately Mary did not specify exactly what she was sending, she only mentioned that she brought some little things.

A few days later, Zagórski asks me my name during lunch. "Jerzy," I reply. To which he says he has a letter for me, but it's stashed at his worksite. He says he'll bring it to me in the evening. He asks me to permanently keep him in my group for the evening work after the roll call because there are beatings in other *Kommando* and my group's work goes on without it. He has been working with me for a week now. He doesn't bring me the letter in the evening, saying that he thought it was for me, but it was actually meant for another Jerzy, who he gave the letter to and he is supposed to find out if it was indeed for him. The next day at noon he doesn't come over to me, pretending to nap, so I go over myself and ask about the letter. He replies that yesterday, during lunch, not knowing who the letter was intended for . . . he tore it up and buried it! I ask him, where? He calmly explains that it was in the spot where he was sitting yesterday. We eat our lunch on the square between Blocks 9 and 10. I need to be smart. I can't look now with everyone around—and later, during work, when the square is empty and you can see every prisoner moving around from far away, it'll be that much harder to dig then.

In the afternoon, I take three trusted men with rakes and we pretend to be leveling out the area in between the barracks which has recently been dug up. I reserve where Zagórski was sitting the day before for myself. I carefully move the soil. After a longer search, I dig out strips of paper—I recognize my brother's handwriting. There are a lot of strips, roughly one-centimeter squares. I look around to make sure nobody is watching. I put a guard at the corner pretending to work and I start collecting the pieces into my pocket, and after turning over the earth some more, I find a few other scraps of the letter. As I do this, some reflections come to me. When the letter had already been torn up and in the ground, Zagórski told me he had it at the construction site—in the evening he said he had given it to some other Jerzy. Why such shadiness? Never mind, what's important is that I have the letter. But where do I piece it back together? If just quickly reading a letter brings such huge difficulty—how do I expect to puzzle these sixty to one hundred pieces into a legible whole? It's impossible outside in the breeze, only in the barracks. But that will take time, I have to carefully study each fragment and look for the continuation on the next. To my misfortune, the letter was two-sided and—as I conclude after a preliminary look, spreading it out on the highest bunk—written on two sheets, so four pages. This will take a lot of time and uninterrupted effort. Putting just a piece together will do me no good. I'll have to gather it up when I have to stop. The situation is almost hopeless.

So I go back to Zagórski and ask him to tell Zieliński to send a telegram to my brother, asking him to resend the letter. He agrees and the next day he tells me that Zieliński demands a slice of bread for the cost of the message. It wasn't my fault, but I gladly give him my piece. Easter starts in a few days and I'm counting on our getting a day off work, and that despite everything maybe I'll be able to put together at least a fragment on my bed. The pieces weigh heavily in my pocket, I can't wait for the holiday. Every evening, I look over the parts of my puzzle-mosaic to familiarize myself with the fragments of syllables. Isolated words— "mourning," "bill"—only excite my imagination. During the day, we cover the flower beds with sod brought over on car trailers. It is Easter tomorrow,[79] at last I will find something out from my brother.

They wake us up an hour later than usual, at 4:15 a.m. We still don't know if we'll be working. After the morning roll call, we learn that none of the *Kommando* will be leaving today, we will all work on the field. *Kommando* Zelent is assigned to pave the entry road and the *Gärtner* is to sod the flower beds. For some unknown reason, the kitchen didn't prepare breakfast. We work hungry, on empty stomachs. They tell us that we will only be working until noon. We get pearl barley for lunch, what a delicacy after so many weeks of rutabaga. I am terribly sleepy. I would be so glad to lie down like the others, but I still have to put the letter together. I barely spread out the strips on the blanket when the doors fly open and the block overseer yells: "*Achtung!*"[80] It must be someone important. We all jump to our feet and stand at attention until the demigod graciously mumbles out: "*Weitermachen.*"[81] As I jump down from the bed, I sweep all the fragments into my pocket. Kapo Henryk Silberspitz walks in and orders a clothing inspection. We are lined up in several rows along the main corridor of the barracks, and he looks over each prisoner, one after the other. He brushes shoulders with his hand to see if dust comes up, if it does—and it happens to almost everyone, they get slapped in the face several times, the same goes for those with muddy shoes. There are no brushes to clean our clothes or shoes, or any shoe polish. There aren't even any carpet beating racks and reeds to dust off our clothing. The only way is to beat our jackets

79. Easter Sunday, April 25, 1943.
80. Careful, at attention.
81. "Continue."

against the side of the barracks. As for the shoes, the kapos instruct us to wash them under running water as a substitute for polish.

The inspection goes on for over two hours—the kapo slapped nearly 80 percent of all the prisoners. I got away with it by jumping over to the already inspected group when no one was looking.

There's not much to say; we are encouraged to have a "Happy Easter." No breakfast at all in the morning, then work—now a general slapping. After the Jewish kapo leaves, I go to the washroom and wash my shoes under a tap. The place is so primitively thought out, even considering that it's still unfinished—there is no floor, no steps at the entrance, doors, etc. Taps have been installed every five meters. Under them there are troughs made from two long planks nailed together, some 10 meters long. Water is poured into the trough and prisoners are all supposed to wash together in this water. But even this primitive washing is not available to everyone. The block overseers and the clerks wash themselves in the buckets, those used to bring water for scrubbing the floor, and in the evening for carrying the extras, such as dried cottage cheese, marmalade, or sauerkraut. Why the use of the washroom is prohibited to the prisoner population at large, is unclear to me—since it has been built.

Once my shoes are clean, I return to the barracks. On the square, I come across an unexpected sight. Two teams are playing soccer. I can't believe my eyes, they are actually wearing sports uniforms. Each man is visibly stout and sturdy. It is not until I hear the words "*tadi*" and "*pojd sem*"[82] that everything becomes clear. These are Slovak big shots engaging in sporting activity to improve metabolism. We, the 99 percent of the camp, are barely dragging our feet and try to avoid even the slightest unnecessary physical effort, we sit, lie down, or sleep whenever we have fifteen minutes to spare, while they need to unload their extra energy and strength. Even in a concentration camp there is no such thing as equality. I walk past them without stopping and lie down on my bed. I have around four hours until dusk, I painstakingly arrange and rearrange the fragments, but I only put parts together, managing an entire sentence here and there, but the meaning of the letter or any concrete piece of information eludes me. The work

82. Slovak: "that way" and "come here."

excited me but I have to give up as dusk sets in. I console myself that my brother is sure to send another letter as soon as he receives the telegram.

This torn-up letter is one of my first lessons in patience at the camp. To have a message from your brother in your pocket but not be able to read it. I don't reproach the man responsible, since this won't get me my letter back and it would alienate him for the future. Nonetheless, his behavior is incomprehensible to me.

I have been told by my friends that those working in *Unterkunft Kommando* who have gotten in touch with their families are now receiving a second breakfast through the civilians, bacon, pork chops, eggs, pancakes, even vodka. They bring some of these victuals with them to the field and eat them instead of the traditional rutabaga. And Zagórski predominates among all. Every day, Zieliński brings him packages from his father. When will Zieliński bring something for me? I know Mary visited him in his apartment and, apart from the letter, also handed him a package for me. Would she really not send me any food? I meditate on this as I fall asleep.

The holidays are over! On the second day we are supposed to work as normal. The prisoners from the January transport from Warsaw had tied their hopes to being released then. There was a rumor circulating throughout the camp called a "parola" in the camp jargon. Nothing to it. I have already been here almost a month and I feel very physically exhausted. My legs are the worst, no sooner has the swelling from hitting my shin gone down than I start getting calluses on my feet from the hard footwear. I developed a kind of garland of thick skin, around one centimeter deep, around my heels, and several of my toenails are dented in, painful and suffused with blood. They are loose and it seems like four of the nails are coming off my toes. I also noticed that ever since I cut my fingernails back at Pawiak, they have not grown at all. This makes me aware of the predatory economy coursing through my body.

Killing lice has become a mandatory morning and evening ritual. Unfortunately, unlike in the days of the Sun King, we have no silver tweezers and tiny hammers; you crush them between your fingernails, quickly wipe your fingers on your pants, and then take bread in your hand.

I have eczema on my stomach and thighs, which itches in the evening. I wake up at night and scratch myself furiously. The abscess on my finger refuses to heal, instead it eats deeper and deeper into the flesh and the doctor cuts out more and more dead tissue every couple of days. I'm in the infirmary the next day. The doctor barely glances at me and confirms my fears: scabies. He gives me some ointment to rub in and predicts that it should be under control in three days. Meanwhile, the scabies spreads across my entire back so that I have to ask a friend to apply the ointment for me. When nobody is looking, I rub my back against the edge of the bed, it itches so much—like a piglet against a post. Behold the former man about town! The doctor gave a very lovely prescription, after rubbing the ointment in for a few days, take a bath, put on a new shirt, and get a new blanket. But it's just the opposite. A bath is out of the question, I am still wearing the same old shirt, the one I got on March 26 after I arrived: it is completely stiff by now, crusted with a mixture of ointment, dirt, sweat, and dust. So I keep reinfecting myself from the old shirt and the old blanket. I keep spreading on the ointment but I can't get these parasites under control.

After Easter, we finally get a pleasant surprise for once. Food packages arrive at the camp which aren't given to anyone. In any case, most of the addressees are either dead or left on transports. One day, after the roll call, the call comes to bring several people from each barracks with blankets. The *Lagerältester* tells me to go and to take two gardeners separately. We go to the window of a small room in the *Schreibstube* barracks where our local bigwig, Rudolf Pietroniec (former bandmaster of the 36th infantry regiment in Warsaw) resides, which serves as the bread storage warehouse. This is where the barracks get their bread. Today, this room is stuffed with packages. An SS man, the *Lagerältester*, Wyderka, and Bubi are there. They open all of the packages, taking out: onions, pork fat, bacon, sugar, tobacco, eggs, etc. and only dark, whole wheat bread is thrown out the window onto the blankets spread on the ground. Each barracks gets two blankets.

A group of curious onlookers gathers by the window. Kapo Silberspitz walks over with his whip and orders them to disperse. They take three steps back but continue to gawk. I move completely to the side. Soon,

Silberspitz charges at the prisoners and starts lashing them in the head. Once they scatter, I return with my men and go back to stand next to the barracks envoys. Silberspitz comes again and asks me what I'm doing there. I reply that the *Lagerältester* ordered me to wait with the gardeners.

"I told you nobody is to wait here," and smacks me across the face with the whip.

I turned away and took my people, giving up on the extra bread we were promised.

Distribution follows at the barracks. It's divided by eye into mounds for each section, and the sections distribute it among themselves. Some bread has a piece of pork fat baked into it or is sliced and spread with lard. Most of the bread is completely green and moldy. Still, hunger is stronger, we pick out the worst parts and eat the rest. We each get four or five pieces of bread. We wrap part of it up in paper and save it for later. Numerous disagreements arise around the dividing of the bread, that someone got a little more, and another less, or that someone had a thicker spread of lard while the other had a thinner layer.

And now the real orgy of thievery begins. Overall, theft is becoming more rampant. They steal shoes, jackets, blankets, so that we try to sleep with everything under our heads at night—but they even pull out bread or shoes from under a sleeping man's head or mattress. More than one victim is forced to go to work barefoot the next morning. It is exceedingly difficult to conduct a search, seeing as you would have to check three hundred mattresses in a short time, while the thief will toss stolen things out the top window, and hurry out right after the morning bell to pick them up and take them to an accomplice in another barracks. Someone like this comes back from work, lies down on his bed, and observes his neighbors to see what they eat and what they have. As soon as they move away to stand in line for coffee, with one swift move the thief pulls out the thing he was eyeing, or he does it at night. Then the cries often ring out "Catch the thief!" But before the lights can come on, the thief has already jumped back on his bed. So we are helpless, and carrying all of your possessions constantly can get tiresome. If you recklessly put a piece of bread down on the bed during supper, a hand from who knows which direction can snatch it from right under your fingers.

Night guards are even posted at the barracks. But those on duty are either sleeping or in cahoots with the thieves. If an alarm is raised, the light usually comes on too late. After being issued our moldy bread, the block overseer recommends that we pack it up, write our name and number on the packet, and deposit it with him during the day. It so happens that at 8:00 a.m., I am ordered to go out for a daylong work assignment outside the wires without lunch, and told to take bread with me. I go to the barracks and find my package. I see that it is tied differently and I establish that a sizable piece was taken out. Since I deposited my food in the morning before heading out to the roll call, my package was plundered not by regular prisoners but a *Stubendienst*—the custodians in whose care the packages were placed.

Theft committed by the *Stubendienst* is one of the constant plagues of the camp. There is no recourse—they have their ways to get revenge. They will crumple the blanket on your bed and put some straw in it, and the block overseer will write down the bed number and you get a lashing. Besides this, they have many other ways to harass you. Some prisoners take their bread with them when going out for work, which is prohibited and fought against by the kapos. Bread is the camp currency, for it you can get cigarettes, underwear, a newspaper. I even used it to pay for sending a telegram.

The rains start again. It rains all night and I dread the thought of what will happen if it doesn't stop before the roll call, will it stop before then, or will we have to work all day in the rain? As I start to get dressed in the morning, I get an unpleasant surprise. Half of my jacket, which I used to cover my legs, is soaked through. Since it is thick cloth, padded with hemp, it will not dry quickly. Too bad, there is nothing I can do, there isn't a spare suit hanging in the closet. I put on the cold, soaked jacket and walk out into the rain to work in it all day. And so it's my bed's turn—the wind must have torn off more tar paper.

Building the Monument

I cooperate very closely now with Zelent, the engineer, and his friend Albin Boniecki, a sculptor from Warsaw. May 1 is approaching, the National Socialist holiday. Kaps decides to erect a "monument" on the field. It is to stand between the kitchen and the washroom, so across from the planned new gate. Zelent builds the foundation under the monument and I am directed to pour a large "roundabout," or a large circle of dirt, around it. So once again, hundreds of prisoners are driven to do more strenuous work after the evening roll call. Barely has the roundabout been poured in the dimensions pointed out by Kaps when he decides, the next day, that it's too small and should be twice as large. The monument has to make a gigantic impression. While we were enlarging the roundabout with five or six truckloads of soil, Kaps only now concludes that the square in this spot is steeply inclined and we will have to level an area of over an acre, removing some forty or fifty centimeters of soil on one side and spreading it all over the square. The prisoners from our field must move this colossal mass of earth in only a few evenings. My work has become worthless because the ground under the roundabout has to be lowered.

The monument itself is worthy of the idea to which it pays tribute. Kaps steals a sewage pipe of some five or six meters in length and fifty or sixty centimeters in diameter from the company working on the sewage system in the *Zwischenfeld*[83] where the administration buildings are. The pipe is made of concrete mixed with fine, smooth gravel. It's taken onto the field in the evening once the civilian workers of the sewage company have left. Standing up the pipe-column presents huge difficulties given the lack of either jacks or scaffolds. The prisoners simply lift one end up to around 45 degrees and then, using two poles connected with a two-meter piece of rope, push the pipe higher. Prisoners on the other side with the same kind

83. Literally, "between field"; here, the area between the barbed-wire barriers of two camp fields.

of poles keep it from being pushed too far and toppling over the other way instead of standing upright. Everyone knows the threat they face if the pipe falls and breaks. Once it's standing, Kaps searches out several stonemasons with specially prepared hammers and chisels to even out the concrete surface, eliminate the visible seams from when the concrete was poured, and create an even, coarse surface. Boniecki designed a hexagonal, three-leveled pedestal and is now preparing the cap, made of wood for now, because there isn't enough time for something more durable. The moving of the earth is carried out feverishly—but without torment, as long as Zelent is in charge. His orders are short, firm, and coarse, like in the military, but he'll never insult the dignity of a friend, even with a word.

One day, Zelent's face is flushed, he has a fever and chills. Our diagnosis: flu. Wyderka allows him to go to Block 11. It is a shelter for the privileged. The kitchen staff lives there. Since some of them work the night shift, they sleep during the day. No one will notice if there are thirty-two or thirty-three of them in bed, which means someone from the outside can be smuggled in and sleep there during the day, if the block overseer allows it of course. On the second day, the flu doesn't subside, on the third his fever is over 39 degrees. Zelent has to go to the hospital. His *Kommando*, consisting of over one hundred people, is broken up into several groups. One is taken over by the bricklayer, Jan Luba, a communist who lived in the Soviet Union for a time and was allegedly locked up for espionage; the second, to Mleczko; and the third to Bolesław Reich from Lublin. The latter has been in the camp for only a few days. Apparently he had some contacts in the SS as he claims to have often had drinks with Kaps in the city's pubs. He claims to be a *Volksdeutsch* and tries to speak German; he murders the language to the point your ears wither. He immediately grasps the atmosphere, takes a big stick, and starts hurling abuse in German at prisoners working under Luba and Mleczko. The other two are also armed with sticks but don't know a word of German. So, since Reich can swear in German and unceremoniously whacks people in the back and head left and right, Reich takes command of the situation on the spot, even though no one appointed him leader. The maxim "*Starszyj—kagda bijot*"[84] wins.

---

84. Russian: "Whoever hits you is in charge."

Within a few days, his *"Führernatur"*[85] draws the attention of the SS men and kapos and he is soon able to usurp Zelent's power. The expression "power is there for the taking" has maybe never been as true anywhere as in the camp. Those without scruples and who want to climb over the corpses of others just have to reach down and take the stick in their hand. He finds himself a piece of wire six to eight millimeters thick and a meter long, orders it wrapped in straw, and starts whipping people with it.

My own men do not worry about Reich of course, since they aren't subordinate to him, so they don't get too wound up when there are no kapos around. At some point he starts to hassle my men as well, in his self-taught German, naturally. This gets my blood boiling and I act perhaps foolishly, from the point of view of camp opportunism. I walk up and tell him in German, with a Viennese accent, to stop interfering with my people. His face sinks and in broken German he tries to explain that it's the job of a *Vorarbeiter* to make sure every prisoner is working hard, even those from a different *Kommando*. I tell him that he doesn't have a *Vorarbeiter* armband on his sleeve yet, and besides, I am here with my people and I alone take responsibility for them. As I walk away, I suggest to him, in Polish now, that in the future he should speak to me in Polish, seeing as German is a problem for him. I speak to him loudly, in the presence of several dozen prisoners. It has an unexpected effect: Reich tries to strike up a "friendship" with me, visiting me during work, and initiating private chats. He confides to me that he confiscated five rubles in gold from some prisoner and gave it to Kaps; they suspected that he took more and only gave up part of it. I immediately recognize the type of rascal he is, I keep my guard up but I feel that his unspoken goal is a nonaggression pact with me. After several days, I notice that Reich gave up the straw-wrapped wire, he tossed it in one of my flower beds. He walks with a wooden stick; they must have forbidden him from beating people with the wire.

Finally, April 30 is here, the monument is standing, the encirclement of earth is finished, divided by four paths forming a cross in the shape of

85. Here, leadership quality.

the *Virtuti Militari*[86] medal. The earth is still bare on the flower beds. The May 1 holiday is celebrated with a discussion between the *Feldführer* and Kaps as to whether the pedestal should include crockets or flat flower urns. I serve as the interpreter in the conversation about this with Boniecki. We both laugh later at the SS men's poor taste. Boniecki prepares a group of three doves taking flight to adorn the column. For material, he uses barbed wire, which he coats with cement dyed bluish-gray. He works in primitive conditions. A partition was placed inside the washroom barracks to provide him with a small work space. He has a roof over his head, I visit him often under the pretext of work. I find out that Zelent has typhus and that all the previous cases of flu and pneumonia—Dr. Jastrzębski, Father Archutowski, Struczowski—they were all typhus. Nice news for me seeing as I inherited his jacket and swapped for his better blanket, of course with its live inventory—so when will I come down with "the flu"? Besides the aforementioned, many others in our blocks are getting sick with "the flu."

86. Poland's highest military decoration.

Thumann and the Beatings

The word "Thumann" means terror in the camp. He is the owner of a golden party badge, which gives him prerogatives above the camp commandant. Thumann is on his feet and in motion all day. Here he rides a motorcycle, there a beautiful black gelding, then he crops up somewhere on foot between the utility barracks under construction. He can appear before the roll call to check if the kapos are up after the first morning bell. He stands at the gate almost every day as the *Kommando* head out for work, stopping and searching anyone suspicious, confiscating second shirts, and demanding that their prisoner numbers be noted down for punishment. At 7:00 a.m., he is already at the guard post by the Chełm road ordering laborers searched who are entering the camp for sewage system work, to check if anyone is carrying too much food or vodka that they could, God forbid, hand over to the prisoners. He stops wagons bringing in cement, sand, brick, and other building materials to make sure no food is hidden under the drivers' seats. And if he finds anything, he stops the wagon, orders the driver's head shaved, puts him in a prisoner's uniform, and keeps him in the camp for several months. If the driver contracts typhus and it takes him to kingdom come, that's his own bad luck. During the day, Thumann stops individual prisoners carrying packages or sacks to make sure they are not carrying potatoes or carrots out of the camp gardens. At noon or in the evening, he stops returning units on the road or by the gate and again the "*filc*"[87] to check if anyone is bringing sausage or vodka with them obtained from the civilian workers. In the evening, after the lights-out bell, when the kapos are gathered in a single room with vodka and an accordion, Thumann appears unexpectedly and sends them running. There is plenty of him everywhere, he always springs up out of the ground without warning, the menace of Majdanek.

---

87. Polish: (from the German *filzen*) body search.

On Field 3, Blocks 1 and 2 house auto shops and garages. It's called the *Fahrbereitschaft*. Mainly Poles work there. Their block overseer is Captain Sławomir Turobiński. The camp commandant's beautiful, eight-cylinder Tatra with a built-in radio is parked there. At night, the Poles take turns getting into the Tatra, to switch on the radio and listen to the Polish broadcast from London. Two lookouts stand in the yard to make sure no SS man catches them listening to the radio. One night, the lookouts failed and Thumann materialized only six or eight steps away while the radio was still on. The listener managed to switch from the London station to some German music and pretended to be cleaning the car's floor mats. Thumann wrote him up—he got fifty lashes, though the offender expected much worse.

Everyone dreads him because they know that he can drop even the strongest man with a single blow to the face, and those called in before him for interrogation for various transgressions sometimes get three hundred or even four hundred lashes in one "session." His constant companion is a large German shepherd, Boris. Thumann never holds his head up high, but always has it stooped forward, his piercing eyes casting their gaze left and right scowling from under the visor of his hat. Pity the poor prisoner who fails to take his cap off when passing him, even at a distance of several dozen steps. Thumann will sic Boris on the prisoner and the specially trained beast will bound toward the offender in huge leaps, sink its teeth into the man's calf, and hold on until he takes the cap off. Then in an instant it lets go. High-class SS training! Out of a crowd of hundreds, Thumann can spot the man standing idly, smoking or flapping his gums. Instantly, the man and the kapo or *Vorarbeiter* are written up and, after the evening roll call, get their payout.

Whips come in different types: bullwhips, whose strike is the most painful; then there are whips made of two to four straps stitched together with an iron wire inside; there are also whips braided together from narrow leather strips, some over a meter long, others shorter. A whip is part of the standard uniform of every SS officer and SS man in the camp, just like his service revolver or belt. Just the same, every kapo and block overseer always carries a whip, which never leaves their hands except when they sleep. It is an external symbol of authority. One day during the evening roll call, the block overseers are told to search the prisoners and confiscate all broad leather belts. We thought they were needed as SS equipment. The following day, they round up several saddlemakers and order them to stitch new whips to be used against us.

Apart from regular beatings across the head and back while standing, and the improvised ones to the buttocks for which you have to bend over and rest your hands on your knees, special tables have been built, called racks, for official enforcement. Each rack has four legs, two are longer and two are shorter. The tabletop is not made of planks but of slats forming a groove. The groove is slanted to one side since the legs are uneven. A slat is nailed to the lower legs just above the ground. The culprit has to stand by the rack and put his feet behind the bottom slat, then two kapos grab his arms, pressing his torso against the groove and strongly yanking his arms beyond the rack. So the buttocks are tightly flexed and the body is totally immobilized. The bottom slat holding the heels prevents kicking or lifting the feet to release the tension in the buttocks. When the rack is standing on the square during the evening roll call where the commandant stands— more than one person's flesh crawls. Before the roll call, the block clerks are notified which prisoners have been called to the *Rapportführer*—and we know what that means.

There is no rule book, so a prisoner doesn't really know what is forbidden. Only the warnings of senior and more experienced prisoners and their own practical camp experience, paid for in slaps, kicks, and whips unfortunately, teach the novice what is permitted. Prisoners get a lashing mainly if money or jewelry is found on them, or two layers of underwear, or secret messages—not to mention for theft and escape attempts. But I know a man who got his butt whipped for picking trees with uneven crowns that were planted at night. So, after the final "*Mützen auf*,"[88] when the *Lagerältester* calls out: "*die zum Rapportführer bestellten*,"[89] the summoned break ranks and run forward, and the execution begins. Most prisoners are first admonished for their transgression and get bloody hits to

88. "Hats on," the opposite of "*Mützen ab*."
89. "Those summoned to the *Rapportführer*."

the face to start. Only then we hear *"Leg dich"*[90] and primarily the *Lagerältester* and other kapo volunteers start beating the miscreant.

There are rules and theories as to whippings. To give a "good" lashing,
you have to spread out your legs and swing the whip slowly from behind
and quickly rip it back from the body. It's "proper" to beat with long whips
and to only strike with the tip. So if the end misses the body and hits the
table, the lashes are not so painful. Sometimes the culprit is expected to
count out the lashes himself. You usually don't know how many lashes
you've been sentenced to. If two kapos are beating together, one on the
left and the other on the right, alternating lashes like peasants threshing
with flails, sometimes a pair of lashes counts as one strike. *Lagerältester*
Rockinger, for example, has a reputation for not knowing how to beat as
he tends to strike too quickly and nervously, without sufficient swing. On
the other hand, the lashes of the former field commandant and current
Blockführer, Groffmann, are very painful. The prisoners know who among
the kapos and SS men is dangerous at the rack and who is sufferable. During collective executions the kapos are drenched in sweat and they switch
off on every offender. After twenty hard strikes the skin splits and deep
cutting wounds form. After the beginning lashes to the buttocks, some
kapos aim higher, near the kidneys, and these strikes are much more dangerous to your health. Very few are able to take the floggings like a man, as
the lashing continues, louder and louder moans of pain escape. Jews utter
inhuman howls and screams, Poles are composed, I admire those who bite
their fingers bloody and don't cry out loudly. Of course, woe unto anyone
naive enough to slip a piece of blanket into their pants. Then the strike
sounds muffled instead of a loud slap, and he gets an additional beating for
it. Unless the field commandant or Thumann, who is assisting, specifies
the number of lashes to be given, the beating continues until the commandant orders it stopped. Those that struggle and try to get away always get
it worse than those who are passive. Finally, the word *"Weg!"*[91] The kapos
let go of the arms, the wrongdoer automatically straightens up, but with
all the pain forgets that his feet are immobilized, loses his balance, and falls

90. "Lie down."
91. "Away!"

flat on his back. Almost every beating ends that way unless someone has experienced it before and remembers to "get out of" the rack first. If the man on the ground doesn't get up immediately—either from passing out or being exhausted by pain—he gets kicked with boots, especially with the tips of the boots aimed at the heart, stomach, kidneys, and sometimes the crown of the head, and besides that he is showered with lashes.

Lashings on the rack also take place during the day if someone is caught red-handed by the field commandant or the *Lagerältester*. The rack is then brought out in front of the office and the whipping begins.

After these executions the prisoners make cold-water compresses, and they go to the doctor to disinfect their open wounds. Unfortunately, disinfectants are in short supply in the infirmary, and anyway prisoners are not always allowed to go. One such case happened at the auto shops where the kapo was Fritz Illert, a professional safecracker. One of the shopworkers was the lawyer and former parliamentary deputy Jan Nosek, tasked with washing cars. Somehow Illert found out that Nosek had received money from home in some illegal way and demanded that he reveal how he got it. When Nosek refused to name the contact who got him the money, Illert personally meted out 150 lashes with his bullwhip. Illert was athletic and often showed off his physical strength. The lashes taken by Nosek were dreadful. After he had finished, Illert forbade the block overseer from sending Nosek to the camp hospital. The primitive "home" treatment in the barracks could not protect Nosek from developing gangrene, and although on the third day he was finally sent to the hospital, before twenty-four hours had passed, his life ended there. When they asked Illert why he had beaten Nosek, he reported that Nosek had sabotaged his orders. This took place in early May 1943.[92] Immediately afterwards, Illert was released from the camp for exemplary behavior and enlisted in the SS-*Panzerjägerdivision*.[93]

"*Der Wonnemonat Mai*"[94] has arrived. Several days after erecting the monument, we learn during the evening roll call that since spring is now warm,

92. Jan Nosek died on May 25, 1943.
93. SS antitank division.
94. "The Merry Month of May."

starting the next day, we are to report to work barefoot, without jackets and without hats. The explanation given is the need to save clothing. On this particular evening, we had mild spring weather, so we didn't worry about it much. We are told to return our shoes to the block overseer with our names and numbers on a piece of paper slipped inside, the same with our hats. Our jackets have to be folded into a square with the numbers clearly visible on the bed. However, the prisoners working outside the *Postenkette*, who are visible to civilians, aren't covered by this order, since why should people beyond the wires know about the conservation of wooden shoes here? Precisely the following day, it's cold and foggy in the morning. We hop from one leg to the other at the roll call and try to stand on just our toes so our feet don't get too cold. We start to persuade each other about Father Kneipp's therapy,[95] air baths, and nudists, so as to prevent from falling into helpless despair, from the torment and frantic production of bronchitis and pneumonia in those whom the lice couldn't finish.

So many of my friends have departed for the Revier that I start to become more interested in the conditions there on Field 1. The patients are segregated by illness: Block 3 is for convalescents; 4, internal diseases; 5, surgery; 6, tuberculosis; 7, hopeless cases; and 8, typhus. At first, the blocks were supervised by Jewish doctors from Slovakia, and after the Warsaw transport arrived, they were replaced with Polish doctors, as well as Polish Jews from the Warsaw Ghetto later. These doctors work with the greatest devotion, to perform their duty with limited medical supplies of poor quality. A private pharmacy is secretly maintained there where they've gathered medicines obtained from various illegal channels.

To get rid of prisoners faster, the weakest and the oldest who are unfit for work are chosen for the gas. So-called selections take place at the hospital every fourteen days. The commissions consist of several SS men, usually drunk; the director of the crematorium, *Oberscharführer*[96] Mußfeld;

95. Rev. Sebastian Kneipp (1821–1897), who developed a method of hydrotherapy.
96. SS sergeant.

and the kapo at the Revier, Benden. The selection consists of having a heavily sick, fevered person walk eight steps in front of the commission. Out of the general population of the sick, which in the Revier amounts to about one thousand people, an average of 30 or 40 percent are selected for the gas chamber, so 60 to 80 percent of all the sick every month. In the first half of May 1943, Captain Antoni Wolf from Warsaw, now a patient, stood in front of such a commission, having been sick with diarrhea in March in the infirmary on Field 3 and contracting typhus fever there. Then he was laid up in surgery Block 5. Despite having gone through two devastating diseases, he passed the test successfully. That day, eighty-four people were taken from the surgery block, including legionnaire Kwiatkowski, so nearly half of the sick in Block 5.

There is a diet on Field 1, barley gruel and tea or coffee for the fevered. The *Revierkapo*, Benden, a waiter from Hamburg, has been interned as a communist at various concentration camps since 1933. He is prisoner number 1. Always dressed in quality clothing, on warmer days he wears white pants and a shirt with a red triangle. All the doctors are subordinate to him and his power is so absolute that in the operating room he often takes a lancet in his hand and performs minor operations. He is the master of life and death, being the most reliable member of the selection commission for the gas chamber.

As much as the medical staff rises to the occasion with great effort, the auxiliary staff, especially the Jewish orderlies, exploit and steal from the sick at every step. The job of a custodian has to be bought, and in May 1943 the price reached five thousand zlotys. The positions were created and assigned by kapo number 1. That's also why his minions have more authority than even a department supervisor or the head doctor of a block. Due to the commonplace hatred with which the (mostly Slovak) Jewish functionaries treat Poles, only on rare occasions are the Poles listened to or get a chance to speak.

I find out from convalescents returning from the Revier that Father Archutowski died of typhus, as did Dr. Jastrzębski.[97] Nobody can give me any information about Struczowski, I describe his appearance, and

97. Marian Jastrzębski died on May 4, 1943.

they tell me that a tall, dark-haired typhus convalescent became a nurse. I assume it's him and I'm happy he found such a good place for himself. All those returning complain about the huge lice infestation in the Revier and that most of the sick contract typhus there. Anyone with a fever and an undiagnosed illness is sent to the typhus block for observation, and fourteen days after admittance he is "100 percent certain" to contract typhus, even if after several days of observation it turns out that the fever was caused by a different sickness, which ran its course and passed.

Categories of Prisoner

Over the course of a month I begin to understand the makeup of the prisoner population. Half of the prisoners are Russians who went to Germany to work, either willingly or as forced labor, and committed some kind of crime there—mostly theft, assaulting a foreman or farmer where they worked, being absent without leave, having intimate relations with a German woman, etc. After they are arrested, they are transferred to concentration camps. Supposedly, there was a ban on swearing and abusive language in Russia. I knew some Russian words from the imperial days of the First World War, and I knew some tongue-twisting configurations of Hungarian, Yugoslav, and Italian curses, but when Soviet youths started showing off their wealth of swear words, I was left speechless. Pups only fifteen or sixteen years old address their elders with the informal "you." Food being insufficient, they have no qualms whatsoever about stealing from their friends, achieving artistry with this skill. Thefts committed by Russians, and particularly Ukrainians, have become a common plague in the camp. Russian soldiers imprisoned for escaping from POW camps are far more decent but they are in the minority and disappear in the mass of these hooligans. Since Russians make up 50 percent of the prisoners, at the same time, in their primitive manners they are noisy, unbridled, and rakish, setting the tone for the camp, raised in the steppes, not being able to speak calmly to one another.

Most of the Polish prisoners consist of people arrested on trains with smuggled goods, people from mass street roundups, people crossing the border between the General Government and other regions of Poland, or hostages from villages that failed to meet the grain quota or located near the site of a train accident. Among them are murderers with the blood of several people on their hands, bandits, professional pickpockets, there are pimps, taking pride in their exploits, like Zygmunt Meller, the overseer of Block 14, there are ghetto smuggling specialists, imprisoned for this, like Janusz Olczyk, the overseer of Block 15. Actual political prisoners incarcerated on direct orders from the Gestapo, the so-called *Schutzhaftbefehl,*[98] constitute maybe 10 percent of all Polish prisoners, that is roughly 5 percent of the overall camp population, since apart from Poles and Russians there are several dozen Germans and several hundred Jews. The way the Soviet prisoners talk is contagious and resonates with the mass of Poles from the countryside. The simple folk didn't want to be left behind the "Russkis," and a vulgar, crude, boorish Slavic camp language was created. Both the Poles and the Russians use certain German terms like "*Mica*" for a hat, "*Deka*" for a blanket, "*antreten*" instead of line up, etc. The Poles use various Russian borrowings, while Russians adopt some Polish expressions. Their favorite word is "*pierdolić,*" which can be used as a synonym for: telling someone off, to screw off, stuffing your face, blabbering, etc. Depending on the prefix: *wy-, od-, za-, na-, z-,* the word is something like the English verb "to get."

The intelligentsia, scattered across all the barracks, drowns and is lost among the rabble. Any educated person, nay, anyone wearing glasses, is treated with contempt by the masses, and since the former haven't mastered the rich dictionary of abuse, they lose every minor argument from the start. Just being in this environment is punishment for an intellectual, when this manner of speaking is the everyday language for most. People from the East, Asians among them, maybe didn't have even the comforts of this place, where they get their own bed and blankets. Being locked in the camp, the change of living space, clothing, diet, doesn't pose as much of a lifestyle change for some as it does for the intelligentsia. Besides this, the intellectual has to level his spirit or at least attune himself to the general standard of the camp if he wants to avoid falling into constant conflicts and reactions to hundreds of different actions and situations, which would be automatic on the outside. A huge proportion of the prisoners address one another as "you" according to the Russian manner and the custom in German crime stories. This is the millstone that crushes individuality the most, and at best, in rare cases, it only polishes away the excess layer of savoir vivre. It's bad enough that "friends" from the common people are unfavorably disposed toward the intelligentsia; the intelligentsia are

---

98. Those under a protective custody warrant.

also especially exposed to persecution by the SS. After all, the whole point here is to exterminate the Polish intellectual elite. So it's life-threatening to admit to being: a lawyer, journalist, officer, priest. At the same time, doctors are in demand and engineers are valued.

Since being a block overseer or *Stubendienst* requires a certain amount of brutality toward prisoners, the answer as to what kind of people are recruited for these positions is automatic, and why most of the well-educated block overseers didn't last long before being replaced. The person willing to beat, torment, abuse, and be absolutely ruthless toward his underlings has a chance to claw up to a management position. The function of *Stubendienst* is a sinecure costing 1,500 zlotys or more, paid to the block overseer. This is why the *Stubendienst* (equipped with whips and bats) wake prisoners before the morning bell to bring water and scrub the barracks. They themselves only check if the beds are made well, fix those that aren't, and write down numbers; they bring lunch, get bread, and the extras, and wash bowls after lunch. For six well-fed chaps, it's not hard work. The kitchens already start serving lunch at 10:00 a.m., so the barracks personnel eat until they are full before the others, they pull out any pieces of sausage floating around on the soup in the cauldron—and the prisoners get only rutabaga soup. The *Stubendienst* cut the sausage—and the next day you can buy an entire rope of sausage from the barracks staff. The *Stubendienst* are mostly Russian, sometimes Poles, but almost no intellectuals. Staying up all night isn't terrible for them since they get enough sleep during the day. They take turns as lookouts standing by the doors which are left slightly ajar, while the overseer, clerk, and other *Stubendienst* sleep on the top bunks at the very end of the building—so that they have enough time to slither down unseen from the beds.

All the more so, the real political prisoners stick together, though there is no habit of asking why someone ended up here, unless they reveal it.

This is not to say that there aren't decent people among the peasants. I have a number of farmer-landholders from the Włodzimierz Wołyński[99] region near Kowel working for me; there are about twenty people from a mass arrest, village dwellers with great civic and social sophistication, very

---

99. Today Volodymyr-Volynskyi, Ukraine.

conscientious and dutiful. I enjoy talking to them during work. But these are pleasant exceptions that deflect from the foul background. Of course the dominant element is unbridled and devoid of self-discipline. To be fair, they only have themselves to blame for 50 percent of the slaps and whippings, by not making their beds, having prisoner numbers coming off at the seams, smoking during work, leaving work without permission and roving around the kitchens, sitting down during work or leaning against a shovel and staring motionlessly at the sky. The clever ones also don't work all the time, but they either pretend to be moving, or set lookouts so they aren't caught off guard.

That's why there are situations where the block overseers have to whip, because there's no other way to tame thieves, or those relieving themselves in the corners of the barracks at night, not wanting to use the crates at the back, or those on the top bunks who urinate under themselves so that it trickles down onto people sleeping below. Sometimes excrement is found in the straw of the mattresses. The lashes given to such a "friend" then are well deserved. In fact, beatings by the block overseers stop making an impression, because they are mostly justified and verbal reminders and warnings rarely resonate with simple folk.

One day, an excited *Lagerältester* Rockinger rushes over to the block overseers during roll call and tells them that carrying whips has been banned and they have to leave theirs in the barracks. As for a clear ban on beatings he says nothing. I have frequent contact with him during my work. He is unbelievably cowardly and subservient toward Kaps. One day, after the roll call, Kaps ordered the gardeners to sprinkle the lawns sown with grass with fire hoses. There were eight hoses, four new and four old. Some of the spots sown with grass are so distant from the hydrant that water from the hose made out of the four old hoses combined doesn't reach. Kaps forbade the use of the new hoses. After Kaps left, Rockinger told me to add the four new ones, and I said that Kaps forbade it. He shrugged and replied:

"I give the orders here now."

So I take the hoses and add them. As I am watering, Kaps returns to the field unexpectedly and asks me why I took the new hoses. I say that

the *Lagerältester* told me to. Kaps doesn't reply. The next day I talk to
Rockinger and tell him that the whole thing with the hoses could have
caused an uproar, since Kaps saw them being used against his instructions.
Rockinger retorts:

"And why didn't you tell me that he forbade it?"

I reply that I did tell him yesterday. Irritated, he says:

"You didn't tell me anything."

Kaps never mentioned the matter but I got an example of the lack of
character and courage by the *Lagerältester* to take responsibility for his
instructions. If there had been trouble, Kaps would of course have believed
the *Lagerältester*, that a common *Häftling* didn't warn him about the ban
on using the hoses and lashes would be guaranteed.

Around that time, in the office I learn that the *Feldführer* and Kaps have
long accused Rockinger of being too lenient and soft toward prisoners,
and that they even nicknamed him "Dr. *Unblutig*."[100] I weigh the pros and
cons of the possible change, in any case Rockinger is unfair, rash, dumps
blame for his mistakes on others in spades, is scared of his own shadow, so
who knows, maybe the next *Lagerältester* will be better? Since Rockinger
only became *Lagerältester* in mid-March, older friends still remember the
previous one, *Lagerältester* Schmuck, with a green triangle, a bandit from
Hamburg, a real lowlife, who would go into a feral rage during beatings,
he also drank and took bribes in cash under the pretext of buying instruments for a planned camp orchestra. But between the time the first transport from Pawiak arrived on January 18, 1943, and the departure of the
first transport to another camp around March 20, 1943, he was unable to
organize the paperwork in the office, and he didn't order the preparation
of name registers and card indexes either in the blocks or in the field office.
So he was demoted to an ordinary kapo at the *Lagergut*[101] and transferred
to Field 4. Even before that, he and the other kapos living together at the
office barracks were *filc*ed and ordered to live in separate barracks.

We hear stories of another terror, Galbawi, who also used to be the
Lagerältester. An athletic build, weighing around 120 kilograms, an ani-

---

100. Un-bloody.
101. Here, the camp's agricultural farmstead. See chapter "A Hand through the Barbed Wire."

mal in man's skin, a bestial tormenter. Apparently he was released and now serves the Gestapo and the SD (*Sonderdienst*)[102] in Lublin. There are rumors that he might come back to Majdanek and all those who know him shudder at the thought of this possibility.

Mary and my brother were back in Lublin and sent me messages, money, and some food through a worker. The messages mean the most to me, since I feel that they are caring for me. They repeat the previous messages, saying my release is moving in the right direction.

At the time, in the first half of May, Wyderka brings us some unbelievably good news, exciting us all. A Polish government has been formed with Prince Janusz Radziwiłł at its head, a Polish Army is being organized, relevant posters are plastered in Lublin; prisoners, other than those caught with weapons, convicted of espionage against Germany, and communists, are to be released from the concentration camps.

The camp is coming to a boil. The releases are to start within two weeks. The *Politische Abteilung* has supposedly started reviewing personal files and preparing release lists. The mood is elevated, everyone works happily knowing that our days at the camp are numbered. Meanwhile, our field has started to fill up again with new transports arriving from Lwów, Włodzimierz Wołyński, Kraśnik, Białystok, Kowel, etc. Some new energy has entered me and I start gazing rosily at the world.

102. Special service. However, "SD" actually stood for *Sicherheitsdienst*, or security service.

Hunger and the Jackals

I'm starving. While planting peas, I eat them raw to feel some weight and fullness in my stomach.

I've gotten pink eye from the constant sandstorms. I remember my brother suffered from the same in Warsaw throughout the summer of 1940. The condition was caused by the dust rising from the ruins and the unswept streets. Despite regular visits to the ophthalmologist and eye drops at home, he still couldn't get rid of it for months. Here in the infirmary there is only one kind of eye drop—universal, of course there is no specialist, there are almost no prospects for healing. But I don't worry about it, since after all, I will be free in May.

I quickly spent the money I received from my brother. The prices on the field are horrendous. A half-kilo rope of sausage is sixty to eighty zlotys, and it's camp sausage, so it's full of water and has little fat, horsemeat naturally. I buy it in secret and after lights-out I eat it under my blanket. Another time I bought a half a kilo of sugar for eighty zlotys. The sugar had been soaked in water to increase the weight, and besides there was no scale and I had to eyeball it to gauge the weight. The sugar was packed into some bag made from female stockings. I also ate the sugar at night after lights-out and with each swallow I felt as if a wave of warmth emanated from my heart throughout my entire body. I ate half the bag, hiding the rest for the following evening. In the morning I wake up invigorated, fresh, and then I was convinced that sugar really "fortifies" and it contains a certain amount of calories. When I go to eat the rest the following evening I see, or rather feel in my mattress, that someone stole the sugar from the straw. My additional distress is that I was supposed to return the bag. My money quickly dissipated from these usurious prices. After all, even with money it's hard to get a piece of horsemeat sausage or sugar. No wonder— the demand is huge and the supply small.

The kapos have loads of money from the theft of jewelry, gold, and cash, as well as bribes. Each has a supplier among the civilian workers who delivers: milk, vodka, raw meat, butter rolls, bacon, etc. They have a ton of money, lightly "earned," and for them high prices play no role whatsoever. Each worker can only bring in a limited amount of products, basically as much as he can fit into his pockets. During the inspection at the main gate they say that it's their meal that they're taking for themselves. Despite this there are maximum limits, but each person can still bring in "only" two liters of milk. Wagon drivers are also suppliers. Hidden in the sand, cement, and bricks, they are able to bring vodka, several bags of cookies from the bakery (ten in each bag), eggs, cold cuts, poultry, as well as larger items, small loaves of stollen, etc. But again, all that goes to the kapos and block overseers, and the most a common prisoner will see is when they order him to take a wheelbarrow to the wagon, they put the products inside, they cover them with sod or bricks, and order him to deliver it to the barracks where the kapo lives. And only the surplus remains for ordinary prisoners. Prices are several times higher here, for example; for a butter roll that costs five zlotys in Lublin you have to pay twenty zlotys; for a newspaper, which officially costs twenty groszy,[103] we pay ten zlotys. Overall everything costs three or four times more in this underground trade than on the outside. The drivers, who earn three thousand zlotys a month from the SS and also get a discounted price on feed, earn extra thousands every month on smuggling food.

And it doesn't end there, laborers and drivers buy shirts, shoes, clothing, not from regular prisoners of course, but from those working in the warehouses as well as block overseers and kapos. The civilians come in torn shoes, held together with string, which they throw out on the field or somewhere in the camp, and they put on new shoes; they wear two or three shirts out, two pairs of pants, etc. They pay relatively low prices to the prisoners, or they deliver vodka and food at camp prices—and they sell the clothing in Lublin for enormous sums. People pay as much as fifteen thousand zlotys for a used suit.

And that's not all: they are also middlemen for selling gold and jewelry. They take it to traders in the city and return with the amount asked for. Naturally, they make money on this, since none of the prisoners control

---

103. One hundred groszy = one zloty.

how much they gain from a sale. As I already mentioned, they charge 20 percent just to deliver the money. Along the way they also collect messages from the camp, demanding fifty zlotys per letter. In fact, the workers don't really do anything. They arrive around 8:00 a.m., make their rounds of the barracks delivering orders to their subscribers: milk for this one, bread for that one, a newspaper for him, bacon, etc. Then, each of them proceeds to the site of the sewage works, they pick around while pipes are being arranged or connected for two or three hours, but it's more of a rallying spot for clerks, *Stubendienst*, etc. to come and buy up the remaining products. Then the "civilian," in "his" barracks, quickly puts on shoes or slips on another shirt and pants, takes a few messages, collects his money, and around noon the workers are already on their way home. Often, already around 10:00 a.m., they are roaming around the field and admit to me that it wouldn't be right to leave for home so early in front of the SS men. They aren't paid by the hour, but according to the job, though it puzzles me why the building contractor isn't interested in the progress of the work and that nothing gets done for weeks at a time. After all, it's about the good of Polish prisoners, so that they'll have a minimum of good hygiene, like lavatories and water with washbasins at their barracks. The civilian workers understand this very well. But these are leeches that don't pay the slightest attention to the terrible hunger, the dying off of hundreds of people, so what should they care about the improvement of conditions for prisoner hygiene. Their only concern is drawing usurious profits out of prisoners under compulsion.

Admittedly, there are other options, namely, your family buying food on the outside and giving it to a civilian worker to hand to the prisoner who they work with; for that they have to take the package to the camp and deliver it to the right addressee. This runs into the difficulties of finding trusted people, the goods pass through the hands of the civilian worker and a prisoner-messenger and only then does it reach the intended recipient. Thumann orders searches of these prisoner-messengers during their march back to the camp, often at the gate, sometimes already on the field during the roll call. Once, in a single evening, they confiscated two bottles of champagne, genuine French cherry Cognac, several bottles of liqueur and Hungarian wine, a few kilograms of chocolate, a dozen or so kilograms of sausage and bacon, vodka, a butchered chicken, eggs, etc. The camp commandant ordered it all placed on a table and photographed.

I finally receive the repeated letter from my brother where he lists everything Mary handed over to Zieliński during her two stays in Lublin, as well as things he passed on to Zieliński when he came together with Mary. It turns out that apart from the handkerchief, soap (which was stolen after only a few days, by the way), and the medicine—I didn't get anything. I show the letter to Zagórski and he promises to bring it up with Zieliński, but over a series of days he tells me that Zieliński hasn't been coming to work. I hear from other friends that Zieliński has been coming to his usual workplace. Several days later, Zagórski tells me that Zieliński is denying it, claiming he never received most of the things, and that the boiled eggs are still at his home at my disposal (for two or three weeks now), but he simply didn't have a "chance" to bring them, and that he got the few slices of bread spread with butter and layered with cold cuts, but he thought they were for him and ate them himself. He doesn't however feel in any way obliged to return any of my things even though he eats first-class delicacies on a daily basis, and to my request that he again press Zieliński to give me what's mine, he erupts with rage and asks if I suspect him of keeping it for himself. I was speaking to the associate calmly and I was far from suspecting him of it, but precisely his outrage betrayed his lack of a clear conscience. His behavior toward me confirms the suspicions expressed by the block clerk Knips about Zagórski, that he had also offered to intermediate the delivery of packages but ate their contents himself, and gave Knips nothing. Knips threatened to inform the *Lagerältester* about the man's embezzlement. Faced with these machinations of a "colleague" with an academic degree, I have no option but to write to my brother to stop sending food and ask him only for money. Even though I pay four times as much, I know that at least I will be the one eating it. In the meantime I chew on raw peas, while others are receiving champagne, and my packages are being eaten by Mr. Trainee Attorney!

Some of the prisoners take to trading in food, buying products from the workers, given that the prices in the camp within the *Postenkette* are lower than on the field, since you have to pass the inspection at the gate.

———————

The news of the planned release of prisoners from the camps after the formation of the Radziwiłł government buoys me up mightily, besides, my brother told me in his letter that my individual case is going the right way, but it hit a snag, since a new transport from Pawiak to Majdanek was derailed near Celestynów by the Polish underground, seven SS men were killed and the Gestapo is focused on the accident—and other cases have been set aside for now.[104] This convinces me and I look toward the future with confidence.

I paint the picture in my mind of when I come home, return to work in the factory, talk to my foremen, I can see their faces, but I can't remember the name—of the person who for many years in a row came to me twenty times a day. I think of my telephone in my office, I can't remember my own number. So I try to recall my brother's number, and my departed mother's, I have doubts about two or three digits. Oh—no good, I see that I'm losing my memory—a lack of phosphorus in my body, a symptom that many prisoners complain about.

The Central Welfare Council (RGO) supplied the Poles with one small bread loaf each. It's colossal aid for us. So, they remember us. Once Knips starts registering Poles, all of the Ukrainians suddenly feel Polish and more than one Russian does too. *Ubi bene, ibi patria!*[105]

104. On May 19–20, 1943, at the railway station in Celestynów, a Home Army unit liberated a group of prisoners being transported from Warsaw to KL Auschwitz.
105. Latin: Homeland is where life is good.

Organization of the Camp

The hierarchy and organization of the camp is as follows: at the head of the entire camp stands *Lagerkommandant*[106] Florstedt, with the rank of SS-*Sturmbannführer*.[107] Everyone recognizes him by the thick cigar that never leaves his lips. He is rarely on the field. He only travels by car.

The camp has five fields with twenty-two living barracks each, i.e., 110 barracks. Each one has three hundred places to sleep, so in theory the camp can hold thirty-three thousand prisoners. This capacity isn't utilized in full since the hospital barracks, occupying half of Field 1, have a smaller capacity; there are hospital wards, pharmacies, infirmaries, housing for nurses and doctors, and Field 5 is only for women.

So only half of Field 1, as well as Fields 2, 3, and 4, are at the disposal of male prisoners. The camp administrative office is located on Field 1. Several of the barracks in Field 4 have been converted to basketmaking and brush-making workshops. They make long baskets as packaging for heavy artillery shells. So a lively bustle and constant crowding is limited to Fields 2, 3, and 4. Field 6 is currently under construction.

Each field has a chief, the *Feldführer*, aided by a *Rapportführer*, in charge of the camp numbers and roll call department, and an *Arbeitseinsatzführer*,[108] who runs the labor department. Their subordinates are the *Blockführer*, stationed at the *Blockführer* gatehouse by the gate, who receive their blocks during the roll call, serve on the field during certain hours, inspect barracks, and meander around the field. The *Feldführer* and his aides almost all hold the rank of *Unterscharführer*, so the rank of corporal, and the intellectual and large-unit leadership skills to match the rank. Apart from the *Blockführer*, there are also guard companies that man the guard towers and supply people to the *Postenkette* to escort *Kommando* sent to work beyond its limits. These are totally raw, unintelligent, mainly *Volksdeutsche*

106. Camp commandant.
107. SS major.
108. The leader of the *Arbeitseinsatz*.

from Romania, Hungary, and Yugoslavia. There are also entire companies of Lithuanians with their officers in Lithuanian uniforms. It makes
me glad to hear SS men speaking to each other in Romanian or Serbian,
since it's easier for them than in the tongue of their "fatherland." Some of
them report from the tower to the noncommissioned officer on duty, riding around the posts on bicycles, saying in broken German: *"Posten Nr. . . .
nichts neues!"*[109]

The most senior of the prisoners on each field is the *Lagerältester*. His
assistant is the *Lagerkapo*. The *Lagerältester* of Field 1 is concurrently the
Lagerschreiber, the head of the camp's main office. The offices of respective
fields answer to him and, indirectly, so do the *Lagerältester* of the three
men's fields. The female camp has a completely separate administration,
as if it were located in a different place. Besides this are the regular kapos.
They are all exclusively Germans and 90 percent of them are common
criminals, so-called bandits who we recognize by their green triangles.
Among the Germans are a handful of political prisoners. They are mostly
communists, and from the leadership rungs of the party, predominantly
workers, but well-read and with a large reserve of general knowledge. Next
are the following functionaries: block overseers, block clerks, office clerks
on each field, and of course the *Stubendienst*. I count the latter as part of
the authorities as they walk around with whips and bats and make heavy
use of them in their barracks.

The *Lagerschreibstube* maintains the numbers of the entire camp, prepares daily and monthly reports, keeps a card index by name and number,
and so on.

The block overseers, clerks, and office workers are almost 99 percent
Jewish. Slovak Jews occupy all the positions in the offices, the political
department, the *Arbeitseinsatz*, kitchens, washroom, laundry, and post
office, and serve as doctors, nurses, and orderlies in the hospital. When
there is no Slovak Jew for a position, then a Polish Jew might get it. On the
outside, the Germans lock Jews into ghettos, force them to take off their
hats in their presence and portray the Jews as social rejects, who have to be
eradicated. Here in the concentration camp, Jews rule over Aryans, Jews

109. "Post number ____, nothing new!"

carry whips, and the Aryans must stand at attention and take off their hats before them. Here, Jews address Aryans as "you" while the Aryans say "sir" to the Jew! Jews and SS men work hand in glove, Jews beat Christians bloody. Everything the opposite of *Mein Kampf*. Where do these Jewish privileges come from?

Majdanek was established in 1941 as a camp for Soviet POWs. Next, Jews were brought in, they were kept in tents in the most primitive conditions and they started to build out the camp. And that's how thirteen thousand Slovak and then Polish Jews were brought in. German kapos were transferred from other camps, such as Buchenwald and Sachsenhausen, and as functionaries, among others, Krzysztof Radziwiłł's middle-school teacher from Jarosław, named Karabanik, and a civil servant from the National Engineering Works in Modlin, named Żurawski. In October 1942, the first transport of Aryans arrived from Lwów. Among them was the lawyer Mieczysław Domiczek. Soon afterward, Soviet officers, POWs from Stalingrad. By 1943, of those thirteen thousand Slovaks, a little over three hundred remained alive. It was then that the last Slovak Mohicans, who had made their way across the entire camp stage, were appointed to all the offices, warehouses, and departments. The Slovaks had then sworn a solemn oath to support one another and not to allow anyone from outside their group into any managerial position. They have been true to their word and form the clique of "the superior ten thousand," which acts with arrogance, exclusion, and condescension toward all foreigners, while groveling before the SS men. With ruthlessness and brutality toward the prisoners they try to document their loyalty, emphasizing that they feel like an integral part of the system ruling the camp and creating the impression that they are irreplaceable. They are all fluent in German, belong to the bourgeois class, and mostly have secondary educations. With difficulty, they can communicate with the Poles and Russians, so to a certain degree they are predisposed to managerial positions. They are always dressed to the nines, and no wonder, because there is a lot to choose from in the clothing taken from the newly arrived transports. They are exquisitely fed, since the provisions taken away from the freshly arrived prisoners before their shower aren't tossed in the trash. And who is entrusted with searching Jewish clothing taken away in the baths, for all the dollars or jewelry, who was instructed to rip apart the soles and heels of Jewish shoes and pull dollars out of there? The Slovak Jews of course! And the dollar is mighty, despite the enforced exchange rate of just four marks and twenty pfennigs!

At the moment of my arrival, the *Feldführer* of Field 3 was SS-*Rottenführer*[110] Groffmann, previously an *Eierkalker*[111] from Gdańsk. Here, he was the commandant of twenty barracks with a normal capacity of three hundred people each, i.e., theoretically 6,600 people. *Schutzhaftlagerführer* Thumann was a carpenter, some kapos remember him from Dachau, then he was still a corporal and stood at one of the guard towers with a machine gun. *Lagerältester* Rockinger (wearing a green triangle), supposedly a philology student, allegedly sat in prison for murdering his lover. *Lagerkapo* Peter Wyderka (from Silesia) was a criminal police officer in Berlin and simultaneously headed a gang, and was convicted for robberies that they committed. Kapo Ossi (first name), a green triangle, Berliner, professional safecracker, of whom hardly anyone knows that he bears the beautiful Polish surname of Radziejowski, and doesn't understand a single word of Polish. Kapo Heini, a young, 18-year-old Jew from Kraków with the surname Silberspitz, and finally, last but not least, the *Lagerjüngster* Bubi, a 13-year-old Polish Jew, son of a tannery owner from near Bydgoszcz or Konin, who denounced and hanged his own parents at Majdanek. This probably suffices for a characterization. I had heard of this little Jew while I was still free back in Warsaw, just before my arrest, when the first Majdanek prisoners were bailed out after the great January roundup in 1943; they returned at the end of the month. This little thickset boy is a fright, he is a sadist with criminal instincts. He carries a whip almost as long as he is tall, dragging it on the ground behind him. No one knows his real name. He owes his camp "career" to the former *Lagerälterster* Galbawi (criminal), a homosexual, who took him under his wing. Even after Galbawi's

---

110. SS private first class.
111. An egg limer; to keep them from spoiling, eggs were preserved in lime water.

release, Bubi kept his privileged position; he was then taken care of by Kapo Wyderka.

These are the masters of life and death of 6,600 people. Kapo Wyderka has earned such a name for himself for his cruelty that his photograph was apparently published in an English newspaper in 1942, a point of pride that somehow ended up in his hands, maybe as a symbol of respect from the SS leadership.

My situation in the camp is made easier in that I speak fluent German and, more importantly, I understand what they are saying to me. Many of my friends speak German but only understand the literary language. And here, some privates or corporals—so peasants and laborers—speak in a Bavarian or Saxonian dialect, or the least comprehensible *Plattdeutsch*[112] from the Danish border region. And each simple SS man thinks that his dialect is the *par excellence* of the German language and everyone should understand him. And when they get frustrated that someone doesn't understand, they turn to violence, asserting that the whip is the best interpreter.

After seeing those red, Austrian cavalry uniform pants that the kapos were wearing, which brought back fond memories, I was able to get into a frame of mind to imagine that I have been drafted into the army again and I have to surrender to the harsh discipline of barracks life. After several weeks in Majdanek I was convinced that everyone who had served in the military adapted much more quickly and easily to the hard regime than those who hadn't.

When I arrived, there were around eight thousand male prisoners at Majdanek, nearly four thousand Poles and Russians each, several hundred Jews, and several dozen Germans.

The prisoners are divided into different groups and categories.

The elite are the *Schutzhäftlinge*, so-called political prisoners. They wear red *Winkel* with the top pointing down. Abbreviated "Sch." The letters printed on the triangles denote nationality, and so: "P"—for Poles,

112. Low German.

"F"—Frenchmen, "C"—Czechs, "I"—Italians, "N"—Norwegians, "SU" (*Sowjetunion,* or Soviet Union)—Russians; the Germans have no letter on their triangles.

The *Berufsverbrecher,* abbreviated "BV" (pronounced "Befau"), professional criminals, referred to in the camp as *"Befauer,"* wear green, upside-down triangles. Having served their sentences in prison, the criminals are sent to concentration camps.

The *Sicherungsverwahrte,* abbreviated "SV," called *"Esfauer,"* "detained for protection" (of society, from criminals). These are recidivists with several convictions (so, the criminal aristocracy), who were free at the time of Hitler's coup or at the outbreak of the war. They wear green triangles, upside down.

The *Asoziale,* abbreviated "Aso," asocials, arrested for avoiding work, violating wartime economic regulations, slaughtering cattle in secret, etc. Black, upside-down triangle.

The *Bibelforscher,* abbreviated "Bifo," Bible students, arrested for not recognizing secular authority and refusal to serve in the army. Violet, upside-down triangle.

Homosexuals, abbreviated "Homo" or "§175," pink, upside-down triangle.

Ausländische Zivilarbeiter, abbreviated "AZA," foreign civilian laborers, arrested for attempting to flee from forced labor in Germany, striking a supervisor, etc. Red rectangle.

Sonderaktion der Wehrmacht, abbreviated "SAW," soldiers dismissed from the army. Red triangle, point facing up.

SS-*Sonderkommando,* SS men expelled from Waffen-SS. Red, upside-down triangle with a black border.

Juden, Jews, reason for arrest: "Jews and cyclists are guilty," red, upside-down triangle over a yellow triangle, forming a six-pointed star with three yellow corners showing from below the red. Abbreviated as "J."

Zigeuner, Gypsies, the same reason for arrest as Jews. Black triangle with a white letter "Z."

Pfaffen, priests, the same red triangles as regular *Schutzhäftlinge.*

Russische Kriegsgefangene, Russian prisoners who escaped POW camps. Red triangle.

The categories are strictly applied only to German prisoners. It's rare for a Polish bandit to have a green triangle or a Polish smuggler to have a black triangle. Red triangles are given to Poles wholesale, so the markings don't indicate their actual crimes. The classification of Russians seems to be the most fluid. Theoretically there is a group of "Russian prisoners" but they don't have separate colored triangles and the tendency exists for them to melt away and disappear in the mass of Russian civilians. At the beginning, Russians were *Schutzhäftlinge*, but later were converted en masse to AZA.

It really doesn't matter what triangle you are wearing, since everyone gets fed the same and has to do the same kinds of work. Although as far as influence is concerned, green triangles have the most sway, because kapos are primarily recruited from their ranks.

There is also a special group among the Germans, the so-called *Ehrenhäftlinge*. The title and associated privileges are granted by the *Reichssicherheitshauptamt*.[113] An *Ehrenhäftling* has the right to long hair, to their own bed, and to other benefits like frequent correspondence, etc. Since there aren't many German prisoners at Majdanek and they all already serve as kapos or other high functionaries, the *Ehrenhäftling* don't stand out very much.

We have something new on the field, each barracks receives several tables and several dozen stools. Also towels for each prisoner. But our joy was short-lived. The tables are set out in the barracks during the day and a stool is placed next to every second bed, and in the evening, before the roll call, they are stacked up on one pile up to the ceiling in one corner of the barracks, out of concern that the prisoners could stain or break them. On Sunday afternoon we have to scrub them, but no one is allowed to sit on them. The block overseer doesn't issue us the towels since he is responsible for them and worries that we will steal them. What good is it that we've been allowed to use the washroom, if we aren't allowed to use towels? And so we continue to sit on the bare ground during lunch and often, during sandstorms, we eat soup with sand that crunches between

113. The Reich Main Security Office, the central SS organization.

our teeth. Thumann introduced another innovation. He ordered the roofs removed from the latrines so that no one shelters there when it rains. At every turn he tries to make our lives repugnant, while creating the pretense of caring for our comfort. I've been here for seven weeks I think, and they still haven't given us new shirts, ours are stiff with filth, full of fleas and nits, some have such clusters of nits on their collarbones it's as if someone spread herring caviar. The prisoners don't even scrape these nits off.

The Russians are subject to special rules. They are not allowed to work outside the wires for fear they might escape. I for one find it strange, since there's a greater likelihood that Poles will try to escape since every other Pole will give them shelter and they won't draw attention to themselves by speaking a foreign language. So Russians only work on the field. The barracks clerks are personally responsible that no one with the letters SU finds their way into a *Kommando* heading outside.

A nightingale has been singing nonstop at night. There isn't a single tree or bush around other than those I recently planted and those have barely turned green. Could a female have woven a nest among the barbed wire and is now nestled on little eggs, while her husband, sitting on the wire, sings to her? It seems that life is stronger than barbed wire. The song of the nightingale brings me much joy.

The Mausoleum and the Turtle

I often drop by Boniecki's workshop to warm myself up. I keep track of his work. For the crowning of the column, he has made a top in the shape of an urn wreathed with laurel. I ask him why he added the laurel. Albin just smiles mysteriously. The doves didn't come out as well, they look more like eaglets. He is working on a pipe tobacco box made out of tin, baking it over a flame to remove the red paint and writing. I learn from Boniecki that once the new top had been set in place, during the moment it was being attached, he dropped a tin can inside the hollow column containing the ashes of a Polish prisoner, he had obtained them from the crematorium. The laying of the ashes was witnessed by B. Jasieńczyk, the kitchen *Vorarbeiter*, and Henryk Szcześniewski, the scout famous at Majdanek for never swearing. Standing at attention for one minute, they silently honored the memory of this unknown prisoner. The monument, intended by the SS to celebrate a National Socialist holiday, became a mausoleum of all the Polish prisoners tortured to death in Majdanek.

The "doves" molded by Boniecki to adorn "their" monument excite the admiration of the SS men and he earns so much credit that Kaps orders him to prepare some decorative sculpture for the garden. "In the blink of an eye" (as recalled by Wiech) Boniecki knows what to do and starts working on the model of a turtle, ten times its normal size, the one that works for the Germans in all of the factories and in every workshop was drawn in coal on the walls and chalk on the ground—as a symbol of slow work. Kaps is thrilled, and the prisoner is too, each for their own reasons—an example of the theory of relativity! As the gardener, I am supposed to choose the right spot in the garden and create the proper surroundings. I choose a place by the gate—so that the turtle can be seen by everyone leaving for work, as well as passersby from other fields. Another reason is that the gate to the auto repair shops is also located on our field, at a 90-degree angle to the main gate. I build a large pedestal of crushed stone, two meters wide and one meter high. There is a large amount of limestone available on our field from our own quarries, as well as gravestones from the Jewish cemetery in Lublin. They were brought by the civilian wagon drivers and were already broken into pieces, destroyed at once. They are mostly sandstone but you'll also find gray marble and expensive black Swedish granite. Weathered Hebrew inscriptions, covered in moss, some of them fresh with glittering gold letters. There is a *Kommando* of around thirty *Steinklopfer*[114] working on the field—prisoners with weak legs, who while sitting, break down these funerary monuments to rubble to pave the entry road and paths. I take pieces of these tombstones to form the pedestal and at least symbolically protect them from final profanation. May they lift the symbol of the camp's resistance and become an integral part of it. I plant a row of junipers as a background and a flower bed of marigolds and irises in front. Then I sow grass around the pedestal and plant out morning glories. The turtle stirs up great cheerfulness among the prisoners and inspires various funny observations. Later I learn that a photograph of our turtle appeared in some underground newspaper. And no man is prouder of the turtle than the *Rapportführer*, Corporal Kaps!

I get in touch with home through one of my "gardeners," Kleniewski. He is a young landowner; his sister, Engineer Janina Ostaszewicz, lives in Lublin at 2d Moniuszko Street. She just located her brother in May through a wagon driver, even though he has been at the camp since January. Kleniewski suggests using this channel, to which I eagerly agree, and I establish contact with my family again. The driver cautions that he won't be bringing any packages. I try to find out how many previous parcels fell through because of Zieliński. I see that my brother writes about it with reserve and undertones, counting on the letter passing through several hands. But I see that he considers Zagórski untrustworthy. I decide then that after the war, I am going to file a complaint

---

114. Stone breakers.

in court against Zieliński because this is plunder deserving of the highest punishment. I have to admit a sad thing, that the workers and the wagon drivers who had contact with the camp didn't pass the test, and I often hear "devout" wishes from the prisoners for each of those exploiters to find themselves in the camp for even four weeks and to experience in their own skins what real hunger means and that they pay the usurious prices for a piece of bread or bacon, as far as they will even have any money.

Homo homini lupus

While I was free, I imagined social conditions in a concentration camp completely differently. The Germans had been sending transports to Auschwitz since 1940, and Warsaw was shaken to the core by the huge roundup and immediate transport of over two thousand people to Majdanek in January 1943. We imagined that there was exceptional solidarity and brotherhood there, that this great misfortune bound everyone into a single family—but those first to be released who returned from Majdanek at the end of January and the beginning of February described how the Jews awaited the demise of their coreligionists in order to take the portion of bread away from the dying.

How true it was! And that's not all—not only are starved inmates lurking around for that piece of bread, but also the "civilians" legally earning several thousand zlotys a month, and more than that on the trade of clothing and jewelry taken out of the camp. They still squeeze out a widow's mite, sent to more than one prisoner by a wife struggling with poverty, for a loaf of dry bread! The SS men and kapos beat and abuse us . . . and the civilians make fortunes and exploit our hunger! *Homo homini lupus.*[115]

I am permanently hungry—hunger is the dominant sensation and thinking of food absorbs my mind completely. While in the *Gärtnerei* to get seeds, which were weighed out, I stepped onto the scale and quickly weighed myself. I was without shoes or a jacket (taken away a week earlier). I had lost nearly twenty kilograms in six weeks. My body had consumed all of the excess fat and my muscles had atrophied as well. All of my ribs are visible, my stomach has completely sunk in, I have no buttocks at all, my arms and legs are skin and bones. At the beginning, my body still had something to draw on, but what will happen in another six weeks? If I lose another twenty kilos, I won't be able to move anymore. And we all

115. Latin: Man is wolf to man.

know what happens next. Every day I see someone else from my barracks lying down on the ground during roll call, he goes to the Revier where they all either die or fail one of the "tests" before the selection commissions, which take place every two weeks like clockwork. We keep finding out about how many sick people were sent to the gas. The few whose families are able to make contact and provide them with food stay in shape, the rest melt away from day to day. There are those for whom families do supply food, but a portion is stolen by the civilians, and another portion by "friends" who eat it by mistake without delivering it. I belong to this group. Deep sorrow wells up inside me toward these hyenas, these jackals. I wouldn't even describe this feeling as anger, but rather sympathy, that someone could debase themselves like this. Could it be that my physical weakening has even caused a change in my psychological reaction and instead of rage I feel pity?

My balance sheet doesn't look good. I have: an abscess on my finger that just won't heal; scabies, which I haven't gotten under control for weeks and is appearing again; pink eye; painful cramps in both my legs every night; nightmarish dreams; memory loss; my nails won't grow, and have also become totally soft; constant drowsiness; and a hopeless lice infestation. On top of this I now have enteritis. A terribly upset stomach, and I can't recall eating anything suspicious. I go to the bathroom eight to ten times a day, a clear mucus. It's my body's reaction to the monotonous diet and depriving it of necessary nutrients. It seems my turn has come. Equal rights for everyone. For many, this is how the journey to the chimneys begins. I gather myself together. In the face of animalistic hunger, I don't eat for three days, which weakens me mightily, but the diarrhea stops. If I could at least rid myself of the lice; it's the end of the seventh week and we haven't bathed or changed our shirts.

Kapo Silberspitz has been released. This causes great agitation on the field. *Lagerältester* Rockinger summons prisoner and lawyer Gacki (former parliament deputy) and forces him to write a letter to his wife, who owns an estate in the Lublin region, instructing her to pay three thousand zlotys to Silberspitz to help him with living expenses in his first weeks of freedom. Outright extortion!

———

The barracks square is starting to look quite presentable. Though my friends tell me that in January and February, during the thaws, it was so muddy on the square that some prisoners, Zelent included, got so stuck during roll call that the wooden soles of their shoes tore off when they tried to move afterwards. The clever guys would prepare two bricks for roll call to stand on as a pedestal in the mud.

Day in and day out, I see dozens of naked corpses being taken out of the field, day in and day out during roll call I see the emaciated breathe their last breath. Hundreds of people idly witness this without raising a finger. The same would await me, were I to die on the roll call square. Death has completely lost its majesty, its mystery, and stopped being terrible. Just a moment ago my friend was talking—and he already stopped breathing, the passing is so easy, so inconspicuous, only that coming back from there isn't possible. This dying has become so commonplace that it doesn't make the slightest impression. It seems even more trivial than getting a tooth filled. We're on familiar terms with death. It has become prosaic, deprived of the romantic halo of a heroic soldier's demise on the field of glory. How much mystery has been swept away from the Greek myth that demanded placing obols under the tongue of the dead, to pay Charon to ferry them across the muddy Styx, which wrapped around Hades seven times? Here, we stand at the Styx every day, the other side is very close, and the passage is free. It's enough to just stop breathing and then the world of SS men, kapos, barbed wire, transforms into ETERNITY. It's so easy! You can truly say that the roll calls take place *sub specie aeternitatis*.[116]

Roll call! The only time of day when all the mouths must be shut, when you don't hear debauched Russian swearing. The only time in the day when I can focus, calmly say my prayers and gaze at the clouds, moon, setting sun, tear myself away from reality and shift myself to my dearest departed and call for their aid. When, in my thoughts, I can visit my beloved in Warsaw

116. Latin: in a universal perspective.

who are looking after me. This is the daily moment of communing with my loved ones, when I draw strength to keep defending myself.

During the full moon, we leave the evening roll call under its light; when we line up in the morning it's still in the sky. Its greenish light doesn't inspire *amoroso*. Every day during the roll call we watch and experience the sunrise, the victory of light over dark, the sight for which nature lovers ask to be woken in the mountains and later talk about it at the table d'hôte as if it were an achievement.

We observe the clouds, the direction of the wind, and try to forecast the day's weather which awaits us, or rather, which we await. The roll call square is located at the top of a hill with a very beautiful view of the panorama of Lublin. Whichever way the wind blows, the roll call square is always breezy and cold. Those that say that this spot was chosen intentionally at the camp's creation for prisoners to always freeze may be right. The first red rays of the sun emerge, the houses of Lublin are bathed in purple light, the windows reflect the rays as if embers burned behind them. Once the barracks are all lined up, the *Stubendienst* lay those who died after yesterday's morning roll call, the heavily sick and emaciated, on the ground, in the mud, by the left wing of each block.

Father Archutowski once told me how he had to hurriedly unload corpses from a wagon under the watchful eye of the crematorium chief, Sergeant Mußfeld. Standing together on the wagon with another prisoner, Obara, they heaved them over some wall where corpses were lying, waiting their turn for the chimney. The Russians manning the crematorium strike a long iron bar with three hooks at the end into the stomach cavity and drag corpse after corpse onto the grills which they shove into the oven. Seeing and hearing all of this I think about what an aristocratic funeral was held for the poorest peasant in the village, who died in his own bed, mourned by his family, washed, and in a clean shirt, reverently placed into even the most primitive, cobbled-together coffin, sprinkled with holy water by the priest and taken to eternal rest in consecrated ground. Meanwhile, here, Mußfeld checks the teeth of every corpse and if they have a gold tooth, it's torn out with pincers. The ash from the crematorium is taken to the compost pile in the *Gärtnerei* and mixed with trash from the entire camp and excrement from the latrines. Any bones that weren't incinerated go to the grinder, they are ground down into bonemeal, carefully packed into fifty-kilogram bags, precisely accounted for in the warehouse register, and sold as artificial fertilizer. The words "Remember you are dust, and to dust you shall return" ring true here literally and at an accelerated pace. Last year's compost was spread on the fields of the *Gärtnerei* in winter, and now they plant rutabaga and cabbage there for the kitchens.

And if the family, notified of the prisoner's death several months later, asks to have his ashes sent, and they pay the fee of ten marks, they get some ashes in a can, which were just gathered out of the oven now. The ashes of their dearest were taken to the compost heap a long time ago!

I wrote to my brother heralding the joyful news that I would be home before long, given the formation of the Radziwiłł government.

There is a change on our field: the kapos replace their winter clothes and red trousers of prisoner-*dompteur*[117] to summer Polish army uniforms. Who knows how those ended up in the camp. They still even have the Polish eagle on the buttons. For us prisoners, the change of clothing is very unfavorable, since this way the kapos become invisible. Before, you could spot the red pants in a crowd of prisoners from three hundred paces away, and now, in moments that I least need it, kapos rise up unnoticed out of the ground. We gardeners also get a change. After Kneipp's two-week barefoot treatment, the *Feldführer* allows us to wear our clogs again, since digging and pushing a spade into the hard earth with your bare foot is difficult.

Thanks to Mrs. Ostaszewicz, my brother quickly sends me money, scabies ointment, and a reply, where he writes that the news about Radziwiłł's government has been greatly exaggerated. At first glance the letter is written very guardedly, so as not to deny at the same time the news of the mass release of prisoners from the camp. He presents my individual case in the following way: my cousin, Ninka, is to come to Mrs. Ostaszewicz shortly

117. French: a tamer of wild animals.

with a suitcase of clothing for me, since they are counting on my personal release any day now, and that Giga was considering whether she could leave Warsaw for Lublin so as not to miss each other along the way. So, excellent news. My brother replies directly to my question that he did not receive the telegram that I gave Zagórski a slice of bread to send. I share the cheerful news with Kleniewski.

When I tell Zagórski that my brother didn't get the telegram, he calmly replies:

"What do you expect? You wanted Zieliński to send a telegram for a slice of bread? That costs a hundred zlotys."

So why did he take the bread from me in the first place? The situation is crystal-clear by now. What catches my notice is that as Zagórski returns from work he takes off his *Vorarbeiter* armband and when the *Feldführer* summons the *Vorarbeiter* after the roll call to discuss various matters and incidents, the trainee attorney is never among them. It's obvious that he has designated himself as a *Vorarbeiter* and he prepared such an armband to have more freedom when working among the civilians. I learn about Zieliński that he took three fees for a single sum of money delivered to a prisoner. Once when he delivered it, again a few days later, saying that he lost the first amount, and then a third time, under some pretext, he weaseled it out of the family, collecting money each time.

The salve sent by my brother is effective and the scabies disappears after three days. Apparently the camp ointment wasn't worth much. My wagon driver doesn't take a percentage for the delivery and refuses my offers of payment outright. Since he rarely comes onto our field, and often visits the neighboring field, or he takes materials to the large garage being built opposite the gate of our field, I suggest to Kaps that we prepare flower beds on the embankments along the camp road by our field and plant flowers around the *Blockführer* gatehouse. The *Rapportführer* agrees to this and Kleniewski goes out every day to care for the flowers and dig around—long enough for the wagon driver to pass him and nod if he has anything for him or not. If he does, he pulls up between the stacks of building materials where Kleniewski collects deliveries and hands over letters. Mrs. Ostaszewicz has money on deposit for me and as needed she sends it through the driver.

Packages begin to arrive for some prisoners, but during the official opening of the packages in the presence of the SS man from the post office and the inspection of their contents, Wyderka takes out everything, leaving only bread. So I write to my brother to send a package as a test, with biscuits made from sweet, greasy flour and eggs, and to also dip them in fat. I don't think these kinds of biscuits will attract the greed of the kapos.

Kaps instructs Boniecki to prepare more sculptures for the garden. He produces several frogs sitting on the edge of a pool of water or climbing out onto its edge, then a penguin with water spouting out of its beak, and his most successful work—a salamander, a meter and a half long, climbing up a wall with one of its legs still on the ground. This is an allusion to the Lizard Union[118]—the lizard's mouth gapes at the window of the "office" of the *Feldführer* located in the corner room of nearby Block 12. Together with the bricklayers I prepare a stone foundation from rocks, a piece of an old wall made of weathered bricks and appropriately placed perennials on one side, from which the salamander is clawing his way up the sunny wall. These are the most pleasant moments of my work in the camp: discussions with my friend Boniecki about aesthetics, arranging allegorical sculptures like the turtle, salamander, and secret mausoleum, and doing work to beautify our field, so work that doesn't benefit the Germans in any practical way.

118. Polish underground organization of the nationalist movement, active 1939–42.

Peter Birzer

The change expected on Field 3 takes place. Rockinger took off his *Lagerältester* armband and they point out the new *Lagerältester* to me. In his forties, a degenerate face, a strangely shaped forehead, the Lombrozian type.[119] After the evening roll call, all the block overseers, clerks, kapos, and *Vorarbeiter* are called to the *Feldführer* for a briefing. The new *Lagerältester* gives a speech with a long whip in hand (despite the recent ban on carrying whips). He calls his whip his barometer, a gauge of work and discipline. His voice is hoarse and drunken. So this is the man the *Feldführer* chose as replacement for "Dr. *Unblutig.*" Too bad that Rockinger left, I feel that the regime will get worse. Rockinger goes to work with some *Kommando* and moves to a different barracks.

The new *Lagerältester* is named Peter Birzer; he has a red triangle. He brings a Slovak Jew, Friedrich, along with him to the field to take over the important *Arbeitsdienst*[120] department in the office, and several new kapos. He controls assignments to particular *Kommando* so he has one of the most lucrative positions. In a few days, while the *Kommando* are leaving for work, Friedrich demonstrates the new order. Slaps in the face rain down, and then brutal kicks to the stomach.

A week after Birzer's arrival, as we are walking out for the morning roll call, we find out that the body of one of the block overseers, Neumeister, was found hanging next to the bell fastened to the pole in the middle of the barracks square (the one with the red light). He was a jolly man around thirty-five years old. An intelligent Jew from Warsaw whose attitude toward prisoners was very decent. The Jewish block overseers deny the possibility of suicide, since he showed no intentions and his personal living conditions were such that he had no reason to take such a desperate

---

119. I.e., having the appearance of a criminal. Named for Cesare Lombroso, an Italian researcher whose theory correlated physical appearance with inclinations toward antisocial behavior.

120. Labor service, responsible for organizing prisoner work in the camp.

step. During the day, Kapo Wyderka tells everyone that Neumeister committed suicide because he couldn't live with the pangs of guilt for crimes
he had perpetrated against other prisoners. This isn't very convincing.
Slowly, the truth leaks out. Birzer and his protégé, Kapo Karl Galka from
Vienna, a former SS man imprisoned for some crime, came drunk around
midnight to Block 5, which was supervised by Neumeister, and demanded
gold from him. Neumeister denied having any, so they started choking
him while he started to struggle and yell. Then they ordered him to get
dressed and come outside with them; they led him onto the field and
started "interrogating" him there. Apparently he confessed that he had
jewelry stashed with a certain Pole. This didn't satisfy Birzer and Galka,
so they hung him on his own belt, and then went to the Pole and ordered
him to give up the jewelry and gold, which he complied with, not knowing what had happened. Since there was no investigation of this "suicide,"
everyone is panicked and scared to mention anything, worried about
meeting the same fate. Neumeister's dead body is cut down after the roll
call and carried away to the crematorium after the Kommando set off to
work. He is placed on a stretcher and covered with an empty mattress, and
the only one brave enough to do him a final service was the overseer from
Block 6, fat Jacob, the Jewish porter from the Warsaw Main Railway Station. He accompanied the body all the way to the field gate. This is the best
indication that something was fishy about the suicide; otherwise, many
more block overseers and Stubendienst would have accompanied the body
on its way out.

After the evening roll call, Zelent and I are called to Kaps. We are told that
he is promoting us to Vorarbeiter of our work squads, and tells us to find
our own armbands—since he doesn't have any spares.

Several days later, Kaps organizes a disciplinary exercise for block
overseers, kapos, and Vorarbeiter, punishment for being too lenient in the
treatment of prisoners and slacking on their duties. After the evening roll
call, the entire field returns to the barracks, we remain, ten overseers, five
kapos, and fifteen Vorarbeiter—about thirty people in total. It starts with
"Hinlegen" (drop down) and "Auf" (up) twenty times in a row nonstop.
By the fifteenth repetition I feel like my heart is going to jump out of my

throat and by the last commands I can't pick myself up properly. Next, a short march and running in fives up the hill of the square. There they command us to lie on the ground and roll back down. The *Rapportführer* stands at attention and orders us to fall in line. We form up in two rows behind him—he turns around—and we are supposed to scatter and form up behind his back again. He commands *"Abtreten"*[121]: everyone runs back to their barracks. Once he sees that the first prisoner has reached his block, he calls out *"Achtung."* Everyone stands at attention. He calls out *"Antreten"*[122] and again some exercise. *"Abtreten"*: we disperse back to the barracks, again *"Achtung"* and round and round he repeats it five or six times. Drenched in sweat, hands covered in dirt, clothing white with dust, we return to the barracks. All our muscles are aching.

Together with another prisoner from the gardener *Kommando*, I am sent to deliver potatoes to Thumann. Indeed, potato delivery is one of the responsibilities of a botanist. We are escorted by two SS men. We load potatoes into sacks in the *Gärtnerei* and put them on a handcart. After we leave the *Postenkette*, the SS men escorting us unshoulder their rifles and hold them ready to shoot. We approach Lublin. At the edge of town, on a hill offering a view of the entire camp, there is—*das rote Haus*[123]—where Thumann lives. His wife comes out (she really looks like the wife of the simple carpenter that Thumann used to be before the war), and tells us to carry the sacks down to the cellar. I feel this is a greater humiliation than carrying the crates of excrement out of the barracks.

121. "March out."
122. "Line up."
123. The red house.

The Arrival of the Jews

The camp gets very busy. In the middle of May, a transport of Jews from Warsaw arrived. Several thousand people came, men, women, and even nursing infants. The SS men turn their attention away from us on the field; everyone is busy with the Jews. They arrived at night and were put in the so-called *Rosengarten*[124]—a very romantic-sounding name—but there is neither a garden there nor roses. It's simply next to the bathhouse building and the gas chamber, a square maybe an acre in size surrounded by barbed wire. The people are kept there in the open air until morning, and then the processing of the transport begins. First of all, the men are separated from the women and children. Suitcases are taken away before they enter the bathhouse, where they are ordered to undress and their hair is cut. Next, the Jews stand before a commission where they have to open their mouths and raise their arms to check whether they are trying to smuggle in any jewelry. The commission sorts the young and healthy to one bathhouse and the older, sick, and adolescents (if they are not with their mothers) to the other bathhouse. They let many more into the latter than there are showers, so that washing would be problematic. Despite this they keep directing more Jews in there until they are stuffed inside, one against the other. The doors are closed with difficulty behind the last one. Unfortunately they don't turn on the water and in a moment, Zyklon gas is released through hidden openings in the ceiling. Through an inspection window in the door, an SS man observes how long the heaped mass is moving, then he closes the gas vents and turns on the ventilators. The chamber stays closed until the evening roll call, after which tractors arrive, each with three trailers, and they take the dead bodies away to the crematorium located almost directly opposite, through the road between Field 1 and 2. The laundry is also next door. Since the gas chamber can't be emptied during the day, because it's in the middle of the camp and everyone

124. Rose garden.

would see the corpses being taken out, the rest of the Jews that are unfit for work are eliminated by being sent alive to the crematorium. There they wait in the shed and when the evening roll call is over and the camp quiets down, the crematorium staff, consisting solely of Russian prisoners, starts liquidating the rest of the Jews destined for the chimney. The doors of the shed open and they are ordered to undress and come out one at a time to the adjacent room. Two executioners stand by the door with iron pipes and each Jew gets several blows to the skull until he drops dead. They call the next one, and his body is thrown on top of the first one's corpse and so on, until everyone is killed off. A trail of blood flows outside from under the walls of the shed. The walls of the execution room are splattered with brains. So many Jews were gassed and slaughtered with crowbars that day that the crematorium wasn't able to consume them all.

In a gorge within the *Gärtnerei* they are building a shooting range. In this same ravine they stack a pile of wood on iron rails, and corpses on top of this, dousing it all with a mix of gasoline and grain alcohol and lighting it. Hair and fingernails begin to burn and fat is scorched in the fire. A tall dark streak trails straight up the day after the arrival of the transport—and when the wind blew into the camp, you could smell the burnt bones, hair, and fat. This fire burns day and night as they throw more and more new bodies on top.

During the day, groups of several hundred Jews are led onto Field 3 and directed to the empty barracks. The familiar procedure of sewing on numbers and so on begins. The Jews are crammed into the empty blocks so that two people sleep in a single bed. For now, we are not allowed to communicate with them, but we find out they were brought from Warsaw where an armed Jewish uprising broke out in early May 1943,[125] that a lot of SS men were killed, that the Germans had to use tanks in battle, and now the entire ghetto is being liquidated. In the following days, new transports of Jews arrive, while at the same time a selection of Jews

125. The Warsaw Ghetto Uprising actually broke out on April 19 and continued until May 16, 1943.

takes place on the field. A given barracks has to undress, while there is a meticulous inspection whether all of the Jews have appeared for the selection. They line up on the roll call square. The commission is composed of the head of the crematorium, Sergeant Mußfeld, Kapo Benden, several SS men, and the *Lagerältester*. Each prisoner stands before the commission and they are either immediately grouped with the *gamel*[126] or ordered to run about twenty meters. Working nearby, I have a chance to observe the selection process. They all sprinted hard, and more than one was racing with death. The segregated *gamel* are sent to Block 19. This barracks used to be well-regarded. The block had its own square on the side facing Block 18, separated by a tall fence made of boards. In March and April, this was where prisoners intended for release were kept. So they didn't go out to work, stayed in the barracks all day, and received better food, to restore themselves. They could sleep all day. In my optimistic fantasies, I had thought about whether I looked bad enough to need feeding and go through Block 19, or would they just let me go on the spot? Now Block 19 has changed its purpose, since they are currently keeping those there who are going to the gas in the evening. Actually, you have to say that the barracks have returned to their original purpose, since its number used to be 15 and in February 1943 it housed over eighty Poles from the first Warsaw transport, who were the first to be sent to the gas chamber in February.

The evening roll call happens quickly; we are ordered to return to the barracks and not leave under penalty of death. Within moments, the field was deserted—but we look outside through cracks in the barracks doors. After fifteen minutes of waiting, we watch as a procession of about 120 Jews forms on the square in the greatest, gravest silence—they move like shadows, without a sound. Not a single cry of fear or spasm of despair—and at the head they carry one on a stretcher who no longer dreads the gas chamber. A scene worthy of Böcklin's[127] brush! A half an hour later we hear the call that we can go outside again.

We are in close contact with the women's field, number 5, because they don't have kitchens—meaning that meals are cooked for them in ours

126. In Majdanek camp slang, a very emaciated prisoner.

127. Arnold Böcklin (1827–1901) was a Swiss symbolist painter, creator of figurative paintings and dreamlike, melancholic landscapes such as *Isle of the Dead*.

and a special column takes food there in cauldrons. This is the link that allows the Jews to contact their wives. They find out something that we, old prisoners, already knew: all the children are taken away from their mothers and sent to the gas chamber. Any mother unwilling to give up her child to the gas can join it in death. Many do it willingly, choosing death in their child's embrace. We hear the crying, sobbing, and wails of mothers whose children were taken from them by force. The groans and sobs hang over the camp. I would say that they are a constant part of the atmosphere, since every day new Jewish transports arrive, so it repeats and the gassing continues permanently, the killing with iron crowbars in the crematorium shed, the selection of the men on Field 3 and among women on Field 5, and irrespective of that also the taking of infants and small children. I still hear their cries and lamentations, mothers for their children, grown women for their infirm, elderly mothers, husbands for their wives who didn't want to part from their children.

A transport arrives that is so large that the rose garden (what an ironic name!) cannot fit everyone and so several thousand people are put on the square between Fields 4 and 5, where coal is stored.

Only from there do they take them in groups with their luggage to the bathhouse and for other formalities. The Jews, having learned through the barbed wire to Field 4 what awaits them, start to rip up their banknotes. But not everyone, since the majority suspects it's a trick by the "bandits," who they take us for at the beginning, and that we want to swindle them out of their money this way. The road from the coal yard to the bathhouse is sown with torn-up 500-zloty, 100-dollar, and even 500-dollar bills. The SS men escorting them rigorously make sure that no prisoner approaches the Jews to take something from them or that after the Jews pass they don't pick something up from the road.

Working outside the field at this time, we find a small, dirty sack the size of a throw pillow near our *Blockführer* gatehouse—rather, the *Blockführer* ordered us to pick it up. We hand the sack over to the SS men and they dump its contents onto the road. There are pieces of dried bread. The SS men tell us to take it. We split it equally between the four of us. The bread is as hard as rock. You have to keep it in your mouth for a long time, until it becomes saturated and then you can slowly chew it. I have that bread for a week, it tastes like the greatest delicacy. From bitter experience I carry the bread in every pocket—and the rest in the sack, which I give to Boniecki for safekeeping in his workshop. The dried bread, collected for a dark hour by some poor Jew, gave me a lot of strength then. It was only at Majdanek that I understood the deep meaning of the prayer: "Give us this day our daily bread."

Others arrive with expensive canned meats and fish, with elegant suitcases stuffed with suits, pajamas, silk underwear, thermoses, musical instruments, like going to a summer resort or a tourist vacation. If a smaller transport arrives they don't take anyone into the camp, but put everyone, without exception, into the gas chamber. The clothing, shoes, and suitcases are sent to the *Bekleidungskammer* where special prisoner *Kommando*, under SS supervision, are busy searching the clothing for any sewn-in jewelry and banknotes; heels and soles are ripped away in search of dollars, the inner lining of suitcases is torn out in search of double bottoms.

Once the Jews are issued prisoner numbers, we can finally communicate with them. They tell us about the heroic acts during the ghetto uprising. Given the colossal influx of thousands upon thousands of Jews, there isn't enough work for them and they have to wait while we find something. Around two hundred Jews are assigned to my *Kommando* and I have to put them to work. Since there is nothing else to do, I tell them to dig up the areas between the barracks, which were already dug up. We don't even have enough spades—so Wyderka tells them to dig with shovels and scoops, in any case the work is light as the earth is soft. I walk among them and search for the intelligentsia. One of them is the vice president of the Zionist Party, a parliamentary deputy and a distinguished historian, Dr. Schipper, living on Tłomackie Street. He is short and around sixty years old, still in good spirits despite digging the earth barefoot. He tells me about the uprising and losing his rich library of historical works. There is the head rabbi of the Polish Army, Posner, a tall, handsome man; Kaczko, one of only three Jewish knights of the Cross of Independence; the owner of several bacon factories; a dentist, Dr. Włodawski, and his son, from Foksal Street; there is Bassis, and many others whose names I do not recognize. I do my best to make the working conditions bearable for the intelligentsia. To those whose legs have started to swell after a few days, I assign seated work pulling weeds from the freshly sown grass.

I showed them what to do and moved on to another group of my people. Half an hour later, they all run over to me with bruised heads. *Lagerältester* Birzer had beaten them with his oak cane and ordered them to stop working. I go to Birzer and ask why he told them to stop. He says they were pulling part of the greenery out, so he chased them away. I tell him that these are weeds that will choke out the new grass. He says that it's fine as it is and not to weed any more. Several days earlier he had bragged in front of me about the large gardening enterprise that he has near Munich, over 250 acres, with several hundred people working for him, and here he doesn't know that sprouting grass needs to be weeded? At the same time, he stresses that he's incredibly fond of flowers and that all of Field 3 must be planted with a sea of them.

During one of the selections, they singled out nineteen Jews that were too weak to work, and locked them up in Block 19. Evidently these were too few to fire up the gas chambers for, so they weren't taken out after the evening roll call. The following morning, two wagons arrive from the crematorium and prisoners start loading them up with corpses from Block 19. All nineteen of them were found hanged; the spin gets to work again and we are told that the Jews committed collective suicide for fear of the gas chamber. Within one or two days later we hear another story, that Birzer and Wyderka got drunk and went to Block 19 at night and hanged everyone. Prisoners from the adjacent Block 20 heard some sort of cries and loud conversations coming from that block. There is no investigation, we hear that the only reaction of camp authorities is the decree that in cases of suicide, no one is to remove the bodies until an SS commission arrives. The whole field is gripped with fear and anxiety. The *Lagerältester* goes around hanging prisoners and there isn't the slightest reaction.

At first, Jews are quartered in the empty barracks and later transports are distributed to empty spaces in already inhabited buildings, jamming two Jews into one narrow bed. A golden era begins for kapos and block overseers. It turns out that despite such strict searches, the Jews were nonetheless able to smuggle in a lot of gold and jewelry. They swallowed five-ruble coins and diamonds and paid the block overseers to allow them to defecate into bowls inside the barracks and search it for the swallowed items. One such experiment costs five dollars. Kapo Wyderka is on the prowl.

He has the experienced eye of a detective and is able to tell just by a prisoner's face whether he has a guilty conscience. He takes a suspect like this to the washroom barracks or to any nearby barracks, orders him to strip down, and meticulously feels every seam of his clothing. There has hardly ever been a case when Wyderka has stopped someone and not found something valuable on them. Bubi helps him with this, as he mingles with the Jews and talks to them in their familiar jargon, and they don't hide anything from him, not realizing who they are talking to. Then Wyderka can extract dollars with certainty, and Bubi gets candy for his services. Wyderka, like the other kapos, hands over some of the jewelry to the SS men, but most of it stays in his sticky fingers. In the camp he has the reputation of a millionaire.

The SS men are looking out for themselves as well. Besides the inspection of clothing and luggage, and the tearing apart of pillows and cushions, where plenty of gems are found, camp commandant Florstedt, along with *Schutzhaftlagerführer* Thumann, First *Rapportführer* Kostial, and all the other fat cats, grab spades and personally dig through the rose garden where most Jews spend their first night at the camp, or wait during the day for their turn at the baths or the gas chamber. They find fistfuls of rings, precious stones, gold dollars, and rubles. The same goes on in the coal yard between Fields 4 and 5. The problem is that coal is taken from here to the kitchen every day. So one SS sergeant keeps an eye on the other, making sure they do not go searching on their own. Sometimes a prisoner makes it into the rose garden or the coal yard. Two of them showed me what they had found in a matter of about fifteen minutes, one was a handkerchief buried in the ground filled with rings and another, dug out from the sand with their foot, a hard-candy tin full of gold dollars.

Now the prices on the field begin to jump. The kapos and block overseers have gold, and the Jews pay unbelievable prices for bread. One day, a young prisoner with a Jewish star approaches me, says my name, and asks if I am him. I confirm and take a closer look at him and realize that it's the son of the owner of the house on Żurawia Street where I lived, and with whom I went through seven years of lawsuits over various necessary repairs, that old Abram Pfeffer[128] didn't want to make. His son managed the building, but he was fully assimilated, spoke correct Polish, and did not look Jewish at all. We forget our past grudges and I take him under my wing. He tells me that he's here with his wife and his seven-year-old son, that they wanted to take the child from his wife, but she declared that she would rather die with him. The news had just reached him a few hours ago from his wife. The next day, he points to the trail of smoke with tears in his eyes and says:

"Look, sir, this is the funeral of my wife and child."

He confides in me that he plans to commit suicide, seeing his fate as also hopeless. I talk him out of it, even though I don't believe what I am saying, but I see him clinging to my every word.

There are neither tools nor work enough for the thousands of Jews, so I tell them to march and exercise on the square all day. Like the rest of us, they wear no shoes, jackets, or hats. Despite this they train for hours: "*Mützen ab,*" "*Mützen auf,*" lifting their hands to their bare heads. A lot of them, unaccustomed to the sunlight, quickly get badly sunburned. Their faces swell up to the point that they can't open their eyelids, that's how bloated their faces are. The men are then ordered to carry rocks, but since there aren't enough handbarrows, they carry rocks in their hands—they order the frenzied sodding of all the slopes around the barracks, the Jews carry the sod, but for lack of barrows they carry it on old doors and boards taken out of beds. The Jews try to make their work easier and shake off all of the soil from the roots, bringing grass with bare roots that momentarily wither in the sun.

It's very hard for the Jews to adapt to the camp regime. You can't start a conversation with any one of them since the rest will instantly stop working and perk up their ears. They also don't know how to speak with one another—unlike those who seem to be working, with backs to each other,

---

128. Abraham Pfeffer was deported to Majdanek on May 3, 1943, and murdered a day later in the gas chamber.

but talking without drawing anyone's attention from a distance. You even have to teach them how to post lookouts. You have to give them credit for one expression though: it's the word "*sechs*," which the Jews say as a warning when some kapo or SS man approaches.

The one "benefit" we have since the Jews arrived is the end of extra work after the evening roll call, since there is such an excess of workers with no work to do that Kaps stopped keeping us up late. Unfortunately, the gardeners are an exception, who are only allowed to water the flower beds and lawns (even on cold days) after the roll call. For this reason our block overseer, Zygmunt, decides to replace me as a section supervisor, since I always come back to the barracks last. My section can't be left waiting until I return for the distribution of bread and extras.

The Jews are treated much worse than the Aryans, and are beaten mercilessly at the slightest opportunity. Birzer has his own special method of beating. He aims his thick oak cane at the nape of the neck, at the medulla oblongata, which controls the respiratory and motor functions; when done just right, this knocks a person to the ground. He often sneaks up behind a Jew standing straight at attention talking to an SS man, and takes aim at a spot on the neck that he wants to hit. If the Jew doesn't fall down and dodges it, naturally he is unhappy, much like a hunter who missed a black grouse. Naturally, the savagery of the *Lagerältester* encourages the kapos to similar excesses.

Various new *Kommando* are formed to push the thousands of Jews off the field during the day. One of them is taken over by Kapo Karl Galka, Birzer's right hand. Supposedly, Galka has been instructed that every day ten Jews shouldn't return. Indeed, every day they carry back one or two dead, as well as several others with battered heads, and cut and crushed skin. He beats with a thick bat. Even if Galka had no such order, his actions would still be tolerated, since no one has uttered a word to him about injuring people so badly for no reason at all. Tragedies play out in the morning as the barracks clerks lead new people to the meeting point for Galka's *Kommando*. They try to run away—but that doesn't help, their numbers have been noted down. That's when the bribery begins.

Every evening, the block overseers receive instructions from prisoner Friedrich, a Slovak Jew in charge of the labor service, specifying the
number of prisoners to be assigned to respective *Kommando*. There are
great *Kommando*, literal gold mines, like the crematorium, the baths, and
the gas chamber (where clothing and underwear are gassed to kill lice);
good *Kommando*—like the clothing and shoe warehouses, shoemaker's
and tailor's workshops, the SS canteens, SS kitchen, *Kompost*, *Gärtnerei*,
and prisoner kitchen; average *Kommando*, like the building of new barracks and camp roads, which means regular contact with civilians; and bad
Kommando, like the *Lagergut*, Field 6 construction, the *Wagenkolonne*, the
penal *Bunkerbau*,[129] *Latrinenkommando*,[130] and those with kapos like Galka.
A bad *Kommando* can change for the good if they take away a hangman like
Galka or *Kommando* leader Private First Class Fritsche, called "the Hawk."
The Hawk is despised even among the SS men. He torments prisoners hor-
ribly. So in the evening, when the barracks clerk reads out the next day's
Kommando assignments, the bargaining gets under way: for one hundred
zlotys you can go from a bad *Kommando* to a better one, and those without
any money to pay are assigned to the worst *Kommando*. People are often
stuck on latrine duty for fourteen days; currently cleaning the latrines and
pulling the excrement cart is a doctor punished for the adverse effect of a
treatment he administered (in primitive conditions without medicines).
If someone wants to get out of a *Kommando*, Friedrich has to make the
change in the office, since he has to change the prisoner number on the list
of a given *Kommando*. The kapo overseeing the *Kommando* gets a list of all
the prisoner numbers, so that in case of an escape they know who got away.
Then the clerk has to take the bribe to Friedrich for reassigning someone
to another *Kommando*, and that's even more expensive.

In order to improve the efficiency of the march of the *Kommando* off
the field, which entails around five thousand prisoners in various groups,
the *Arbeitseinsatz* decrees that every *Kommando* has their fixed assembly point and order of departure from the field. Each *Kommando* has a

129. The bunker-building unit.
130. The latrine-emptying unit.

permanent number and an unchanging amount of people. Every day, it receives an *Arbeitsdienstzettel*[131] with its name, number, and prisoner total. This card is presented at the gate by the kapo while loudly reporting the unit's number and amount of people; meanwhile, the *Kommando* marches through the gate without stopping, and the *Blockführer* write down the number, and check how many prisoners are marching out, hitting any-one that's out of line in the head with a walking stick. The prisoner-labor report is received by the SS *Kommando* leader awaiting the arrival of his assigned *Kommando*, together with several other SS men with their loaded *Empi* pistols. The number of SS men depends on the number of prisoners. In any case, even three prisoners have to be escorted by two SS men. There can't be any stopping at the gate and the several thou-sand people have to march out of the square within ten minutes of the "*Arbeitskommando formieren*" command. If there is a delay, such as there not being the right number of people in a *Kommando*, the block overseer and clerk are responsible for not providing enough prisoners. But because the *Kommando* has to go out, they grab the first prisoner they see from the reserve group still standing on the square to have a full complement. And when the "replacement" can't go because he has sick legs, he gets beaten with the stick and kicked and ultimately the able-bodied prisoners take him on their shoulders and carry him out so that the number that's writ-ten on the prisoner-labor report marches out the gate. Thumann stands at the gate almost every day and watches over the march out; if there are delays and breaks between the leaving work squads, Thumann reproaches the field commandant, who then tells off the *Arbeitsdienstführer*. Conse-quently, soon afterward a messenger comes onto the roll call square and calls out: "*Sämtliche Blockältesten, sämtliche Blockschreiber*."[132] All the pris-oners present on the square must repeat the order aloud and a moment later the block overseers and clerks come running out toward the office and form up, usually in a row in front of it. The *Arbeitsdienstführer* and the *Lagerältester* come out and the punitive exercises begin. Depending

---

131. A report on the number of prisoners employed in a *Kommando*.
132. "All block overseers, all block clerks."

on their mood, they can last from fifteen minutes to an hour. Recently, they were all ordered into the pool of water and then, in wet clothes, to roll along the main entry road paved with crushed brick, covered in a layer of red dust. They were all red from head to toe.

The march out after the lunch break must happen the same way within ten minutes.

They segregate the prisoners between Jews and Aryans. The Aryans move to Blocks 14, 15, and 16. The entire Aryan population of my Block 9 goes to Block 15, overseen by Janusz Olczyk. I regret parting from overseer Zygmunt Stauber, the most solid block overseer in all of Field 3. I rank him higher than all the Polish, Aryan block overseers. The clerk, Knips, leaves Block 9, he works his way up as he is taken into the *Schreibstube*. He doesn't deign to notice me when he comes to the old barracks sometimes. His replacement is one of my gardeners, Jerzy Noak, a middle-school teacher from Białystok, twenty-eight years old, skinny, nearly two meters tall. He came with the Białystok transport at the end of April and as an educated man, I brought him in as a gardener. The poor fellow just stood there, barefoot, and jabbed with the spade in one spot, deep in thought. He wasn't much of a "botanist," but he is a very erudite person, fluent in German, French, Italian, and English, interested in every aspect of life. A first-rate conversation partner and great at finding new topics to discuss. He was arrested by the Germans for his care of the municipal library and for the eminent influence he exerted over the cultural life of the Polish intelligentsia. *Lagerältester* Rockinger took an interest in him as a "fellow professional" and made him the clerk of Block 9 in place of Knips. Of course he didn't have the slightest qualifications for it, since he wasn't brutal or indifferent, and was too soft, too subtle, and couldn't gain authority among the masses. After the Aryans are moved to three barracks, a Jew comes as the clerk in Block 9, and Knips returns to Block 15, whom the Slovak Jews schemed out of the office. It is a preeminently unfriendly unit.

Herr Knips

The first packages start arriving through the camp post office. I receive the biscuits I requested. They are remarkably nourishing and give me a lot of strength. Other prisoners, who are sent eggs, bacon, sugar, or onions, have them confiscated in whole or in part, with Wyderka and Bubi leading the way. The distribution of packages is organized like this: during the evening roll call, prisoners receive numbered slips for packages, and they line up in front of Block 13 where they are handed out. Last names are not called out, only numbers. This leaves a lot of room for abuse. The clerks don't hand out all the numbers to the prisoners as they should, but keep some for themselves, then they send trusted prisoners from the *Stubendienst* to pick them up. This is what our clerk did, the *Volksdeutsch* Knips, who kept nineteen numbers which he distributed among his toadies, led by the *Volksdeutsch* Stanisław Bonder from Okęcie. Then begins the mass opening of packages and the aggregation of bread, fat, sugar, etc. Bonder starts selling bread right afterward and keeps half of the agreed-upon price, and Knips buys vodka with the money collected. Janusz Olczyk accuses Knips of the theft of nineteen packages in front of Block 15 during the morning roll call, and Knips shoots back the charge that he stole gold teeth from the *gamel* who in February went from Olczyk's barracks to the gas chamber . . . And both fall silent. At the evening roll call they are already friendly, as if nothing happened between them.

I notify my brother not to send anything besides fat-dipped biscuits for now, since it would be a shame to give anything to Wyderka and Bubi. My property manager and landlord's son all rolled up into one, Pfeffer, who threatened me with eviction so many times after I counted my rent toward the costs of necessary furnace or floor renovations, finds out that I receive packages, and asks me to share with him. I let go of the old conflicts, which seem so distant and inconsequential now, and give him a few biscuits. He goes on and on about how tasty they are.

Within a few days the Jews figure out which *Kommando* are bad and where there are beatings. Loads of them, who never held a spade in their lives and at most had a potted flower in their home, declare themselves gardeners. They treat the work very condescendingly. But a certain Jew, a journalist, comes to me and proposes the hiring of a certain group of Jews into my *Kommando* for an ongoing payment of one hundred zlotys per head, and he lists certain names, some of whom already work for me. It's consistent with the overall attitude and habit. He learns to his surprise that the moment he's made such a proposition he can no longer work for me at all, and others, like Rabbi Posner, must stop working for me, since on the one hand I don't want to enrich myself through the misfortune of my fellow prisoners, but also I want to avoid even the suspicion. Knowing the speculative sense of the Jews, which they can't get rid of in the camp, I have no guarantee that the middleman, despite my refusal, won't pocket a weekly fee from his protégés who are already working for me. Depending on the instructions received in the morning, I select a certain number of Jews to my *Kommando* from the reserves. Every day I am met with imploring stares of completely emaciated people, pleading for work with me. I never held a stick in my hand, a mandated attribute of a *Vorarbeiter*, and yet my *Kommando* impeccably carries out all the work they are instructed to do. The pleading stares and the importuning is a signpost for me that I chose the road in line with my conscience.

We get a new "improvement": our headrests, which we had just gotten in Block 15, are taken away. We have to sleep on bare mattresses, we aren't allowed to fold our clothes under our head. It's terribly uncomfortable, but you come back so tired in the evening that you drop like a log onto your hay.

Kaps leaves with a promotion and takes over as commandant of Field 4. A new commandant arrives with a new *Rapportführer*, Sieberer. It's a big

change for the better for us, the departure of Kaps, he was an enthusi-
ast of evening work after the roll call, which was more like keeping the
prisoners working overtime, since there really wasn't much work to do.
We gardeners often have evening work anyway, since *Lagerältester* Birzer
goes over to the *Gärtnerei* almost every afternoon and brings a few sets
of flower seedlings. He keeps emphasizing how fond he is of flowers, and
with nearly every crate he asks me what kind they are, not knowing how
to distinguish asters from marigolds or snapdragons by looking at their
leaves. Noticing my surprised expression, he casually mentions that in his
business he only trucked vegetables. At the same time he asks whether I'm
certain those tiny plants with only two small leaves will have time to blos-
som this year. I see that something about this horticulturalist doesn't add
up. The seedlings brought in have to be planted the same day of course, by
order of the *Lagerältester*. What doubles my workload though is that I get a
hodgepodge of flowers every day, so I plant them in mixed batches. Then,
depending on what new flowers arrive, I complete older flower beds with
matching varieties, to avoid a medley. They can't tell me in advance how
many crates I'll get, but they bring them every few days and I am ordered:
plant. As a result, certain varieties were planted and removed several times
to achieve a harmonious look, which I am responsible for.

All the flowers and shrubs brought over from the forest and peasant farmsteads several weeks ago have taken root. Even the lilacs have
bloomed. Of course the old junipers didn't take, their needles are yellow-
ing and falling off, so every so often I take one at a time out of the ground.
The ash trees don't want to get going, even though we give them dozens of
buckets of water each day. The fat overseer Jacob keeps badgering me into
conversations and asks:

"So, gardener, what's going to grow there, dates or oranges? Oh, you'll
get your ass kicked if they don't take."

Luckily, Kaps left, so maybe the new *Rapportführer* won't know who
planted them. Just two or three days after taking over the position, he
meets me by the vegetable patches and asks me if I am the gardener and
why the beets haven't been thinned yet. I tell him that there is still time
and it will get done in the coming days. I am dealt a tremendous blow in

the face, so hard that I stagger back, and since there was a shallow drainage ditch right behind me, I lose my balance and brace my shoulder against the barracks. I straighten up and get hit again, then Sieberer leaves. So I call over my people, we drop our other work, and we start thinning the beets. The work really wasn't being done late. The next day a messenger calls out on the field:

"Gardener *Vorarbeiter!*"

Other prisoners repeat it like an echo. I reply and the messenger calls me to the *Rapportführer*. What fun, I think to myself, and run to the office. He is sitting in his room by the desk, I stand "*stramm*" at attention by the door and mutter the obligatory:

"*Ich bitte um Erlaubnis eintreten zu dürfen.*"[133]

His gaze rises up to look at me, then he lowers his head and shows me a little bundle on the desk and says curtly:

"Take it."

I take it, thinking it's some seed to be planted. I do another *Stellung*,[134] click the heels of my wooden shoes, and step out. I carefully unravel the bundle outside, but it doesn't appear to be seed, I look, it's glazed poppy-seed cake, maybe a kilo of it. I'm dumbstruck. Just four months ago I would have thrown the package back in the face of the person who actively slapped me in the face, and here I see an unbelievable thing for a concentration camp—a Styrian highlander's notion of restoring my honor. Could it be that he had some afterthoughts? I think it's unlikely, rather I suspect that someone else he trusted must have said something flattering about me as a professional who knows what he's doing. I split the poppy-seed cake with several of my best coworkers.

A most unusual sensation took place in the camp today. They call all of the overseers, *Schreiber*, and *Vorarbeiter* for a shower. Several dozen people have gathered up in a few moments and several dozen people march to the bathhouse. It was such a pleasure to cast off that shell of filth, that

133. "I ask permission to enter."
134. Literally, position; here, a position of standing at attention.

armor, that corset, everything different already, just not the shirt. What an unbelievable reaction of my skin after rubbing it under the hot water with kaolin soap and washing away the layer of dirt, since washing under the faucet couldn't substitute for a hot shower. The bath lasts fifteen minutes, I get a mended shirt, the same long underwear (slightly gray in color due to its being washed in lukewarm water without enough soap)—but it's exquisite compared to what I just took off minutes ago. What splendid blood circulation after the bath. I feel ten years younger. They tell us that every Wednesday at 2:00 p.m. our group will go bathe.

Food Packages

Birzer invented a new sport: beatings during package distribution. The table where the opening and inspection of packages takes place stands by the open barracks doors with a wooden doormat in front of it. When a prisoner's number is read out, he has to break ranks, run up to the table, and take off his hat. Everyone mechanically stands on the mat and then gets Birzer's favorite strike to the neck with his cane. There was no command as to where they should stand, so once they get hit in the neck, more than a few people don't know what they did wrong and get hit again, until they simply move to the side before the next strike. You can stand on the doormat (according to Birzer's delusions, although it's not explicit) if you come up to the table to receive an already inspected package, but if the opening and checking lasts a long time, you have to stand on the ground next to the doormat. I figured this out by observing who he was hitting and when he would stop, and I tell all my comrades nearby, but those further away who aren't as observant, or who do know what's going on but fail to pay attention, get the cane. A typical example of a beating in the camp for nothing, thinking up something, and then the deviant doesn't tell anyone what the line is that you get beaten for crossing; on the other hand it exemplifies how by paying a little attention and grasping the situation you can avoid several blows.

The inspection of packages entails taking out certain items and cutting open bread and breadstuffs in search of any letters baked inside. Wyderka and the kapos assisting him take food less and less. Without exception, though, they take any medicines, tobacco, and letters loosely placed inside the package. Letters like these are subject to censorship and aren't handed over to the intended recipient. The task of unsealing and unpacking the contents is carried out by a prisoner from the *Poststelle*,[135] Adam Panasiewicz, a radiotelegraph operator from the Warsaw post office. He

135. Camp post office.

is a person of exceptional integrity and honesty who privately informs each of his acquaintances about their packages that have arrived in order to thwart the clerks who try to steal them. There have been cases of people finding wrapping paper from packages in the garbage with their names on them—and the packages were taken by the barracks clerk, who sent trusted *Stubendienst* with the numbers to pick them up. Since complaints about stolen packages are piling up, the "authorities," i.e., the Slovak Jews, introduce another innovation, that the man whose number is called out is to state his first and last name for verification. But that does not change much as the clerks know to whom the package is addressed, so they just pencil the first and last name on the number that their trusted accomplice uses. So now some people without numbers group up near the package distribution point, and listen for whether someone else is using their name. They catch these thieves, but the reaction of the SS men is surprisingly soft, so it doesn't discourage the clerks continuing their thieving procedures. Naturally, they know very well whose packages they cannot take. You can't mess with someone who can communicate in German and could go straight to an SS man with a complaint, or with a smooth operator in general. But the vast majority are poor, simple people, helpless against the *Schreiber* who is like what the police officer was to the peasant in the countryside. They prefer not to make a fuss, and if they even find out about the theft, they go to the man with a humble request and gratefully accept a piece of bread from the stolen package as a full settlement of their claim.

This isn't the only form of embezzlement. The prisoner files don't have their surnames spelled correctly, instead of their actual names they appear how the SS man or Gestapo agent wrote it when the transport was sent off to the camp. Some people's names are extraordinarily distorted, but sometimes just one letter is switched or dropped. The statement of packages comes onto the field. The clerks from all the blocks come together and the reading of names begins, each checks in their block register and if they have that name they take the number for the package. If the spelling of the name doesn't match, the package is considered undeliverable. The statement then goes to Fields 2 and 4 to be read; unidentified packages are nobody's property and are divided among the SS men, prisoners working in the post office, the Slovaks in the office, and the block overseers and clerks. Some of them receive official numbers to obtain these unclaimable packages, and sometimes they are generously handed out at the end of the distribution. There are so many scams and people interested in stealing that this extensive gang reinforces itself. People go to the office specifically to find out what their "official" name is and in messages to their family they notify them what surnames to include on the packages so that they get delivered to them. Professor Noak is recorded as Nowak in the files and until the time he "straightened out" the spelling of his own surname in Białystok, he lost a lot of incoming packages. You can feel an undisguised ill will from the Slovaks. Adam Panasiewicz deserves a special page of honor in the history of Majdanek, since after two or three package distributions, he remembers, as a consummate postman, the surnames and faces of his fellow prisoners and notifies each of them without asking, calling from a distance:

"You have a package today, sir!"

On request, he will go and check the list to see if a package came for someone. He fights against the Jewish abuses and hundreds of prisoners owe the maintenance of their strength to him. Now that packages start arriving through the official mail, the thieves have a lot of room to maneuver. The packages are stacked up in the barracks in one place, near the bed of the block overseer, and a night guard is posted there, but packages are still stolen at night. They steal it from under your head too, and the professional thieves do it much more elegantly, since they slice open the side of the box hidden under the head of the mattress and take out the contents, leaving the empty box. Whatever the thief doesn't steal at night the *Stubendienst* and more than one overseer will take care of during the day. After all, the overseers also take a tribute from the packages, since on the distribution day they sit next to the entrance to the barracks and inspect every box, picking out the things that they like. They do this quite moderately, but if there are one hundred packages for a barracks and the overseer takes one egg and one sugar cube from each, then in a single swoop he has a hundred eggs and a hundred sugar cubes.

One day, during the evening roll call, the barracks clerk Knips informs us that we are all to write home and that he has a postcard for each of us, and instructs us on how to correctly write the sender's address: "*Schutzhäftling* X . . . Nr. . . . born on . . . son of . . . (parents' names) *Konzentrationslager* Lublin." We cannot include the field or block number. The postcards are to be returned to Knips before the morning roll call the following day, and he stresses that they have to be written in German. We are not allowed to describe our lifestyle, to mention any diseases, and the text must include the sentence "I am healthy and doing well," and the censor would most like to see letters in which the prisoner says he is doing so well in the camp that he doesn't want to leave. So the postcards mostly convey requests for things to be sent in packages and different questions. There are maybe twenty prisoners in our barracks who can speak German, and maybe ten who can write it. I am mobbed by people asking me to write their cards, I visit the adjacent barracks and I find out that they are writing in Polish and that according to the office no more than 50 percent of the correspondence should be in Polish. I go to Knips and ask him why he announced something totally different to our block. His wholly cynical reply:

"If I had announced that only half can be in Polish, everyone would write in Polish, and this way maybe only a few will write in Polish."

I accuse him of preventing people from giving a sign of life to their families by providing false information, and that it's impossible for everyone to write a card in German in one evening hour. Knips, the applicant for the Upper Silesian Cross, replies with an icy stare:

"And what do I care if they write back home?"

Meanwhile, his own wife writes to him in Polish, it's the only way she knows how.

Germanic blood awakens in a scanty few. The pimp, Zygmunt Meller, the overseer of Block 14, claims that his real name is "Raoul von Möller" and applies for enlistment in the German military. Two *Stubendienst* from his barracks, both with Polish surnames, do the same, characters known around the block for stealing bread and other camp frauds.

Finishing Off the Jews

We are alerted at noon, the soup had just been given out when the roll call bell rings, we leave our full bowls, there is the command of "*Antreten*." The SS men come and receive the roll call. We don't know what happened. We stand for maybe an hour—Thumann, Florstedt, and other high-ranking SS men arrive by car. None of the block overseers know what happened. At last I see SS men leading a Polish Jew, around forty years old, a stout, balding, blond-haired man dressed in an old German military police uniform, barefooted, walking toward the roll call bell. Many Jews walk around in these old uniforms. The Jew looks completely calm. There are a few more barracks between ours and the pole with the bell, so you can't see what's going on there. After fifteen minutes the command is heard, "*Arbeitskommando formieren*," and then, we are terrified to see the Jew in the uniform hanging next to the bell. It was announced to those standing closest that the Jew was being hanged for attempting to escape. The escape attempt consisted of the man falling asleep in some corner within the *Postenkette* during the construction of barracks, and not coming back to the field for lunch. At the gate, the kapo had to report, of course, that a prisoner from his *Kommando* was missing, though in any case the SS men themselves would have figured it out when counting the returning unit. So a search with dogs commenced immediately, naturally in the work area of that *Kommando*, and the sleeping prisoner was found. The sentence of hanging was issued right away by the camp commandant Florstedt. Kapo Wyderka did the hanging. Florstedt, Thumann, the *Feldführer*, *Rapportführer*, and others ordered stools to be set up around the improvised gallows and with the hanging man in the background they had a photo taken. *Sieg Heil!*

New transports of Jews arrive from time to time. The gassings and selections in the field are constant, since those who were strong two weeks ago can't all nimbly run the twenty paces today. They are intensively finishing the construction of the new crematorium near Field 5. Luba, the bricklaying foreman, a prisoner on our field, works on erecting the chimney. The old crematorium has been shut down, and bodies are taken to the forest where they are burned on pyres. This is done by the *Waldkommando*.[136] They also dig up corpses hastily buried in the past and burn them in the forest.

The *Rapportführer* sends me to the SS corporal who is the head of the *Gärtnerei* to ask for some climbing plants, which Sieberer himself can't describe. This gives me the opportunity to visit the three gigantic, modern greenhouses filled with a wide assortment of flowers. All the SS men in the *Gärtnerei* are professional gardeners and they treat prisoners leniently. Which is why everyone tries to get into this *Kommando*. The work is slow, it is easy to get lost among the up to two thousand prisoners, and you work together with women from Field 1. While working the parcels located right by the road, on the edge of the village-suburb of Dziesiąta, you can see or talk to someone from your family walking down the road or standing in the gate of one of the farmsteads. Prisoners have lookouts in the greenhouse. Couples are sitting in recesses all over, tenderly embracing and kissing, paying no mind to their surroundings—I, as a prisoner, though a stranger, don't count. I saw scenes like this on the street in Paris in broad daylight, and I was surprised. It was explained to me, a foreigner from "the East," that this is the capital of the world and that's the custom. I shook my head in disbelief. Here in Majdanek I understood that you can smother someone else with kisses in front of strangers, totally blind to God's green earth. Working in the *Gärtnerei* also came with the advantage of eating all the new spring vegetables and fruit—radishes, lettuce, cucumber, strawberries, etc.—and also bringing them back to the field for their block overseers and clerks.

The *Gärtnerei* buildings are located on a hill, and as I wait for the boss, who just left before my arrival on his motorcycle to ride through the *Gärtnerei*, I see an image which reminds me of a scene from the pharaonic film *Sumurum*.[137] One thousand Jewish women carry composted earth from one end of the *Gärtnerei* to the other. Two women carry a single handbarrow, and that's how a snake of five hundred handbarrows is mov-

136. Forest work squad.
137. He is referring to *Sumurun*, a 1920 film starring Pola Negri.

ing along. It extends along the rolling landscape. The women move like
ghosts, some of them beautiful, young, statuesque figures dressed in rags,
their hair hanging down, dirty, grown out, eyes hollow, fixated somewhere
in the distance, looking for their husband who was ripped away from her
or her child who was gassed—they pay no attention to their surroundings. And this is how they walk, day after day, with handbarrows, there
and back. This is how women are worked to death in the camp, and the
ashes of the dead also don't experience peace, as they are thrown out on
the compost, and loaded on handbarrows from there and carried back and
forth across the grounds of the *Gärtnerei.*

On my field, the SS men from the labor section come up with the most
idiotic jobs for the Jews, to keep them moving, and the rest, for whom
they can't find any work, have to march all day. Taking people to the gas
has become so commonplace that it's not done after the evening roll call
anymore—when prisoners were locked in the barracks previously—but
just in the middle of the day. The Jews go to their deaths with great compo-
sure and self-control. Recently a group like this was waiting in front of the
gate at 5:00 p.m. since they needed one more Jew to complete the group.
We gardeners happened to be working near the gate. Then one Jew asked
for water from the bucket, another for a piece of bread, so—their exact
words—that they could have a drink or eat before dying.

Volksdeutsch Bolesław Reich has a field day with the Jews. It's now in
fashion to beat and abuse the Jews. Jews are ordered to carry earth from
the left side of the field to the right, and from the right back to the left, at a
fast pace. During this urgent work, Reich positions himself at the narrow
passage between Block 22 and the washroom barracks embankment. The
path is so narrow that two handbarrows can't pass each other and one set
of people has to go down into the sewage ditch alongside the path in order
to pass. And since they are taking dirt past Block 22, a traffic jam forms
there. Reich sets himself up on that path and pounds everyone in the back
mercilessly. He hit one Jew in the back of the head so hard that it cut open
his neck. The Jew lost consciousness, or fell onto the ground from the
pain; in any case he was lying there motionless. The path instantly emptied
and the news started to spread around Field 3 that Reich had killed a Jew.

They moved the corpse onto the embankment so that people could pass. An hour later, when no one was around, the dead body came back to life, jumped to his feet and hid somewhere in the barracks so that no one could find him until that night.

Dr. Włodawski works for me, and he is getting weaker day by day, and every day he expects to be released. He tells me that his father, back in the czarist days, bought a plot of land in Nicaragua or Ecuador on the basis of an advertisement, part of a primeval forest settlement; every plot (each worth several hundred dollars) came with citizenship of that country for the buyer. Włodawski's parents maintained that foreign citizenship. Decades had passed since then and the third generation had already grown up. Back in the ghetto these "citizens" of Nicaragua, about thirty to fifty people, had tracked each other down and took steps to be interned as foreigners and then exchanged for German citizens interned in Allied countries. Włodawski got a message from one of his sons, who managed to stay free and was working on the matter with the Germans, that any day a car was coming to Lublin to take his father, mother, and brothers from Majdanek. Meanwhile Dr. Włodawski is fading away before my eyes, he has swelling from water retention. I arranged with the overseer of Block 11 (where the kitchen staff sleeps), Engineer Szachowski, for him to lie down there during the day, since if he goes to the Revier, they'll send him to the gas on the spot. He lies there for two or three days. Włodawski is already sitting at the morning roll call, I talk to him and buck up his spirits, after the roll call I give his son about a dozen sugar cubes to strengthen his father. After lunch the son comes to me and says that his father ate a few sugar cubes but he just died a moment ago, unfortunately. When they saw that he was dying in Block 11, they quickly moved him to Block 9 so that the Block 11 overseer wouldn't have to explain how the corpse of a stranger ended up there. The overseer of Block 9 demands that the young Włodawski give him the gold bridgework of his dead father. The son asserted that his father didn't have a gold bridge. All evening they haul the young guy to Wyderka, to the *Lagerältester*, then to the *Rapportführer*, about the allegedly stolen bridgework, instead of letting the boy calmly sit by his father's side and say his goodbyes. When he asks for his dad's piece of bread, which the block received, the overseer denies it to him. The next day Dr. Włodawski "stands" at the roll call for the last time. He lies in the dust of the roll call square, and his face has a gentle, contemplative expression. The poor fellow didn't live to see his release. In two days they really do take all of the "Nicaraguans," including the young Włodawski, and bring them to another camp.

There are over one hundred young Jewish boys aged eleven to fourteen on our field. All boys up to ten years old were taken by their mothers to the women's field when the families were separated. These children had their own clothes taken away from them, and the warehouse doesn't have children's clothing, so they receive adult clothes. A kid like this, who gets the pants of an adult man, has his feet reach halfway down the pant legs at most and literally walks "in" them, trailing half of the pant legs along the ground behind him. At first the kids were scattered across the barracks, which was beneficial for them, since every block overseer made sure they got a second bowl of soup and extra pieces of bread. Then the commandant ordered them consolidated in one block. There are several singers among them from the choir of the Warsaw synagogue. Beautiful voices. The ingenious boys started a barbershop quartet and in the evenings, and especially on Sunday afternoons, they make their rounds through the barracks and sing different lyrical and humorous songs, for which they collect various donations. The most popular song is one describing the wedding of a rabbi: "They ate geese, they ate ducks, until they all, got the dumps, mazel tov, mazel tov, mazel tov."

Since the packages are now being given out on a more consistent basis, I ask my brother to send some other products besides the biscuits, like bacon, dried sausage, lard, onions, eggs, etc. I also ask him to write the consecutive number of the package and date it was sent next to the address so I can see how long they take to reach me. I suggest that he send packages through the RGO in Lublin so that they deliver them to the camp, because my friends are convinced that packages sent this way arrive more reliably and without their contents being tampered with.

I get a message from my brother that Hańka, my faithful and unfailing friend from my student days who is currently living in Lwów, has taken steps on her own initiative to secure my release, and that some "well-connected" German took a down payment of twenty thousand zlotys from her. Hanka notified my brother that the question of my release is a matter of days. My brother and Mary notify me of this in their messages, in which I can sense the excitement with which they were written. This mood is contagious to me, of course. I let a few of my friends in on the secret, including Noak, and I grant him the authority to receive any packages that might arrive after my release. My brother reports that the clerk Goerke, from the Warsaw Gestapo, who interrogated me and conducted my case, was transferred to another city, and he considers this a positive factor. During the investigation, Goerke tried to persuade me several times to confess to the acts that I had been accused of—that he understood the patriotic activities of Poles and that what I did was not such a terrible crime, and that it would make his job easier to just admit it. A few times he interrupted the typing of the report and inserted the line: "Admonished to tell the truth, he testified . . ." and I kept holding my ground. Finally he got irritated and said:

"Well, in that case you'll feel on your own bones what a concentration camp is."

I remembered his name because the last page of the report included the note: "Prepared by Goerke." When my transport from Pawiak was being sent off he was actually there, representing the Gestapo. While personal data of the prisoners was being read as we stood outside, I was used as an interpreter; he recognized me, and as we were returning to the cell, he waited for me in the stairwell. I didn't notice him. He grabbed me by the lapel of my jacket and then I recognized him. He said to me:

"Why did you lie? Now you're going on the transport."

I didn't reply and kept going. I thought to myself: "Little clerk, my friends are working on this from the top." I could sense, though, that he felt a grudge toward me. From later messages I learned that all subsequent conversations had been happening strictly with him, and that Goerke felt animus and hostility toward me. Maybe now, since he has left, my chances will improve, though now we generally understand that releases can't be carried out by the right Gestapo office, but by the *Reichssicherheitshauptamt* in Berlin.

The Gallows and Selections for the Gas

An order comes to erect gallows on all the fields. This is carried out by amateurs, which means they attach a wooden triangle to the pole where the bell hangs and the red light is mounted, with a loop at its end for a rope. I have never seen an execution by hanging—but from what I gather from the press, death is not by suffocation, but by the breaking of the atlas caused by the sudden drop of the body, from under which a bench has been kicked out. Here the loop is at a height of maybe two meters above the ground. The roll call bell, above which is a small roof with a life-size crowing rooster on top, cut from wood and painted red, is mounted on the southern part of the pole. The gallows are attached to the opposite, northern side. The phlegmatic joke that immediately springs forth labels the execution site "under the rooster." The rooster was designed by Boniecki and echoes those placed on church spires, and the little roof symbolizes a chapel. It is where prisoners direct their gaze during roll call while they pray.

The day after the gallows are built I see Wyderka walking before the evening roll call with a long rope slung over his shoulder like an executioner; he does a pull-up on the gallows, testing its strength. The roll call is over in a flash and afterward the blocks are ordered to line up in a *carré* [138] around the gallows. Camp commandant Florstedt arrives along with Thumann and other bigwigs, preceded by the "*Mützen ab*" order. They lead some Jew under the gallows and the commandant announces that the Jew will be hanged for attempting to escape. They call for an interpreter to translate it into Polish. Wyderka steps out and in a mixture of Czech and Polish says:

"*Ta osoba benzie obwiesona . . . ,*" [139] etc.

The Jew puts the noose on his neck himself, I lower my gaze and look at the ground, not wanting to observe the torture of someone being hanged.

---

138. French: a square or quadrangle.
139. "This person will be hanged . . ."

In silence I pray the Eternal Rest. The silence on the square lasts maybe ten minutes. Then the command *"Mützen auf."* The SS men start their motorcycles and ride away. The body is hanging motionlessly, his toes almost touching the ground. Kapo Galka assisted Wyderka with the hanging. We march back to our barracks and from ten steps away, I see Galka kicking the corpse in the buttocks, twisting the body around several times in one direction, letting it untwist back the other way, and then, before the eyes of thousands of prisoners, Galka urinates on the hanging man's legs. Today, the former SS man and current kapo, Galka, convinced me of the superiority of the Nordic German race over the Semites.

I find out from the friends of the hanged man that the escape attempt consisted of the Jew lying down among building materials during work and falling asleep inside a long drainage pipe where he was found during the day. Those who watched the execution relate that Wyderka pulled the convict up on the loop, the poor fellow began to suffocate and was desperately flailing his arms and legs. The execution lasted a long time since they waited until all of the twitching stopped. He was simply strangled.

A few days later, right before the evening roll call, I see the field commandant assisting several prisoners, who, standing on a ladder, are taking down the gallows. What does this mean? The gallows are raised to about four meters since at its current height the dead body was almost touching the ground with its feet. It's probably that the SS men want all of the prisoners to see the entire execution and for it to be a more effective educational experience. There is no clock on the roll call square, it must have been late and the roll call was about to start any moment, or maybe the camp commandant was to appear, but something is happening that is inconceivable to me at first. The field commandant himself climbs up the ladder and personally nails the gallows into its new place. My first reflection was whether this person doesn't respect his uniform, after all the Waffen-SS is the elite of the army, Hitler's cohorts, but in a moment all is clear: that in the veins of every one of these SS men flows the blood of thugs, cutthroats, executioners, and torturers. The flair of the executioner fascinated the field commandant to such a degree that he wanted to at least pound a few nails into the gallows.

After the roll call, there is another execution. A Jew tried to escape from the Jewish *Kommando* but was caught. Since it was a genuine escape attempt this time and not just a man caught sleeping, the camp commandant decides to punish the entire *Kommando*. The *Kommando*, consisting of fifty people, has to undress and one after the other have to get into the pool with cold water, and then each of them gets twenty-five whips on their wet, naked bodies. Inhuman howls reach our ears. Our block is the sixth from the front, so we hardly see anything. About a dozen curious people go to the side, nearing the barracks to get a look at what's going on in front. When the field commandant notices this he takes out his revolver and starts shooting into this group of prisoners. He hits one Pole in the thigh and the rest scatter. You can see the sadistic frenzy that overcame him while whipping the Jews that just for looking he shoots at prisoners—since he forms us up into a square around the hangings. After the beatings they order us to form up in a *carré* around the gallows. Of course, the delinquent also gets a helping of twenty-five lashes. Taking advantage of the chaos of the blocks forming up, I back up to the rear rows. After all, you don't have to push much. It's enough to let yourself be shoved aside by those from the back rows trying to move up to the ranks of a different block standing in front, just to get a good view of the death spasms of the condemned. More than one of us rebukes this primitive lust for sensation and bloody thrills, but those we say this to push forward undeterred, replying with filthy Russian swear words. Maybe the future of the world does in fact belong to these people, who have no sensitivity, subtlety, or internal brakes? A martyr's death by strangulation begins again. Wyderka elevates the hanged person up the loop to a height of three meters. The execution is a little shorter today, we hear the command: "*Mützen auf, blockweise abrücken.*" The dead man is taken down and carried to the front of his barracks. In the morning, I hear that the corpse came back to life, but what happened to him—we don't know; in any case, there is no corpse lying next to his barracks.

I'm in the infirmary to see Dr. Lewiner, a radiologist from Warsaw, who administers my eye drops every day and because of our frequent contact we've come to trust each other. I tell him about the biggest whopper— a hanged man coming back from the dead. Dr. Lewiner looks around to make sure no one can hear us and whispers to me:

"I was called to the one hanged at 9:00 p.m. last night. He really did come back to life, he only lost consciousness on the gallows." In any case, the convict was filled in on a lot of details of the course of his own execution.

He looks around again to make sure no one is there, and whispers:

"They hung him again at night."

The news from the Revier is that the selections to the gas chamber are still taking place, the only thing new is that starting in June 1943, they will only conduct selections among the Jews. It often happens that a heavily sick Jew, such as an overseer or his son, will appear on the field. These are prominent Jews, who are notified of a selection commission a day in advance, so they leave the Revier and return to the field as "healthy" to avoid the commission. Being big shots, they have their ways of hiding from the selections.

During the evening roll call, I see that the camp road is densely packed with companies of SS men, as far as the eye can see in either direction. Trouble is brewing. I look to see if they have rifles—no, they are unarmed. Well, it doesn't seem as bad now. The roll call ends in the blink of an eye. The camp gate opens and four SS companies march onto our field. At the same time we hear the command: "*Sämtliche Blockältesten, Blockschreiber, Kapos, und Vorarbeiter.*" We run to the front. But aside from our group, the SS men start selecting other prisoners from the ranks of different blocks by sight and form them up next to us. Damned if I know what's going on. Are they choosing at random for execution by firing squad? The *Feldführer* is standing near me so I observe him, thinking I might catch a word that will tell me what's happening. The SS companies form up in various parts of the field. The field commandant turns to the leader of the nearest company which is standing by the pool and utters the mysterious words:

"Here you have the designated men, now you will carry out the instructions."

Chills run down my spine. Some SS corporal takes me and five other prisoners and leads us to Block 8. All the blocks, i.e., the prisoners, are formed up on the field in rows, and the barracks are totally empty. On the way, I ask myself what he's going to do with us in the barracks, the silliest thoughts bounce around my head. There, the SS man tells us to search all of the beds for "forbidden objects." He doesn't say what we should be looking for, whether they be weapons or dollars or underwear. He orders us to throw all the mattresses on the ground and shake out the straw. I sigh with relief. Admittedly, he threatens us that if we conceal something, we will be shot, but we've already gotten used to the threats. Moments later other SS men arrive, each with a group of six prisoners, and soon the entire block is teeming. We have to throw all of the shirts, socks, scarves, towels, etc. into the middle of the barracks. The straw dumped out of the mattresses produces unbelievable dust. I start thinking about my bed, who is digging through it, I didn't have anything hidden there, but just stuffing the straw back into the mattress and dusting out the blanket, and so on, will consume a lot of time.

Rummaging through the mattresses lasts over two hours, until late dusk. Somebody comes and calls out to stop the work. I go to my barracks which is in perfect order, and I ask if there had been an inspection; there had, but the SS corporal in charge only ordered them to look under mattresses and some blankets. Just my luck to have gotten an eager beaver. My face is dusty, I go to wash up first of all. Supposedly nothing was found, in any case they didn't find any weapons, and you can't assume that the camp leadership mobilized so many SS men to confiscate extra socks and shirts. Wyderka is hit with a loss, he had a package of seventy-four thousand zlotys in 500-zloty banknotes in a package with another prisoner that was taken. It seems that was the one real result of the great *filc*, also known as the "*hipisch*."

I was a witness to a tragicomic situation. A transport of Jews arrived from Międzyrzec, famous for its brush-making. This trade also includes specializations in sorting and braiding hair, etc. They organized a brush-making workshop in two barracks on Field 4 and some German civilian businessmen accompanied the *Feldführer* in choosing a certain number of these brush makers. There was a crowd of maybe three hundred of them there. Everyone wanted to get this calm, indoor work. Everyone was crowding, and they almost smothered those German civilians. Strikes from the whips of about a dozen SS men and firing a revolver into the air didn't do the trick. Finally, all of the Jews were ordered to lay in rows face down to the ground; the SS men spread out with whips; and if any of the brush makers tried to get up he got lashed in the back. Only then did the commission walk through these lying rows and choose the necessary craftsmen from among them.

The suicides begin among the Jews who see the hopelessness of the situation in the camp and have much greater anxiety than the Aryans. Every second or third day they report that once here in this barracks, or once there, some Jew hung himself at night. They do it so quietly that someone sleeping in the same bed as the desperate person doesn't notice it. Some don't have the courage to hang themselves, so they go to the wires. They go through in broad daylight, mainly before the morning roll call, over the single wire bordering the death zone and, ignoring the calls from the towers, they walk up to the fence of barbed wire called the "*Schlauch,*" the coils of which they wouldn't be able to cross anyway. When calling out fails, the posts shoot—if they hit the head or heart it's ok, if they shatter the leg and the Jew lies on the spot for a few hours, until a commission comes to take him to the Revier to finish him off—it's worse. The SS men aren't as hasty to shoot; up until 1942 they got six days of vacation immediately for every prisoner that they shot, but now they don't get this bonus.

One of the Jews chose a disgusting way to die: just before the morning roll call, while the blocks were lining up in the field and there was no one in the latrine, he jumped into a cesspit and drowned himself in excrement. The roll call lasted several hours and after a frantic search of every nook and cranny, someone had the idea to use long sticks and check the cesspits, where they found the body. He was the son of some rabbi. Another man hung himself inside a narrow drainage well still under construction. After slipping inside, he placed a piece of pipe across its top and hung himself on it. The riddle was how he had managed to pull himself up so high, since his feet were a good meter off the ground and the sides of the well offered no visible footholds for him to have elevated up before hanging himself.

During one such extended morning roll call, while the body of another suicide victim is being sought for the roll call to add up, one of the intel-

ligent Jews says: "They count us like gold, but treat us like shit." There is so
much truth to this comment and it so accurately reflects the entire camp
mentality that I would gladly use it as the motto of my memoir.

My Jewish gardeners have set themselves up nicely. The vice president
of the Zionists, Dr. Schipper, was accepted to the potato stores to peel
potatoes. Several weeks at the camp have taken their toll, but the robust
older man manages to stay in good spirits and lifts others up. It's always
satisfying to talk to this perpetually smiling and courageous man. Kaczko,
recipient of the Cross of Independence, managed to buy an assignment
in one of the warehouses. On his last day working for me, Bubi torments
him, climbing on a ladder and dumping an entire watering can's contents
into the collar of his shirt.

The kapos are truly terrifying in how they abuse people. When they
catch someone nosing around the kitchen during the day to beg out a
bowl of soup or steal a few potatoes, or if they find someone with a lit
cigarette or find a few carrots in someone's pocket, they begin the beating. The first strike is supposed to knock the prisoner to the ground and
only then do the boot-tip kicks to the heart and the skull, and the heels
to the kidneys, begin. Sometimes a poor devil gets ten to fifteen full-force
kicks to the skull and lies motionless, I think that the skull is fractured and
he is already dead—but more than one rouses and drags himself off after
an hour-long blackout. It also takes my breath away to watch Wyderka,
Birzer, Galka, and Bubi curse the very sick people lying down during roll
call and then kick them in the skull and heart to wake them up and get
them to stand. This kind of torment is almost a daily component part of
the morning roll call ritual.

Zelent returns to the field having recovered from typhus. I am happy for
his return, I don't know him very well, but intuitively feel the need to make
friends with him.

The Golden Calf

Rumors start to circulate on the field about the enormous fortunes amassed by the camp commandant Florstedt, the *Schutzhaftlagerführer*, and other SS men, taken from the Jews, through confiscations, digs in the rose garden, from tearing apart clothing and footwear, etc. Gossip has it that they only passed on part of the valuables to their superiors and kept the rest for themselves. Of course, nobody has ever seen it. The kapos also conduct searches of their own and allegedly hand the findings over to the *Feldführer*, but they say that Wyderka and kapo "Ivan," a Russian immigrant, Konstanty Bielski, who feasts on Field 4, have millions. Wyderka has his treasure buried somewhere near the washroom barracks and prowls near it in the evenings and at night. Kapo Ivan bribes SS men to take him to Lublin where he has a mistress with whom he stashes the gold or who forwards it on. They talk of two Slovak Jews, Marmorstein and Fuchs, who also have millions in jewelry. Fuchs lives on a different field, but I meet him when the SS sergeant who is the head of the coal yard asks the commandant of Field 3 to lend me out to design a decorative garden for him in the empty, one-acre field in front of the coal heaps. Fuchs is elegantly dressed in sports clothes, clean and groomed, he leads the *Kommando* that chops firewood into small billets. The coal and firewood yard is located near the so-called *Zwischenfeld*, between Fields 4 and 5. The cords of wood are piled in such a way that they form a small hiding place, where a large table is placed. Fuchs lies on this table during work hours and reads the newspaper or sleeps. So many offenses committed at once. There is no one else on the site besides the woodcutters. So the lookouts can see from far away when the head of the coal yard, the SS sergeant, is approaching. I notice that Fuchs is almost overly familiar with this SS man. Fuchs gets a thick and substantial soup for his people in the SS kitchen around 10:00 a.m., which he sometimes invites me along for. Basically a camp baron. He tells me how he managed to save his own brother through the head of the crematorium Mußfeld, after he had been selected for the gas in the Revier. He has access to up-to-the-minute radio news and can tell you what Churchill or Beneš[140] said, he is informed on the progress of the war, fascinating in his abilities and contacts. They say he has close to four kilos of jewelry. It's very possible, since more than a few brooches can be found while dispensing coal for the kitchens. And that job belongs to Fuchs.

Another camp Croesus is Marmorstein, also a Slovak Jew, who supposedly, while searching through Jewish property, found and turned in jewelry worth two million zlotys to Thumann. But this was just a part of what he actually found.

While meeting with Fuchs and supervising the daily progress of the earthworks, I observe life through the wires on the neighboring Field 5, where the women stay. I see both the sunlight and the shade of the camp. Here is the elegant millionaire Fuchs—over there, in rags, the women who until recently wore the jewelry which is now in the hands of Fuchs. They live in a state of the greatest self-abnegation, slovenliness, and neglect. Twenty meters away through the wires from the prisoners organizing the garden are the latrines on Field 5 without any screens or protective walls. The women don't pay the slightest mind to the working men, they lift their dresses and take care of their physiological needs, as if they were inside four walls. These aren't people anymore, they are mannequins, husks of people who lost their spiritual lives and each and every feeling, descending to purely vegetative functions.

Camp commandant Florstedt lives in the so-called *Weisses Haus*,[141] a villa with a huge veranda not far from the road. We can see it from our roll call square. The villa's interior was renovated in a luxurious manner, the parquet floor was laid and torn up three times because the commandant's wife didn't like the pattern. It has been equipped with state-of-the-art electric heating, cooking, and cleaning appliances, Frigidaires, even electric cigarette lighters in each room. There is a permanent *Weisses Haus Kommando* which goes to do housework in the commandant's residence.

---

140. Edvard Beneš, president of Czechoslovakia in exile (1939–45).
141. White House.

Releases and Contact with the Free World

The information about the releases are indeed true. A Gestapo commission arrives from Lwów to release certain prisoners caught in street roundups in the city. After the evening roll call, they set up tables, and order prisoners from Lwów to gather around them, and start reading out the names of natives of Lwów. Those from the Lwów transports whose names aren't read out are to step forward themselves. We learn a new nomenclature, *Aktionshäftlinge*, prisoners captured during mass street roundups. Once their personal data is written down, private interviews are conducted asking about the man's trade and whether he committed any crimes under German standards. Violating the penal code leads to prison, while being in conflict with the *"Volksempfinden,"* the uncodified, custom law—which the Gestapo tend to stretch like elastic according to their own *"Empfinden"*[142]—lands people in concentration camps. This test of loyalty lasts five to ten months and then prisoners are released, if there is nothing else that can be pinned on them—provided, of course, that the *Aktionshäftlinge* is still alive. Around seventy people from the Lwów roundup are released. The others become full-fledged, "gilded" *Schutzhäftlinge.*

Right after this, the Warsaw Gestapo arrives and in a similar way, the names of about 150 people are read out from the January roundup in two groups. Among others, Kleniewski leaves; it's through his sister that I had contact with my brother. It's high time that he left, because he has a nasty infection on his bare foot and he's afraid to go to the Revier since it's still not absolutely certain that they won't take Aryans to the gas anymore. I ask Kleniewski and my other departing friends to contact my brother and tell him about the conditions here—about everything that's hard to write in a letter. I can't give him a letter, since released prisoners go through the same inspection in the bathhouse as when they were admitted to the camp, and after the shower they get decent, civilian clothing. Then they

142. Feeling.

are taken to the *Politische Abteilung* where they sign a declaration that they will not disclose any information about conditions in the camp to anyone.

I wonder when my turn will come. There have been two or three cases of individual releases of real *Schutzhäftlinge*, but those released got no advance notice. The block clerk receives an order from the office in the evening for the prisoner to come to the field office in the morning, right after roll call, shaved and with a fresh haircut. By itself, this does not mean anything yet, as prisoners are often summoned for interrogation to the *Politische Abteilung* or *Abteilung* III to sign some power of attorney document sent from home to the camp authorities, etc. Once the SS man escorts the prisoner to the bathhouse along the way then he knows "what's going on," but he can no longer communicate with his friends to get some instructions to take outside. Of course, those who are to be released already had notices from home sent through civilians, so they have an idea when they are called to appear having shaved and with their hair cut. But there were only two or three such sudden cases. And how many such notifications of my release have I gotten from home already?

There are other releases, but only from Field 4. That is where they keep a special category of prisoner, the *Geiseln* (hostages) taken collectively from some village for failing to meet a supply quota or for an act of sabotage committed nearby. Such prisoners are interned for a specific (but unknown to them) period of time. Their numbers are printed on red, rather than white, scraps of cloth; they are kept in separate barracks and have certain minor comforts in their treatment. They are all peasants from the countryside.

My contact with the outside world is becoming more frequent. Due to Kleniewski's release, I delegate Kazimierz Wszelaki from Kraśnik as an observer beyond the wires, he is related to a head judge and legal adviser to the Ministry of Foreign Affairs. He is a real crafty fellow, having fully adapted to the camp regime, he doesn't like to work but he doesn't let himself get caught, he'll carry any package in full view of the SS men. A watering can serves as his hiding place, which he carries everywhere as a matter of principle, even when it's raining—since the *Blockführer* on duty at the gate see it as a tool for work. Besides this he has a dull sickle that he pretends to cut grass with on the escarpments, stuffing some of the grass into the watering can, under which he carries what "our" wagon driver handed over. He was heavily compromised in underground warfare. The Germans burned down his house and brickyard. His wife and children had to hide for a long time. He also makes contact with home through the driver and since the clerks steal packages so brazenly, he asks that they be addressed under my name, since Knips doesn't dare steal from me.

I also get to know one of the laborers from the sewage works company who my friends praise as an exceptionally reliable and helpful person. He brings me twenty postcards. I reason that letters written on postcards don't draw as much attention as messages on scraps of paper. I want to pay him for taking my postcards, but he refuses to take money, asserting that he feels obligated to help prisoners. I arrange with him to have my brother write to his address, and he will bring me his letters from there. Without mentioning it to him I ask my brother to send him a certain sum every month for his trouble. This is a splendid contact since I get mail from my brother when it's fresh, whereas the wagon driver would carry it for days at a time because he didn't have a route past Field 3. Sending replies also works very well. I read the letters in Boniecki's workshop— Wszelaki keeps watch—and if necessary I immediately write a reply, so that by 1:00 p.m. my letter is in the mailbox. I get letters three days after they are written in Warsaw.

Sometimes I send Wszelaki on reconnaissance missions. Some say that there are ways to make contact with your family in the *Gärtnerei*. So I send him along with four men carrying two handbarrows to bring "bearded" carnations. So many of these were sown that they don't know what to do with them all, so anyone who asks for them gets as much as they want. Of course it's just a pretext to move around freely through the several-hundred-acre area. There, where the compost *Kommando* works, and the compost piles are heaped, it's around 150 meters from the road that runs along the Dziesiąta suburb. The *Postenkette* stretches along this road, with a guard post every one hundred meters, thirty meters inside the field, and on the camp grounds, there is a well from which the civilian population draws water. There are specialists in the compost *Kommando*, who, while pretending to work on the flower beds right by the road, got to know the women living in the nearest houses. One of these women will give notice that the relative of some prisoner is in her home and wants to see him. Of course if she can specify his field and block number and which *Kommando* he works in, he can be fetched by the afternoon. Then the prisoner in question leaves at noon with the compost *Kommando*—and a friend from the compost squad leaves with the other's *Kommando*. Naturally the kapo has to be let in on the secret and get paid for it. When the prisoner arrives, a messenger gives a sign to the woman, who has been sitting in the window or chatting by the gate all day. She waits for the moment when there are no prisoners by the well (an empty bucket sits there), she approaches the well with her bucket filled with victuals, fills the empty bucket with water, and leaves. Then a courier comes over and takes the bucket full of goodies. After a while the SS men get wise to this and from then on an SS man needs to be paid off. The tax is one hundred zlotys, half a liter of vodka, and a piece of sausage, and for that price the SS man takes care of the two neighboring posts, from the left and right sides. Prisoners who have regular contact with family living in Lublin have predetermined places where they pick up their packages from. After the evening roll call, the *Postenkette* is brought in and the entire *Gärtnerei* is accessible to the civilian population. That's when the families hide packages for their loved ones under some shrub, in the corner of the compost pile, or between rocks. This connection is only possible for those who regularly work in the compost *Kommando*, since you have to take or eat the contents of the package first thing in the morning or otherwise hide it so that an SS man doesn't find it. The SS men who go out as the *Kommandoführer*[143] of the compost *Kommando* lead charmed lives, since everyone pays them off to not pay too much attention.

This would have been tolerable. But then other SS men found out about the arrangement. All of them that aren't on duty come to the compost area and look around at the prisoners or at civilians who get near the *Postenkette* line, to see if they are bending down or leaving something. A friend from my block, Baran, a chauffeur from Lublin, has it made. Almost every day he eats pierogi, pork chops, fruit, and vodka supplied by his wife. During

143. SS supervisor of a work squad sent outside the camp.

the delivery of these care packages, you can't talk, and at most exchange a few words. So these meetings are limited to seeing each other. These contacts are only valuable for Lubliners—and since the mail has started working normally, it's more reliable and cheaper, because you don't have to pay a bribe. Wszelaki meets with his wife by the compost several times, but he can't say much to her. It depends on the guard posts. Sometimes you have to wait two days for good posts, and even then you have to keep your eyes peeled since various higher and lower SS dignitaries are patrolling the *Gärtnerei* by bicycle and on foot.

Our surveillance of the messages going out of the camp determines that the two *Stubendienst* from Block 14, Eugeniusz Grudziński and Tadeusz Szymkowiak, under the overseer and pimp "Raoul von Möller," are snitches and secretly working for the Germans. Besides, the very fact that both of them and their boss volunteered for the German army disqualifies them. I receive the warning through Zelent and pass it on to my trusted friends.

As a result of the efficiency of postal deliveries and the large amount of food being absorbed through the compost *Kommando*, prices for bread, sugar, and more are falling by the day. Bread stopped being something special for the Aryans, nobody demands it and it is no longer accepted as payment. The camp currency of choice is now bacon, measured in quarter-kilo monetary units used to buy clothing, shoes, vodka, tobacco, etc. Thanks to the regular packages my physical condition begins to improve. Directly after arriving in the camp our overseer, Zygmunt Stauber, did say that the first three years in a camp are the hardest, which we considered a joke at the time, but it seems like now I can endure the camp these days compared to that first week. I've gotten used to a new way of life.

During the battles of the Isonzo during the First World War, in 1918, I was sick with hay fever with quite serious symptoms at the beginning. In order to relieve it I ordered an antiallergy toxin from one of the European pharmaceutical factories, in Rostock, which I took every year from March to May in twelve graduated shots. The shots brought me relief—yet from time to time, when the grasses and crops blossomed in June and July, my sinuses and eyes got inflamed, and I would get asthma and other symptoms. Admittedly, the factory brochure stated that in 30 percent of cases the condition is cured, but since I had light allergies every year despite the shots, I didn't have the courage to stop them even for one season. I was arrested in February 1943 and totally unable to continue my treatment. I grew anxious thinking about June 8th, my birthday, when the first symptoms regularly manifest. This year I had no symptoms on my birthday, already a valuable birthday gift. Usually the first ten days are the worst, then my sensitivity drops in proportion to the shedding of the blossoms. This time I sneezed maybe fifteen times in the same time period and my eyes really itched. And that's it. It will be for the doctors to judge—but I think that those shots intensified my idiosyncrasy,[144] instead of immunizing against it. And right here, in Majdanek, I'm out in the fresh air for eighteen hours a day, surrounded by fields and meadows in every direction. I made another interesting observation about myself. I didn't possess any soap for a long time; when I got some soap for washing laundry, I used it only to wash my hands. I didn't wash my face as an economizing measure. It's likely that as a result of not using soap to wash my face, the years-long skin inflammation I had, which the most various professors and dermatologists treated with multifarious creams, mixtures, oils, oats, powders, special soaps, and light therapy, completely disappeared. The concentration camp demonstrated the suitable and simple therapy for my inflamed skin, which no one else thought of: avoiding all soaps, creams, etc. and washing your face with clean water.

All of us in the camp have an abnormal craving for garlic and we all order it from home. I can eat an entire bulb in a day. After several weeks of gorging on garlic I notice that my fingernails, which had softened over my time in the camp, are hardening again, and might be even harder than when I was free, and they aren't crumbling. The top edges of my ears are peeling and thick strips of skin are still coming off. The doctor tries to cheer me up that it's just from frostbite. I had no idea that I had frozen my ears in the first

144. Kwiatkowski here means the body's oversensitivity to something.

days in the camp. The abscess on my finger healed in no time after eating a few portions of sugar. I got rid of the scabies, the fleas are only passing through from other beds, since I change my shirt every week. Thankfully the universal eye drops help and my pink eye calms down. Thanks to the warmer weather my nose stopped dripping, which had lasted for two months and irritated my nostrils.

The weather is beautiful—it rarely rains, dream weather for a concentration camp, but what will the poor farmers do, everything will be dry as a bone. We've all become meteorologists. We observe the clouds in the morning, the direction of the wind, and then the most diverse sunrises in a gamut of colors and shades. Pouring rains aren't so terrible, like three-day drizzles, since when it pours you can stand by the wall of the barracks, and we've noticed that the wind always blows from one side so if you stand by the wall on the opposite side you won't get soaked. I start to wonder why I carried an umbrella in Warsaw, since I could have just not gone out in the rain, or used a trolley car or taxi—or stood by a wall as a last resort. Here we've learned to get by without umbrellas and waterproof Burberrys.[145] The worst is a rainstorm during roll call, then we're defenseless. When a light rain falls and you have to work, that's when you get soaked the most.

One day, the evening roll call just won't end because the *Feldführer* hasn't arrived so there is no one to report the roll to. Eventually, First *Rapportführer* Kostial comes over and receives the roll call. The following day and for the following week, the *Feldführer* is gone. Some saw him being led without his belt on—others say in secret that he was arrested and imprisoned in the Lublin Castle. The reason? "Jewish gold." A week later, though, the *Feldführer* is back. Still, the kapos stick with the version that he was under investigation in the castle and that other SS men from the camp are still locked up there.

I enjoy relative freedom of movement on the field, the SS men know me as the *Gärtner*, the murderer Birzer is kind to me, and when he's drunk—

---

145. A reference to a waterproof gabardine invented in 1879 by Thomas Burberry.

which happens a lot—he treats me with respect, since he shakes my hand—unheard of . . . to a *Häftling*—while others run from him when he's drunk, since that's when he is the most dangerous! When he's in this state, mumbling, he brags that he is a reserve officer and apart from his gardening business, he has twelve thousand acres in Hungary, in the Carpathian Basin, etc. When he's sober and I do my regulation "*Mützen ab*," he passes by without even noticing.

One day Wyderka comes to me and says:

"Did you know that the ash trees have taken root?"

I nod even though I hadn't noticed. I go to them and I can't believe my eyes, they've all grown shoots and the buds have opened. My reputation as a gardener is saved.

I am slowly learning who the most prominent people in Majdanek are. There is Professor Poniatowski and Prince Krzysztof Radziwiłł, both on Field 2; the province governor of Kraków, Gnoiński, on Field 4; and in our Field 3 kitchens—Jagodziński from the Polish Socialist Party, who planned to assassinate Marshal Józef Piłsudski; and among the women there is Irena Pannenkow, the parliamentarian Prauss, Iłłakowiczowa, daughter of the mayor of Warsaw Słomiński, and Kurcyuszow. The well-known fraudster from Warsaw, Prot-Kadzidłowski, is on Field 4.

Fluchtpunkte

A new transport arrives from Lublin Castle to Field 3, most of the new-comers get *Fluchtpunkte*,[146] i.e., red marks (the size of a 10-zloty coin) against a white background painted on the left breast, on the pants, under the numbers, and on the back. It means that these prisoners are consid-ered potential escapees and they are not allowed to leave the field for work. If a newcomer gets "points," it means that the Gestapo considers them big fish and recommends "special care." And if a prisoner attempt-ing to escape is caught, the camp command gives them *Fluchtpunkte* at their own initiative. Almost the entire transport of eighty-five prisoners gets "points," as I learn at the *Schreibstube*, since they were sent to the camp while awaiting trial before the *Sondergericht*.[147] That's serious business. The specter of death hovers over them. They get the special, isolated Block 3, supervised by Pietroniec, and they are to form a penal company. The guys need to be taken care of so I ask Pietroniec to select a few "on the level" fel-lows as gardeners. I get Wacław Lipski from Pomerania, a lawyer and jour-nalist for the Warsaw *Dziennik Narodowy*;[148] Józef Serafin, a lawyer from Kraśnik; his brother-in-law, Tadeusz Kaszubski, a lawyer from Lublin; and Szwajcer, a first lieutenant from the air force. The first pea pods are ripen-ing, so these *Fluchtpunkte* are working "in peas."

The first Aryan prisoner tries to escape, he is captured, and brought to our field having been severely beaten. Here, the SS men and kapos pile on. A terribly mauled mask stands in front of the office. Wyderka and Bubi bring red and white oil paint and paint his face, or rather his wounds, with a large *Fluchtpunkt*. On his nose, temples, and upper lip they paint a red circle, and around it, on the forehead, near the ears, and on the chin—a white border. They paint the same, oversize markings on the front and

146. Literally, escape points.
147. Refers to the Nazi special court.
148. Polish: "National Journal."

back of his jacket. They take him to the *Politische Abteilung* for interrogation, which refers him to the Revier, where he receives an injection that puts him out of his misery.

I learn of a new custom in the camp. If someone is caught committing any sort of transgression and they are to be punished, they "arrest" him, which entails putting him in between the wires next to the *Blockführer* gatehouse by the entrance. They stand on the crushed stone with a bare head, without food, until twilight, and if any trickery needs to be prevented, the prisoner is taken to spend the night on Field 4.

My former house manager, Pfeffer, got some work in an *Aussenkommando*[149] where he has contact with civilians, and tells me that he got in touch with his Polish friend in Lublin. Several times I have given him postcards to forward. One evening I write a postcard to Mary and I look for him the next morning in the barracks before roll call, so he can take it. He's not here, they say he might be in the washroom barracks, I run there and indeed I find him. He gladly takes the postcard, unbuttons his zebra shirt (camp stripes), and puts it in the pocket of his civilian jacket underneath. I looked at him, I don't know if he understood my stare. I squeezed his hand. We heard the bell for the roll call. In the evening I come to his barracks and ask for Pfeffer—I get conflicting replies. Fat Jacob, who took over this block, is sitting down and asks:

"Who are you looking for, gardener?"

"Pfeffer," I reply.

He freezes and stares back at me.

"How do you know him?"

I say that he used to be my landlord, and other Jews, who have started listening to our conversation, nod their heads in agreement. Then the overseer replies:

"Pfeffer is gone."

"What do you mean, gone?"

"Escaped," Jacob says.[150]

---

149. External *Kommando*, working outside the camp.
150. Jerzy Pfeffer escaped the camp on June 21, 1943.

I do my best to keep myself composed, not to blush or otherwise reveal the joy I feel at the news. I express interest in the escape and wonder if he managed to take my postcard for Mary with him. They tell me he left his striped uniform at his workplace, and apparently changed into civilian clothing provided to him. I do not admit to having already seen him in those clothes in the morning. So he took the postcard for Mary . . . Safe travels.

I don't think they captured him, because he never came back to our camp, and escapees are always returned to their parent camp for both bureaucratic and educational considerations.

Kapo Meierovitz is moved into my barracks, a magnate, since he's in the *Arbeitseinsatz* and makes decisions about all the transports, work assignments, etc. He is totally informed about everything going on in the camp. His name does not seem very German to me, and the way he acts is also different from other Germans. I believe he is from Frankfurt, a highly cultured journalist with a first-rate education, good manners, and broad horizons. We stand next to each other during the roll calls and those thirty minutes take me back to my past interests and way of expressing my thoughts. In a short time, he comes to trust me and starts telling me in confidence about certain events.

There are squads that work after the evening roll call and don't stand for it. These detachments are "commandeered," and during the receipt of the roll call by the *Blockführer*, the block overseer reports however many prisoners from *Kommando* X have been commandeered. Only at night, once a given group has returned to the field, the *Blockführer* at the gate will note that the unit has returned to the camp. One day, all the commandeered squads unexpectedly return for the evening roll call. This draws the attention of those in the know, so I ask Meierovitz about it and he tells me in secret that not all of the "commandeered" units came back, and that the *Effektenkammer*[151] *Kommando* was stopped and sent to the shed next to the shuttered crematorium between Fields 1 and 2, and that the entire crematorium crew is also slated for extermination. They live separately to

151. Here, the prisoner-property warehouse.

prevent contact with other prisoners. The SS men sneak snacks and vodka in for them—after all, the Russians from the crematorium have plenty of their own gold—but it's a tradition in the camps that from time to time you liquidate the crematorium personnel.

I receive news from home that my release was delayed because the *Reichssicherheitshauptamt*, which decides on the matter, moved out of Berlin due to the bombing raids—allegedly to the Sudety mountains. A totally convincing argument—nothing to do but wait.

One of the prisoners escaped from Block 16 at night. As a punishment, all the Block 16 prisoners are locked in the barracks. They aren't allowed to go out on the field during the day, they get no food, and they don't even come out for roll call. We are very worried about what might happen to them. The entrance to the barracks is nailed shut with a board. Guards stand in front. Most of the prisoners inside are Polish. After twenty-four hours, the Polish blocks, 14 and 15, get organized and set aside a certain number of cauldrons of soup and coffee and smuggle them over to 16 at night. Kapo Wawrzyniak, a Pole with German citizenship from Westphalia, takes care of it. At noon on the third day, *Lagerältester* Birzer removes the board and goes inside the block for an inspection. Seeing this, I run back to my barracks, stick two loaves of bread under my jacket, and run to 16. Birzer has already come out and wants to nail the doors closed when he sees me running toward him. I stopped and hesitated.

"What do you want?"

Haltingly, I explain that I want to hand my friends some bread.

"*Aber selbstverständlich*" (but of course), he replies.

I am pleasantly surprised that he is tolerant of human kindness. The next day, the barracks are opened and everyone comes out "to freedom." We breathed a collective sigh of relief, since we feared that Block 16 would face collective responsibility.

On our field, every day it's the same scene at the evening roll call. They always carry in several dead people and a few that are so gravely injured that healthy prisoners carry them on their backs or support them with their shoulders. Mostly their heads are injured and split open. If I don't recount these murders and mutilations every day it's not because they have stopped, they've just become commonplace. A person gets used to it and starts thinking that's the way it has to be. In our block, a prisoner from Lwów, Lutman, draws all of our attention. He works in a good *Kommando*, the compost, he has a PhD in philosophy and worked for the Ossolineum publishing house, but he is terribly helpless. He has totally given up, he gets loads of packages, but he can't get his life together or even try to get a new shirt or a towel. He walks around covered in lice, he has a dull, frozen expression, he's totally absent, like a sleepwalker. Despite several attempts from friends to snap him out of it, he doesn't react. He's fading away before our eyes—he's completely, psychologically crushed.

Killing the *Effektenkammer Kommando*

In secret, I learn the facts about the liquidation of the *Effektenkammer Kommando*. The prisoners assigned to this *Kommando* collaborated in the plunder of gold, jewelry, and cash from the Jews and they knew all the secrets. The *Reichssicherheitshauptamt* received a report about embezzlement in Majdanek, in which SS men and certain officers from the camp command were involved. The *Effektenkammer Kommando* prisoners and higher-ranking prisoner functionaries could potentially provide damning testimony. So, the SS men involved decided to cut off any possibility of an investigation and destroy the entire *Effektenkammer Kommando*. They were taken to the old crematorium. One by one they were let into the wooden shed where they were shot. After two or three days, Jews from the *Bekleidungskammer* and *Entlausung*[152] *Kommando* recognized, by the numbers and elegant, bloodied clothing, that their friends from the *Effektenkammer*, who had vanished without a trace, had been murdered. But on the day of the massacre, one Jew from the *Effektenkammer Kommando* had been laid up sick in the hospital. A commission from Berlin was already on the spot in Majdanek and was conducting an investigation. They came to the Revier, determined that the man was living and issued a stern warning to take care of this star witness under penalty of unpleasant consequences. The Jew was taken from the Revier and interrogated.

We get a new business proposition. We've gotten used to the collections of five zlotys for the clerk to furnish the office, etc. We have cash, it doesn't cause us distress. But now we get a bolder proposition, to buy rutabagas, cheese, or juice. The *Lagerältester* is the seller and the products come from the SS canteen, and the *Lagerältester* charges triple for it. Again the same hypocrisy: you aren't allowed to have money—but you have to buy the merchandise.

152. Delousing.

Several days after this transaction, the SS men carry out a general *filc* after the roll call—we have to empty our pockets and toss everything into our hats lying in front of us on the ground. They confiscate handkerchiefs, pocketknives, money, mirrors, etc. They take fifty zlotys that I recklessly had on me and a pocketknife. The next day, the *Lagerältester* hands me another pocketknife, for the gardener.

The block overseers do their own trading. There are a few categories of prisoner that are allowed to wear leather footwear, as well as the kapos, overseers, *Schreiber*, and *Vorarbeiter*. Every Wednesday they get to exchange their torn shoes for undamaged ones. The block overseers have turned this into a business. They get ripped shoes from civilian workers who wear them into the camp. Each Wednesday they send an entire contingent of leather shoes allocated to a given block to the *Bekleidungskammer* to be exchanged, the same day they sell the newly obtained shoes to the civilians, who came in old slippers and leave in new shoes. Then, when a prisoner who has the right to wear leather shoes goes to exchange them, he's met with enormous difficulty or gets equivalent replacements, so he would rather just keep the old ones. I can't regard this as a patriotic deed, as "depleting German supplies" like some overseers pat themselves on the back about, since they gain a personal benefit from these "patriotic" acts, and besides, this is Polish property, and the fewer shoes there are in the warehouse, the fewer are left for prisoners . . .

They read out a notice at the evening roll call and order it to be translated by interpreters, saying that the work of those prisoners who attain average productivity will be compensated from now on. Those that exceed the norm, will get a bonus. Various rumors crop up right away, some even gather that our camp will be transformed into a labor camp. The announcement is posted in the office, I take a close look at it the following day and what catches my eye is that there is no header which would note the name of the department that issued the notice, nor is there a signature, just a date from two months ago without a locality. The end of the notice doesn't sound like an official announcement, but more like a propaganda leaflet: "and so, work."

I suspect that this is a German propaganda trick, necessary perhaps for neutral countries to see or for other aims of the SS.

The trend of bowing has established itself among the prisoners, without taking off the cap, just nodding your head, at most tipping your cap . . . And that's in order to differentiate a friendly greeting from the bow we are forced to give to our hangmen.

They move all of the *Fluchtpunkte* formerly concentrated in Block 3 onto Field 4. As they stand in front of the barracks, ready to march out, Pietroniec gives a patriotic speech and calls on them to maintain their dignity. I lose my friendly helpers: Lipski, Serafin, Kaszubski, Szwajcer, and others.

Some company from Lublin is carrying out a general roof renovation. As a result, the camp is flooded with civilian workers hired for the project.

The field commandant conducts surprise searches of packages deposited in the barracks and confiscates various scarves, sweaters, etc. hidden inside food containers. The same goes on in Boniecki's workshop, where a sweater received from my brother is taken away from my hiding place. Luckily, they didn't find the 500-zloty bill stuck into the sugar. All the confiscated items are thrown inside a large crate with dirty underwear in the washroom barracks and are to be sent to the *Bekleidungskammer*. I manage to find my sweater inside the crate and for the price of a quarter-kilo of bacon, the warehouse keeper lets me have it back.

Unknown SS men enter the field and order the roundup of all Jewish children. This isn't the first time, so it's nothing out of the ordinary; nonetheless, the children, as if driven by instinct, instead of gathering—scatter across the entire field. With the help of the overseers and *Stubendienst*, the SS men begin chasing the children and grabbing them like a dogcatcher picking up strays on the street. I won't detail how many tears were shed in connection with this. Some of the kids sheltered in the kitchen. There the head of the kitchen, the short and stout Corporal Wellmeier, stood in front of the door and forbade the SS men from entering the kitchen. The SS men leave empty-handed, taking just ninety children from the field. We know where they are leading them—to the gas! The next day the kitchen chief gets the order from Thumann to give up the rest of the kids who sought refuge with him.

Pietroniec contracted typhus fever. He is lying alone in empty Block 3, the doctor visits him every day, the *Stubendienst*, Chyliński, the pastry chef from Tarnopol, an older, very decent and sensible man, takes care of him. I visit him daily to share the latest news from the camp.

The Camp Administration

The respective camp administration departments that answer directly to the camp commandant are as follows:

1) The *Politische Abteilung*, which receives the personal data of prisoners from the Gestapo, including those under a *Schutzhaftbefehl* (protective custody order), and a short explanation of reasons for imprisonment. A dossier is created for every prisoner which compiles all of their documentation and arriving correspondence pertaining to them. The *Politische Abteilung* maintains its own prisoner index, receives transports, handles related correspondence, and decides which category a given prisoner is assigned to. The department is headed by *Kriminalsekretär* Grundmann.[153] Additional interrogations are carried out there at the request of the appropriate Gestapo office. The *Politische Abteilung* also receives orders to carry out death sentences decided by the Gestapo as well as release orders.

2) The *Abteilung* III is headed by *Schutzhaftlagerführer* Thumann, having the rank of second lieutenant. This department deals with internal camp life, so keeping various records, daily reports, and prisoner numbers; exercising disciplinary power over prisoners, conducting investigations into internal violations; and maintaining prisoner files with particular focus on punishments meted out. All daily reports, the so-called *Stärkemeldung* (prisoner counts), are signed by the First *Rapportführer*, Sergeant Kostial. He is Thumann's right-hand man, like they are cast from the same mold. And he has the same dog as his boss.

3) The *Arbeitseinsatz* handles prisoner work assignments. The department signs contracts with various factories and enterprises which it provides with prisoners. Since these businesses pay six zlotys daily for an unskilled worker and eight zlotys for a skilled specialist, or sometimes more, it's important for the *Arbeitseinsatz* to maximize the camp's

---

153. Detective sergeant; the name here should actually be Kloppmann.

profitability. It tries to get as many prisoners hired for paid work and to pull the most qualified workers out of the camp's own *Kommando* so that those units remaining are kept to minimum numbers and largely consist of *gamel*, that is, the weak and sickly, thus not very productive workers. In the outside *Kommando*, none of the camp authorities concern themselves with prisoner productivity, that's for the factory to worry about, and it has to pay the predetermined rate either way. It's an unrivaled rate, since civilian workers, despite rates set by the German labor bureaus, are paid incomparably more. Taking into account the lower productivity of prisoners due to poor diet and a lack of interest in efficiency, their work still pays off very well for the businesses.

Whereas the weak, picked-through human material has to unconditionally carry out a certain pensum of camp labor, and the poor result of the work is the best measure of its efficiency. Besides this, in the camp there is control at every step, from the official SS supervisors to those casually walking by, and the guards in the towers will often even yell at lone prisoners to work harder. These ones are under the most strain and since their strength has already been so depleted, more and more of them are exhausted and finished off.

The *Arbeitseinsatz* prepares lists of prisoners assigned to various *Kommando*, those hospitalized, and those working as barracks personnel, then it determines that the numbers don't add up. Namely, the number of prisoners who the *Arbeitseinsatz* can determine are employed in various places is always lower from the actual roll call count. It is absolutely unavoidable that a certain number of prisoners roves around, and loafs about the camp, and despite various measures remains elusive. They hide behind the barracks, in the barracks, they keep an eye out for SS men, which is itself tiring and requires constant vigilance. It often comes down to the *Arbeitsdienst* having to reduce the numbers of *Stubendienst* and even *Schreibstube* to have more bodies for work. At the head of all this is SS-*Hauptscharführer*[154] Troll, whose kapo is the German journalist Meierovitz, who provides a helpful contrast to all the other Germans.

154. SS staff sergeant.

You are not allowed to change your *Kommando* assignment on your own. There are *Kommando* which people yearn to get into, and others which they run from.

Finally, the *Arbeitsdienst* puts together transports to other camps, so they decide the fate of every prisoner. It also maintains its own files taking special account of each person's profession and the *Kommando* where they work.

4) The hospital, known as the *Häftlingskrankenbau*, abbreviated HKB, or as the Revier, is headed by SS-*Lagerarzt*,[155] Dr. Rindfleisch. It maintains records of the sick.

5) The crematorium, headed by the infamous Mußfeld. Prisoners sentenced to death by the Gestapo are executed there by firing squad.

6) The *Effektenkammer*, the warehouse where, theoretically, each prisoner's belongings are kept in a paper bag. In reality, however, only the clothes of German prisoners are stored and, if one of them is transferred to another camp, the bag goes with him. The *Effektenkammer* also maintains files.

7) The *Bekleidungskammer*, a warehouse that stores striped prisoner uniforms and various old articles of clothing obtained from unknown sources, since none of the arrested ever arrived at the camp wearing such rags. All the clothes have the letters KL painted in red. The pants have red stripes. The warehouse keeps a card index with the specifications of the clothing issued to each prisoner.

8) The *Poststelle* maintains the records of the incoming and outgoing mail in a special card index that contain columns for each of the twelve months, and the SS men employed there conduct censorship of letters.

9) The *Bauhof* is the building materials depot, which also plans the expansion of the camp. It is not subordinate to the camp commandant for administering building materials and has a certain autonomy, which causes antagonism between itself and the camp headquarters.

10) The *Standortverwaltung* is the camp's administrative department: it supplies food, and it manages the kitchens in the respective fields,

155. The SS camp doctor.

the vegetable gardens, and the lands adjoining the camp, as well as the *Lagergut*, shoemaking workshops, carpentry workshops, the laundry, etc. They are again at war with Thumann and they forbade him from collecting vegetables from the *Gärtnerei*; they sequestered the dining room set that Thumann had ordered made in the camp's carpentry workshop, etc.

11) The *Unterkunftskammer* is a warehouse of various types of equipment required to maintain the camp: soap, scrubbing powder, bowls, buckets, brooms, brushes, seeds, lubricants, chains, wires, etc.

There are also the SS-*Küche* (the SS kitchen), SS-*Kantine*, SS-*Unterkunftskammer* (SS warehouse), and the bathhouse and gas chamber, for gassing bugs and people.

We have a new, unusual *Zugang*. Around fifty prisoners arrived from the Buchenwald concentration camp.[156] All Germans with green triangles. They came in striped uniforms and have small bags slung over their shoulders with various knickknacks. They remind me of trolley-car drivers' bags. The Varsovians jokingly label them "trolley-car drivers" on the spot. We learn that they were brought in to increase the kapo cadres. They despair at the living conditions here and tell us about life in Buchenwald. There, the barracks are divided into sleeping and dining areas. The dining room contains long, tall cupboards. Six prisoners share one cupboard, where they keep their towels, underwear, food packages, bowls, cups, spoons, and knives, since each person has their own table setting there. The beds have straw pillows, so-called pillow-cased headrests. The bed has a sheet, and the blanket also has a cover. The prisoners are assigned to particular tables, each with a table manager. They have their tables prepared with portions of bread and extras after the evening roll call. So the distribution of bread is very efficient. The barracks are models of cleanliness, there isn't one louse in the camp, the food is much more tasty and plentiful, the prisoners get paid a bonus for their work with which they can buy cigarettes, bread, vegetable salad, marmalade, soap, beer, etc. from the canteen. A movie theater is operating, and radio loudspeakers are installed there that

---

156. The prisoners mentioned were deported from KL Buchenwald on a transport on July 26, 1943.

broadcast news and music. There is a large orchestra in the camp consisting of several dozen prisoners, who play every day during the march out to work and upon the return. There is "even" a *Puff* [157] for prisoners. Medical care and the hospital there are very good. The "trolley-car drivers" are depressed at the primitive conditions in Majdanek. On the other hand they say that while the *Bettenbau* has been brought to such perfection in Buchenwald, the requirements are so high that many prisoners prefer to sleep on the ground next to their beds to save themselves the work of making them. The blanket cover, which has a blue-and-white checkerboard pattern, has to be folded on the edge of the bed at a 90-degree angle so that the crease runs in one line along the border between the white and blue squares. They also tell us that in Buchenwald they have a bunker (underground prison), where prisoners are locked up for violations and they often don't emerge alive. Finally, that they don't have a gas chamber, instead they have "shots," injections of gasoline and Lysol that lead to death after a few minutes. They walk around the barracks and choose prisoners randomly for "shots."

At the beginning of July, a transport of approximately one thousand prisoners bound for Buchenwald is formed, and influenced by the stories told by the "trolley-car drivers," many prisoners volunteer to go willingly, to improve their living conditions. Admittedly, *Lagerältester* Rockinger had previously said that he is keeping me in Majdanek for two weeks to complete the spring gardening work, and now the current *Lagerältester* tells me that my departure is out of the question, since I am indispensable as the camp gardener. Meanwhile, Rockinger left as a free man, since he volunteered for the SS at the front and his application was favorably taken care of.

---

157. German slang for brothel.

The Move to Field 4

Unexpectedly, after the roll call, they order us to take all of our food packages and form up on the square. Another surprise. They are taking us off the field, to where? They lead us toward Field 4—then the columns marching in front of us turn into the gate of Field 4. Field 3 is left completely empty, only the *Lagerältester* and the office staff remain. We stand on the roll call square. The assignment of barracks begins—it lasts over two hours. Unbelievable turmoil and yelling on the square. Finally, they take us to our barracks, Block 1, where there isn't a single bed, just a bare floor, which we lie down on to go to sleep. It's so cramped on the floor that when I turn from one side to the other, I have to do it at the same time as my neighbor. I get up in the morning as if I've been trampled. Forget about washing up. The block overseer woke us up an hour early to form up for the roll call, where there are already controversies, since on Field 3 we lined up on the right side and here the trend is to line up from the left. The block overseers from Field 4 have taken command, and they treat us like cattle. The prisoners who belong to *Kommando* that work outside the wires set off for work; the rest are ordered to march and exercise on the square. During the march I observe the appearance of the field, and above all the layout of the lawns and flower beds, and to my satisfaction, I see a huge difference in favor of Field 3. The flower beds here are full of weeds, the flowers have shed their blossoms and are uncut, the negligence and carelessness shows.

Later that morning a messenger arrives and calls out several dozen prisoners to cross over to work on Field 3, including Zelent and me. We return for lunch to Field 4. The same for the evening roll call and to sleep.

The evening roll call lasts over two hours. Some Jew escaped and the flogging of all the Jews from that *Kommando* begins. They whip more than the requisite twenty-five lashes per person, the extra being for those they want to force a confession out of. Since I am an outsider here, I can't find out the details of the escape. I spend the night on bare boards again.

Field 3 seems like the home that I was evicted from. The next day, they order the entire gardener *Kommando* to go to work on Field 3. For lunch I return to Field 4. It's very uncomfortable to gather at the sound of the bell, some loser is always dragging about—and the entire *Kommando* stands on the square and can't go to lunch, which is short anyway, since the break only lasts fifty minutes. Luckily I learn that about fifty prisoners, including me, are to be taken back to Field 3 by the evening roll call. I return with my packages and I am glad, it's like coming home.

Each *Kommando* has a certain number of people they reserve for themselves—they allocate twelve people to me, but the *Schreibstube* forces me to include three strangers in that number for whom the Slovak Jews pulled some strings. I save the most solid people for myself, and they are certain to be excluded from the transport. All of the *Fluchtpunkte* remain concentrated on Field 4, which means I can't bring back four of my workers. They had excellent contact with the city. It got to the point that a civilian worker appointed for the task brought lunch for four or five people in mess tins, consisting of soup, meat, and vegetables, and still warm, so that you didn't even have to reheat it. Once they invited me for beef roulade with kasha and another time for pierogi.

The next day, around eighty people come from Field 4 to our field. There are over one hundred of us altogether. We are all grouped in Block 14, but I sleep in Block 3, where only the overseer Pietroniec, who has recovered, and the clerk Gregorowicz, remain. Currently, the roll call lasts five minutes. I have ideal sleeping conditions. Silence in the barracks—fresh air, there is only one new scourge: fleas. They don't let us sleep, even though we splash the blankets with caustic disinfecting liquid. Field 3 isn't empty for long.

Fourteen Thousand Peasants

We see a large column marching down the main road on a sweltering day, a cloud of dust rising over it. The column turns into the camp. It barely fit in by the barrier to the camp gate—then a new caterpillar begins moving down the road half an hour later—a multitude of people. They stand there for a long time, then they turn into the camp. I am working with my people to cut the weeds along the road leading from the main road to the camp, within the *Postenkette* of course. I see several of these columns up close. All of them peasants, old people, women, children, relatively few men. All of them loaded with big packs, sheepskin coats, pots. The sweat is pouring from them, they are carrying all of their belongings. On top of this, many women are carrying infants in their arms. They are being driven to the *Entlausung*, but they aren't changing their clothes, the guards limit themselves to taking away their packs, pots, etc.

They are taken to Field 3 and 1,000 to 1,200 people are transferred into each barracks. Two people in each bed, so six hundred people in the beds, and four hundred sleeping on the floor in the walkways between the beds. They are from the districts of Biłgoraj, Zamość, and Hrubieszów.[158]

They say that the army came and ordered them to take all the livestock from every village by a certain deadline to neighboring towns to have it registered. There, the cattle was taken away while they were kept outside. Then the people were ordered to leave their villages and they were sped onward by foot or by train to Majdanek. The peasants have no idea that they are in a concentration camp.

Within a few days, Field 3 fills up completely. Some fourteen thousand peasants have arrived. The camp's total population is twenty-seven thousand people, a sizable town, concentrated on several hectares.

158. In July and August 1943, nearly nine thousand displaced persons from the Zamość region were temporarily settled in Majdanek.

The flea plague is ridiculously annoying; forget about catching them. During the day I take off my shirt every hour and sometimes more often, and shake out thirty or forty of them. Then I drop my pants and do the same. Since everyone is doing it, and the weather is dry and hot, the fleas jump up from the ground again on people passing by and the game begins anew.

Despite the war, the peasants are used to abundant and substantial nourishment, and here they are starving like mad. We save the children with the contents of our packages and I divide all of my sugar, biscuits, eggs, etc. among the mothers with infants in their arms, in a matter of five minutes. My friends do the same, but there are a hundred of us Polish *Schutzhäftlinge* for fourteen thousand people. It gets crowded around the pool, where mothers are washing their children's diapers. They were forbidden from going to the washroom barracks, and several days later the *Lagerältester* chases them away from the pool. Under the pretense of watering the flowers, we draw the dirty water out of the pool, which has no drainage, and we keep pouring fresh water for the women. I explain that the water has to sit in the sun before watering.

The peasant children are looked after by the scout, Szcześniewski, who shares his food with them (even though he doesn't receive packages) and takes up collections of food for the children among his friends.

Among those who came from Buchenwald we got *Lagerkapo* Krause. He is a very respectable person, he defends prisoners and doesn't chase after us to work.

Lagerältester Birzer found himself some woman, whom he bought for himself with a bowl of potatoes ... He hangs out in her barracks all day and has no reservations about sharing a bed with her surrounded by a thousand people.

At night, near Block 3, we hear groans and yells, "Countrymen, save me!" Pietroniec and I jump to our feet and we carefully peek through the crack of the front doors of the barracks. The pool is nearby. There we see the silhouettes of three figures. The person yelling for help, the tall, thin figure of Galka, and the thickset figure of a shorter man. In a moment we hear the hoarse voice of Birzer. And so it's him. They both pull the person into the pool, who is fighting with all his strength . . . At a certain moment the cries stop. Upset, we go back to bed, since Birzer could come into the barracks. In the morning, before the roll call, we go to the pool and to our terror, we see a corpse floating with its hands tied with rope. It was classified as a suicide. It turns out that it's the husband of Birzer's betrothed. And again there is no reaction from the camp authorities. A degenerate murderer runs rampant around the field and chooses his victims.

The displaced peasants are afraid. Any thug who chats up a woman in German has her eating out of his hand. Like that, in heat, you can spit or cry. The peasants don't have to form up for roll call, since you would be counting them all night, instead they are kept in rows on the field for most of the day. There are never enough torments.

Unexpectedly, they shut off all the water to the camp. During the evening roll call they announce that whoever uses water to drink or wash will be punished by death. Thumann comes on the field and orders the water supply to be cut off from the piping system and takes the key with him. The women are deprived of the ability to wash diapers, there is no water to drink during the sweltering heat reaching 55 degrees [131°F] in the sun. The air in the wooden barracks is like a baker's oven. There is just one well with a hand pump, but it's where they draw the water for the kitchen nearby which the SS men guard to make sure no one enters the fenced-in area where the pump is. Tragedies play out. Women go in tears to beg for half a bowl of water to drink. There is no way to get the water and we ourselves, besides the morning and evening coffee, have nothing to drink and we work in the broiling heat.

After two days Thumann comes to the field to reprimand the *Feldführer* that the flowers by the *Blockführer* gatehouse have not been watered. They alert me and I am ordered to organize a column of fifty people who have to take fifty-liter buckets from the kitchen, which are used to carry soup and potatoes, and carry water in them for watering. It turns out that the water in the fire hydrant by the pool has a separate line and works. But the *Lagerältester* has the key. So we carry the water beyond the gate to water the flowers, what a waste, your heart breaks that you can't use it to drink and wash underwear! The peasants aren't allowed to go near the pool, and if a few of them dash over to a bucket unnoticed, they empty it in moments and they are shoving each other so much that they spill water from their bowls. What knavery to abuse innocent people like this, above all women and children.

The effects don't take long to manifest themselves. Older women lie down on the roll call square and every day I count eight to ten bodies, even though these people aren't beaten or starved. What did these peasants do wrong? They are Poles, and their farms are right now being settled by *Volksdeutsche* from Croatia, Slavonia, and Serbia. And these naive peasants are worried about who will cut the hay that's still standing on their meadows, who will harvest the rye and wheat. They are gullible, fooling themselves that they'll return to their farms!

The carnations in my flower beds have bloomed gorgeously. I didn't have such beautiful ones back in my place in Komorów. No wonder: no flowers anywhere have ever had such care and so many unpaid workers around them. A riot of colors, blood red, crimson, amaranth, bright red, various shades of rose, creamy, white, and mottled. Thumann comes over and orders a bouquet made of thirty or forty flowers. He warns that they have to be lovely, vibrant specimens. He is breathing down my neck and after a while he mutters in his bass:

"*Schneller.*"[159]

Damn it—the scoundrel sees that eight to ten flowers are blooming on one bush, one in its bud, others shedding their blossoms, so you have to pick out the nicest flower, run your hands down its stem to the ground and cut it by the root. I stand at attention and say that I can cut out the whole plant quickly, but if I'm supposed to choose the nicest flowers, I need time. He scowls at me:

"In that case, you'll send the flowers to my office immediately," he says, and leaves.

The Red Cross and the RGO organize relief for the displaced persons, but it is limited to supplying milk for the small children. However, by the

159. "Faster."

time the milk passes through the hands of the various layers of SS men, *Lagerältester*, and block overseers, there's more water there than milk.

Gestapo commissions come from Lublin every day, preparing lists of the displaced. The transport to Buchenwald hasn't left and keeps being postponed. On Field 4 in Block 1, interrogations of prisoners by the Gestapo often take place. The beatings of those being interrogated are inhuman. The barracks is about fifteen meters from the garden I'm working on, so I hear the groans of those being tortured up close.

They move various *Kommando* back onto our field from Field 4, so now I have people to talk to, since before I had to communicate with my friends from Field 4 through the wires. Some toss packages to each other over the barbed wire, mostly with food, but this is risky since the guard posts shoot and they totally shattered one prisoner's knee. The prisoners hide behind the corner of the barracks and from there they heave the packages over with a great swing. There are those who throw across bottles of vodka and those of us, jugglers, who always catch the bottle in midair.

As a result of the confusion that reigns on our field thanks to the location of so many thousands of displaced peasants there, the attention of the SS men is diverted away from us prisoners. People take advantage of this and they start to slowly, one by one, put on wooden shoes—and they get away with it. Over the course of a week, the entire field is walking in shoes.

Work in the baking sun is torment. Before 1939 you got foreign passports; obtained extra permissions for taking money out of the country through the foreign exchange commission, thanks to friends; and you sunbathed in Lido in Italy. And then, in your swimsuit, at the Excelsior, you ate "breakfast," consisting of more courses than lunches here. Beautiful women from all the corners of the world paraded around in gorgeous pajamas made of lamé and brocade, more chic and sumptuous than ballroom dresses. The snobs lathered themselves with oils to tan more and then to be able to brag about it. Here where it's 55 degrees in the sun we have an excess of the sun's rays, but there is no colorful umbrella or roofed wicker beach chair to hide from the heat. Here, no one will marvel at my tan!

———

On July 26 an agony was inflicted on Field 2. All day long every prisoner working in the *Bekleidungskammer* and the *Entlausung* was whipped, eighty people altogether. Each of them was asked whether they were selling clothing from the warehouse, if they had money, etc. Regardless of the answer, each one of them received an untold number of lashes. Twenty SS men took turns doing the beating. Among others, Dębski got 208 lashes. The beaten were taken care of painstakingly by Dr. Zembrzuski and Dr. Klonowski, making bandages for them, giving shots for pain, and more.

We get a new *Arbeitseinsatzführer*, Gosberg, an obese giant. He walks around with a bamboo cane that's cracked at the bottom and as a type of greeting he hits prisoners twice on their bare head. The force of the strike depends on whether it's supposed to be a "tender" joke or a sign of contempt. Gosberg shows us what punitive exercise really looks like. He bans my people from sitting on the ground while pulling weeds. They have to squat, which causes terrible numbness in the legs.

Marmorstein

The millionaire, Marmorstein, is moved to our field as part of his punishment. But a donkey loaded with gold can surmount the highest walls.
He serves his "sentence" by living with the *Lagerältester*, for whom the
cook prepares special lunches. He doesn't attend roll call. He acts arro-
gantly toward us, like a wealthy upstart. He is called to Thumann several
times as part of the investigation and after his return, I sometimes hear
fragments of his conversations with Birzer where he gives accounts of the
interrogations, the course of which apparently pleases him. Marmorstein
moves to Block 5 to sleep in, where the overseer is a Polish Jew from Łódź,
Rajchman, chairman of a restaurateur's union. His son is laid up there sick
with typhus; he is afraid to hand him over to the Revier.

Birzer is almost constantly drunk. His ladylove isn't very loyal to him.
He chases around the barracks in search of her. Once, he catches her
in flagranti with the *Volksdeutsch* Stanisław Bonder, in bed in the half-
empty Block 15. Bonder gets a severe beating from his jealous rival and
for days afterward his face is totally bruised blue. One night they take me
from Block 3 to Block 15 (the one I belong to), since Birzer is checking
the prisoner count. I have permission from him to sleep in Block 3. He
counted us, started talking about something, mumbled, and left. We're
standing barefoot in our shirts. After he walks out we want to lie down,
but the overseer won't let us, since Birzer didn't give the *"Weitermachen"*
command when he left. We stand like this for two hours, until we resolve
to send someone to Wyderka. The overseer is afraid that if Birzer comes
into the barracks again, and sees that we've gone to bed without permission, it could turn into a big brawl. Wyderka arrives and orders us
to go to sleep, but in the meantime Birzer comes over and drunkenly
explains that he has seniority and commands us to go to our beds. Something is carrying him around the barracks, what victim will he search out
tonight?

On the morning of August 3 at breakfast, I hear that someone committed suicide by hanging near the latrine. Nothing new in Majdanek. Before the roll call I make my way, one way or another, the daily walk that even kings take, and I see the body hanging from a leather strap in an almost kneeling position. How could they have hung themselves? The legs and pants are covered in dust and dirt, the face is bruised—who's that—it's Marmorstein! The feet and calves are lying on the ground. I inspect the entire positioning of the corpse, it's a fiction, you can see that the body was dragged and hung on the strap to fake a suicide. The matter is clear, I have a suspicion about who the perpetrator is.

During the roll call, everyone is talking about Marmorstein. After the roll call, the latrine is closed. I stand by the flower bed near Block 18, adjacent to the latrine, pretending to work. The *Feldführer* comes over with Birzer and tells him:

"You have to clean his pants with a brush, so they aren't so dusty."

I guessed it right! But I didn't suspect that the *Feldführer* was in on it, the one who had already been arrested "for gold" and kept in the Lublin Castle for ten days. Then I am working near the office, cutting withered marigolds—it's a good observation point. Thumann approaches and orders to see Birzer, who is somewhere on the field, probably with his betrothed. Birzer comes running. Thumann calls him over to the entryway of the office and asks him who murdered Marmorstein. Birzer replies that he knows nothing. Then Thumann orders him to lie on the rack and starts whipping him. Birzer, the old, hardened *Häftling*, doesn't make a single sound. He gets maybe fifty lashes. At last, he stops whipping and orders the block overseer, Rajchman, whose barracks Marmorstein was sleeping in, to come over. Ten meters away, I keep fervently cutting the wilted marigolds. Rajchman claims that he doesn't know anything, that no one came to the barracks at night, and that Marmorstein left the barracks in the early morning. Thumann orders him to lie down and starts whipping. Rajchman groans and cries. Thumann halts the lashing and says:

"I'll keep hitting you until you tell the truth."

The Jew pleads that he doesn't know anything. More strikes fall on him. He gets maybe sixty lashes. Thumann is out of breath, he stops the whipping. He orders Rajchman's son (the typhus convalescent) to come over, who happens to be the barracks clerk for his father. I know if I mentioned the brushing of the corpse's feet, Thumann would stop whipping those two innocent Jews, but I also know that tomorrow morning I would be hanging like that "suicide" in the latrine!

During lunch I visit the Rajchmans to express my sympathy and ask about their health. The elder Rajchman suffered worse than his son. With tears in his eyes he admits that, after all, he couldn't rat out Birzer, since he knew that he would hang him that night.

At noon they summon Birzer for an interrogation with Thumann, and in the afternoon the news spreads that Birzer admitted to the murder. And what a surprise, the punishment? He is demoted from *Lagerältester* to a kapo! He changes his armband and the next day he goes out to work with some *Kommando*, though he continues to live in the office where Aleksander Kaźmierczak, the cook from the MS *Batory* ocean liner, continues to prepare his meals.

Kapo Ott becomes our new *Lagerältester*. He used to be on Field 3 and was recently convalescing in the Revier, where Thumann brought him from. He has a red triangle, he is an *Oberlehrer*,[160] maybe even in a middle school. The whole field breathed a collective sigh of relief after the defanging of Birzer the murderer.

I learn from Meierovitz and the prisoners working in the bathhouse that we had a new *Zugang*. The entire *Kommando* from the crematorium in Auschwitz arrived. Several dozen people, mostly Jews, dressed to the nines and well-fed, with the armbands of kapos, *Vorarbeiter*, etc. "to take over work in our crematorium." Of course they needed to take the regulation shower. They were taken to the bathhouse, but they were led into the gas chamber. The information is confirmed that the SS men personally liquidate those that know too much. These dangerous *Kommando* include: the crematorium crew, the gas chamber crew, and those who work in the *Politische Abteilung*. An assignment to one of these is equal to a "suspended" death sentence.

Another transport arrives from Auschwitz: Jews who fell ill with malaria

160. Senior teacher.

there and were sent here as a camp that's in a dry, mosquito-free environment.[161] They come to Field 3. These are mainly Greek and Albanian Jews; there is also a handful of French and Polish Jews. They were sent here not so much to convalesce, but to rid Auschwitz of disease carriers. They say that Auschwitz is very malarial, that there is a terrible plague of mosquitoes, and that the camp command has two airplanes that spray the areas surrounding the camp every day with anti-mosquito chemicals. Naturally, the most important factor is maintaining the health of the SS men themselves. It's touching that the Auschwitz camp command took the trouble to send those sick with malaria away to Majdanek instead of straight to their own chimney! From them I learn about the existence of Rajsko,[162] where up to five crematoria work day and night. Overall, the Jews praise Auschwitz and say that it is a cut above in every way. There are multistory brick buildings with rooms containing fifteen to twenty beds, and even bigger halls. They all have tiled stoves, double windows, decent washrooms, and lavatories in every building. The Revier is organized very well, medical care there is first-rate, and there is a rich variety of medical treatments. Food is much more plentiful there, with side dishes of cheeses, honeys, liver sausages, etc. There is a movie theater, library, and orchestra, and on Sundays soccer games take place. Prisoners subscribe to different newspapers, they get money mailed from home. There is no overtime work. During roll calls you don't take your caps off in front of SS men. It's inconceivable that a block overseer would strike a prisoner. No one takes off their cap in front of the *Lageraltester*. The Jews from Auschwitz judge Majdanek to be terribly primitive in every way compared to Auschwitz. Not long ago I heard the same opinion out of the mouths of the prisoners from Buchenwald.

The ban on Russians working outside the wires has been lifted. Some of this scourge will flow out beyond the fences and the atmosphere on the field will be more pleasant during the day.

A new sensation. A Russian prisoner denounced two fellow Russians for planning an escape at night. Both Russians are promptly taken to the office

---

161. The transport reached Majdanek on June 4, 1943.
162. A subcamp of Auschwitz-Birkenau.

and tied to a roof support post inside the building, and a young Jewish office boy is ordered to stand watch. At night the Russians tear off their fetters, crash their bodies through the locked door, and escape through the wires. But instead of going straight out to freedom, they climb through the illuminated wires onto Field 4; there, they steal knee-high boots from some barracks, climb through the illuminated wires onto the *Zwischenfeld* with the coal dump, and from there again get through the floodlit wires onto Field 5. Either their strength failed them or morning had broken, but for some unknown reason they didn't cross the final wires to escape, but hid in the cockloft above the kitchen. Trained dogs find them there before noon. The SS men lead them in shackles to Field 3, and in those shackles they tie them to the same post they broke away from. Now an SS man stands guard. Their faces are terribly bruised. All of us respect them for such a feat: prisoners put food in their mouths and lit cigarettes to their lips. Overnight they tie them seated to the post, without taking off their handcuffs. The next day they take them to Thumann for interrogation, from which they don't return. They murdered them.

The transport to Buchenwald left.[163] Zygmunt Godlewski, a civil servant who came in the first transport from Pawiak, is one of those who left. Now they start forming several transports of Jews to Auschwitz.

Thanks to the transfer of our entire field onto Field 4 a few weeks ago, that little Jew, Bubi, got stuck there and the *Feldführer* isn't bringing him back. His star has faded. Wyderka doesn't have his snoop any more. Bubi calls through the wires to his friends, badgering them to throw over a piece of bread or a sack with some stolen potatoes.

Thumann has ordered that a scale model be made of the entire camp with the surrounding terrain. The model is to be two by three meters in size. First we have to take leveling measurements to represent the terrain in relief, and only then build a model of the camp. The work is entrusted to Zelent, who is the technical *mädchen für alles*.[164] The *Vermessungskommando*[165] is

163. Five hundred prisoners were transported out on July 30, 1943.
164. Girl for everything.
165. Measurement *Kommando*.

created, some of its members go and take measurements with a theodolite, take blocks of wood and cut out miniature barracks with windows and chimneys, guard towers, etc. A splendid occupation.

I get a message from my brother that my unfailing friend Hańka is continuing the campaign in Lwów for my release. My brother has found another route and was going to Kraków, where he paid an advance of ten thousand zlotys to some German intermediary. He sends me a *résumé* of all the activities and lists five actions being taken independent of him in the effort to secure my release. At least one of them probably won't fail! The matter of my release, according to my brother, is a matter of several days. I tell him about the possibility of seeing each other in the *Gärtnerei* and I call on him to come.

My first cousin Stefan (an assistant professor of dermatology in Lwów) sends me a present from Professor Weigl. A series of anti-typhus shots. A gift worth 1,500 zlotys. Dr. Lewiner administers the injection, the next two are to be taken a week apart.

In a roundabout way, I learn about the horrible things the communist Jan Luba, whom I only met in Block 15, is saying about me. This bricklayer told Zelent that I only spoke German in Pawiak, that I only became a Pole when I got here, that I am Birzer's spy, and that while I am pretending to work, stooped over the flowers by the window of the *Lagerältester*, I am whispering information to him. The normal reaction would be to go and knock him in the mouth. But not in the camp. Various *Dementi*[166] won't help. Only my own conduct can confirm or deny this slander. I keep to myself and don't look for friends. I am in regular contact with Zelent but I feel that something unspoken stands between us.

It becomes established that we both identify educated Polish people from among the new transports who need help, and until they are set up we hire them in our *Kommando* and we often exchange people with one another who need a temporary stay under the roof of the workshop.

---

166. An official denial.

Auf der Flucht Erschossen[167]

The morning roll call brings a real bombshell. Birzer was gunned down last night. He's lying in cherry-red silk pajamas in the garden that I installed between the office (in Block 12) and Block 13. Another mystery. One of the kapos invited him around 9:30 p.m. to come to the garden and sit down for a talk ... It's such a gorgeous August night. Birzer came out in the company of Kapo Erich,[168] a young German communist, and they sat down on two chairs. Two shots rang out. Birzer was hit in the heart and fell to the ground. Erich was hit in the shoulder.

No one is allowed near the corpse. During the day a commission arrives, photographs the position of the body, and studies the entry and exit wounds and the mark left on the wall of the barracks. Supposedly, they established that the bullet came from the tower near the auto repair shops.

What we have is a mysterious scandal: the death of Marmorstein, the shooting of Birzer. Now I remember his words when I spoke to him about the retreat of the German armies and the possibility that we could leave Majdanek. Deep in thought, he told me:

"I'm not leaving this camp alive."

I hesitate for a moment as to whether, after the commission finishes, I should walk up to his body and lay a few of the flowers that he liked so much upon his chest. He was good toward me, he recognized my work and once, when he knew about heavy punitive drills for the kapos and *Vorarbeiter*, he demoted me for the afternoon and took my armband, returning it to me the next day. Another time, after the roll call, he singled me out and told me to go with my *Kommando* to do some immaterial job. It surprised me but I got to work. Then I heard all of the overseers, clerks, and *Vorarbeiter* being called for punitive exercises. He had bailed me out again.

167. Shot while trying to escape.
168. Referring to Erich Hornung.

He did the same for Zelent. I concede all of this to him in my thoughts, but I have to show solidarity with my friends and countrymen, whom he drowned and tormented. I loudly tell myself "no" and walk away in another direction. The prisoners are universally delighted that he has been rendered harmless. I'm shaken by the words of those who cringed before him, supplied him with vodka, and drank with him, such as my overseer, Olczyk, who now speaks of him with contempt. He could at least stay silent and not slight himself.

The prisoners are afraid to talk about the incident, but Pietroniec tells me in confidence that Birzer was shot from the tower by our former *Rapportführer*, the current *Feldführer* of Field 4, Kaps, who shot crows mid-flight so well from his rifle. I learn from my friends in the Revier that the camp doctor recorded the cause of death in the *Totenmeldung*[169] as "shot while trying to escape," and even more interestingly, Marmorstein's was listed as "pneumonia." This confirms the murkiness of the affair and the desire to cover it up. It's evident that powerful forces behind the scenes came into play. This explains everything that Marmorstein possessed, millions in jewelry. The plundered gold didn't bring good fortune, two people have paid for it with their lives, and it seems like it's not over yet.

With Birzer gone from the scene, a huge relaxation takes place on the field. Ott is courteous, polite, shakes our hand, joins in conversations, issues orders in the form of questions: "Wouldn't it be better to do it like this?" … "Wouldn't it be advisable?" The nightmare that weighed on the camp has disappeared. People lie down to bed peacefully. The only deplorable thing is the sight of the displaced peasants who are deteriorating from the camp's room and board. They don't get any packages; who would send them, as entire villages were evacuated? Many infants and small children die, and the same goes for older women. They are fortunate that at least they haven't been forced to work. They are cooped up in the stuffy air and stink of the sunbaked wooden barracks, consumed by fleas and bedbugs. Every day the Gestapo and SD come from Lublin to register them. Next, they read lists of names. Why, nobody knows. They hint at sending the

169. Report on the death of a prisoner.

peasants away, but where, nobody knows. They lead people in groups to the *Effektenkammer* and return their bundles, sheepskin coats, pots, and pans. A week later trucks and Polish Red Cross (PCK) ambulances arrive and take around a thousand people. Half the roll call square by the office where those leaving are gathered is isolated, and no *Häftling* is allowed near. While this group is getting onto the vehicles and leaving the camp, the SS men are checking to be sure that some prisoner hasn't strayed among them. While the Gestapo is on the field and talking to the *Feldführer*, he calls me over and reproaches me for the sewage drain not being clean. This is Luba's job. I reply that the work doesn't belong to my *Kommando*, which gets me two strikes with a reed to my bare head and the order to call over the right people. As I leave I hear the voice of the Gestapo agent from the castle behind me:

"*Vielleicht möchtest du laufen.*"[170]

I find out that the Red Cross is placing the peasants in nearby villages. Thank God that they aren't being taken to Germany.[171] Every day a thousand or more leave. Unfortunately, no one will resurrect those infants and seniors who wasted to death from thirst and the most primitive hygienic conditions. I see the remains of an old woman sprawled in the dust of the roll call square and her daughter crying over her for hours. A southern-looking raven-haired woman is roaming around the field—she lost her mind in the camp. She seems like a country teacher. She's the subject of ridicule and cruel jokes by the Russians.

While one of the last groups is being transported away, they turn the water back on for the field. But every day during this period I had to take several dozen buckets of water from the hydrant so that the marigolds by the gate wouldn't wilt!

Certain *Kommando* from Field 4 move into the empty barracks and new transports also arrive. Normal camp life resumes, it's almost pleasant under the regime of the new *Lagerältester*, Ott. Block 15 fills back up with the same Poles. I set myself up so that I lie down to bed in the highest bunk

170. "Maybe you'd like to run."
171. Some of the displaced persons from the Zamość region were released, but the majority were pressed into forced labor in Germany.

at the back of the barracks, falling into a deep sleep instantly and I wake up to the work bell. I form up my *Kommando* and we head out for work, then I return to the barracks and eat my lukewarm soup set aside for me by the *Stubendienst*. I eat, hidden between the beds. I keep several gardening tools in the barracks, so that in case of an inspection I can explain myself for being inside during work hours. A forty-five-minute nap during lunchtime really refreshes me.

Because of the surplus of people and the inability to put everyone to work, a selection takes place every morning before the *Kommando* head out for work. The sick, *gamel*, emaciated, those unable to work because of a beating or the redundant, are ruled out. The overseers lead them to a square surrounded by a tall fence by Block 19 (which is again a rallying point for Jews being sent to the gas chamber). There they sit on the bare ground or stand, in the sun or rain, and a surly guard stands by the gate with a bat and doesn't let anyone out before the evening roll call. When some extra work comes up during the day, the *Vorarbeiter* go there to get more people for the job. The prisoners pester us insistently to take them for work. The reason isn't a spontaneous urge to work—but the opportunity to break out of that prison within a prison and the ability to move around freely during work, to see other people and maybe to organize some potatoes or a bowl of soup. Some of these "volunteers" bolt once they pass through the gate and just rove between the barracks.

The golden calf Moloch has consumed another sacrifice. The commandant of Field 4, Kaps, was arrested. Talk is getting louder that he shot Birzer. He certainly didn't do this for ideological reasons; rather, he wanted to neutralize someone who knew about the looting of Jewish jewelry carried out by Kaps.

Another blockbuster. Kapo Steiner from the camp auto shops has escaped.[172] He went to Lublin with an SS man, with whom he regularly drove to some local auto shop. He wore gray riding pants, without red painted stripes, in elegant, knee-high boots, a silk sport shirt, and, as a

---

172. Fritz Steiner was removed from the camp rolls on July 12, 1943.

German, he had permission from the commandant to wear his hair long. Having taken off his number and green triangle from his pants, he didn't attract any attention on the street. The SS man often let him go on his own in Lublin and Steiner always came back. Once, he betrayed his trust. Since Steiner sometimes visited the sister of one of the prisoners, as a reprisal for his escape, that prisoner was placed between the wires by the gate. He stands there for several days on the gravel, without meals or his cap.

Lagerältester Ott tells me that his predecessor, Rockinger, who went to the SS, was again sent to a concentration camp, this time to Buchenwald, from where the notification came. It's understandable to me. Rockinger was bragging in June that he spent fifty thousand zlotys in the past month. Of course everything came from robberies and bribes. But when he went to the army and got a few marks in pay, he couldn't afford to satisfy his whims like he could in the camp. So he likely continued to steal and ended up behind the wires again. It turns out that calling those with green triangles *"Berufsverbrecher,"* or habitual offenders, is on the mark.

One of the people working in my *Kommando* is Wiktor Domański, a film actor in Warsaw. A big lazybones—but first-rate in finding out all of the latest rumors on the field. When he leaves at 2:00 p.m., he returns at 6:00 p.m., even though he was excusing himself for "half an hour." It turns out later that he was shaving, sleeping, etc.

I get a message from my brother that he was in Lublin but he couldn't get ahold of me. He was in the wrong place, not near the composts. He left a bountiful package at the RGO to have delivered to me. He says he'll be back in a week. I'm living in unbelievable excitement, anticipating the moment I see him. I prepare a long list to my cousin Ninka, which I want to give him.

Thumann orders that the potatoes planted between the barracks be dug up and given to him. *Tableau.* He has some dispute with the head of the *Gärtnerei* who was flippant toward him in some matter. So Thumann decided to supply himself with potatoes from us. And here, *Lagerältester* Birzer and all the German kapos had already ordered potatoes dug up for themselves, and following their example, all the block overseers and clerks did the same in secret. I pretended not to see any of it. Ultimately, other prisoners started tearing out entire unripe potato plants. Now, when ordered to dig out all of the potatoes, I gathered about five bushels, and I had planted fourteen. Ott comes to me in despair and asks what we should do—at the same time alerting me to hide about two bushels for him for later. Upon seeing the miserable result of the potato harvest, he orders the Solomonic verdict of having every block overseer whipped fifteen times. It's almost a just sentence, but since the kapos who were doing the lashing also didn't have a clean conscience, and Thumann didn't administer any of the whips himself, the flogging was more of a ceremony of symbolic punishment.

There are still complaints about the mail. Packages don't arrive, especially the most valuable ones. The Slovak Jews came up with a new method. Packages that they can see are wrapped well, are unpacked at the post office, repackaged into different paper, and addressed to their trusted friends. The Jews are still forbidden from receiving any letters or packages.

Seeing My Brother

The *Lagerältester* is told by Thumann to plant the former potato patches with lettuce or kale. It's an excellent excuse for me to go to the *Gärtnerei*. But I put off these expeditions until my brother arrives, so that I have a reason for being in the gardens.

On April 8, around 4:00 p.m., I get notified that my brother is waiting for me. I drop everything and report to the office that I'm going to the *Gärtnerei*. I go to the composts, but a messenger tells me that my brother had waited all afternoon and left, and that he will be back at 7:00 a.m. The lookouts will be the same people. I spend the night in eager anticipation, I wish the meeting had already taken place, since it causes me a lot of worry. Finally the morning bell, roll call, I can't wait until 7:00 a.m., I take my assistant Wszelaki and another friend with a handbarrow. The messenger-observer leads me to the lookout, who calls out with joy that my brother is waiting and he was here yesterday. I am ten meters from the edge of the camp. Wszelaki finds a vantage point on a hill thirty meters away to keep an eye out for any approaching SS men. My brother appears in the gate of the village farmstead and walks out to the middle of the road. The lookout advises him to stand in the gate so that he draws less attention to himself and encourages me to talk with my brother. What should we talk about, what should I ask him, what should I say. What's crucial in my situation? The conversation is heavy going. I ask him about my release. He tells an incredible story, that the Organization Todt[173] has the right to select a certain number of prisoners from the concentration camps, that Hańka paid twenty thousand zlotys to put my name in sixth place on the list, that only the first three were taken under consideration, and that in the next application I'm supposed to be first. The lookout orders me to back up since someone is driving by. Then he gives the sign and I approach and bend

173. Created in 1938 in Germany, Organization Todt was tasked with building military installations. Work was initially done by Germans, later also by forced laborers from countries occupied by the Third Reich.

over, pretending to dig. My brother tells me that the organization issued a death sentence against Sobczak, the informant who ratted me out. Now, Wszelaki calls out from behind for me to move back, since some SS man is nearing the composts. My anxiety goes through the roof. After fifteen minutes I come back to the same spot. I tell my brother that he doesn't look good, I see he's also stressed. I throw my letter to my cousin onto the road, some kids run over, pick it up, and take it to my brother. He tells me that the Gestapo agent, Goerke, the one in charge of my case, searched my place on Żurawia Street and took all of my awards and medals, as well as the medals of our dearly departed father. My brother asks me if I'd like vodka. I reply, gladly. He buys a liter bottle from the owner of the farmstead right away and the woman carries it out in a bucket in the direction of the well, placing it between the cabbage heads. I tell my brothers that I'll use the expression *"gajowy"*[174] in my letters as a euphemism for SS men. Wszelaki calls out again that an SS man is approaching. I bid farewell to my brother and I'm happy that our meeting is over.

I am exhilarated. We didn't say much to one another but I was shaken out of my internal lethargy. I think about whether it was good that we saw each other at all, since we communicated the most important things in our messages. My brother is standing by the gate—I back up to Wszelaki. A female prisoner—working on the field—who observed the entire conversation that I had with my brother backs up and takes a handbarrow with her friend, they are picking cabbage. They go to where the vodka is and place it under the cabbage. The SS man is roving around nearby, they retreat into the terrain where the women are working. Finally, they make a turn and near the mounds of compost with their handbarrow—in one motion Wszelaki grabs the bottle and shoves it into a heap of trash. The SS men are roaming, sniffing around, sensing that something is being passed around. I see my brother from a distance, he's leaving at last. Thank God that it's over.

An hour later we go back, with handbarrows full of something green, to the sand mine, that's where our column is, taking sand for the concrete slabs on Field 3. The vodka goes into the sand and in an hour it's on the

174. Polish: gamekeeper.

field, it disappears from the wagon during the lunch break into my package of food. I give Wszelaki a gulp, give some to the drivers, and the squeeze to the clerk, Knips, leaving half a bottle for me. I treat it with care and only take one gulp, leaving the rest for a number of evenings.

I lie down to bed and start calmly digesting the sensations and the news my brother gave me. The story about the special privilege of the Organization Todt to claim a certain number of prisoners from concentration camps looks like a big scam to me. Too bad that they let themselves get duped out of twenty thousand zlotys. Good that the informant Sobczak got a death sentence. Those kinds of bottom-feeders should be dealt with mercilessly.

Sobczak was the "innocent" head of the disciplinary department of the Warsaw Insurance Company, nominated by the German receivership manager, Kurth. Sobczak bore an unbelievable grudge against me for asking for his identification in my office in my "Pioneer" machine tool factory when he showed up there in November 1942. He refused to show his ID to the doorkeeper or to sign the factory's visitor log, which the doorkeeper immediately informed me about by telephone. I made speaking with him conditional on his showing his ID. He spoke to me in German, foaming at the mouth, claiming to be an SS officer and that it was the first time that a Pole asked for his identification. He was either ashamed of his Polish last name, or wanted to conceal it completely. Steam was coming out of his ears when I wrote his name and ID number into the calendar on my desk.

He had shown up because of a complaint I had filed to the receivership administrator of the insurance company against the company inspector, a Ukrainian. After inspecting the list of payments and deductions to the insurance company he had threatened my staff, even though no problems were found. He said that in the case of any discrepancies the factory's women bookkeepers would be hung and they could choose where they were to be hung, in the Okęcie or Żoliborz districts. This was during the period of mass public hangings of fifty people at a time, while the accompanying proclamations of Governor Ludwig Fischer stated that communists had been hung. During the conversation with Sobczak, who was interrogating my staff and determining the course of the incident, I said that alleged communists had been hung. Then he jumped out of his chair:

"*Halt!*" he exclaimed and turned to the clerk accompanying him: "You are a witness to what this man said." And turning to me, saying: "You questioned the validity of the official announcement of the Governor of the Warsaw District."

I was already expecting to be arrested back then, and all the more so a few days later, while I was still in the insurance company, when I learned from one of the department heads that Sobczak had been the commissioner of the Polish Criminal Police in Poznań before 1939 and now he was in the branch office of the Gestapo in the insurance company, that's why he was the head of the disciplinary department.

On February 18, 1943, I was typing propaganda articles in my office in the factory when I heard heavy footsteps on the stairs. I managed to pull the half-typed piece of paper out of the typewriter and hide it in the drawer of the typewriter stand when Sobczak entered my room, without knocking, alongside some other officer. I didn't have time to sit down at my desk before he was already in the middle of the room. He asked about Pietrzak, the electrician. I picked up the receiver to call the foreman in the assembly hall—the line was dead, it didn't work. I called for the office boy, he didn't come. So I had to go to the hall myself and ask the nearest worker to call Pietrzak. This took maybe a minute. When I came back to my office I saw the drawers of my desk had been pulled out, and right then Sobczak was pulling out the drawer under the typewriter where I put away what I was writing. He started to read. At that moment, Mary called and asked me about the results of the search by my friends in the *Arbeit-samt*[175] as to whether her cousin, Marchwicki, who vanished without a trace a few days ago, is being held on Skaryszewka Street,[176] or whether he was sent as forced labor to Germany. I'm half-conscious while speaking to her, and I tell her I didn't find any information. Next, Sobczak took the receiver and connected to someone, saying that he found compromising documents and asking whether he should bring the culprit in with him immediately. He put down the phone and told me that I'm coming with

175. The Nazi German state employment office, established in occupied Poland in September 1939, it enforced mandatory work requirements and supplied forced laborers.

176. A transit camp in Warsaw on Skaryszewska Street 8, for Poles detained during round-ups and sent as forced labor to Germany.

him and if I try to escape he'll make use of his firearm. I used the internal line to call to the other manager, my partner, to come to me right away. When he saw Sobczak, the blood drained out of his face. I told him that I wanted to say goodbye, he became pale, I shook his hand in silence. We got into Sobczak's car on the courtyard of the factory and we drove to Szucha Avenue. There he handed me over to the clerk on duty and threw the papers in question on the table, saying:

"Ones like him are the most dangerous for us."

I was taken to the so-called trolley car in the basement of the former Ministry of Education. While sitting there in silence for four hours, facing the wall, I realized where I was and what awaited me. Two floors up there is an elegant office where my brother used to work as the head of the legal department. His tenure ended with the arrival of the Germans. Now I had started a new stage of my life in the depths of that building.

Infandum, regina, iubes renovare dolores![177]

All of the memories of the past six months came to life in front of my eyes. I remember all of my courageous friends from Pawiak, who returned brutalized from interrogations on Szucha Avenue, I remember meetings with various academic luminaries and dignitaries of the Warsaw city government in the underground cells of the VIII and then VII units of Pawiak—I recall the meeting with my adversary in a cramped cell, whom I didn't "notice" in the nine-square-meter space, until he came up to me with an extended hand and apologized. Yes, even the best film directors with the most vivid imaginations can't compare to what life has in store.

I remember the details of my disgrace. I was already in Unit V at Pawiak, the so-called transport unit. I was acting as a translator there, and Schuch-Börzel (half-Pole, half-Swede) was the clerk. Zygmunt Łempicki, a professor of German studies, submits a letter to the Gestapo where he asserts that his arrest was based on a misunderstanding, since he was an official guest at the *Parteitag*[178] in Nuremberg several times. There he was

177. Latin: "Great queen, what you command me to relate renews the sad remembrance of our fate." A quote from Book 2 of Virgil's *Aeneid*, the beginning of Aeneas's story of the capture of Troy.

178. Party convention.

introduced to Hitler as the protector of the Union of German Students of the University of Warsaw, and despite the recommendation of the Polish government, he did not resign his position. He states that in his published writings he promoted the idea of National Socialism, that he is very sympathetic toward the Germans, that he gave Germans shelter in his home during the wartime operations in 1939, and this fact can be confirmed, among others, by Dr. Grundmann, the head of the propaganda department in the Warsaw District (he once published a German guidebook of Warsaw).[179] Schuch-Börzel and I read this letter with disgust at the time, telling each other that we both have to remember it well in order to reveal the compromising content at the appropriate time. This is how characters broke down, and not just those of lesser mortals, but among outstanding, educated personalities with venerable, armorial surnames. During the war he had worked in the *Kommissarische Verwaltung Sichergestellter Grundstücke* (Receivership of Appropriated Jewish Homes) headquartered in the *Bank Gospodarstwa Krajowego* (National Development Bank), and when other university professors were availing themselves of aid from the RGO so as not to die of hunger, he could afford to eat breakfast every day in the most expensive restaurant in wartime Warsaw, Taverne on Świętokrzyska Street.

No wonder scoundrels like Knips, Silesian "insurgents" who correspond with their wives in Polish, send their sons as volunteers to the Luftwaffe and become *Volksdeutsche*. The Germans themselves rightly called them "*Konjunkturschwein.*"[180] Someone like Zelent, a descendant of Dutch colonists, a young academic, assistant professor of the Warsaw Polytechnic, could have taken a lucrative position in the armaments industry. Instead, he preferred to work for his daily bread as a motorman in the Warsaw-Grodzisk Electric Access Trains, which elevates his stature monumentally in comparison to the others . . .

179. Karl Grundmann, *Führer durch Warschau mit zahlreichen Abbildungen, Verzeichnis der Deutschen Behörden, öffentlichen Einrichtungen, Angaben über den Distrikt und Stadtplan mit neuen Deutschen Strassenbezeichnungen*, Kraków, 1942.
180. Opportunistic pig.

This is how I spent the entire night in bed, and like in a movie, all of the past months played out before the eye of my soul.

On September 12, 1943, Albin Boniecki, the sculptor, a dear friend of Zelent's, is released. He is ordered to present himself the following day with a shaved head—but someone revealed to him that he would be set free. We all congratulate him. Each of us gives him some verbal instructions. Three days later, Bielecki is released, the retired civil servant from the Ministry of Transportation, and a member of the executive committee of the National Party. We consider it to be the beginning of some larger series and that the releases are proceeding alphabetically.

The stolen gold, to which so many tears and curses have clung, consumes another victim. Our *Feldführer* disappears, the one, it was persistently told, who had been locked up for a couple of weeks in the Castle while he was being investigated and who recommended that Marmorstein's pants be cleaned with a brush. They hint that Thumann is also mixed up in this affair. It keeps spreading its reach. The new *Feldführer* is *Arbeitsdienstführer* Gosberg, which means that *Rapportführer* Sieberer gets skipped over for promotion.

In place of *Lagerkapo* Krause, who leaves with Wyderka for Field 4, we get Tomaschek, a Czech from Vienna, a carpenter by trade. Intelligent, very humane, and favorably disposed toward us Poles, speaking to us in Czech, and replying to our greetings.

In the sheds of the old crematorium, next to the laundry, where prisoners were shot or killed with crowbars, a storehouse for old clothing and underwear has been set up. Dębski from the *Bekleidungskammer* tells me that the walls of the shed are thickly perforated from revolver bullets. They are the traces of the executions carried out.

Domański took part in a spiritistic séance with a small saucer and "he" said that a truce would be signed on September 21, 1943. Great happiness and expectation for this day. The news from the front is such that you can guess that the German army is retreating across the entire front.

The *Gärtnerei* is being difficult as far as giving out seedlings for planting out the potato fields. The *Arbeitsdienstführer* comes running and says that thanks to the intervention of the camp commandant with the *Gärtnerei*, we get the seedlings. It doesn't matter what we plant, the main thing is to plant something, since Thumann is coming back from his vacation in three days and all the plots have to be seeded. Before I could prepare the ground for planting, prisoners from the *Gärtnerei* unexpectedly bring me about ten handbarrows of lettuce and turnip seedlings and dump them in the sunniest spot. In the camp, everything is done backward; instead of preparing the ground in advance, the work begins by digging out the seedlings. I still have to carve several dozen pegs, make a line out of ropes, and find people who may have once planted something in their lives. These preparations take half the day. The effect of the work was about right. Despite pitting the plants, only half of them took, since the process lasted two days. The young plantlets couldn't bend to the concentration camp method of planting. In any case, what's the point of planting lettuce in the middle of September? The nights are cold, it's planted in the shade. But the end result is not the issue, it's just a matter of rushing the prisoners along with work, which is free after all.

Lagerältester Ott tells me that he will be leaving his position, to be taken over by the *Lagerältester* of Field 1, Hessel. At the same time, the *Lagerschreibstube*, the camp administrative office, led by Hessel who is also the First *Lagerschreiber*, is moved onto our field. I see Ott showing Hessel around the field. He is a tall, broad-shouldered, blond-haired main in gold glasses, around thirty-five or forty years old, with the appearance of a typical Prussian officer. He moves with the entire office, staffed by the Slovak Jews, and the next day, all of Field 1 moves to our field as well. The Revier from Field 1, which took up half of the barracks there, is moved to Field 5. The women move from Field 5 to Field 1. It's a gain for the Revier, as it now gets the entire field. Whereas the women get the most nicely organized field of them all, since Field 1 has modern living barracks, while on Field 2 the *Lazarett für sowjetrussische Kriegsversehrte*, a hospital for Soviet invalids, has recently been set up. Fields 3 and 4 are what remain for male prisoners.

After the move, Hessel holds a meeting with all his functionaries, and by the manner of his speech, I see that he is an eminently unpleasant type. After a personal brush with him, the reputation that he brought from Field 1 is confirmed.

How idiotically people are engaged in work just to keep them in constant motion. At the end of September on an area of several acres in the *Gärtnerei*, carrots are planted! Don't spare the seed, don't spare the human effort, as long as the prisoners work: tempo, tempo!

I Get My *Fluchtpunkt*

It is September 26, 1943. Six months ago I arrived in Majdanek. I believe that the hardest times are behind me. During the evening roll call they call Knips to the front. He returns with three *Fluchtpunkte* in his hand and tells me:

"You are to sew these to your clothes."

"Why?" I ask.

"I don't know anything, they told me nothing."

What happened? I run over to the office to Dr. Horowitz after the roll call, but he can't provide any information either. The next day I see the new *Lagerältester* and ask why I received the *Fluchtpunkte*. He doesn't know anything as well, but he presumes that either I wanted to escape while I was being arrested or that my illegal communications with the outside world were uncovered here in the camp. But neither one applies in my case. Something else must be behind it. I sew a point on my chest below the triangle, in the place where you would wear a medal of distinction on a tailcoat; I sew the second point on my pants under my number, and the third on my back. I ask *Feldführer* Gosberg if he knows why I was given the *Fluchtpunkte*. He only laughs and says that he doesn't know anything about it. I don't give up. I ask Pietroniec, who knows some of the Slovaks in the *Politische Abteilung*, requesting that they discreetly take a look at my files. It's a very risky thing and prisoners working in the *Politische Abteilung* are strictly forbidden from sharing any information. Nevertheless I get a message that Thumann used a red pencil to write *"Fluchtverdacht"*[181] on my files, and what's most interesting—the directive came from the Warsaw Gestapo. Goerke is a scumbag! On the one hand he's negotiating with Broniek Albinowski and assuring him that he's sending the factory's application for my release to the *Reichssicherheitshauptamt* with a positive

181. Flight risk.

recommendation, while at the same time sending a dispatch to Majdanek to "put a black mark" on me! I also learn that I am classified into *Lagerstufe* I. What this means, no one can tell me.

I can't say that I'm happy about these points, but I am proud of them, since the Gestapo now counts me among the "big fish," and I get the feeling that my close friends treat me with greater respect as a result. The immediate consequence for me is that I can't leave the field without an SS man accompanying me. Never mind, though, I work on the field and I don't have much business outside of it. What's more unpleasant is that I might have to move to Field 4, where all of the other *Fluchtpunkte* are concentrated. The *Feldführer*, who has known me for three months, assures me that I will stay on Field 3. This is very valuable since I have friends and established relationships here, whereas there I would have to start camp life all over again.

At the end of September, a large transport from Lwów arrives. I get a hold of Alojzy Stamper, a member of the National Party's supreme council, and Jerzy Meinhardt, an articled clerk, to be part of my squad.

Field 3 is drowning in flowers. The rows of flowers along the length of the entire roll call square have bloomed in every color. Since the square rises up onto a hill, there is a wide swath of blooming asters visible across its length. The rows of asters and snapdragons in front also display every color. As I work by the wires, I hear the admiration of the SS men and prisoners from other fields over the riot of colors. Now I have a very pleasant occupation. For several weeks, on an almost daily basis, I am asked to bundle together several bouquets of flowers. They are mostly for various *Schar-* and *Sturmführers* and I know what they like, since they mostly pick up the bouquets themselves. Back in my student days in Vienna I marveled at the gorgeous flower arrangements in florists' shops and the indefinable talent for tying even a modest bouquet of violets in a way that was unrivaled by any other capital. Now I am learning how to arrange and tie flowers myself. The SS yokels mostly demand medleys. But if I have a free hand, then I take delight in matching two or three pastels, but arranging each bunch with different shades. I am most glad to put together subtle arrangements of hues for Kapo Meierovitz, who falls in love with some nurse on Field 5. He has exceptional sophistication and appreciation of beauty. While tying these flowers I forget about where I am and it seems like I am in my garden in Komorów. Yes, Komorów was also a preparation for Majdanek. Back then, when my guests (including dear "Fendruś") walked around at night in cloaks—I kept wearing shorts and a sleeveless sport shirt. Maybe that's why I was able to survive the freezes here in a jacket without a vest.

I went out today with a unit of Jews to get limestone for the borders of the flower beds. We were beyond Field 6 which is still being built. We pass the new crematorium, which is being finished. Next to it, behind a makeshift fence, lies a stack of corpses and a pile of wood heaped up on rail track, ready for burning. Since the time of the World War, 1914–1918, I have been familiar with the smell of dead bodies. But this mass of corpses emits such a foul odor that despite covering my nose with a handkerchief, I vomit.

Zelent came up with something new. Among the members of his *Kommando* is Engineer Eustachy Gorecki, a person of remarkable talents. He can draw just as well with his left hand as his right, and he is prodigious at playing chess from memory, winning matches while sitting backward to the chessboard. When I announce the moves made by his opponent, sometimes he asks him why he played it that way and gives him a chance to take it back. Gorecki is adept at mirror writing with his left hand.

At the same time, Szcześniewski, who worked on the restoration of the castle in Zamość, knows its layout and architecture by heart. So Zelent suggests to the *Feldführer* that a miniature of the castle could be erected as a decoration on the field, since other fields have set up crude miniature strongholds in Gothic style in their gardens. The *Feldführer* is enthralled by the idea. Our belief was poured into the work. Of course, we don't say that it's Zamość, just a figment of our imaginations. We produce thousands of tiny, quadrangular cement bricks, and pentagonal ones for the wall recesses. We erect the castle on the embankment near the washroom barracks. The foundation is made out of concrete. The stronghold is about seven meters wide, battlements are made, drawbridges and slopes. The master bricklayers conjure up a gem. A miniature of the Zamość Castle is being built inside a concentration camp! What joy. We are raring to go. I already thought through the design to include the planting of trees, using dwarf conifers, cotoneasters, and rock plants, which I saw in the *Gärtnerei* nursery. Gorecki drew up coats of arms with decorative borders, which are different for each gate. Hessel spends hours observing the work.

He is a very harsh boss. He sets a pensum of work that has to be done and ends his instruction with the sacramental clause:

"If it's not done by the roll call, *bekommst du den Arsch voll.*"

The sewage ditches alongside the barracks are laid out with concrete slabs. If in Ott's day the laborers laid fifty slabs, Hessel currently demands seventy-five slabs laid down. Before, the slabs sat out and dried for a week after they were poured; now, because of a lack of materials, he orders us to take the slabs three days after they were poured. Of course, loads of material cracks during the work. Because of this, the top edges of the ditches have to be sodded again. Since the work has to be done according to Hessel's deadline, it's done for show in the evening, since he runs around and checks if everything has been finished, and the next day the makeshift section is taken apart and put together solidly.

We are sentenced to be locked up in the camp until the end of the war (assuming we survive)—and the work is carried out in such a tempo as if we were leaving the camp in two weeks. Hessel has an idée fixe when it comes to concrete borders. It drives poor Zelent crazy. After laying out the sewage ditches on both sides of the roll call square, he orders all of the flower beds to be bordered with concrete slabs. What a waste of cement! I couldn't get a bag of cement for my factory in 1942 in order to patch the pitted concrete floor—and here the SS uses wagonloads of cement to surround flower beds and pave gutters. It's sabotage—from the German perspective, but the SS stands above these rules. Unexpectedly, the chief of the *Bauhof* visits us, an SS officer independent of the camp commandant. When he saw the building of Zamość, he ordered the work halted and the structure dismantled, and for the bricks to be crushed to rubble and used to line the roads and paths. Too bad we couldn't finish the project. Those masons working on the construction, Zelent, Szcześniewski, and Gorecki, swear a solemn oath to each other that they will build the miniature of Zamość in the exact spot if they live to see freedom and independence.

When I ask to be excused for half an hour on Wednesday to go shower with the regular group of functionaries, Hessel denies me, justifying it by saying that I have too much work for me to go bathe.

The Plan to Liberate the Camp

Lipski, Serafin, Kaszubski, and Szwajcer are moved from Field 4 to our field. I take Lipski on to work for me and assign him to husk dried flower seeds in the metalworker's shop, where the furnace has been lit since the morning, ostensibly to stoke the fire for heating steel. Zelent takes on the three others.

My relations with Zelent have finally warmed up. He started conversing with me, mentioning the rumors about me circulated by Luba, admitting that he has been observing me for a while and came to like me, while Luba lost face in front of close friends. His moral values became clear. Luba's friendship with Wyderka went to his head and he started beating prisoners from Block 15—something I often witness—knocking them to the ground, kicking them in the ribs, and throwing stools at their heads.

Frozen stiff, I sit down next to Lipski one day and help him husk the seeds. Our families are connected by bonds of friendship, since his uncle was a Jesuit superior and often visited my parents at home. I was in middle school then. We talk about prewar life in Warsaw, we learn that we have many mutual friends, he tells me about his conspiratorial work in the Lublin region during the war, I tell him about how I and my commercial representative, Jerzy Terpiłowski, armed trusted workers in the factory with revolvers, of shooting practice on Saturdays after closing time, and the unrealized attempts to buy an automatic rifle, interrupted by my arrest. After a few days he asks to speak with me, but cautions that it has to be after the roll call so that we are free to take a walk around the square.

We meet in the evening and Lipski declares to me that a liberation of the camp by underground soldiers is being planned, and that he is heading the operation. First Lieutenant Szwajcer is charged with commanding Field 3, and the task of the prisoners is to help on the inside, to take over the guard towers, while the rest of the work, such as dealing with the guard companies, the so-called *Standarte*, will be taken care of by the partisans.

He also confides in me that the Russian group in the camp, among whom is a Russian general, has been in contact with the outside and that the two actions are to be coordinated. The prisoners are to get hand grenades. It's a matter of creating units in each barracks and on each field who would be ready for action and would know what to do when the signal for liberation was given. He asks for my opinion and whether he can count on my cooperation. Without a second thought I swear to help him, but I start to critically analyze the different phases of the action. The way of getting into the camp and storing a large amount of grenades raises doubts for me. We take note of the large number of Jews in the camp, whom we can't let in on the secret; an element that was not combat-ready would create an unbelievable panic once things set off. Freeing two to three thousand people might work, but not fifteen to eighteen thousand. Of course it's not just a matter of smashing open the camp, but of leading all the prisoners to the forest, where they could change their clothes and spread throughout the region or defend themselves there. I ask how we could get immediate help if the SS men suddenly decided to gas the entire camp, which is what the worriers tell each other. Lipski replies that if necessary, one barracks on each field is to be successively set on fire and help from the neighboring forest would come right away. This kind of operation would cost lives, but it would be a one-time event and fewer prisoners would die than the number dying every month from being worked to death.

In the end, I inform Lipski that my intuition tells me that Zelent should be initiated into all of this and I will ask him whether he wants to talk to Lipski about it. Zelent agrees to talk, but mentions that he hasn't heard anything from beyond the wires about it. I can sense that the work of the underground on the field is concentrated in his hands.

The conversation between the two takes place the following evening. Zelent represents the ZWZ,[182] Lipski the NSZ,[183] but they come to a basic understanding. Lipski's subordinate in underground work on the outside was Pietroniec. I don't fill him in on my conversation with Lipski but, chatterbox that he is, he brags to me in secret that he got a confidential

182. Union of Armed Struggle, a Polish underground organization.
183. National Armed Forces, a Polish underground organization.

code for Lipski. I tell Lipski about this immediately to admonish Pietroniec right away about the need to stay silent, since these matters shouldn't be revealed to people unnecessarily.

Zelent, Lipski, and I are all open with each other.

The plan to liberate Majdanek was thought up by the NSZ, which, however, didn't have enough people to carry it out. Because of this, they made contact with the ZWZ in the Lublin area. The communists also had designs to liberate the camp. The NSZ and ZWZ wanted to work out the operation in detail, to prepare identification documents, clothing, and transportation, and think through the liberation down to the last steps of dispersing the freed prisoners. The communists, on the other hand, wanted to just initiate a prisoner uprising and escape without further planning, believing that things would develop somehow. The date set by the ZWZ and NSZ for the freeing of the camp was Christmas Eve 1943.

Among the more serious operatives in Majdanek who, beyond their personal affairs, are interested in the fate of the whole, besides Zelent and Lipski, include: Orpisz,[184] Krupski, Dębski, the lawyer M. Pruszyński, Dr. Sztaba, and the scout Szcześniewski. It doesn't mean that everyone is in agreement as far as the specifics. Sometimes there are controversies, like between Orpisz and Pruszyński, where the former, whetted with alcohol, almost blows his cover in the barracks during supper. Among the important figures on Field 3 are Colonel Łabędzki and Krupiński.

Hessel won't let me bathe again, putting it off until next week.

A high-ranking guest comes to the field. Theo Papst, formerly an SA *Gruppenführer*[185] and an SS major, has been transferred to the camp. He last lived in Kraków and was, according to his story, arrested for having too close of a relationship with a Polish aristocrat. The news makes its rounds throughout the field. The communist German kapos are angry with him. Georg Gröner, a German journalist who lived in France for a long time and was arrested after having emigrated to Yugoslavia, after drinking

184. A reference to Witold Ignacy Orzechowski, code name Longinus, arrested and interned at Majdanek under the name Witold Orpisz.

185. General in the *Sturmabteilungen der NSDAP*, the assault detachments of the NSDAP, the paramilitary arm of the Nazi Party.

on Sunday (two shots are enough), hurls abuse at Papst on the roll call square, calling him a party swine and such. I walk away since I don't want to be a witness to this incident, but, what a surprise—there is no reaction, he avoids any punishment.

Our *Blockführer* is Private First Class Müller, who my friend Malanowski (a civil servant in the Tobacco Monopoly Administration) knows by sight from before the war. A *Volksdeutsch* whose parents owned a store on Rybia Street in Praga-Kamionek. He is a specialist at searches. Whenever he pats someone down, he always finds something. The naive consider it "luck," but in fact he has his plants among the prisoners who spy on and denounce others. Then Müller goes in on a sure footing. I saw him walk into our barracks one evening and without looking around, went straight for some bed, and pulled a bottle of vodka out from under the mattress, and took a ring out of some person's pocket. Of course Müller pretends that he doesn't understand Polish. He often walks around drunk.

I was witness to an ugly scene today. The runner by the gate to Field 3 is Eli Szydłower, a young, 12-year-old Jew from Łódź. A fine boy, with an excellent upbringing, and decently dressed as a *Läufer*.[186] It is rewarding to converse with this child, who has proven uniquely immune to absorbing the vulgar atmosphere of the camp. He does not fraternize with older prisoners, is always clean and washed up, and acts like he would still be under the wholesome influence of his mother who was able to raise him so superbly. Müller comes to the office looking for his bicycle. He is totally wasted, he can barely stand up. With a nasally voice he cries out, "*Llll . . . äufer!*" Eli runs from the gate to him, Müller asks him where his bicycle is, which he left in his care. Eli replies that Corporal X took the bike even though Eli advised him that it was Müller's bike, and that SS man replied by hopping on the bike and calling over his shoulder that he'd be back in fifteen minutes. In response, Müller slaps the boy in the face and asks him why he allowed the bike to be taken. The boy's eyes well up with tears. Müller pulls his revolver out of its holster and announces that unless the

186. Messenger.

bike is found within ten minutes, he will shoot him. How is the poor lad to find the bicycle when the SS man rode it out of the camp? The boy runs to one of the barracks and hides. After ten minutes, Müller starts looking for him, and someone hearing him call out *"Läufer!"* obligingly points out where the boy is hiding; Müller pulls him out and takes him in front of the office. There he orders the rack to be brought out and starts mercilessly beating the boy with a thick, oak cane. Then he whips him, the boy is screaming at the top of his lungs, while Müller, in a drunken mania, keeps repeating: "Where's the bike, where's the bike, where's the bike," while he lashes. Finally the boy gets away and bolts. Müller pulls out his revolver and aims . . . but he doesn't pull the trigger. Poor Eli, totally innocent but so brutalized.

The morning roll call is dragging out. We learn that someone escaped from one of the barracks at night. Several weeks ago, night watches were introduced, which are supposed to guard against anyone leaving the barracks at night. The guards simplify the work for themselves and put a table in front of the barracks doors and go to sleep on it. The doors squeak in all of the barracks so this way the guards are alerted. The *Feldführer* announced that the block overseer and clerk will be held personally responsible for an escape from their barracks at night. So after the escape, they call the overseer and the clerk—two Slovak Jews—over to the *Feldführer*. Hessel manned most of the barracks with his toadies from Field 1. The interrogation starts, combined with slaps to the face, then whipping on the rack. Finally, they take the two to empty Block 13. *Feldführer* Gosberg and Hessel go in. Moans emanate from the barracks, silence has fallen over the square, you could hear a pin drop. The groans from Block 13 cease. A moment later, the command comes: *"Arbeitskommando formieren!"* While our units are forming up, we find out that Hessel said that both Slovaks hung themselves out of despair that a prisoner escaped from their block at night. I saw these "suicide victims" being carried out with bloody faces. Their clothes are covered in clotted blood and dusty from being dragged on the ground. I don't think a single prisoner believed in this act of despair, brought on by the overactive sense of responsibility of two Slovak Jews!

The *Feldführer* is often so drunk that he staggers when he walks. Everyone runs away when he's like this. He boozes it up with several SS men and the inseparable Hessel in the office. Tipsy from vodka, he calls some random Jew and puts him against a wall, places an apple on his head and plays William Tell with a swastika, shooting at the apple. The next day he gets ten days of house arrest; somebody denounced him. The conditions on the field are very unpleasant—what a bed of roses it was back in the times of *Lagerältester* Ott, who became the kapo in the *Poststelle*. He is now designated as the *Lagerältester* on Field 5, which has been totally neglected, since the women have not planted much there, and the area is woefully overgrown. After his nomination Ott wants to take me as the gardener to Field 5. While Dr. Horowitz tells me again that he is to become the head of the office on Field 6, which is still under construction, and is to consist only of workshops, he wants me there in the office.

The atmosphere on Field 3 is unpleasant in every respect. Practically all of the barracks are manned by Slovak overseers, the same goes for the entire *Lagerschreibstube*, only Slovak Jews, all of them arrogant with unbelievable nerve and self-confidence. All Hessel's talebearers, with the overseer of Block 13, Ferdinand, a fat, slaver type, at the forefront.

Szwajcer has come down with typhus and leaves for the Revier. Several days later, Lipski also gets typhus and departs as well. The entire plan to free the camp is underwater—or is on hold at least.

Thanks to the RGO, Polish prisoners are provided with anti-typhus shots, because the disease is intensifying again. There is a limited amount of serum but some of the prisoners are afraid to get the shot since someone started a rumor that the SS men were trying to poison us.

Meierovitz is taken to the Revier with the flu. Several days after he left, rumors swirl that Hessel brought about the reclassification of Meierovitz from an RD (*Reichsdeutsche*)[187] to J (*Jude*) and that he was ordered to sew on a star. They then deny this news and say that the order was annulled.

---

187. A German citizen living in the Reich.

Hessel calls all of the prisoners to the office who speak German fluently and can type it. Out of the entire field, eight or nine prisoners come forward, me among them, but Hessel rejects me because I can't be a clerk, since with my "points," my movements around the camp are limited.

I sleep next to Knips. He has constant diarrhea because of his uncontrollable gluttony, and he is so lazy that he orders a bucket placed next to his bed. He is too much of a slug to go to the crate, the so-called *Kübel*, but also too sensitive to have the bucket stinking under his nose, so he sticks it by the neighboring bed of some no-name *Häftling*. None of these common people has the courage to protest against using a bucket for fulfilling your bodily functions, which is then used the next day to pass out marmalade, curd cheese, or other side dishes. Knips has better food, I don't take the extras either, but 90 percent of people do. Passion gets the best of me one day when several of my scathing remarks have no effect and an argument starts, during which I am yelling for the whole barracks to hear. A few days later he is transferred to the *Poststelle*. Thank God that slimy character moved out of our Polish barracks.

Coming over as our clerk is the factory owner from Łódź, Krongold, a very cultured individual about thirty-five years old, who finished his studies in Belgium. He takes Knips's bed—we spend pleasant evenings together, lying in our beds next to each other and after the lights are out we share reminiscences of Paris, Brittany, and the Côte d'Azur. Unfortunately, the lights don't always go out, since the overseer, Olczyk, often invites several "Russkis" from the crematorium to gamble. The pot amounts to several thousand zlotys. The game often drags on until midnight. The light shines right into my eyes. But it's hard to war with the overseer.

As a result of the dramatic spread of typhus fever, they open a branch of the Revier on Field 3 and designate Blocks 20, 21, and 22 as the typhus wards. Dr. Hanusz, Dr. Matera, and Dr. Tomszewski are moved also, as well as Engineer Sopoćko, one of my first gardeners, who, after surviving typhus, stayed in the Revier as a nurse. These barracks are surrounded with barbed wire, partially extended into the roll call square, with a gate leading onto the area of these three isolated blocks. The entire enclosure, including the digging in of the posts and gate and the nailing of more than a dozen rows of barbed wire, had to be done by Zelent in a single evening. He got the order around 4:00 p.m. and finished the work after midnight. Hessel was screaming, "*Schnell, schnell!*"—and then the barracks stood empty for three days before the typhus section started to move from Field 5 to Field 3.

For weeks, the prisoners have been digging deep trenches near the crematorium and they assume that they are meant to be defensive positions in case of a surprise attack on the camp by partisans. Allegedly, these kinds of trenches are to be dug around the camp. In any case, several machine gun nests have been built in the *Gärtnerei* and several more on the side facing the main road, dug into the ground and covered with thick roofs and soil.

Gosberg got drunk again and for no reason took a bamboo stick to the overseer of Block 13, Svoboda, a Czech *Volksdeutsch* of Russian descent (quite the combination), beating him so badly in the head that he has to be sent to the Revier. Gosberg doesn't let him go to the hospital, so his friends get the SS doctor to come to the field under some pretext, and when he sees the wounded man he orders him taken to the Revier. There they make a report with Svoboda and another inquiry is opened up into Gosberg.

I learn that Pryłucki, the son of a Jewish editor and parliamentary representative, escaped from Field 4. He had a gold tooth removed with which he bought leather shoes. He already had civilian clothing. While working in some *Aussenkommando*, he fled, supposedly a Polish woman was waiting for him in a carriage. After two days, Pryłucki was captured and, surprise, surprise—he wasn't hanged, but only whipped, given a *Fluchtpunkt* and assigned to Field 5.[188] This change in the attitude of the SS men toward Jews is a sensation. Could it be that after hanging thirty or forty Jews for

188. This event took place on October 16, 1943. The escape was aided by Helena Pawluk, who was arrested, imprisoned at KL Lublin, and subsequently sentenced to death by the German Special Court on March 6, 1944. She awaited execution in the Lublin Castle prison and survived until the end of the occupation.

"attempting to escape," a fundamental change has taken place in the treatment of the Jews?

The frosts come at night, and in the morning there is a thin layer of ice on the water in the buckets standing inside the barracks.

A tremendous and pleasant surprise, we get jackets or coats, which we aren't allowed to wear for now. But it makes you look more calmly toward the impending winter, since we will be able to go around covered. The freeze already cut down the late varieties of asters, my work as a gardener is ending. What kind of job will I find in the winter with my *Fluchtpunkte*?

Blockführer Eberle often stops by to observe my work and chat with me. He is a Bavarian and lives right on the Swiss border. He likes to tell stories, but unfortunately it's hard to understand him. He never had a bat in his hand, his face always has a smile. He's the most solid SS man, generally liked by all the prisoners.

Lagersperre

We find out that *Lagersperre*[189] has been ordered on Field 3 because of the spread of typhus. Starting tomorrow, October 25, all contact between our field and the outside world is to be cut off. I immediately think of the letters which I won't be able to send and receive through my secret channels. Certain essential *Kommando* are moved to Field 4, such as the mailmen. Noak goes there, he is taken along with Knips to work in the post office. The field is totally isolated. A column of strangers brings food to the gate and leaves it, from there our people pull in the carriages. All of the sick are sent to the Revier branch established on our field. Most of the prisoners are unemployed, but the morning and evening roll calls are carried out just the same. The morning roll call is moved back a bit.

It starts at 6:00 a.m., so we wake up at 4:30 a.m., always going out onto the square in the moonlight though. This is how I remember the view of Lublin—I saw it in the spring, the summer, and now in the fall. I could draw the panorama of Lublin from memory today; I have the order of every building, roof, and tower etched in my mind. Every day I look at the massive form of the silo standing near the train station, although I can't see the station itself. The silo—maybe the first in Poland—was built by the State Grain Industry Corporation, with construction carried out by the "Engineer Mieczysław Szydłowski and Ska" company, and financed by the Polish Industrial Bank, where I was a vice president. Ancient history, 1928/1929! Once a week I came from Warsaw to the construction site to inspect the progress being made, depending on which the company would get further payments for the work. Standing on the scaffolding of the sixth floor, I gazed thoughtlessly and indifferently at the green hills surrounding Lublin where Majdanek now stands.

All of Field 3 must go to the bathhouse for delousing, and there we are supposed to get "clean" underwear and different clothes. At the same time

---

189. Quarantine.

the delousing of the barracks is to take place. How it's supposed to be done, nobody knows. Orders weren't issued. It isn't until 10:00 p.m. that they call the overseers to the office and they get instructions about how the delousing will be carried out. They are typically SS, unclear, unrealistic, mess-inducing, and put the lie to the opinion that Germans are great organizers.

At 4:00 a.m., while we are still half-dressed, they unexpectedly dump the straw mattresses from other barracks into ours. They heap them up chaotically, creating high obstacles in the passages between the beds. Our block is one of those where all of the mattresses from the entire field are to be gassed. A layman would realize that the gas won't reach these crushed mattresses. They order us to leave our recently issued jackets, which we still aren't allowed to wear, in the barracks. I wait until the last moment by the doors so that my jacket doesn't get stolen. They place a glass containing live lice in the barracks. They carry in several cans of Zyklon, used to gas people; the crew in gas masks opens the cans, closes the doors to the barracks, and nails them shut. At the same time others seal all of the cracks in the walls and doors with paper. It's hopeless work, since there's a crack in between practically every board.

We know what kind of rags we'll get after delousing. Whoever has decent clothing and doesn't want to lose it grabs the first piece of tattered attire that he can, one that he won't regret leaving in the bathhouse, he'll get different rags there, and once he returns he'll put on his old clothes. I get pants that reach halfway down my calves, and Pietroniec, who just took over one of the storage rooms, called the *Gerätekammer*, gives me an ostensibly good-looking summer jacket. But what matters to me is saving my quilted spencer that I got from Struczowski back in April—I sweated in it through the summer, since *Vorarbeiter* were allowed to wear jackets, but not to just have to give it up in the fall. We are walking around dressed up like for a masquerade and one person is laughing at the other because of our bizarre look. The good clothes are hidden deep in the recesses. I feel something crawling over me, a familiar sensation, I go to another barracks, take off my shirt, and see about twenty lice. I smash them, go back out on the field, and again something is crawling on me. Once more I smash about a dozen of them. There isn't a single one on the jacket. Where are they coming from? Ultimately I discover that there is a hole in the collar of the jacket, and they are coming out in throngs from the lining of the jacket. There's no helping it, I have to wait until the heat causes the last louse to wake up and crawl out onto my shirt. After an hour I have peace. It illustrates the condition in which clothing is supplied from the *Bekleidungskammer* to the respective field storage rooms.

Blocks 14, 15, 16, and 17 are packed with mattresses and blankets and gassed, and the rest, stripped bare of bedding, stand empty. The blocks go one after the other to the bathhouse. Around 5:00 p.m. it's our block's turn. We strip naked in front of the bathhouse in the open air and line up to several barbers sitting outside. They cut off all of our body hair (except on our head, since that's always trimmed short). Luckily it's a sunny and windless day, but it's still the end of October. We take our shoes in our hands and before entering the baths we go into the gas chamber. We are crammed in there, like the Jews were, waiting to be gassed. We walk out individually to the baths, they check at the door to make sure no one takes in any piece of cloth, no socks, handkerchiefs, etc. After the shower (three to a head), we get "clean shirts" and various old tattered clothes. We are to sleep in the empty barracks on the beds without mattresses, on bare boards, without blankets or our jackets. The nights are cold; after all, water was freezing inside the barracks at the beginning of October.

I search for another way to spend the night. Inside the washroom barracks is a metalworker's shop, located in Boniecki's old workroom. Since my flowers are drying there and my seeds are being husked, I consider it my condominium. Just a few days ago they brought bales of compressed wood shavings to stuff the mattresses with. Along with Wszelaki, we push the bales together, creating a kind of futon, I sleep next to him, next to us are Serafin, the technician Barański, called "Stryjek,"[190] a retired train engine driver, and others. Altogether, about fifteen people. It's much warmer in the little chamber than in the barracks, more so since we lit the stove. We found a few blankets. And so the sleep is tolerable. On the other side of the wall is Zelent's measurement *Kommando*, which is making the scale model of the camp. Zelent invites me over, but I've already arranged

190. Polish: uncle.

a place to sleep. Everyone who slept in the empty barracks is complaining in the morning about the annoying cold.

And that's what the disinfection of Field 3 looked like. Even if all of the prisoners had gotten perfectly deloused underwear and clothes, putting them on lice-infested beds that only had the mattresses and blankets removed cancels the whole purpose of washing and changing clothes. A typical SS way of solving problems. In a couple of days they open the gassed barracks, the lice in the glass are still strolling around. And wait until you see those sandwiched under a layer of a dozen or more mattresses. So all in all, it was one big humbug, done only to exhaust us.

All Saints' and All Souls'—normal work days. My thoughts are at the graveside of my wife and daughter, by the grave of my father, and my mother, who was killed during the last bombing of Warsaw on September 25, 1939, the day before the capitulation. I know my brother will take flowers and tidy up their graves at Powązki Cemetery, but I can't pray at their side.

And that's that, the typical fate of every Polish family, the mother killed by German bombs and the son sitting in a concentration camp!

The Massacre of Seventeen Thousand Jews

On the morning of November 3, before the roll call, we notice that behind the wires, machine guns have been placed at regular intervals with the barrels aimed at the camp, next to them are groups of SS men in cloaks and battle gear. Apparently, they've been standing there all night. We say to ourselves: "*Dicke Luft*."[191] The roll call takes place as normal, then each block is ordered to move back so that there is more space between each one. We therefore take up the entire square. Then, the Jews are ordered to step out of individual blocks and create separate groups. SS men come over to check if there are any Jews left among the ranks of the Aryans. They lead the Jewish groups forward, and gather around the hydrant, while the Aryan groups are ordered to step back into the heart of the square, so the area between the kitchen and the washroom barracks.

What does this all mean? I hear my heart thumping in my chest. Trucks, driven by SS men, drive up to the Revier branch, located in Blocks 20, 21, and 22. Hessel with the *Feldführer* drive all the Jews out of these blocks, barefoot and wearing only shirts, and order them to get into the trucks. Some try to explain that they are of mixed descent, Hessel nods and says that they can explain it "there." Some, seriously ill, with high fever, unable to walk, are carried to the trucks and brutally thrown inside. The sick are naked, the barefoot only in shirts, without even a blanket to cover them, they shiver from the cold. My decimated Block 15 stands ten steps away from the nearest car, so I observe from up close the merciless loading of the sick. The cars leave and stop at the front of the square, where the Jews are grouped. We stand like this for maybe an hour. Finally, the gate opens and the Jews are led out to the left, and so to the crematorium. Perhaps two thousand departed from our field.

They had barely left and here, along our field, other large groups of men are moving in the direction of Field 5. On Field 1, there are women; on

191. Literally, "thick air"; an idiom meaning something threatening is in the air.

Field 2, there is a hospital for Soviet invalids, so these people are strangers. We look at the road leading from Lublin, the road leading to the camp, everything is swarming with masses of people, and rising above them are clouds of dust.

Numerous passenger cars drive toward the crematorium, some military units are marching. There is incredible movement, with everything flowing in one direction. Suddenly, I hear music, some woeful milonga tango, then a waltz by Strauss, it's music played from records through a loudspeaker. The sounds carry from the direction of the crematorium. Where did this loudspeaker come from, we never heard it before. The music plays continuously. Record after record. A plane is circling low around the camp, so that sometimes you can't hear your own voice. There are short breaks between the records and then I hear a muffled "ta ta ta—ta ta ta," just like the sound of a machine gun.

Private First Class Eberle comes to the square. We form a circle around him and ask what's happening in the camp. He emphatically answers that today, Jews are being finished off in the entire territory of Europe occupied by the Germans. We reply that it will be our turn next. He swears that it's out of the question. But how can he know? He tells us that the Revier was moved early in the morning to Field 4 and that all the Jews are being grouped on Field 5, from which groups of one hundred are led to the crematorium grounds, where they are executed by firing squad. He adds that transports of Jews from nearby labor camps are coming. We are overwhelmed by an indescribable tension and depression. Everyone has flushed faces. The *Kommando* didn't go to work of course, we nervously walk around the square. I hear my friends calling to go back into the barracks. I go back to my block where everything is OK. But, God have pity—the Jewish barracks look as if a horde of Huns had passed through them.

And indeed, a horde of bastard Huns did crash through there, speaking today in Ukrainian. Then, when death began to collect its harvest by the thousands, the jackals threw themselves on the Jewish barracks and ripped apart hundreds of mattresses, plundering everything of any value. It's impressive how hundreds of beds could be searched in twenty or thirty minutes and ten barracks turned upside down, without being noticed.

This is the moral and ethical visage of the Soviet youth, who sucked out communist slogans together with milk from their mother's breast. Even a dog will whimper when he stands above the still-warm body of another dog, a companion in his play. The saying by Tuwim comes to mind: "I won't even call you a dog, since that would be an insult to a dog."[192]

There is no lunch today, because all the kitchen staff was taken, but no one thinks about food today. The office ceased to exist, everything is disorganized. The speaker plays throughout the day and from time to time you can hear a series of shots from automatic weapons. New columns of Jews and Jewesses keep coming, streaming along the road near our field.

Dusk falls, the sounds of music still fill the air. Reflections come . . . The all-powerful Friedrich from the *Arbeitseinsatz*, a good man left, Dr. Horowitz, Polish Jews went: vice president of the Zionists, Dr. Schipper, Kaczko, my block clerk Krongold, Dr. Lewiner, the degenerate Bubi, and the newly minted Jew Meierovitz . . . and so many other personal acquaintances. Night comes, the music stops, the slaughter is over. I spend the night restlessly, the bed next to me is empty, my neighbor Krongold, a friendly *causeur*,[193] is dead.

Only when I wake up the next day do I fully realize what has happened. Like with the loss of a loved one, it takes a few days before you realize that the person is dead, when you come into contact with objects belonging to that person, with issues concerning that person, which you answer yourself: not ever, never! The flocks of crows circling over our heads on the day of our transport's arrival, this ominous sign came true in a terrible way.

On November 4, the feverish formation begins of new *Kommando*, office personnel, block overseers, clerks, postmen, the *Politische Abteilung*, the baths, kitchens, SS canteen and SS kitchen, the *Effektenkammer*, *Bekleidungskammer*, and so on, all of the choice *Kommando* previously occupied by the Slovak Jews. Panasiewicz and Noak are assigned to the *Lagerschreibstube*. Knips is now the overseer of Block 6. I stay a gardener,

---

192. Reference to an epigram by Julian Tuwim, *"Na pewnego endeka, co na mnie szczeka."*
193. French: a conversationalist or storyteller.

because I can't leave the field, so there's no other use for me. I'm not worried about it since I'm settled here.

We slowly learn the details of the massacre. Yesterday, the camp was completely cut off from the world, and even the SS officers and Gestapo agents who were entering the camp had to give the guards a password that was specially issued for this day. The camp SS men didn't have access to the execution site, outside Gestapo and SD units were there. Around 6:00 a.m. yesterday, all block overseers from Field 5 were called to the Revier office—before submitting the daily report (there is no regular roll call at the Revier). The evacuation of all of Field 5 was ordered, with the exception of the sick Jews who would stay. The sick Aryans were moved to Field 4, and by 8:00 a.m. they were all gone from the field.

Captain Antoni Wolf, the block clerk in Block 21 on Field 5 (with Dr. Sztaba), tells me that near Block 22, just beyond the wires by the crematorium, unknown SS men with automatic weapons and breakfast in their haversacks gathered around 6:00 a.m. at the crematorium. The barbed wire on the fence near Block 22 was unwound, and in this way a gate was made as a passage to the crematorium. The Jews were driven into particular barracks, then groups of one hundred were taken into Block 22, where they undressed, and then, naked, arms raised, ran single file into the "defensive" trenches, where they were mowed down with machine guns. The next one hundred ran out onto the layer of bleeding and still-twitching corpses.

Wolf was in Block 21 until 8:30 a.m. and from the windows of the barracks, at a distance of fifty meters, he saw the first shootings. The entire operation was directed by the Jew, Friedrich (from the *Arbeitseinsatz*), to whom the SS men swore that he would come out of it alive. He lined up and counted out the hundreds in the barracks, then he hurried them to Block 22 for quick undressing. We all know that in a concentration camp everything has to be "*schnell, schnell,*" you even have to rush to your death. There were seventeen thousand Jews gathered there, and only one incident where a Jew lunged at an SS man with a pocketknife and wounded him, the rest went like sheep to the slaughter.

There were 4,300 Jews liquidated from Majdanek itself, the rest were from other camps. Several Jews smuggled themselves onto Field 4 along with the sick Aryans. After they were found, they were transported to Field 5 during the day. All of the Jewish doctors were shot, and the number of sick fell on November 3 from 1,500 to 712. After finishing the butchery, the SS men unexpectedly shot Friedrich through a door. He gained in that at least he did not have to undress, and death came suddenly.

On November 3, late at night, three hundred Jewish women who they didn't have time to execute before dark were led from Field 5, back onto Field 1; they were finished off on the 4th.[194]

There is a version circulating that on November 3, in the afternoon, a telegram from the central Concentration Camps Inspectorate in Oranienburg ordered a halt to the executions; supposedly many Jews survived because of this. I don't know how, perhaps further transports were to arrive on November 4, and maybe these transports were turned back—but at Majdanek, not a single Jew interned there remained alive. The pits filled to the edges with corpses were covered with a thin layer of earth.

On November 5 I see *Feldführer* Gosberg leading a Jewish messenger from Field 3. Did he rise from the dead—no, it turned out that he somehow got onto Field 4 and hid there for two days. He was found, and Gosberg graces him along the way with various questions and then triumphantly leads him to the crematorium.

The office is a complete mess. Noak tells me that Hessel can't get a handle on the situation, he isn't able to instruct the newly assigned prisoners on how to deal with ongoing matters. He gets furious because the novices don't know the usual manipulative tricks of "office work" and he has already beaten a few. I feel the benefit of this disorder in the office, since before, Hessel would spend hours prowling around the field, looking for some piece of straw on the ground or a bowl thrown in the bushes, now I don't see him for days at a time.

194. The women were kept alive to sort through the belongings of the victims. On April 13, 1944, they were transported to Auschwitz, where they were murdered soon after arrival.

The Gehenna in the *Lagerschreibstube*

On November 13, they call me to the office. Hessel tells me that I've been assigned there and that my work begins at once. I'm not at all pleased by this, having already heard from Noak about the chaos prevailing there and having experienced Hessel's nasty character firsthand. He tells me I'll be sleeping in the room next to the office where all the clerks sleep and to bring my things from Block 15 at once, so I go get my blankets and food packages.

I begin my work. Hessel informs me that I will be in charge of the camp records: the numerical files, corresponding to twenty thousand numbers, the alphabetical files, and the records of the deceased, hostages, and Germans. At the same time, he attempts to explain how documents circulate and the fundamentals for adding record entries. But he is rambling so much that despite my focused concentration I can't make head or tail of what he's saying. From what I'm able to gather, the office work is at the level of a municipal *diurnista*[1] and mostly entails manipulation and knowing which binder is where and what each contains.

The office is swamped with papers, since new groups of workers, who don't know the work techniques yet, were improvised on each of the fields after the Jews departed. Instead of letting us work in peace, Hessel runs around between us, looking over each person's shoulder, orders us to stop what we've already started, directs us to begin something else and gives what we've done so far to someone else to continue; an hour later he again tells us to stop our work and to start something else. Everything is started, but nothing is completed, a single document is passed on to five prisoners in turn to take care of and then taken away in the middle of it and no one knows who did what. Every five minutes Hessel raises his voice, yells and screams; he hit Noak in the face. Every fifth word is "*Scheisspolacken*," he sits down in his room next to the office and every moment he tears

1. Polish (archaic): a junior clerk.

one of us away from our work and we have to run into his room. It's not office work but a devil's mill, consisting mostly of counting prisoner rolls, records of moves from one field to another, incomings and outgoings—above all, the evening roll call on every field has to add up. It's not peaceful here, not a place where we can focus on the work. I feel knocked around by the chaos and yelling.

In the afternoon, Hessel shows me a list of last names, the twentieth of its kind that I've held today, and asks who put check marks by the names. Taking a closer look to see if in fact I did make the check marks, I try to recognize whether I had seen those names today—suddenly I get a smack to the face and the menacing question:

"Maybe dwarves did it?"

I keep working, an hour later another misunderstanding, Hessel wants to kick me in the rear end—but I'm standing just a few centimeters too far away—and he misses. He curses at me about doctors and directors and boots me out of the office. Thank the Lord my soul, I quickly take my blankets and packages and go back to the barracks. I meet Zelent along the way and, clasping my hands in prayer, I thank God that I could break out of that lunatic atmosphere in the office after just one day. I had barely settled back in at the barracks, occupying my old bed and eating supper, when a messenger came around 9:00 p.m. and said that Hessel has ordered me back to the office and to spend the night there.

Gehenna begins. I am responsible for the state of the files, which no one can give me an accounting of, since the person who used to manage them is dead. The numerical file runs from 1 to 20,000. In Majdanek, there is a tradition of assigning the same number multiple times as it becomes available again. In other camps, sequential numbers are issued, so by knowing the last number given, you know how many prisoners total have been through the camp from its founding, or when numbering started over. While in Majdanek, numbers are assigned once they've been freed up by death, transfer to another camp, or release. So in the numerical files, each successive owner of a number is listed. Each card has room for eight entries. If a card is totally full, it's set aside and a new one for a given number is inserted. From a cursory review of the card index, I see that each number has been assigned eight times. I want to check what the names of my predecessors were who bore the number 8830 before; what happened to them? My name is beautifully handwritten in space 1. So I am number 9! What happened to those before me? How many left for different camps, and how many went through the chimney? I go to the card file of the deceased. I look for the names of those whom I couldn't ask in person. I find Struczowski there, dead from typhus fever in April; Horodyski, beaten by *Lagerältester* Rockinger; Krzyżanowski, the gardener who suffered from ulcers (sycosis); Dr. Jastrzębski, the landowner; Respond, who worked for me in August. The death report of Marmorstein, murdered by Birzer with the understanding of the *Feldführer*, really does list "pneumonia" as the cause of death.

The head clerk in the office is Stanisław Olszański, a civil servant from Zamość, previously the clerk from the Field 1 office; he already worked with Hessel there. He deals with current matters, writing daily camp reports—so-called *Stärkemeldung*—and provisioning reports—so-called *Küchenrapport*, and more. Olszański moved from Field 1 to Field 3 several weeks ago and he was the clerk in Block 6. I knew him by sight. Matters with the *Arbeitseinsatz* are handled by Tetych, a clerk from the Bank of Poland in Zamość. Noak maintains prisoner files according to their age (*Alterseinstufung*) and free numbers; Panasiewicz works as a typist. There is also Węglarz from Lwów, who is lying in the bedroom with a high fever, probably typhus, and he's leaving for the Revier today. Olszański's German is weak. He's reserved toward me. The *Stärkemeldung*, which is complicated because it has many fields, is typed by Hessel himself at first. We temporarily have a medical student, Lech, working with us. A calm, level-headed, likable colleague. After being beaten by Hessel, he gets sick and leaves for the Revier. The doctors keep him there as a nurse. Hessel's protests to the *Arbeitseinsatz* and his demands to send him back to the office don't work, since they explain that as a medic, Lech is predestined for the hospital, not the office.

The *Stärkemeldung* is divided into: the *Schutzhäftlinge, Berufsverbrecher, Asoziale, Sicherungsverwahrte, Homosexuelle, Bibelforscher, Juden, Zigeuner, Ausländische Zivilarbeiter,* and *Sonderaktion der Wehrmacht,* and each of the categories is subdivided into national groups. Newcomers are added to the previous day's roll, and then the outgoing, including the dead, released, and shot (*"exekutiert"*),[2] are listed by name. Outgoing transports get a transport manifest as an *alegat*,[3] and you collectively subtract, for instance: 307 Sch (*Schutzhäftlinge*), including 15 RD (*Reichsdeutsche*), 254 P (Poles), 20 Fr (Frenchmen), 17 It (Italians), plus 18 BV (*Berufsverbrecher*), including 15 RD and 3 Tsch (Czech), 104 J (Jews), including 4 RD and 100 P, and so on. The general head count of the prisoners indicated in the *Stärkemeldung* has to add up from the numbers reported at roll call on each field. Additionally, a roll call plan is prepared for each field, listing the number of prisoners on every one, and finally, for your own field, a detailed record of the number of prisoners in each block, including those commandeered who don't stand for roll call. The office workers do not themselves stand for roll call as information is often needed while it's happening and the office roll call is received by the *Rapportführer* himself in the office. That's where the *Blockführer* also come to report the head counts of their barracks. This is a huge convenience for the office, of course, especially now in the rainy, wintry season.

Since nightfall comes earlier, the lunch break has been canceled and the evening roll call takes place at 4:00 p.m. Lunch is only handed out afterward and coffee is distributed at 7:00 p.m.

Because the Jews are now gone from the camp, an inventory is taking place. All the fields, that is 3, 4, and 5, prepare prisoner name and number lists, which are checked against the camp card file as to whether the names are present there and matched with the right field. The card index contains the number, full name, category of prisoner (*Häftlingsart*), nationality, date and place of birth, profession, block and field number. In case of transfer from one field to another, the record must be updated. It's extremely important (from the perspective of the camp, of course). Every afternoon, just before the roll call, the *Politische Abteilung* and *Abteilung* III, headed by Thumann, send the prisoner numbers of those who are to be called

2. Executed.
3. Polish: here, appendix.

the next day immediately following the roll call. The card file is checked
for where a given prisoner is located and a notice is sent to the appropriate field offices to deliver the prisoners in the morning. The summons is
signed by Hessel and, since you can't leave the field after the evening roll
call, the *Blockführer* take the summons to the appropriate field. There is
no contact with neighboring fields after the evening roll. For the moment,
due to the ongoing quarantine on Field 3, contact with other fields is broken off even during the day, and SS men serve as messengers.

Woe unto you if you notify the wrong field. A reply comes in the morning that the prisoner is not on that field. You have to look for him and in the
meantime the *Kommando* have left for work and the prisoner might have
left on a truck to a job in Lublin or in Piasków. It's hopeless at that point, but
if the sought-after man went to the *Gärtnerei* for example, you can find him
within an hour and blot out the mistake in the index before Thumann sees it.

Checking the lists of prisoners in the camp against the card index takes
up huge amounts of time, it lasts a week, with work being done in the
evenings and at night, since during the day, current matters need to be
addressed. We sleep from four to five hours per night. What's interesting
is that Jews are still present on the *Stärkemeldung* and haven't been struck
from the rolls.

Hessel is exceptionally unpleasant, nearly every day one of us gets
slapped. We had barely finished checking the lists, which was very arduous,
when Hessel announced that we had to count the number of Jews in the
files by the following morning. There are five of us, so each takes five hundred cards and we count the Jews. Hessel leads this method of counting. I
naively ask whether I should count Kapo Meierovitz as a Jew. Hessel replies:

"Obviously. He was a half-breed after all, his mother was a Jewish
prostitute."

You can hear the joy in his voice that this person had been killed. Hessel
played a large part in it. I share what Hessel said with Noak and say:

"Much respect for the Jewish prostitute if she was able to impart so
much culture, erudition, and subtlety to her son. German *Mutti*[4] should
learn how to raise their sons from this Jewish prostitute."

4. Mothers.

Then, in the morning, we check each other's results, and before the roll call we come to the conclusion that we can't give a definite number. In the morning we tell Hessel (since he went to sleep at 11:00 p.m.) that each time we counted, different totals came out. In the afternoon, in other words after our daily work, Hessel tells us that we'll have to count the Jews again. The previous night we hadn't slept a wink. We're totally spent since we've only been sleeping four or five hours lately—and here we have to carefully count all night. I propose that the Jewish card files be separated out and then counted, so someone can check whether any Jewish files are left among the Aryan ones, but Hessel rejects this, saying it would take too long. I already know from experience that during group work there is no sense of responsibility, since if there's some discrepancy, you can always insinuate that someone else made the mistake. We exhaust ourselves until the morning, different numbers are still coming out, finally we decide that we'll give Hessel the number from the *Stärkemeldung*. Once I give him the number, I see the satisfaction in his eyes and I get the patronizing reply:

"I knew that would be the number."

The Jews are still listed as living in the reports.

The checking and searching of the clothing and shoes of the seventeen thousand murdered Jews takes place on Field 5. An entire *Kommando* is sitting there, tearing and ripping everything to pieces. Purportedly, great sums of money are being found there. Captain Grudowski, the main clerk in the Revier, had to pay Hessel a ransom of ten thousand zlotys.

Who shows up at the office? Herr Knips. I don't know how he managed to call attention to himself—but he was probably the only one of us who actively tried to get into the office. His nerve and confabulations have made an impression on Hessel. We, who are daily called "*Scheisspolacken*" by Hessel, avoid any conversations with him unrelated to work, while Knips brownnoses without reservations, stressing several times that he's a *Volksdeutsch*, that he was a clerk in the Warsaw District, that his brother, Leon, is a high-ranking functionary in the Lublin District, and that his boys volunteered for the German air force. For this reason we uniformly ostracize Knips. Noak tells us that when he used to work with Knips in the post office, Knips was under observation since he was seen opening packages and taking various things for himself. Kapo Ott had already ordered that if he were caught again, an official report would be submitted and he would be kicked out of the post office. Knips was lucky since he came on November 3, and after that bloody day, there was a reshuffling of all the *Kommando*.

Knips takes my ideas for streamlining our work, which I freely tell my friends, and he runs to Hessel, presenting them as his own. They become infatuated with one another and after a few days, I hear Hessel tell some SS man that Knips is his best worker. I make way for Knips to claim the spotlight without any regrets, I have no ambitions to be in first place here, since in life, amid real competition, I was at the head of more serious institutions than the office. But when you have to work, and not just talk, Knips fails and gets knocked so hard by Hessel that he breaks his glasses.

We get another special job: checking the card file of *Abteilung* III— Thumann's department—against our records, especially as regards compiling the number of Russians. An SS man comes over from that department, a *Volksdeutsch* from Croatia, Eggi, a decent person in any case. Checking the files lasts from the morning until late at night, and only after it's done can I do my regular work. It lasts another week. I work with Knips and the SS man. I notice that the department has several prisoners listed as Jews that we note as Russians—meaning Aryans, so I pay it no mind. After all, I'm supposed to check and reconcile the numbers of Russian prisoners, not Jewish ones. Human lives are at stake. Knips, on the other hand, finds the card of a Russian in his stack by the name of Szymon, a dentist from Odessa. And he's already jumping up to the SS man and saying:

"If he's a dentist, a native of Odessa, and is named Szymon, he must be a Jew."

During a break, my friends and I tell him off for taking human lives onto his conscience. Knips replies flatly:

"I have a different viewpoint in the matter and I won't change my approach to it."

I tell Zelent about the incident right away, so that this fact will be remembered and that this turncoat will be held responsible when the time comes. The next day, Knips discovers another Jew; he talks about it loudly all day, so that, nolens volens, the SS man must note it down and both prisoners are called to be interrogated by Thumann. Both "Russians" are wiped off the face of the earth. Zelent tells me that Lublin has been informed about Knips's excesses.

There is a general campaign against concealed Jews on the field. There is a Jew in the kitchens, he currently goes by the last name Krawczyk; it's enough to look at him to know, and before the massacre he didn't really hide it, but in the card index he's listed as an Aryan. Someone denounces him. Gosberg calls him to the office, examines his genitals, ascertains that he's circumcised, and begins to savagely beat him. Krawczyk explains that it was a surgical operation. Gosberg orders him to tell where his family lives. He replies that none of them are alive. When asked where they are buried, hesitating, he names some village. Gosberg asks him what his nationality is, and he replies that he's Ukrainian. They order him to say the Our Father, and he stumbles through it inaccurately in broken Polish-Ukrainian. Some prisoner I don't know is called as an interpreter, he has a serious expression and he doesn't question the authenticity of the prayer or the language. They command Krawczyk to stand in the office all day, but they release him back to the kitchens at night. They weren't persuaded that he's a Jew. I've been convinced more than once that the Germans, who are so attuned to the subject of being Aryan, don't have a sense for who is a Semite, while we Poles, who constantly rubbed shoulders with Jews, are quicker and more accurate in identifying those with Semitic blood.

Kapo Silberspitz is back on Field 4. It turns out that his presumed release in the spring was really a transfer from Majdanek to the Lublin Castle, where he has been ever since.

The camp commandant has ordered that all the civilian laborers working on the camp toilet installations be expelled. It only pertains to Fields 4 and 5, since the quarantine continues on our field.

I have to give credit to Hessel for his unflattering barbs, saying that the civilian laborers sabotaging the sewage works at Majdanek were only doing harm to the prisoners, 50 percent of whom are Polish.

"They could have smuggled and traded," says Hessel, "but they should have also built toilets and a water supply system at the same time. It's all the same to me whether the prisoners go to the latrine under the open sky or to the washroom barracks."

Because of the quarantine on Field 3, Zelent was directed to continue the work, and indeed, within two weeks he finished three barracks, 14, 15, and 16. Each one had eight toilets installed, built-in cement troughs with water flowing in from symmetrically placed openings in the water pipe fastened above the washbasin. All of this is separated from the dining room by a brick wall. The room is separated on the other side from the sleeping area by a partition. The gate/barn doors have been boarded up and sealed, the entrance is now on the side of the barracks with normal doors and an entrance hall. Barracks furnished like this will make the winter easier to bear.

We have a stove in our bedroom where we cook in the evenings, mostly fried potatoes and onions. Noak brings in his friend as a *Stubendienst*, Sergeant of Artillery Jan Małyszka from Białystok. He makes our beds, brings us food from the barracks, cleans the room, and fries the potatoes. He sits in a warm room all day. Obviously, we treat him as a colleague, not as a lackey, it's a good assignment, better than working in the rain and cold, or next door under the direction of Hessel.

"The best office worker," Knips, gets shivers, telling himself that it's the flu; the next day the shivers subside, but on the third day he has a high fever. Typhus. I'm sorry he's leaving, not because I hate to see him go, but because he was a buffer between Hessel and me.

They start retrieving the Jewish bodies from the trenches and burning them on piles in the open field. The crematorium can only cope with burning the "regular" output. They estimate that burning all of the Jews will last until March 1944. The southeasterly wind carries the fetor of decomposing corpses and the smell of burning bones, hair, and fat. The air that we are constantly breathing is horrible.

Our office takes up almost half of the barracks; it's very big. Five of us sit there and there is only one stove. When the temperature drops the stove isn't enough to warm up the room. My hands are all blue, as if frozen through. It's difficult to pore over the card files for hours on end with numb fingers. Hessel sits in his room all day with the door closed, ordering the stove to be stoked until it's red-hot. He has some grievance toward me again and hits me; it happens to each of us in turn for that matter, whoever happens to be nearby gets it.

After one such incident, Olszański comes over to me and extends his hand, saying that he has to apologize for what he thought about me. Surprised, I look at him and wonder what this is all about. He tells me that right after he came with Hessel from Field 1 to Field 3, someone told him that I was Hessel's intermediary and informant, and that he should always keep up his guard around me. He admits that one day, when I approached the group in which he was standing, he stopped sharing the latest radio news, fearing my presence. Now he has observed me every day in the office and convinced himself that nothing ties me to Hessel. Olszański's German is weak and he often doesn't understand Hessel's rapid-fire instructions. He asks me to listen in whenever Hessel is speaking to him and then submit the right paperwork. I agree to this and take care of all the outgoing correspondence besides routine documents, which he then presents to Hessel as his own work.

Stanisław and Julia Kwiatkowski with their sons Zygmunt, Jerzy, and Stanisław.
Hoover Institution Library & Archives.

← Jerzy Kwiatkowski. Hoover Institution Library & Archives.

Class IV b of the I. *Staatsgymnasium* (state secondary school) in Czernowitz. Jerzy Kwiatkowski sits in front of Director Klauser (in dark glasses). Hoover Institution Library & Archives.

Warrant Officer Kwiatkowski
in the Imperial Third Dragoon
Regiment with his medal of
bravery. Hoover Institution
Library & Archives.

→

Kwiatkowski in the uniform
of the Imperial Third Dragoon
Regiment. Hoover Institution
Library & Archives.

Kwiatkowski in a Polish
cavalryman's uniform,
Czernowitz (then Cernăuţi),
1919. Hoover Institution
Library & Archives.

First Lieutenant Kwiatkowski
in the Cipher Bureau, Warsaw,
1920. Hoover Institution
Library & Archives.

Maria (née Horodyński) Kwiatkowska, Ciechocinek, 1938. Hoover Institution Library & Archives.

Jerzy Kwiatkowski, 1937. Hoover Institution Library & Archives.

Q u i t t u n g

Datum   18.2.43.

Name   K w i a t k o w s k i

Vorname   Jerzy

Namen d. Eltern: Stanislaw - Julia

Depositen: 909,oo Zl
    1 Taschenuhr gelbSeneta, 1 Ehering gelb,
    1 Ring weiss mit weissen Steinen.,.....
    ...

Übernommen:

Deposit receipt issued for items
taken from Jerzy Kwiatkowski
at Pawiak Prison, February 18,
1943. The State Museum at
Majdanek.

III. Innerhalb des Lagers:
  I. Lagerzwecke:
    Küche   149
    Stubendienst /Blockpersonal/   130
    Schreibstube   17
    Läufer   12
    Kapos   4
    Geräte-Umtauschkammer   5
    Zaunreiniger   3
    Krankenpfleger
    Kinder
    Leichenträger
    Sonstige Lagerarbeiten /im Lager/

  II. Lagerwirtschaft:
    Jauchefahrer   10   VA 12370
    Gärtner   20   VA   8830
    Fahrbereitschaft   60   2405

IV. Unbeschäftigte Häftlinge:
    Arztmelder   46
    Vernehmungen
    Entlausungen
    Quarantäne   17
    Verstorbene   88

Zusammenstellung.

I.   Aussenkommandos   95?   + 7

II.   Innerhalb der Postenkette   + 9

III.   Innerhalb des Lagers   2405

IV.   Unbeschäftigte Häftlinge   88

     Ausgerückte Kapos   28

     Feldstärke am 6.9.1943 4294

I.c.A.no.3/7   Der   ...hrer Feld III:

A list of work squads, *Konzentrationslager* (KL) Lublin. The State Museum at Majdanek.

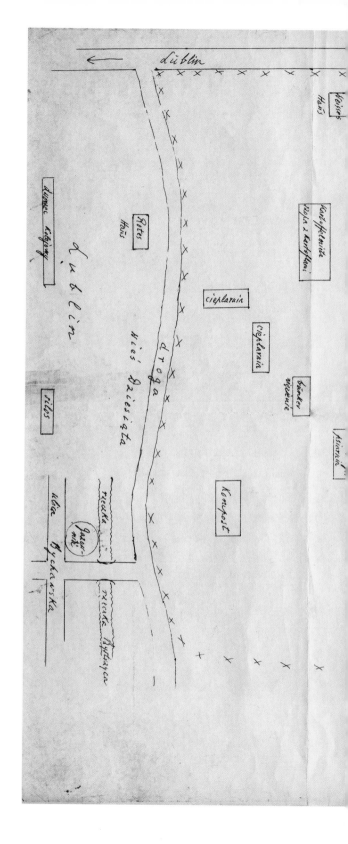

The general layout of the Majdanek concentration camp drawn up by Kwiatkowski. The State Museum at Majdanek.

Plan sytuacyjny obozu koncentracyjnego Majdanek

Sporządził więzień Nr 8830 Jerzy Kwiatkowski

Szosa → Chełm

Koszary SS

Koszary SS

Komenda   obozn

Politische Abteilung

Wład do Komeny

Droga do wsi

Bahnhof

Baracki budlijii

Komora gazowa i łaźnia · Rozpornia

Transformatoria

poczta   Thuman Abteilung III

Lagergut

Kamienie Łomy

I Pole — Stare Krematorium

II Pole

III Pole

IV Pole

V Pole — Zwischenfeld Pole ogólne

VI Pole

1 2 3 4 5

Warsztaty filmajdings kanmes

nowe Krematorium

palenie trupia na stosach

rowy z trupami

Legenda

xxxx Grosse Postenkette naeży stojące w dzień
ooo Kleine Postenkette naeży stojące w nocy
Barak Nr 1 Effektenkammer Nr 2 łaźnia
Barak Nr 3 Rewir Nr 4 SS Küche Nr 5 garaże
□ więzie. strażnice
⇨ Wachtürme / Bewachungsturme

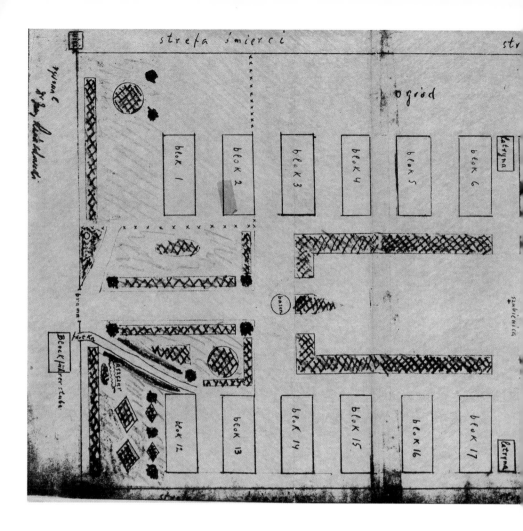

A map of prisoner field 3 drawn
up by Kwiatkowski. The State
Museum at Majdanek.

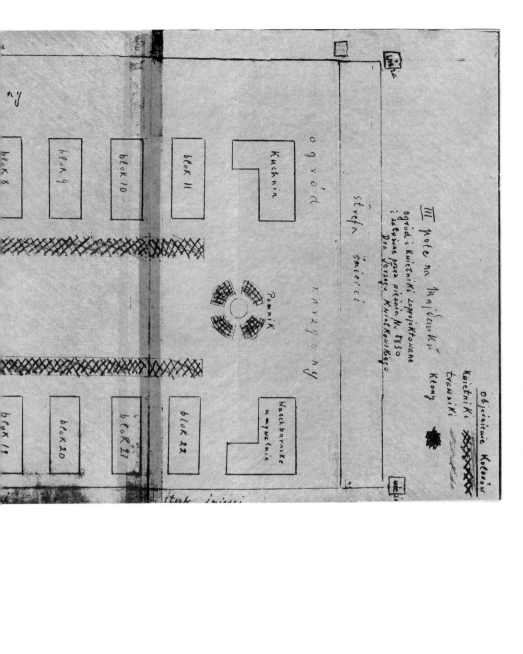

Alexander
ruster Franz

5792 Banaszek Stanislaw
40 Bargielski Georg
3o2 Bartzies Herbert
8145 Bednarski Taddeusz
822 Bełlak Walter
den Ludwig
aut Jan
Bogen Karl
Borowski Mie yslaw
k Jol
187o Be
384 Bre ne Kar.
5947 Burc n Anto

C
4623 Cieply Franz
3817 Cynkin Napoleon
1o92 Czerski Franz
9955 Czerwik Marian
6 Czop Michal

D
813 Dombrowski Siegfried

E
67 Eckert Heinrich
5 Einicke Ludwig
83o Elsbacher Franz
6 Enke Willi

F
29 Fietz Richard
1834 Florian Josef

G
el Fra
aruc

12 Ba orth
2 He
Hawlicek
essel Th
tt Otto
ann Paul
Erich
en

IJ
835 Ja ski Stanislaw
3304 Janiszek Andrzej
2083 Jankiewicz Stanislaw

K
4o Kauer Alfred
15 Kazmierczuk Aleksander
5167 Kli sh Myron
25 Klorowski Johann
11o K potek Karl
1758 Klosowski Jerzy
2722 Klukewicz Aleksander
1o5 Knipp Fritz
4115 Kowalski Richard
2463 Krausl Karl
1438 Kruk Henryk
4o48 Krupski Wladyslaw
5438 Kruszewski Nikolaj
898o Krygowski Mieczyslaw
39 Kuhlemann Hermann
3974 Kulesza Czeslaw
2261 Kuzmitsch Metscheslaw
883o Kwiatkowski Jerzy

L
77o Laskowski Waclaw
3319 asocki Henryk
1163 asanowski Michal
150 entner Jose
480 stmann Julius
2729 Li owicz Wlodimier
54 Ladislaw

6797 Majchrzak Stefan
9962 Maliszewski Bohuslaw
8526 Mankiewicz Czeslaw
832 Mayer Ernst
4881 Mayer Rudolf
3o57 Merta Ernst
61 Mettbach Johann
163 Mistelberger Josef
3088 liszewski Kazimierz

N
957 Nadolski Peter
23o Naumann Paul
1978 Nedelkow Josef
Noa erzy

2954 Olszanski Stanislaw
18o Olszewski Bruno
5o1o Orpisz Witold
13 Ott Hans

P
3399 Panasiewicz Adam
2529 Panz Mieczyslaw
1676o Pasieczny Stanislaw
292 Passow Wilhelm
3865 Pawlak Stanislaw
36 Pejsar Franz
4156 Pietronec Rudolf
41 Pilar Andreas
248 Plintsch Oskar
3 Pluczynski Hermann
153 Popowski Karl
9300 Porzeczkowski
2595 Przybysz Edw

←
A fragment of the list of the last prisoners evacuated from KL Lublin, July 22, 1944. The State Museum at Majdanek.

Left to right: Albin Maria Boniecki, Henryk Szcześniewski, Jerzy Kwiatkowski, Maczków, 1945. The family archive of Krzysztof Szcześniewski.

Kwiatkowski (standing third from left) at the founding meeting of the Society of Former Political Prisoners in German Concentration Camps and Prisons, in the British occupation zone in Germany, Maczków, July 3, 1946. The State Museum at Majdanek.

←
Kwiatkowski in Maczków,
late 1940s. State Archives
in Lublin.

Kwiatkowski with family,
Washington, DC, 1970.
Hoover Institution Library
& Archives.

Jest to tylko pewien nadmiar wilgoci w nosie skutkiem czego nozdrza sa
stale mokre a czasem z nosa i kpnie kropla. Na wietrze nos obsycha,znow
sie saczy sluz i skorap pierzchnie, robia sie na koncu nosa strupy. Nie
ja jeden na to cierpie, widze,ze wielu z nas obciera sobie przez przerwy
rekawami lub czapkami nosy. | | Dostajemy lozka w in-
nem miejscu - ale znow spi nademna Struczowski - a faktycznie spimy w
jednym lozku. Niewiem dokladnie jak dlugo juz jestem na Majdanku, ale
dotychczas sie nie mylem | |

Przyłączam | się następnego dnia rano do grupy ktora nosi wode do szorowa
nia podlogi i korzystam z tej okazji i myje sie poraz pierwszy - bez myd
la i szczotki - ale co za rozkosz ze lepki brod z rak i twarzy zszedl.
czuje sie tak orzezwiony po tej toalecie pod kranem. Czapka sie wycie-
ram. Czuje ze mi porzadna broda wyrosla, zreszta widze to tez po moich
kolegach. W niedziele mieli nas golic, ale poniewaz codziennie pracowa-
lismy do wieczora, wiec stracilismy rachube co to za dzien w tygodniu.
A golenia nie bylo.
          Mamy pierwsze dni kwietnia, temperatura nic sie nie ociepla,
bardzo silne wiatry i mrozy nocne. Pocieszam sie, ze od 21 marca juz
jest kalendarzowa wiosna. Co tu zrobic, by sie uchronic od zimna. Wpadam na pomysl. Biore rano garsc slomy z siennika, chowam sie za lozkiem

niernie i wtykam ja sobie za koszule na plecach i na piersiach i ja równoczesni
rozprowadzam.Sloma troche kluje. Przy rannym apelu czuje ,iz mnie ona
troche grzeje.Wieczorem ja wytrzasam, jest juz sama sieczka. Tak sie slo
ma pokruszyla. Po kolacji odbywa sie kontrola zawszenia.Gdy mnie Dr Jastrzebski oglada,dlugo przeglada koszule, znow mi sie przypatruje ,stawi
mnie na bok i kaze mi czekac. Zauwazylem ze cale cialo moje jest jak w
pokrzywce, tak sloma poklula mi piersi i brzuch. W cztery oczy powiada
mi dr Jastrzebski, ze jestem strasznie przez wszy pogryziony, tylko dzi-
wil sie ani jednej wszy nie znalazl Powiadam mu, ze wszy niemam i ze od
slomy jestem pokluty. Kiwa niedowierzajaco glowa i powiada, ze to jednak
zaognienia od ukaszenia przez wszy.   *Komendant pola*
          Na drugi dzien po odjezdzie transportu wola mnieyFeldführer
Groffman do kancelarji, wskazuje na worek i powiada, ze tam jest trawa
parkowa do siania. Otwieram worek,ale widze ze to nie jest trawa, lecz
nasienie jakiegos rodzaju koniczyny. Z worka wydziela sie zapach stech-
lizny,nasienie jest zbutwiale. Tlumacze mu ze to nie trawa parkowa i daje
nasienie do wachania - powiadam mu, ze przeprowadze probe kielkowania,
ale potrzebuje do tego waty lub ligniny oraz stalej temperatury cieple
Widze ze mu tem zaimponowalem, idzie ze mna do Izby chorych i kaze wyda
lignine. Odliczam loo ziarnek, klade do wilgotnej ligniny i umieszczam
miske w "Schreibstube"kancelarji III pola. Blogoslawie go za to. bo
w kancelarji cieplo, w piecu az huczy. Co pare godzin, wpadam na 5 minut
do kancelarji, by skontrolowac czy juz ~~~~~~~~~~~~~~~~~~~~~~~~~~~~~~~~
~~~~~~~~~~~~~~~ iz dzialam z po~~~~~~~~~~~~~~~~~~~~~~~~~ pat~~~~~~~~~~~
~~~~~~~~~~,a mnie przy nie~~~~~~~~~~~~~~~~~~~~~~~~~~~~~~~~
nika kancelarji slowackiego zyda Dr.Horowitza dyrektora banku. Wyjatkow
skromny,cichy i taktowny czlowiek,ktory sie nietylko do mnie,ale do
wszystkich wiezniow ~~~~~~ bardzo przyzwoicie odnosił.

ZYCIE OBOZOWE

          Pracujac na polu i to w poblizu bramy a równoczesnie ~~~~~
~~~~~~ ktorym pierwszy~~~~~~~~~~~~~~ ~~~~~~ cho~~~~~~~~~~~~~~ ~~~~~~~
~~~~~~~~~ i "Schreibstube" widze co sie na polu dzieje. Rzucaja mi sie
jako nowicjuszowi przedewszystkiem w oczy "Wagenkolonnen".Sa to stare
wyranzowane niemieckie wojskowe furgony z ciezkimi kolami, siegajacymi
do wysokosci piersi, z koziem umieszczonym 2 m nad jezdnia.furgony ciagnione przez 4 ciezkie konie artyleryjskie. Otoz te wozy sa obecnie bez
koni, a ciagnione sa przez wiezniow. Sa porobione"szleje" z drutu,wrzyna
jacego sie gleboko w tego piersi i ramiona, a pozatem po bokach wozu sa umoco
(dodatkowo) wane tez druty (po 4 na kazdym boku) z wplecionym kawalkiem drzewa dla
uchwycenia. 20 ludzi *za orczyki* ustawia sie w nastepujacy sposob: 2 prowadzi dyszel
4 ciagnie sprzodu, 8 z boku, a 6 popycha z tylu. Wioza przewaznie kartof
le do kuchni. Woz taki pomiesci najmniej 2 tony. Jest kilka takich wozow
i jezdza one przez caly dzien na teren gospodarstwa warzywnego,gdzie sa

The typescript of the camp memoir, 1945.
Hoover Institution Library & Archives.

202

Praca w skwarze jest męczarnię. Przed 1939 r. wyrabiało się
paszport zagraniczny i człowiek opalał się na Lido, a potem w
kostiumie kąpielowym zasiadał do "śniadania", składającego się
z większej ilości dań niż tutejszy obiad. Snoby smarowały się
olejkami, by mocniej się opalić i po powrocie do domu chełpić
się swą opalenizną. Tu, przy 55 stopniach gorąca, mamy aż nadmiar promieni słonecznych, ale nie ma tu barwnego parasola ani
kosza, w którym można by się schronić przed spiekotą. Tu nikt
nie będzie podziwiał mej opalenizny!

z za drutów takiej informacji nie posiada. Wyczuwam, że w jego ręku
koncentruje się podziemna praca na polu. Rozmowa między oboma odbywa
się następnego wieczoru. Zelent reprezentuje Z.W.Z., Lipski N.S.Z.
ale dochodzą do zasadniczego porozumienia. Podwładnym Lipskiego w pra-
cy podziemnej na wolności był Pietroniec. Jego nie wtajemniczam
w moją rozmowę z Lipskim, ale Pietroniec gaduła przechwala mi się w ta-
jemnicy że dostał drogą poufną dla Lipskiego szyfr. Donoszę o tem
z miejsca Lipskiemu, by pouczył Pietrońca o konieczności zachowania
milczenia, gdyż w takie sprawy nie powinne być niepotrzebne osoby
wtajemniczone.

Zelent, Lipski i ja gramy teraz w otwarte karty.

Projekt odbicia Majdanka powstał w N.S.Z. /Narodowych Siłach Zbroj-
nych/ które jednak nie rozporządzały dostateczną ilością ludzi do
akcji. Wobec tego nawiązał N.S.Z. kontakt z Z.W.Z. /Związkiem Walki
Zbrojnej / okręgu lubelskiego. Również komuniści projektowali odbicie
obozu. Ale NSZ i ZWZ chciały plan odbicia opracować ze szczegółami,
przygotować dowody osobiste, ubrania, środki transportowe i przemyś-
leć odbicie obozu do końcowych faz dyslokacji uwolnionych więźniów.
Komuniści zaś chcieli jedynie wywołać sam odruch buntu więźniów i wy-
zwolenie ich bez dalszego planowania, uważając że dalsza akcja sama
się jakoś rozwinie. Jako termin odbicia ustaliły ZWZ i NSZ wilie
1943 r.

Do poważniejszych działaczy na Majdanku którzy poza swoimi osobis-
temi sprawami interesują się losem ogółu należą prócz Zelenta i Lipskiego : Orpisz -Krupski, Dębski, adw. M.Pruszyński, Dr Sztaba, har-
cerz Szcześniewski. Nie znaczy to ,by wszyscy byli zgodni co do wytycz-
nych. Dochodzi czasem do kontrwersji jak np. między Orpiszem i Pru-
szyńskim, podczas której Orpisz podniecony alkoholem prawie się na
bloku podczas kolacji konspiruje. Do wartościowych jednostek na III
polu należą płk. Łabędzki i Krupiński.

Hessel znów nie pozwolił mi pójść do kąpieli, odraczając to na
przyszły tydzień.

Typhus Fever

Wszelaki contracted typhus, the same with the technician Barański, Serafin, and the train driver called "Stryjek," so the entire gang that slept in the metal workshop after delousing. They got sick right in the incubation stage, fourteen days after that night. Typhus has passed me by again. Only now, after reading Struczowski's death report, do I realize that I should have come down with typhus in April. We slept in the same bed to stay warm. When leaving for the Revier, he gave me his warm spencer and I traded my torn blanket for his thicker one; mine didn't lack for lice, but I still managed to make a deal! Lipski came back after the typhus passed. I visited him in Block 21 while he was sick.

Knips is lying in Block 21 on our field. He sends me a card asking me to visit him: since the package sent by us to the Revier was allegedly missing sugar, he asks to be supplied with food and so on. I show the card to my friends and declare that I will leave this appeal without a reply. Remembering the hundreds of packages stolen by Knips meant for various poor, hungry, good people, stolen first of all from those who weren't present on the field because they were in the Revier, more than one of whom died of emaciation, I refuse to help this scumbag. I stand in solidarity with my friends who have been robbed. Let him waste away and learn what it means to be hungry.

The quarantine ends on November 25. We'll finally regain contact with the world. The SS men have served as messengers to other fields and offices thus far. Now, appearing as a messenger from Field 4 is—oh irony—a young boy with a *Fluchtpunkt*. Such is the shortage of people after the murder of the Jews!

I am in close contact with Dr. Hanusz, head of the Revier branch on our field, as well as with Witold Sopoćko, my former gardener. His wife moved to Lublin after his arrest—like many wives of the arrested—and almost every day he receives letters or packages from her. During the quarantine, his trusted worker brought messages onto Field 4 and from there, he threw them over the wires onto Field 3. Thanks to Witold's help, I sent letters to my loved ones so that they wouldn't become alarmed by my silence. Unfortunately, I wasn't able to get a reply from them during this period.

I met Dr. Hanusz in passing in March, when the infirmary was in Block 12, where the office is now. Back then I learned that he is a major in the Polish Army, a prisoner of war, who since his capture in France has been hauled to various concentration camps. He is a native of Przemyśl. He has specialized in treating typhus in the camp, but he complains about the lack of a laboratory where he could carry out research. He created a groundbreaking treatment. In heavier cases, he uses a syringe to puncture the spinal cord in the lumbar region of a typhus convalescent, aspirates cerebrospinal fluid, and injects it into the meninges of the sick person experiencing a crisis. He has nearly a 99 percent success rate, mortality has dropped to a minimum. But it was difficult for him to conduct scientific experiments as to what doses were appropriate and on which day of the recovery that taking fluid was most effective. He doesn't have a microscope or even the most primitive test tubes. He was indeed able to send samples for analysis in Lublin, but he suspects that the Germans deliberately sent him false data. In any case—by strange coincidence—he happened to read in the *Münchener Medizinische Wochenschrift*,[5] which found its way into the camp, where the head SS doctor of the Majdanek concentration camp, Dr. Rindfleisch (who sent the samples to the lab in Lublin and knew Hanusz's method), was describing it in the medical journal as his own discovery. They robbed us of our independence, our country, our property, factories, and furniture, why wouldn't they also appropriate our scientific achievements?

When I have a spare moment in the evening, I visit—despite an official ban—the typhus block and see Hanusz, Sopoćko, Matera, and Tomaszewski, who live there. Of course they are not in danger since they already had typhus. Sometimes Hanusz has genuinely good news to share.

5. German: "Munich Medical Weekly."

He is a great patriot and is very devoted to the sick. He's a bit of an edgy person, but after so many years in the camps and the conditions in which he performs challenging work, it's no surprise.

Lagerkapo Tomaschek was moved to Field 5 to finish the construction of a large barracks containing an operating room and various doctor's offices. They say that the outfitting of the operating room as well as the X-ray equipment is to be donated by the PCK.

On December 8, around 6:00 p.m., they alert us that a transport of women has arrived and that we have to fill out the *Aufnahme* in the wash-room. Why us men, when the women always receive their own trans-ports? It is a clear night, snow crunches underfoot. We set up tables for writing in the dressing room. There are a lot of SS men; it turns out that we aren't completing questionnaires with personal details, but forms for the *Effektenkammer*. They bring in ninety-seven women, mostly in peasant clothing, maybe ten in city garb. They came from Sierpc (Sichelburg) and Ostrołęka (Scharfenwiese). The SS men order the women to undress; they do so partially, the Germans shout to take off their shirts too. There are large paper bags next to the table. The women get into two lines, approach the table, give their full names which my colleague writes on the bags, and then step up to me with their bags in one line, and to Olszański in the other. We write down personal details and note each article of clothing placed into the bags in front of us on a lengthy questionnaire. It takes quite a long time to process one person. The rest are standing naked in tempera-tures of 4 or 5 degrees and shivering from the cold. The peasant women are so terrified and shocked that they forget their nakedness and move quite freely. A young, attractive girl stands in line; when she approaches the table for a bag, the SS man sticks his cane into her crotch and pokes around. The brave girl asks in broken German:

"And what would you do if someone did that to your sister?"

The SS man turns red and lowers his cane. A pretty thirty-year-old woman with an intelligent look comes up to me. Her beautiful, hazel eyes are unnaturally wide with fear. In one hand she holds a bag, the other is draped with all her things. While giving her personal details, she drops the bag and tries to cover her womb and breasts with her shaking hand. She is a seamstress from Ostrołęka, and they have also brought her husband. She looks at me, terrified; after all, she does not know who I am. I tell her:

"You have to grit your teeth. You have to hold tight for the first three weeks, and if you endure that much, it will work out somehow."

I try to put all my strength of persuasion into these words. I see the woman unconsciously straightening up and that I was able to lift her spirits.

I recall the first night spent at the Pawiak Prison, from February 18 to 19, 1943, in a windowless basement, on a bench with the director of the technical department of the Warsaw city government, Engineer Olszewski. In the morning, we were taken for delousing, and the person running the disinfection oven, Engineer Żurowski (the owner of Leszkowo), an older gentleman with glasses, asked me in passing who I was, and after hearing the answer, he said:

"Too bad, it happened, you must forget about what was, keep your head up, you're starting a new life."

He was half turned away when he spoke because an SS man was approaching. I blessed him and today I still bless him for these heartening words. Afterward, he smuggled a copy of the New Testament into my cell.

After the women have bathed, they bring in over two hundred men and the same procedure is repeated. There are two minor noblemen with the last name Mizgier among them, born and raised in the Mizgiery village. The work ends around midnight. We return to Field 3 under the escort of two submachine guns.

Various German kapos converged on the registration of the women, apparently having asked the *Blockführer* on duty if they could escort them to the washroom. They flocked over as if they were heading to a brothel to look at the exposed women. My "witty" friends callously ask me what impression the nude women made on me. I smile and say nothing. What am I going to say, that I was disgusted to witness the humiliation of the dignity and honor of Polish women?!

The most valuable material in the office is the card file. Thus far, the Slovak Jews were the ones who exclusively worked with it, so it was inaccessible to Poles. Divulging any information from the files to an outsider was and is

strictly prohibited. But practically from my first day of work, I started getting questions from my personal friends about the fate of various people.
If you know their number, then it's very easy to determine where a given
person is, whether they left or died. For the most part, they only give me
the last name. Then you have to look in the name index, which contains
only the number and last name. It was compiled in summer 1943, and in
cases of death or departure, the relevant cards were destroyed. So it only
contains those who are currently in the camp. If nothing turns up in this
file, I look through the cards of the deceased in the alphabetical index. The
card file doesn't give a 100-percent-certain answer, since Polish last names
are often mangled and the death certificate is issued not according to the
correct spelling but to the official spelling under which a given prisoner
was handed over by the Gestapo to the camp—or however the Slovak Jew
wrote down the last name of a deathly sick prisoner sent to the Revier. If
the person you are looking for isn't there either (and I try different spelling variations), it's still possible that they were in the camp and left with
a transport. I get the same sets of names, occasionally two or three times
from different friends, to check. I tell Zelent about it and he tells me not to
answer any questions besides those that he asks, since everything is cen-
tralized with him. Besides this information, I supply Zelent with various
data in relation to the numbers in the camp, the breakdown of national
groups, mortality, etc.

Only now do we learn that the commandant of Majdanek, Florstedt,
was arrested in Krynica because of the embezzlement of Jewish gold
and jewelry. The investigations of the murders of Marmorstein and
Birzer are bearing fruit and have consumed another victim of the golden
calf. Hitler's satellites, his faithful SS, having gone through an excellent
Nationalsozialistische Erziehung,[6] are performing well. The blood of the
massacre of the Jews on November 3 is on his hands. They tell each other
that Florstedt was sent away as a kapo to Dachau. The new commandant
is *Obersturmbannführer*[7] Weiß from Dachau. The senior kapos know and

6. A National Socialist upbringing.
7. SS Lieutenant-Colonel.

praise him. You can see the regime change right away since Weiß allows aid from the RGO and the PCK to enter the camp.

Five times a week they send us very nourishing soups, like pearl barley with meat and pea soup with bacon, bread for all the prisoners, and white rolls, apples, compote, and milk for the sick. The distribution is directed by Zelent; the Germans harass us and call the soup "*Scheisssuppe*,"[8] angry that they don't get any. All of the Poles receive packages; we give our soup to the needy. Since certain block overseers (Polish ones, unfortunately) start to trade in RGO soup, Zelent decides to appoint trusted men in the barracks and centralizes the soup distribution, helping with it personally. Kaszubski and Korabiowski help with this.

Among those who failed the test of good character is the overseer of Block 16, Skiba, an oil man from Borysław. He was a small fry in the oil business, but he never lost his Borysław mentality in the camp. Word of his excesses even reaches his wife, who pleads with him in letters to rid himself of his characteristic approach toward people and to be fair with his fellow prisoners in the camp. He beats people and doesn't return deposits of cash and valuables entrusted to his care by simple people who refer to him as "Mr. Engineer—a Pole," and carries out various scams at the expense of his subordinates. He has a bad reputation. I'm polite to him but I keep my distance.

The actor, Wiktor Domański, who left my employ to become a *Stubendienst* for the pimp, Meller, has gone sideways, and prisoners have started to complain about him in every which way. I've disassociated myself from him.

Soviet flyovers of the camp started in November. The camp siren gives the signal, but ten to fifteen minutes earlier, the lights on the wires go out. If a light is still on by accident in one of the barracks, the guards from the towers yell out, "*Licht aus*."[9] If no one hears the shouting and the light stays on, they start firing directly at the barracks. Some of the barracks are rid-

---

8. "Shit soup."
9. "Lights out."

dled with bullet holes, but luckily no one has been injured. Then—much later—the sirens in the city sound. But they are all flyovers, and usually you can't even hear the sound of the engines.

The lights on the wires, the so-called *Schlauch*, are on from 3:00 p.m. to 8:00 a.m. the next morning. If these lights weren't on all night, as well as in the fog and during the day, and if the fences weren't electrified, all of Warsaw could have certainly lit their homes and people wouldn't have to sit in the dark, illuminating individual rooms with smoking kerosene lamps or exploding carbide lamps.

Hessel the Fiddler

Our situation in the office is nightmarish. Every day we come to work wondering whether one of us will catch hell from Hessel. He comes toward you screaming, and then you can't hear what he's saying anymore; only one thought dominates—will he hit me or not? People that don't even interact with Hessel try to get away from the field. That's what Ryszard Rode does, going from working for Zelent over to Field 4 in the *Bekleidungskammer*. He does it by signing up as sick with Dr. Hanusz, who moves him from the Field 3 Revier to the one on Field 5, and there, another Polish doctor signs him in to Field 4. When he gets there, he lauds the idea. Panasiewicz also wants to escape the office this way. He pretends to be sick and goes to Hanusz. He helps him with keeping the records and correspondence in the Revier branch. Hessel finds out about Rode's trickery, calls Hanusz, and beats him mercilessly. I hear everything through the thin wood wall. He gets maybe twenty slaps and then punches to the face, then I hear Hanusz's head slamming against the wall. He comes out with cuts and blood all over his face. Hessel orders that Panasiewicz be sent back immediately. Hanusz holds on to him for two more days to keep up appearances and sends him back. Exactly eleven days after Panasiewicz went to Hanusz for his fake illness, he gets a fever and actual typhus! He got it his way.

In Block 12, where our office is, half of the barracks makes up a sleeping area and dining room for all the kapos. It's the site of nightly drinking binges presided over by Hessel. The Germans talk to one another about the most immaterial things so loudly that at first, ignorant of what's happening, we thought they were arguing. Only now do I see how much thieving and plundering the kapos have done, given the consumptive lifestyle they lead. Every day they get: meat, chicken, fish, cakes, vodka, liqueurs, etc. We keep away from them, since they continue the *Herrenvolk*[10] principle, referring to us as "you," while we have to address them as "sir."

10. Master race.

I find out from the former *Lagerältester* Ott who Hessel really is: a coffeehouse fiddler who was sentenced three times for various crimes. Right at the outbreak of the war, on September 1, 1939, he was locked up in a concentration camp as an SV (hence a green triangle) and thanks to various machinations with SS men that he served, he swapped his triangle for a red one (political). He has the unconditional support of First *Rapportführer* Kostial, for whom our office prepares all of the reports to sign. Kostial, who works in the *Abteilung* III, is the right-hand man for its chief, Thumann—so the camp is ruled by this triumvirate. No one can question Hessel.

He is unscrupulous and his method is to create the impression that everyone is incompetent and they don't know how to do anything, and he alone knows how to get the job done, making him essentially irreplaceable. Whenever an SS man approaches, Hessel begins yelling for no good reason, raising his voice, and if he can't glom on to anything at that moment, he remembers some issue from a week ago and starts going off about it, but as if it just happened at that moment. When Thumann shows up unexpectedly, Hessel has no shame in grabbing a few dozen old death certificates or irrelevant papers right in front of us, just to pretend that he's working. It seems like he's convinced his superiors that he is working nonstop for eighteen hours a day and that he does nothing else but correct the mistakes made by these *Scheisspolacken*. Olszański writes the *Stärkemeldung*, which are complicated daily accounts, flawlessly. But in order to hide it from Kostial that Hessel doesn't write them, he forbids the report from being written before the evening roll call, since Kostial visits us immediately prior to it. When the time approaches, Hessel sits down at the typewriter and types the heading and waits for Kostial to find him there. After the roll call—so once our free time begins—he tells Olszański:

"OK, now you can keep writing."

The work lasts at least two hours when there's normal traffic in the camp. On days when there is no movement or changes, Olszański will start asking at 3:00 p.m. whether he can begin writing the *Stärkemeldung*, but Hessel says no, using the excuse that Kostial might still order some changes. But Kostial can't order any changes, since they happen automatically when someone is moved, dies, or is released, or when new transports arrive. What it's all about is keeping Kostial from seeing, God forbid, that someone else can write the reports also.

Once, after he had been drinking, he bragged about having been a block overseer in Dachau in 1940. Every barracks there had a thousand prisoners; his was full of priests. The priests were mostly Polish, including the entire Gniezno chapter, with its suffragan bishop. He sneers at the fact that the priests hid behind the stove in the evenings after work and heard one another's confessions and prayed the rosary. He brags about being an atheist and how he schooled those "*Pfaffen.*" He mentions the example of the time when the priests tracked snow into the barracks from their wooden shoes. How could they be punished? You can't hold back their food. So he forced the *Tischältester*[11] to declare that the entire barracks will willingly give up its next four Sunday dinners and offer them to the neighboring gypsy barracks. Triumphantly, Hessel adds:

"After all, they were permitted to give them up; my hands were clean."

He also says that Polish "partisans" from 1939 were kept in separate barracks that were surrounded with additional barbed wire. A camp within a camp. The windowpanes were taken out and each person got only one blanket, and half the amount of food. In the winter of 1939/1940, most of them died out. Hessel has a violin which was looted from some Jew who naively came to Majdanek with his fiddle. He plays every couple of days, just five or six bars, usually of the same melody, and then puts away the violin. It's indicative of his inner turmoil. He's a technically competent player, but the pull of the bow is soulless. His petty cash, a wallet with twenty thousand zlotys, is kept by a young Czech who serves as a waiter for the kapos. He's anticipating the possibility of a search of the kapos. He hands his wallet to the Czech as if it were a pair of galoshes. It's not a huge sum for him, since he spends one thousand zlotys a day on food and drink. Admittedly, he pays for all the food for the *Feldführer* and *Rapportführer* of Field 3. Kostial never eats anything at our place.

11. The senior prisoner at each table.

Hessel is hated among the German kapos. In the spring, they organized a concert on a Sunday, improvised with an accordion, violin, and guitars, and they invited Hessel. He ordered that the musicians must come to him. When the kapos didn't comply with this, he dashed into their barracks and forbade any playing. A fight broke out and Hessel got it good from the kapos, and he reported them for revolting. An investigation was carried out and several kapos were sentenced to whippings; the punishment wasn't actually meted out, while officially they announced that it had been.

That's only a silhouette of our boss's character. Any minor suggestion or casual comment on how to streamline the office operations is seized by him immediately and he has no shame in loudly reporting to Kostial in our presence about the new improvement that he introduced. He is openly contemptuous toward us Poles, accentuating it at every step, and seeking to injure our pride at every opportunity. Every third word is *"Scheisspolacken,"* and every disorder and shortcoming that he tells Thumann and the *Feldführer* about he blames on the Poles, even though most of the mess comes from the Russians.

The evening roll call has been moved to 2:00 p.m. The morning roll call still takes place at 6:00 a.m. It doesn't matter either way for us in the office, since our work finishes when there are no more new arrivals—around 8:00 p.m. Only then do I go for a walk around the field and visit Zelent to tell him about all of the relevant occurrences in the office. But even then, a messenger often comes to call me back, because Hessel demands some explanation or "urgent" work, which could easily be done a couple of days later. Tomaschek has been replaced as *Lagerkapo* by Lang, the camp interpreter up to now.

On December 19, 1943, a transport arrives from Minsk and Borisov.[12] There are about seven hundred Belarusians and Russians with women and small children, suspected of *"Bandenzugehörigkeit"* (membership in partisan

12. Today Barysaw, Belarus.

gangs).[13] We take down their personal details all night long. There is a general directive from the Gestapo that all Russian last names must be written according to phonetic German spelling, so "Shcherbachev" is written as "Schtscherbatschow," while Polish last names are written according to their authentic spellings. But not every German knows the correct spelling of Polish last names. So if the Gestapo misspells a prisoner's name, that's how it's entered into our files.

The next day I write the card files for the new arrivals. It's freezing outside, and in our room it's maybe 8 or 9 degrees, my fingers are totally numb. I try to legibly write the letters of the Russian last names, which are so hard for the Germans to read. I already finished a whole stack. I'm calligraphing the surname "Awratschenko." Hessel comes over with the *Feldführer*, takes the card, and asks him whether he can read it. Gosberg starts to read it letter by letter, since simple Germans are only used to Gothic script and have difficulty reading the Latin alphabet. Then he throws Avrachenko's card onto the table and I get a sudden blow to the face; my glasses fly somewhere behind me onto the ground. I get a sweet taste in my mouth. Blood is dripping from my nose onto the files. I'm sitting there stunned, I get another punch to the nose and the abusive words:

"So this is your handwriting, double doctor?"

Gosberg pulls him away by the sleeve. I stand up and wipe the blood from the stained cards. I don't wipe the blood off of Avrachenko's card, I let it clot, I'll keep it as a memento and promise myself to pay for blood with blood. My friends pick up my broken glasses. I walk to the bedroom; in the mirror I see my cut lip and my swelling nose. I make compresses and return to work. Olszański tells me that Gosberg was reproaching Hessel in his room behind closed doors about why he was beating me without cause. If an SS man, a sadist in the mold of Gosberg, is criticizing a German prisoner for unfairly beating a Pole, well, then, that best typifies the character of my boss, whom the kapos don't refer to by his name, but as "Stapo," short for Gestapo.

13. The transport from Minsk and Borisov, consisting of 548 men, women, and children, was received in Majdanek on January 3, 1944.

A death report arrives stating that the block overseer Svoboda, whose head Gosberg pulverized, has died. They were treating his wounds and he came down with typhus, which is what killed him. So the intermediary perpetrator of his death is Gosberg.

The next day my nose is violet, by the third day it's almost black.

The deadline for freeing the camp has been moved to New Year's Eve. Communist cells are operating on different fields and want to trigger an immediate reaction. The signal is supposed to be simultaneous fires in barracks on all the fields.

Christmas Eve, 1943

Christmas Eve is in two days. The PCK has sent gingerbread to all Polish prisoners, alongside Christmas wafers, holy pictures, apples, honey, bacon, eggs, etc. The auto shop prepared a die, a steel engraving of a Nativity scene: prisoners with the letters KL on their backs are kneeling in front of the crib, and one of them is holding a long stick with a kind of banner on it in the form of a triangle with the letter P (the symbol for us Poles). It's the size of a postcard; I also find a few dozen nice, smooth, cream-colored cards among the office supplies and deliver them for typing. I send several cards in envelopes to my loved ones. The last batch of packages before Christmas arrives, and I don't get anything, despite the otherwise regular deliveries of packages.

The diorama needs to be done by the holidays, since Thumann designated it as the Christmas present for the SS mess hall. Rain and snow are falling. Since it's an order from Thumann, the SS men don't concern themselves with anything else and load the table, made out of wood chips held together with plaster and meticulously glued-together houses, towers, and barbed wire (imitated with thread pulled through needles), onto the back of a truck, putting it on its side since it doesn't fit otherwise.

The RGO provides us with some exceptionally good borscht, as well as cold cuts and cheeses for making sandwiches, beet and horseradish salad, white rolls, and more. Not having known about it, we made a collection among ourselves and bought various appetizers and a row of vodka bottles. The Polish political prisoners gather at Pietroniec's place in the warehouse. Zelent orders us to set up tables and benches in a semicircle there. The Red Cross delivered many Christmas trees with shiny decorations, which were divided among the barracks. One of them is in Pietroniec's place, of course. I go there around 6:00 p.m. They already distributed the RGO soup in the barracks, so we can leisurely enjoy Christmas Eve. When

I arrive, most are already there, maybe fifty people. My friends seat Zelent and I in the place of honor near the center of the table by the tree. Father Przytocki from Stanisławów, who works in the *Entlausung*, stands up and, putting on a brave face, says in a joyful voice:

"Now we will say the traditional prayer."

He says the Our Father. My jaw is shaking, tears are streaming down my cheeks and falling on the Christmas wafer. We share the wafer with one another, remember our loved ones back home, embrace, and kiss each other on the cheeks. The atmosphere is dignified—ceremonious— sublime. We sit down at the tables, it starts bustling. Father Przytocki and Lipski speak, pointing out the collapsing might of our oppressors. I drink a *Brüderschaft*[14] with Zelent, Lipski, and Pietroniec. We sing Christmas carols. I'm sad that I didn't get Christmas wishes from home in time, but I know that everyone is remembering me during the breaking of the wafer. But I have been given a gift. The ideological elite of the prisoners have put me in the honorary place today, and it's the most valuable gift that they could have given me. It's my most beautiful day in the camp. The scale and tension of my inner emotions on this day can only be compared with receiving Holy Communion on Calvary in Jerusalem in 1927.

After a two-hour stay, I bid farewell to my friends and I am invited to Dr. Hanusz's in the typhus block. Just today, Tetych was admitted with a high fever. Here I find a formally prepared table set for ten people. It's covered in lignin, which is what the napkins are also made from. Dr. Hanusz, Dr. Meter, Dr. Tomaszewski with his son who is a nurse, Sopoćko, the Revier clerk Czarnecki,[15] Olszański, the scout Szcześniewski, me, and a few other nurses are all there. They serve borscht with dumplings, then eggs with roasted onions, fish, vodka, wine, cookies, and tea. Hanusz intones "The Anthem of Underground Poland." In an undertone:

Onward to battle, soldiers
of Underground Poland, to arms!
The Polish might protects you,

14. Toast of friendship.
15. An alias.

The bell calls you to the fight.
The hour of vengeance tolls
For crimes, torment, and blood—
To arms, Jesus and Mary,
The warriors' call resounds . . .
. . . To arms, Jesus and Mary,
The warriors' call resounds . . .

With great feeling and lovely diction, Olaszński recites "The Gray Soldier's Coat."

It is impossible to understand the spirit that permeated that night unless you were there. We leave around 10:00 p.m. and visit our home barracks, Block 15 for me, and then with Olszański to his, Block 6. They treat us with vodka everywhere we go. My head is really spinning by the time I get back to the bedroom. That was my Christmas Eve 1943!

I remind myself that last year I received several lovely English handkerchiefs from Ninka for Christmas. Doesn't the old superstition hold true that this foreshadows tears?

December 25 is a day off work. But Hessel announced that the office would be working as usual, all day. The roll call takes place an hour later than normal. *Rapportführer* Sieberer, who took over command of the field during Gosberg's leave, conducts a head inspection during roll call. Dozens of prisoners are slapped for their hair being too "long," meaning about two or three millimeters. He calls the barbers and orders that everyone must have their heads shaved by 3:00 p.m. The shaving takes place on the square. This is the "festive" atmosphere that accompanies the first day of Christmas. We eat a potluck dinner at the holiday table—but in light of the surprise that Sieberer dealt us, the mood has soured.

We don't work in the afternoon, *Lagerkapo* Juliusz Lang[16] put in a word for us. He lives together with the kapos and claims to have been an officer in the Polish Legions, served in the light cavalry, been a military attaché in Washington, D.C., and left the army in 1934 after marrying a German

16. Actually Julian Lang.

woman. We suspect that he is Jewish. He's friends with Hessel and plays cards with him regularly. After Marmorstein, Fuchs, and Wyderka, he's considered the wealthiest prisoner on the field; he made a fortune trading in jewelry, which Olszański helped him with. He doesn't mix with the Poles, he keeps the exclusive company of the Germans and the Russian, Victor (Hessel's lackey, an agronomist engineer, the manager of some *sovkhoz*[17]). He spends all his free time playing cards. Lang intervenes with Hessel and we get off work for the afternoon.

I write a letter to my family and tell them that I don't regret spending Christmas Eve in the camp. I don't know if my loved ones will understand me; they will certainly be shaking their heads in disbelief when they read this passage of the letter.

Christmas Eve included an ugly incident on Field 5. There are two barracks there for sick female prisoners. After the Christmas Eve supper, our former *Lagerkapo*, Tomaschek, and kapo No. 2, Schommer, went for a visit to the women's barracks. No one is allowed to walk around the field after 9:00 p.m. They were drunk, of course, and ignored this rule—like mating grouses. Two shots rang out from the guard tower, two bleeding figures lay on the white background of snow, Tomaschek and Schommer with their legs shot through.

A similar situation took place at the same time on Field 1, where Thumann came over drunk in the company of some other officer. They went into a barracks, roused several women out of bed, and started "interrogating" them in just their shirts. The fiancée of the scout, Szcześniewski, was among them. It lasted a while. The *Lagerschreiberin*,[18] Ms. Stecka, called over the *Oberaufseherin*[19] to help, and she ordered Thumann to leave the women's camp and said she would submit a complaint against him.

On the second day of Christmas, all of us in the office are invited by the cooks for dinner. It's more modest than we imagined, evidently they wanted to demonstrate how simply they live, which we know a thing or two about. The overseer of the cooks is Engineer Szachowski from

17. Russian: a state-owned farm in the Soviet Union.
18. The main female camp clerk.
19. Head supervisor of the female prisoners, a female member of the camp staff.

Warsaw. He always has a lot of new information, which he always presents in a rosy way. We joke with each other about his way of expressing himself: "The situation is woooonderful," and yet he infects all of us with his optimism, if only for a few hours.

Lipski informs me that the deadline for freeing the camp has been moved from New Year's Eve to January 9. The reason for the constant delays is that the NSZ and ZWZ can't come to a final agreement on what to do with the freed prisoners. Both organizations are too weak to carry out the plan on their own, though.

Olszański tells me in confidence that the communists are preparing to liberate the camp on January 9, 1944. When he has wetted his whistle— and he does like to drink—he raises his fist in the air as a greeting.

On December 26, Hanusz moves with his Revier to Field 5. On December 27, he gets a summons to the *Politische Abteilung*. Is he going to be released?

Some SS sergeant whom I don't know asks me if I own homes in Warsaw on Chocimska and Dolna Streets. I confirm it. He says:

"Your brother was here before the holidays and wanted to see you so that you could sign a power of attorney for him to administer the houses. But since visits are forbidden, I told him to leave the documents. But really, think it over whether you can sign it for him."

I waved it off and signed them, knowing that this was, after all, a false pretense that I had personally advised my brother to use to try and meet me officially. Counting on the fact that both of us could be arrested, back in 1941 we had granted each other power of attorney through a notarized deed, and had also empowered our attorney to manage all of our property.

Before New Year's Eve I finally get my Christmas package, so I count it as my New Year's delivery. We drink a lot that evening. Around midnight, shooting begins; we even hear automatic weapons. Colorful rockets shoot into the sky. We turn out the light in the room, raise the blackout curtains, and open the windows. The fusillade has lasted for half an hour already and is intensifying. We start to get excited. Olszański, already under the influence, says emphatically:

"Gentlemen, we are witnesses to a historic event . . ."

I yank him by the arm in the dark, since I see that he wants to reveal the secret of the camp's liberation, which has now perhaps been accelerated from January 9 to the previous time frame, New Year's Eve, while most of the Germans are drunk. The firing quiets down, and it turns out that it was only celebratory shooting. The boozed-up kapos come to us and are drunkenly effusive, practically kissing each other. We receive them formally and coolly. Hessel is totally out of it and goes to sleep. The kapos carry him, bed and all, to the middle of the office and he doesn't feel a thing.

The new year, 1944, starts with a barracks fire on the *Zwischenfeld* between Fields 1 and 2, in the laundry and the shuttered crematorium.[20] The fire broke out around 6:00 p.m., so after dark, and lasted over two hours. I remembered what Lipski had said, that a fire in Majdanek would signal the partisans in the forest to immediately come to the camp's aid. I can only establish one thing, though: within fifteen minutes the camp is surrounded by a heavy cordon of SS guard companies, which formed up beyond the barbed wire. The SS is on alert!

Several days later, a fire breaks out on Field 5. It was taken as the battle cry for the uprising and this could have resulted in tragic consequences for Majdanek. A communist from Białystok on Field 4 thought it was the signal and ran with a candle to his mattress in Block 5 and started to light it on fire. Władysław Dębski scared him off. The zealot ran to the neighboring Block 6, pursued by Dębski and several friends who prevented the barracks from being set ablaze. The prisoners on Field 3 had already asked those on Field 4 through the wires whether it was the signal. The overseer of Block 5 reported to the *Lagerältester* of Field 4 (a communist) about the attempt to set the barracks on fire. The *Politische Abteilung* carried out an investigation, but the *Lagerältester* buried the matter, testifying that the man from Białystok was just drunk.

On the Feast of the Three Kings, the *Rapportführer* gets punished for the harassment inflicted on the entire field on the first day of Christmas.

20. The drying-room barracks on the inter-field burned down on January 7, 1944.

A search is carried out at the place of his lover, the sister of the SS man Toruński, and they allegedly find twenty thousand zlotys there. She is arrested, and Sieberer meets with the same fate two days later. The money came from the well-known source: the rose garden . . . And Sieberer had been making such preparations for the arrival of his beloved. He ordered Noak to compose a tetrastich in German to welcome his dearest and then have our draftsman (a Russian) paint it in Gothic script on a large sheet, which, festooned with a garland border, was hung on the door of his room. He had me type a request to the camp commandant for the allocation of beds, sheets, curtains, table settings, and so on—not imported from the *Vaterland*, naturally, but looted from Jewish homes . . . and meanwhile, they locked his dearest in the cooler! Poor, broken SS man's heart!

The complaint lodged by the *Oberaufseherin* of the women's field gives an unexpected result. Thumann—the demigod of Majdanek—and all the SS men in general are strictly forbidden from entering Field 1.

The Dead Arrive

A transport of gravely ill prisoners from Auschwitz arrives in the evening. There are about a thousand of them. During the unloading of the railcars, 290 corpses remain inside. They died on the way. The transport consists of people that are so sick that they can't walk, they are driven to the bathhouse in cars, there they lay them on the concrete floor in an unheated room. Another twenty-seven died by morning. The washing lasts all day. They bring them to Field 4 and we go there after the roll call to fill out questionnaires. The clerks from Field 4 help us. The new arrivals are mainly tuberculosis sufferers in the final stage, many of them have phlegmon, dysentery, enteritis, or other chronic, incurable diseases. The condemned! We wonder why these people were sent to us, instead of letting them die in peace in Auschwitz. All the nationalities are among them: Poles, Germans, Frenchmen, Dutchmen, Italians, Albanians, Yugoslavians, there is a professor from a university in Paris, an Italian composer, an opera conductor, doctors, and a large proportion of intelligent people in general. The sick are deprived of even a pretense of medical care. In the end, modern medicine might already be useless for the majority of them.

A few days later, the same kind of transport arrives from Dachau—1,200 people. Then, over a thousand prisoners from Sachsenhausen (Oranienburg); several days later, six hundred from Buchenwald. There are many among them who went blind while working underground, digging caverns in Dora to house new factories being built there. They tell us that the transport that left Majdanek for Buchenwald in July mostly perished in the undergrounds of Dora. The prisoners have barracks underground, so that they don't see the light of day at all. It is terribly stuffy and humid there.

Dr. Sztaba, the doctor for Field 5, collects information from the Poles that came from different camps about the conditions and types of work there. He finds out that in the camps in Dora, Ellrich, and Nordhausen, in the Harz highlands, all branches of Buchenwald, some kind of flying rocket-torpedoes of enormous proportions with steering mechanisms are being built.[21] He writes down this information in invisible ink and passes it on immediately through the wires to the hands of our released friend, Albin Boniecki, who is again working in counterintelligence for us.

After Field 4 fills up, the new arrivals are placed in the former typhus barracks on Field 3, which was abandoned by Dr. Hanusz less than two weeks before. Not even a superficial disinfection was carried out. All of the transports brought with them a huge amount of corpses, and the mortality is terrifyingly high. We figure out that the act of moving these prisoners from various camps is intended to finish off the chronically sick. That's why the depths of winter were chosen for the moves. Here, they want to do them in with typhus. Zelent and I decide to give up our RGO soup for the benefit of these poor Lazaruses. Most of the Poles accept this. The soups and side dishes go to these three barracks and are given to Poles, Frenchmen, and Yugoslavs. In this way we want to emphasize the friendship and solidarity that unites our nations. The widely advertised National-Socialist NSV[22] and the German Red Cross have greater funds at their disposal than the PCK, but they aren't interested in the German prisoners. Dr. Zakrzewski is made overseer for these three barracks, but his daily functions as a doctor are limited to collecting several dozen aluminum neck tags taken from the deceased. Identifying the sick according to the transport list is very difficult. They are mentally ill, unconscious, and feverish. They are written up while lying in bed. Some of them give the wrong last names or aren't on the list. It happens that a sick person who has already been recorded will get up to relieve themselves, and on their way back, gets lost in the labyrinth of densely packed beds and lies down somewhere else in a part of the hall that wasn't yet registered. There they register him again. So there are more last names on the registered list than on the transport list.

The dying are indifferent to what's going on around them. Attempts to reconcile the lists by Noak aren't successful. Then Hessel gives the order to force all the sick people out of their beds, line them up in their shirts

21. A reference to the A4 ballistic rockets assembled at the Mittelbau-Dora camp complex, known by the propagandistic name "V-2" (from *Vergeltungswaffe*, "retaliatory weapon").

22. Short for *Nationalsozialistische Volkswohlfahrt* (National Socialist People's Welfare).

and blankets in freezing weather in front of the barracks, and individually let them back in, noting down the last names. This lasts several hours; you can imagine how many people caught a deathly cold because of this. The sight of these poor fellows makes us aware of what we are, numbers: nothing more, just numbers to be liquidated at the fastest rate and in the largest amount possible. *Memento mori!*

Thumann orders a doghouse made in Zelent's workshop for his German shepherd Boris. The walls, roof, and floor are all double-layered, and the gap is filled with cotton. The entrance to the house is covered with a two-way flap. A dog's life; they are taken care of well.

Hessel demands that all the files be ready the morning after a new transport has arrived. There's a lot of them, because they go to: 1) the *Politische Abteilung*, 2) the *Abteilung* III, 3) the *Arbeitseinsatz*, 4) the post office, 5) our numerical file, and 6) our name file. Each form is in a different format, according to a different system. Even the order of the points in the description is different on each form. In the beginning, we work all night, despite the fact that the SS man Müsch from the *Politische Abteilung* clearly stated that there is no rush and the files can be delivered in several days. But Hessel wants to show how "he" works. Naturally, he goes to sleep leisurely at 10:00 p.m.

We're jolted by the news that they've ordered new trenches dug by the crematorium. We're even more shaken by the information that two loudspeakers have been installed on top of the crematorium. Battles are ongoing in the region of Rivne and Dubno. A rumor spreads that before the Germans abandoned the city, they shot all of the inmates in the prison and penal camp in Rivne. The same information arrives from Kowel, spread by German kapos who have contacts with the SS. We get the news from Kapo Gröner, the only one that we tolerate in our bedroom. He is learning Polish, sings "*Góralu, czy ci nie żal*,"[23] and takes care of a Polish woman on Field 1, who he delivers packages to and intends to marry. He

---

23. Polish: "Highlander, do you not regret."

sits with us every day and gloomily repeats that *"Splittergraben"*[24] awaits us all. Those in the know tell us that enough reserves of gas have been stockpiled in the camp to kill fifteen thousand people, and just as much alcohol mix to burn the bodies. Moved by this news, I write farewell letters to Mary and my brother. In the evenings Hessel starts to talk with the kapos about an evacuation march beyond the Vistula to Radom.

In the meantime, another transport of goners from Neuengamme arrive. Out of 290 people, thirty corpses were removed. I don't think I have to mention that all the transports consist of cattle cars, and people lie on the bare floor without blankets or even straw.

There are three thousand new sick inductees to the camp (not counting our own sick). The mortality rate currently stands at 0.5 percent of the entire camp population daily, so at this rate, in a matter of two hundred days, or a little less than seven months, fifteen thousand prisoners will die.

The *Arbeitseinsatz* work squad is put into our sleeping quarters, i.e., Kapo Neumann, a German with a green triangle who took over the unit after Meierovitz, as well as several Poles: Engineer Krygowski, another oil man from Borysław, Andrzej Janiszek, Klosowski, and others. It gets cramped but our roommates are civil. The only foreign body is the Kraut, who observes every detail and is always running to Hessel.

The multitude of transports have created a huge backlog. We work regularly until midnight since *à la longue*,[25] you can't stay up every night. We divide what needs to be written up among us and sometimes it happens that a file is created twice. Because of this feverish work and sleep deprivation, we're so tired that sometimes mistakes like this are made. When a duplicate file is returned a few days later, Hessel goes crazy, we've discredited him and the slaps to the face and throwing of stools begins. It's also a tragedy if an inspection of the files shows that a different number of individual incoming prisoner categories was reported in the *Stärkemeldung*

24. Slit trench.
25. French: in the long run.

than it shows in the card files. For example, a Czech BV was reported as admitted when it should have been a Czech SV, or a Russian was written down as "Sch" instead of "AZA." The Jew was right who said, "They count us like gold, but treat us like shit." Who really needs to know the breakdown of how many homosexual German prisoners are forty to fifty years old, and how many male, Polish Jehovah's Witnesses are sixty to seventy? It's only to justify the employment of so many hundreds and maybe thousands of SS men and protect them from service at the front.

Because of the mountain of work, Hessel expands the office. Before the holidays, Majewski had already come in as a draftsman to write up various dossiers and registers in ink; Wacław Laskowski, freshly arrived on a transport from Sierpc, now comes as a writer to create card files; Stanisław Jabłoński, a former civil servant in the Ministry of Justice who just arrived from Daniłowiczowska,[26] becomes a typist; and Henryk Zalewski, a technician from the Avia factory in Warsaw, brought here back in January 1943 from Pawiak, is now my special assistant. He creates card files and crosses out the names of the deceased and adds the date of death. Sometimes, when we get death reports from several days of transports all at once, that is to say three to four hundred notices, we have to automate this function as well. Zalewski makes a stamp out of rubber in the shape of a cross, similar to the Cross of Independence, with two long, crossed lines as a symbol of crossing out the name and a dotted line for the death date. Czesław Mankiewicz comes on as my second assistant; a former student at the Warsaw Polytechnic, he arrived from Pawiak with me. He came back from the Revier where he was laid up for ten months with tuberculosis. Benden asks Hessel to take special care of Mankiewicz, so that's why he took him into the office. I find out that Mankiewicz had been injected with tuberculosis as an experiment and was then painstakingly treated.

After distributing the RGO soup among the goners in Block 20, Lipski slips on the frozen stairs on his way out and breaks his leg. He goes to Field 5 the following day.

---

26. The prison on Daniłowiczowska Street in Warsaw.

Plenty of Germans arrive on the transports who are still more or less upright. Hessel decides to Germanize the office, which we Poles are pleased with, we'll get away from this nightmare. Węglarz came back from the Revier recently after recovering from typhus, he's a bit deaf now, like everyone else dazed by it. Hessel sits at the typewriter and orders that someone start dictating. He does it when he wants to speed things up, since he thinks that we work too slowly. He usually makes a mistake mid-page because of the rush and pulls out the paper from the typewriter, crumples it up, throws it against the ground, swears "*Scheiss,*" and beats the innocent man who was dictating to him in the face. Afterward, one of us starts the job again and then it's done well. Now Hessel takes Węglarz to dictate. He makes a mistake and flies into a rage, hitting Węglarz in the face and knocking him off his stool onto the ground; he kicks his legs, walks away, turns around, and, from a distance, throws a stool at him but misses. He punches the young Czech, who works as the waiter for the kapos and who carries his wallet, so hard that he ruptures his eardrum. This Czech had been arrested and was locked up in the Castle because, while working as a waiter in a German mess in Lublin, he spoke in Czech to the Polish kitchen staff, despite being warned several times to only speak German. He tells us about sitting in the Castle in the same cell as a fat German, Galbawi, but that this German was sometimes let out of his cell and went out on the town. Galbawi is of course the former *Lagerältester* of Majdanek who was said to have been released and had gone to the Gestapo. We have confirmation. What role did he play? He sits in various cells, pretending to be arrested, to extract confessions from his cellmates. The young Czech didn't even realize that he was sitting alongside an agent provocateur.

Rapportführer Sieberer was released, but he doesn't return to Field 3, he is assigned to the *Standarte*, the guard unit.

Every couple of days, Hessel brings in a few Germans for a tryout. These are school principals, office clerks, etc. The tests end with a beating and kicking these Germans out after just twenty-four hours. Hessel kept one of them for longer and assigned him to the *Arbeitseinsatz* as an assistant to

Serafin and Tetych. What one of those two can do in an hour, a German needs three hours for. Corporal Tempel slaps him once, then again a short time later, and the third time he beats him until he draws blood and boots him out on the spot. It turns out that the *Herrenvolk* isn't so agile to grasp the situation on the fly and the "*Untermenschen*[27] *Scheisspolacken*" turn out to be the smart ones.

All of the correspondence for Field 3, and all of the undeliverable letters for all of Majdanek, come to me to distribute among the barracks or to determine where the unknown addressee can be found.

Occasional inspections of the correspondence sometimes reveal unbelievable trickery. A Polish working woman writes to her brother-in-law and curses him out, asking what is going on with her husband, his brother. Both of them were at Majdanek. It seems that the brother-in-law had previously written to her to say that the husband was sick and that she should address packages to his last name, so that he can take them to his sick brother in the hospital. The woman complains that it's so difficult with four children, and that it's such a huge effort to regularly send packages. I check; his brother died five months ago. The letter, addressed to the brother-in-law, bears the number of the deceased. He's clever: he said to address it to him, and to provide the dead man's number at the same time. This way he could secure all of the packages arriving under the number of the departed for himself. The matter is clear—the guy's a jackal—a hyena. I present the matter to my friends Zelent and Olszański. They acknowledge that there should be no mercy or national solidarity shown to such a leech, and that what he's doing should be brought to the attention of the field commandant. The vulture gets the honest, deserved twenty-five lashes in the ass and confesses to bleeding the poor widow dry for the last five months.

Andrzej Stanisławski lives with us, Thumann's *Läufer*, the son of the director of the Bank of Poland in Poznań. An intelligent, handsome, twenty-year-old boy. As a messenger he has to be well-dressed, and Andrzej likes to dress up. As a messenger he also gets to go to Field 1 where the women are and he heads there often for little breakfasts. Of course, he gets lucky.

27. Subhuman.

Sexualnot

Sexualnot[28] (I don't know if there's an equivalent in Polish) is very strong among the women. It's actually the same with us, but based on accounts of those who had direct contact with them, for them it's more unruly and less controlled. They even get excited by words; they don't call us men, but males. Every one-on-one opportunity is taken advantage of, matter-of-factly, without needless preludes. Whoever can't get onto Field 1 rushes to the *Gärtnerei* or the *Kartoffelmieten*,[29] spots where both men and women work. There is a big cellar there where these tête-à-têtes take place in a spot completely lacking in ambience or entourage.

I have known Andrzej since last summer. Back then when the main office was on Field 1, he covertly checked various names for me that I had received questions about in secret messages. He fell in love with a medical student who works as a nurse in the women's infirmary. Besides frequent visits, he writes letters to her. When most of us lie down to sleep, he sits down to write and spends an hour or more composing a letter. The light shines in my eyes, but despite my urgings, he doesn't stop writing until he's finished. In the morning he gives the letter to Noak to read and evaluate; Noak, at 28 years old, is quite naive in this area (he doesn't reveal much, and when the spirit moves him, he talks about his experiences in the form of the adventures of "his friend"). Andrzej delivers the letter in the morning and brings a reply in the afternoon, which Noak extends his hand for from a distance. With a professorial expression, stroking the place where a professor's beard should be and nodding his head as if he were grading a school essay, he studies the love letter. He consults with Andrzej, and in the evening another letter is being composed. It loses the charm of a secret, romantic correspondence—and it becomes a stylistic exercise, not

28. Literally, sexual need; the sex drive.
29. Potato mounds.

springing from feelings, but the result of a discussion or inspiration of a professor.

But even my older friend Olszański has fallen for someone on Field 1 (*nomina sunt odiosa*),[30] a woman who paints pretty miniatures. He can't visit her like Andrzej, so our messenger delivers letters and brings back replies.

I know when he's writing these letters at the side table, since whenever someone approaches, he reflexively covers up the letter and draws attention to himself just like a schoolboy in love. He is excited and overjoyed when he reads me fragments of "her" letters. Over the course of their correspondence, they start speaking to each other using the informal "you." What a success! I tell him my honest view that licking a lollipop through a windowpane like this doesn't make any sense. It's an unnecessary teasing of the imagination. I'll admit, I'm one of those who would "have women by the spoonful," but not just in the physical sense, but to stay faithful to someone who misses me and might shed a tear for me sometimes.

My home is my castle when it comes to our bedroom. There, we are cut off from all boorishness, great friendship reigns, and package communism, where you can take something from another's shelf if you happen to like it, is fine. Hessel enters infrequently, just sometimes during the day to check if we are keeping the closet tidy and to complain to the *Feldführer* out loud about how these Poles live.

Noak is an expert in coming up with various topics for discussion, with the favorite and most often debated subject being the difference between culture and civilization. After the lights go off, Serafin recites passages from *Pan Tadeusz*.[31] The two or three hours of friendly coexistence come at a high price, since every morning our personal and national dignity is denigrated.

Dr. Lutman, an employee of the Ossolineum, died of typhus. Letters addressed to him from his wife come for weeks, full of concern for his

---

30. Latin: names are undesirable.
31. "Master Thaddeus," an epic poem by Adam Mickiewicz published in 1834.

health. In letters to the deceased, each word takes on such a different, deeper meaning. From these letters I see that his wife treats him like her older son—indeed, he was really helpless and in need of care. Since I know that the *Politische Abteilung* doesn't immediately send death notices, I try to inform the family by, instead of destroying the letter, writing the date and a cross by the last name of the recipient in colored pencil, and writing "*Zurück*"[32] and including an arrow pointing toward the name of the sender. The camp post office returns these letters to Lublin.

We get a new roommate. A small transport from Lwów brings us a certain Lippmann, a German first lieutenant from the First World War. He possesses an Iron Cross First Class and a gold emblem for wounds suffered, which was only given to eighty soldiers throughout the entire war. He has mixed ethnicity, his father was a Jew and he himself married a Jewess. He's a cousin of the well-known American journalist Walter Lippmann. The Gestapo sent instructions for him to be treated especially well, and he was supposed to be made a kapo, but someone objected and he was sent to the office and assigned to our sleeping quarters. Another foreign body spying on us and, what's more, getting irritated, because we speak a language that he doesn't understand. He walks around with a red triangle, but after a few days Hessel forces him to sew on a Jewish star.

Serafin comes down with gingivitis and oral ulceration, he can't swallow anything. I cook my noodles with milk for him, which is the one thing he can choke down. After a few days of lying in our bedroom, Hessel forces him to go to the Revier. The Russian doctor Abratumov, a Tatar who heads our infirmary, visited him in our room every day. He gave him vitamin injections and some kind of oral rinses. Serafin was also taken care of by me, the *Stubendienst*, and his brother-in-law, Kaszubski, who visited him frequently. Another example of Hessel's ruthless treatment of prisoners.

Since the kapos consume vast quantities of vodka, and they can't take the bottles out to the trash, they get into the habit of smashing them into tiny

32. "Back."

pieces and throwing them into the toilets. After a while, all of the pipes are backed up. Hessel raises a storm and dumps the blame on who? Of course, the "*Scheisspolacken.*" He curses us out in the evening in front of all the kapos and forbids us from using the toilets and washrooms in our barracks. We have to go to the neighboring Block 13. This doesn't change the situation with the kapos' toilets, they still get clogged.

The field doesn't have a telephone line. The only one is in the *Blockführer* gatehouse where they call Hessel over to receive various instructions.

Hessel's friendship with Thumann is very cautious and the former is perpetually on guard, striving to maintain the impression that things are always going smoothly. In the camp language it's called "*Nicht aufgefallen.*"[33] He's in league with the SS men who all hate and fear Thumann. Hessel orders a bell installed from the gatehouse to the office and vice versa. Officially, one is used to call messengers from the office to the gatehouse, but in fact it announces Thumann's approach to the Field 3 gate, which is when the long, buzzing tone of the bell sounds. The opposite bell is for Hessel to use to call for help at night if he is attacked—really! We have nothing to hide from Thumann. But when the long bell rings, Hessel jumps to work and a messenger or one of us has to run to the kapos' quarters where an iron oven stands, an improvised kitchen where "Olek" Kaźmierczak, the chef of the MS *Batory* ocean liner, cooks for him. Hiding places have been installed in the floor there, and the washroom has a movable partition behind which is an empty space. The cook is so well-trained and has his work spread out in such a way that within a minute, all the saucepans and food supplies disappear. The personal cooking of food is strictly forbidden. The best measure of Hessel's stature is the fact that he doesn't bow to SS men, all the way up to the rank of corporal, and they don't dare demand that he remove his cap in their presence.

Corporal Albrecht is an interesting character. He is used as a translator and every day he escorts prisoners called for interrogation, to be released or to be shot. He speaks Polish and Russian fluently. He is a noncommissioned officer in the First Light Cavalry Regiment. He presents himself

33. Not to fall afoul of.

well, is polite toward everyone, but they say that in 1942 he was a mad dog. He speaks to us in Polish, delivering liqueurs to Olszański, taking twenty dollars per bottle without giving change. A sly fox. You can see that he's trying to gain our favor. His wife lives somewhere in Lithuania, where a search was carried out to look for hidden wealth in her home; his promotion has purportedly been blocked for him being a Polonophile, at least that's what he says. Zelent warns me to be careful around him. I don't admit to him that I was a captain of horse in the Third Cavalry Regiment. Albrecht spends days at a time idly sitting in our office, since he has nothing to do, and even if Thumann gives him some confiscated secret message in Polish or Russian, he gives it to us to translate and only signs off on it. He likes to drink. Once, the kapos invited him for vodka. He drank, they brought over Pilniak, a Pole from the auto shops, with an accordion, and Albrecht began to dance solo. He danced a first-rate mazurka, oberek, and kujawiak, and then he crooned a song with the refrain, "Every German [*Niemiec*] is a pig." As early as 10:00 a.m. the next day, he was called to report to Thumann for disciplinary action. Someone who understood Polish—and practically no kapo does!—managed to inform about this incident. You really have to be careful. He doesn't return until around 4:00 p.m.; he's subdued—but the clever fox came up with a good defense. He explained that he was actually singing: "Every prisoner [*jeniec*] is a pig . . ." and someone who didn't know Polish well misunderstood it. Though he wasn't able to deny having shown off his Polish dancing skills.

My pants have worn through so much on my left knee that you can see my long johns. I use a safety pin to close the hole. *Feldführer* Gosberg is surprised that I, as an office worker, don't have intact pants. I inform Pietroniec about this. His intervention with our countrymen in the *Bekleidungskammer* brings no result. I know that articles of clothing are sold by the dozens in the warehouse and it rains vodka there. If I were to send some vodka or bacon then some pants would be found for me. But I consider my prisoners' outfit to be a uniform of honor. A hole on my knee won't bring me any disgrace. I'm not going to pay for replacement pants. Pietroniec managed to get a piece of cloth of the same color and I ask to have patches sewn onto both knees.

We learn from the prisoners that came on the sick transports that there were no mass executions on November 3 in Auschwitz, Buchenwald, or Sachsenhausen. So this confirms our assumption that the mass murder in our camp was triggered by anxiety over the sudden advance of the Bolsheviks near Rivne and Dubno. This also increases the likelihood of the version that says that the Concentration Camps Inspectorate stopped the executions by telegram, from which you can conclude that the executions were ordered independently by the local camp command (to which nearby camps are subject), or by the premature execution of some secret orders in case the Bolsheviks unexpectedly drew near.

Exekutiert

Around 8:00 p.m. I get a note with ten prisoner numbers without last names handwritten by a near illiterate person; it's from Hessel. I have to determine the names and call them by the following morning. They are all Poles from Field 4. I take the summons signed by Hessel to the closed gate, call for the *Blockführer* on duty, Corporal Fritsche at the time, and ask him to have someone take it to Field 4. He refuses and asks why I am bringing it so late. I reply that the *Blockführer* just brought the telephone message with the numbers. "*Hau ab*"[34] is the reply. I return to Hessel and he orders me to go there again. I go and call out Fritsche who flies into a rage and says that if I don't leave immediately, he'll start shooting. I leave and communicate Fritsche's refusal to Hessel. Then he goes there himself— he's pissed because he has to interrupt a game of blackjack—and Fritsche accepts the summons from him. The next day Hessel reports the incident to Gosberg, who calls me in and has me describe what happened. I don't feel good about it, since all the wrath will be directed at me, but Hessel had to demonstrate the difficulties he encounters, and from what I find out now, he has a bone to pick with Fritsche. They call in Fritsche for a confrontation, and he lays into me, saying that I misunderstood, he was just warning me not to approach the gate since one of the guard towers could have shot me. I stay silent, Gosberg tells me that I can leave, and I see that he believed me since he reprimands Fritsche. I know that from now on I have a mortal enemy and he's one of the worst beasts. My friends confirm my intuition that the matter has taken a turn for the worse for me.

Hessel orders that the files of the ten men called at 7:00 a.m. to the *Politische Abteilung* be brought to him, he marks down a cross on each of them with the note "*exekutiert*." The first executions by firing squad ... The hangings stopped after the mass murder of the Jews. The execution of ten

34. "Buzz off."

prisoners stirs up immense worry. Those to be executed had been in the camp for almost a year, though they were all from the same transport. One of them apparently had revealed that he was sentenced to death, but after a year in the camp he assumed that the matter was over. A couple of days later, prisoners working in the city bring news that days before the execution, there was a posted notice that as a reprisal for underground activity, fifty named hostages were shot; several of our friends were among them.

After a few days, Hessel brings me a note in the evening again, this time with names and numbers. Before he hands it over, he asks me what my number is. I tell him 8830.

"OK, because your namesake is here," he says, narrowing his eyes, "*Ich sehe schwarz für sie.*"[35]

Hessel orders me to keep quiet; nonetheless, after locating the fields and barracks where these people are, I notify Zelent about the names. By a strange coincidence, these people are from Field 4 again. The next day I find out that one of them, who was bedridden, was taken on a stretcher to the crematorium.

Even worse, gray buses filled with civilians start arriving at the crematorium. The buses enter through the back road behind the fields, so from the side with the kitchens and Block 22, and after they are unloaded, they leave empty through the main camp road. The workers building Field 6 are withdrawn then and taken into barracks, but there's always someone who manages to hide and have a look. You can also observe the surroundings of the crematorium from the windows of Blocks 21 and 22 on Field 5. My friends say that the condemned have to run in pairs into a deep trench where the SS men shoot them with automatic rifles. When only two or three people are brought, they are led into the crematorium where they are shot in the room where corpses are already lying, waiting their turn for the oven. Our network determines that the buses are mainly bringing prisoners from the Lublin Castle, but in some cases people are brought from villages where a German was shot. These buses are notorious. Our *Stubendienst*, Sergeant

35. "The future looks bleak for them."

of Artillery Janek, sits at the window and counts. Then he comes to us and whispers, four vehicles have arrived . . . The sixth one has come.

I bring Zelent the news that his brother, the administrator of an estate in Radzyń, was named among those shot according to the announcement in Lublin.[36] Among them is another person from Majdanek. Zelent is shattered by the news. He knew that his brother had been arrested, and that he offered armed resistance. A couple of days later, just like every Wednesday, a small transport of older people arrives from Lublin to the concentration camp. The transport is directed to Field 4 after the formalities are taken care of in the office. One of them is a prisoner who had been in the same cell as Zelent's brother. After finding out that Stanisław Zelent is on Field 3, this prisoner writes a lengthy message to him. He describes the fate of his executed brother, and what he was subject to in his final months. Zelent calls several of his trusted friends and reads the letter. His face is drawn, all the tendons and veins are tense. In a hoarse voice he reads off the agonies that his brother suffered. Besides normal beating he was stuffed into a hot oven used to disinfect clothing. At the end, Stach (Zelent) says:

"I read this to you because I don't know if I will leave Majdanek alive— and in the event of my death, I want you to spread on the outside what these sons of bitches did to my brother."

We squeeze his hand in silence.

A transport from Dachau arrives,[37] this time with a little over three hundred healthy prisoners: Germans, Frenchmen, and Dutchmen going to the DAW (*Deutsche Ausrüstungswerke*—the carpentry workshops in Lublin with their own prisoner barracks).[38] Kapo Enders comes as their *Lagerältester*, he's also a carpenter and an intelligent man. We are struck by the friendly relations that the prisoners have with him. Enders moves into our barracks, he does not stand for roll call as he has been commandeered. He brings a fox terrier for camp commandant Weiß, whose home he visits out-

36. In accordance with the proclamation of the chief of the security police and security service in the Lublin District, Witold Zelent was shot on November 23, 1943.
37. The transport reached Lublin on January 26, 1944.
38. A reference to the labor camp in Lublin on Lipowa Street, a sub-camp of Majdanek from January 1944.

side the *Postenkette* without an escort. Some say that he's Weiß's brother-in-law, others that Weiß married his friend. Enders catches Hessel's attention—after three days in the camp—for inappropriately fraternizing with prisoners and Hessel warns him that he will intervene with Weiß. We have high hopes for this since Weiß is considered a good commandant, but he's unreachable, he comes to the camp once a month for a few minutes, and Thumann serves as a screen between him and the camp.

Knips returns from the Revier. After surviving typhus, which was so hard on him that Hanusz doubted he would make it, post-typhus heart complications have developed. I found out that as a convalescent, he blackmailed Polish nurses, demanding RGO soups that were meant for Polish prisoners, threatening them with denunciation to the camp command. Since he is from the *Schreibstube*, the Polish nurses were afraid of him. The main clerk for Field 5, Grudowski, is a daily visitor to the office. I tell him about Knips and give him a thumbnail sketch of who he is. Grudowski calls him in, rakes him over the coals, a Polish doctor receives instructions—and two days later Knips is on Field 3. He comes back to the office and takes the bunk below me. We demand that he get deloused since he came back in dirty underwear, to which the rat calmly replies that since he had typhus, let others experience this pleasure. We check and it turns out that besides Lippmann and I, everyone else has already had typhus.

The lice start showing up in our beds again. As a habit we start to check our underwear every evening; the only ones who don't do it are Knips and Lippmann. We see that Lippmann is scratching himself and while making the beds, Małyszko finds Lippmann's dirty shirt crawling with lice. He sleeps next to me. Now I know where the lice are crawling from. Our coaxing doesn't help, Lippmann is fine with his lice. So we order Małyszko to demonstratively take the blankets out of our bedroom at 8:00 a.m. and load them onto a cart. We arranged with the *Entlausung* to have our blankets disinfected within two hours. The perceptive Hessel immediately asks whether there are lice. We confirm it.

"And whoever has lice," he commands, "should go for delousing."

A pause. That's how we maneuvered Knips and Lippmann into getting deloused.

Laurich, "the Angel of Death"

Not long afterward, scabies shows up on my hands. The head of the infirmary, Dr. Abratumov, a very nice Muslim, gives me two liquids in two bottles, which I alternate rubbing onto my hands. The solution is excellent, the symptoms disappear after two days. Abratumov came to Majdanek with other military men from a POW camp and whenever Hessel sees him in the office, he runs to the closet with indexes and locates the Gestapo document transferring him to the camp, and he reminds him that he is a Jew. This isn't what the document states at all; it only says that he is suspected of being a Jew. It came up because as a Muslim he is circumcised. He absolutely is not the Jewish type, he looks more like a Kalmuck or a Tibetan. Hessel repeats this kind of talk with Abratumov whenever the *Feldführer* is present. He finally pumped up the *Feldführer* to such an extent that he calls the doctor over and starts slapping him, then he orders him to strip and triumphantly states that he is a Jew. They call me to be the interpreter and Abratumov affirms for maybe the tenth time that he is a Muslim and that the Gestapo couldn't have identified him as a Jew. Gosberg orders him to put on a Jewish star. I am at the doctor's in the afternoon and he declares to me, with tears in his eyes, that he'd rather be shot than put on the star, and he keeps going around without it.

I'm happy that Knips is back, since I want to pass him the torch, let him take responsibility for the card index as the "best" office worker, according to Hessel's declaration. During the first few days, Knips says that he just wants to ease back into the work, and after a few days, he rejects the gesture, I see that he has come down a peg or two—it's not the old Knips with his impudence and pushiness—now he wants to lead a calm existence, hiding behind an accountable coworker.

I get a written order from the *Politische Abteilung* to mark down Henio Silberspitz as a Jew in the card index. Hessel warns that this is a secret, and that Silberspitz absolutely can't find out about it. Hessel certainly has had a hand in this. I have to admit to myself that this is a uniquely correct decision and I think that what Silberspitz says about his father being a colonel in the Polish Army is nonsense. He's a little barracks clerk now on Field 4, his hair is shaved and he's first to bow his head toward me.

I visit Lipski and Tomaschek in the Revier several times. Lipski's leg is mending very well—but he's terribly bothered by the thousands of lice that have nested under his cast, which he is helpless to do anything about. Tomaschek's gunshot wound to his calf is festering.

Two SS men come to us from the *Politische Abteilung*. Private First Class Müsch, from the Rhine region, a very decent person who takes care of card-index matters, determining prisoner categories, etc., and Private First Class Laurich, a scoundrel from under a dark star who deals with interrogations and executions. Laurich escorts the condemned to the crematorium. He's a half-wit who rides his bicycle into the office, sending the messengers from the gate in front of him to run ahead and open the doors. He rides into the office, then to the kapos' dining room, and then to the room where the kapos' barber has his workshop, where he sits down or turns around and rides into Hessel's room. His bonds of friendship with Hessel are strong. "*Zwei gleich gestimmte Seelen*,"[39] in the words of some German classic. Whenever Laurich shows up, he calls for Pietroniec right away, who then gets twenty-four hours to conjure up boots, horse-riding breeches in specific colors, leather gloves, or several suit jackets. Laurich goes to the kapos' bedroom and takes a nice silken down quilt from one bed and a sweater from another. All of this finds its way to Lublin on the black market, where Laurich collects exact orders. Woe to Pietroniec if he doesn't deliver what is ordered. Since Pietroniec has to furnish the *Feldführer*, all of the higher-up SS men, Hessel, etc. in clothing and shoes, even in women's wear, stockings, and slippers, which are packed in our office and sent to the Reich, he has to have connections in different warehouses. All of the SS men need Pietroniec, and so with the knowledge that he is carrying products for them, they don't hassle him at the gate, which

39. "Two souls with the same mood."

Pietroniec takes advantage of, bringing his prisoner-suppliers other products to be exchanged that would normally be confiscated. He's a wholesaler and takes on the job of bringing ten to twenty bottles of vodka and dozens of eggs onto the field at a time.

Laurich is known as "the angel of death." If he comes for you, you can bid your life goodbye. One time, he comes to Field 1 for a Polish woman. Not having an inkling of anything, she ties a handkerchief onto her head and goes with him. They pass Field 2, Field 3, Field 4, the young woman thinks they are going to the Revier, but they pass Field 5, after which the road only leads to the crematorium. She doesn't want to go any further, she struggles, then she lies down on the ground in despair and convulsive lament. The *Blockführer* comes out of the *Blokhauz*[40] in front of Gate 5, and together with Laurich they pull her into the *Blockführer* gatehouse and phone for help. She gets taken by force, screaming to high heaven. The next day, one woman figured on the *Stärkemeldung*: "*exekutiert.*"

Laurich shows up at the office before noon and Hessel orders Dr. Abratumov to be summoned. I think: they'll check whether he sewed on the star. Abratumov comes, he's white as a sheet. Laurich tells him that they'll go to the *Politische Abteilung*. Laurich doesn't even glance at his red triangle. They leave—I run to our bedroom, which has a window facing the front, and I look at where they're going, will they turn left or right—a human life is in the balance. Laurich motions to the left. My God—he's taking him to the crematorium. I hear Hessel's voice, he calls me, and he orders the doctor's card. I hand it to him and while I wait, he draws a diagonal line across it, marks in a cross and date and signs it "*exekutiert.*" The blood is all on Hessel's hands, one day he will pay for this. A shame about Abratumov, a kind, courteous, cultured, thirtysomething Muslim who lost his life only because this SS lackey, Hessel, wanted to document his zeal.

After a ten-day stay, Knips returns to the Revier with heart complications: probably the aftereffects of typhus.

---

40. *Blockhaus.* As in some other cases, the author's spellings are not always consistent with either German or Polish.

They Count Us Like Gold, but Treat Us Like Shit

The order comes down that Poles must be recategorized from "Sch" (*Schutzhäftlinge*) to "AZA" (*Ausländische Zivilarbeiter*); the same as those Russians who were still listed as such. The Czechs stay as "Sch." An elite is evidently being formed: the western nationalities are "Sch," and the eastern "AZA." Some optimists pin their hopes on it being easier to release us as "AZA" than as "Sch." We were just as happy as we were in May or June of 1943 when they read out loud that we were supposed to be paid bonuses for our work. We deluded ourselves then, thinking they would convert the concentration camp into a labor camp—nothing doing. So far none of us have gotten a single zloty in pay yet. They didn't even check whose work was more productive. Some people read into it a likely international protection for concentration camp prisoners, since the Germans are taking into account their many countrymen interned in the United States. So in order to avoid retaliation, they'll want to treat their "Sch" well—but they previously eliminated Poles and Russians from this category. I suspect something different, that several gentlemen in the *Reichssicherheitshauptamt* who were slated to go to the front lines preferred to come up with a reorganization scheme to create some activity, new statistics, rearranging the registers, and so on.

And these registers! We shudder at the thought of every 1st and 15th of the month, when we have to prepare the *Monats-* and *Halbmonatsberichte*.[41] There are separate tables for men and women. The prisoners are categorized—again by nationality. The head count from the previous report is at the top, then the incoming and the outgoing prisoners with different specifications: departures, deaths, executions, releases, escapes. Another roll divides each category of prisoner into age groups by ten-year increments, another is a special register of Czechs with their health

41. Monthly and half-monthly reports, respectively.

conditions and the number of people in the hospital. These kinds of rolls aren't created for Germans, Frenchmen, and others, apparently it was a one-time question that keeps repeating as a matter of inertia. Besides this there are lists of *Rotspanier*,[42] like those who fought in the Spanish Revolution against General Franco. They are classified according to nationality and age. Finally, the listings of Russian prisoners who were transferred here from POW camps in the last month and were converted to "AZA," depriving them of Geneva Convention protections.

Normally we don't prepare reports for the women's camp. But we do have to prepare monthly reports that go to the Inspectorate in Oranienburg. The women send material every month with mistakes and sometimes it's difficult to figure out where and how to fix them.

I prepare five copies of these reports, but you have to write them twice since you are not allowed to write through four pieces of carbon paper. The reports are taken by a special courier to Oranienburg.

Hessel maintains a convoluted accounting of all of the changes, which in the end don't add up to the actual head count of the last roll call. Then you have to look for the mistake. He doesn't sit down to the work until the afternoon: when the count doesn't add up, he labors over it for several hours and when he becomes hopelessly exasperated, he calls us to help. But he doesn't allow us to work in peace, he breathes down our neck and keeps interrupting. He mostly makes addition mistakes, even rushing through this important step, since he doesn't add one number to another but instead combines three of them together and adds it to the previous one. Then we waste hours at a time to find the mistake—but he believes that only he can work fast.

Sometimes we have to send the rolls that we receive from the women back to them on Field 1 through the *Blockführer* late at night to be corrected. Not until the numbers add up around 10:00 p.m. can we start writing. The rubrics on the forms are so narrow that only three-digit typewritten columns fit there, and we have four- or five-digit numbers. Is it possible that the SS man who drew up the forms didn't anticipate such growth in business? Hessel makes a fuss that the five-digit columns spill

42. Red Spaniards.

over the lines. The forms are created on some kind of "pedaler,"[43] and when two copies are lined up exactly, the lines don't match up perfectly. Hessel blames us for the fact that the numbers on the copies don't fit perfectly in the blank spaces. Corrections are not allowed, nor is using an eraser. So we write slowly so as not to make a mistake. Hessel roves around the office nonstop, looks over our shoulders, yells that we are writing "very slowly," and sometimes he hits us.

In general, leading up to the 1st and the 15th, he is notably irritated. This exasperation is passed on to us and you'll accidentally press the wrong key on the typewriter and you have to take the list out and start all over. Sometimes I start the work three times. We beg God almighty that Hessel will go back to his kapos and keep drinking. In that case we finish the work in two or three hours; otherwise it can last as late as 2:00 or 3:00 a.m.

They've started giving us cigarettes. They are made out of hops. Each package of one thousand cigarettes includes the label: "Harmful to health—only for Russian prisoners." The cigarettes are so disgusting that no one wants to smoke them, but every day complicated requisitions need to be filled out for them. I write these orders in the evening. The block overseers don't even come to pick up their allotments, and we don't know what happens with them.

I get a notification from the *Poststelle* that I am not allowed to put a cross and the death date on letters to the deceased, I can only write *"Nicht mehr im Lager."*[44] In a matter of three months I was able to smuggle through many—though sorrowful—notices to families about the fate of their loved ones. At least they stopped sending packages which the SS men laid their paws on once they were marked undeliverable.

A conflict arises between *Feldführer* Gosberg and Kapo Papst, who had been a lieutenant general until recently, so an SA general. He works in the *Bauhof*. Gosberg ordered that he organize the theft of several dozen toilet bowls, pipes, and fixtures, as well as a huge number of bags of cement,

43. A foot-operated printing press used for small format printouts, a pressure press.
44. No longer in the camp.

to install sewage works in Field 3 on his own initiative and on a broader scale than in the officially approved plan. Papst refused to carry out the heist and Gosberg removed him from the joint kapo bedroom and put him in Block 3, occupied solely by Russians. He sleeps among them. Now Papst is looking for contacts amongst the Poles. I run into him on Sunday afternoon over at Zelent's. He laments the defiant attitude of the Russians toward him. I think to myself: "Now you have a foretaste of what you and your friends in the SS were up to with the 'conquered nations.' Now the lack of submissiveness from the *Untermensch* bothers you." I try to extract information from him about the general mood, since he must be familiar with various directives from the time when he was still at the trough. We discuss the future of concentration camps. Several times Papst warns against any attempts to free the camp and mass liberation. In that case all the prisoners could count on merciless elimination.

Two labor camps have been subordinated to Majdanek: Budzyń near Kraśnik and Bliżyn near Skarżysko-Kamienna.[45] Both camps consist solely of Jews.[46] We get daily telegraphic reports about the head counts, which are added to our *Stärkemeldung*. Olszański often waits until 8:00 p.m. to start the work, once they hand him the cable. I help him with it in the evening, even though it's not my area of responsibility. Olszański has hardly any work during the day, he collects papers for the evening report, stands by the stove and warms himself, and sometimes stealthily smokes a cigarette, blowing the smoke into the stove. He often affirms his friendship and our mutual understanding.

---

45. The camps were subordinated to KL Lublin in January and February 1944, respectively.
46. According to the information collected by the resistance, in mid-March 1944, there were 372 Polish and 2,380 Jewish prisoners in Bliżyn.

Every SS Man Carries a Baton in His Bag

A course lasting several days is to take place for noncommissioned SS officers somewhere in Germany, at the end of which they are to become full officers, i.e., second lieutenants. Kostial, Gosberg, Laurich, and others will attend. One of them managed to get the course text and now the office has to make ten copies for them. The text details various uninteresting military regulations, but there's also a section intended to impress the essence of a general education into those thick skulls in a matter of weeks. It includes: the Seven Wonders of the World, names of musical compositions, the operas of Wagner and Puccini, though for some unknown reason *Tannhäuser*[47] has been left out. At night they bring several typewriters from the SS offices, typists are brought together ad hoc, and the texts are copied all night. During the day some things are written on our three typewriters as well, but in any case we also have to proofread. The Russian draftsman does nothing but draw colored borders for the covers and the title pages of various chapters. Certain covers are speckled with different colors. The SS students come together every day to inspect the work, not taking any interest in the content of the text but the appearance of the covers and they caution the Russian—using me as an interpreter—not to draw identical covers for other SS men. They act like women at the store who warn the store owners not to allow an identical ball gown to find its way out into the world.

The Soviet armies keep moving forward, every day there are reports about the latest "*Abwehrsieg*,"[48] German strategic losses at the front. Will you, SS corporals, make it in time to finish the course and sew on officer's epaulets?

Our draftsman, Majewski, died after a lengthy bout with typhus fever.[49]

47. An opera by Richard Wagner from 1845.
48. Defensive victory.
49. Andrzej Majewski died on March 18, 1944.

———————

Thumann shows up at the office unexpectedly on Sunday afternoon, or rather for an inspection of the kapos' bedroom. There he finds *Lagerkapo* Lang, completely plastered. Thumann immediately orders the rack brought into the office and orders Hessel to whip him. Hessel complaisantly asks how many times. Thumann replies:

"Until I say, enough."

Hessel lashes his most trusted friend, with whom he plays cards every day, with all his strength. He has to show Thumann his dedication after all. The clerks are present for this, but we pretend that we are working with our papers. Thumann stands leaning forward, feigning indifference, in general he strikes the pose of a distinguished phlegmatic, and from the twitching of his cheeks you can see the sadistic pleasure that he takes in the swish and smack of the whip and the quiet moans of the delinquent. Lang keeps himself together exceptionally well. Perhaps his heavy inebriation serves as an anesthetic. After maybe sixty lashes, Thumann quietly says: "*Genug*,"[50] and without looking around, leaves. Lang is demoted the next day. His place is taken by a green bandit from Field 4, Edmund Pohlmann. Short in stature, perhaps thirty years old, with chestnut hair and a low forehead. The owner of a large brothel, he had thirty girls in his employ. In the first few days an argument breaks out between him and Zelent, whom he cracks in the head with his cane, splitting the skin to the bone. His head is bandaged in the Revier, they want to file a criminal report but he asks not to, since it will come back to bite him in the end. The *Feldführer* is "shocked" when he sees Zelent with his entire head in bandages and learns about Pohlmann's beating, but there are no consequences. Pohlmann, known as "Feluś," becomes the terror of the field. "Feluś" looks askance at me, but since the office is not under his jurisdiction, he has to limit himself to sinister glances.

Today is Candlemas—my wife's name day.[51] Did my brother get my card with the instructions to place red carnations on her grave? On that day

50. "Enough."
51. I.e., her patron saint day.

our home turned into a florist's shop: thirty to forty baskets of flowers and wreaths. Today she is in the Powązki Cemetery and I am in Majdanek!

They keep burning piles of bodies of Jewish prisoners executed on November 3, 1943. For weeks the odor of burning hair, bones, and fat has hovered over the camp; the wind brings the stench of corpses despite the freezing weather.

"Feluś" came down with typhus, we are all happy, to hell with him. His place is taken by the green bandit Lipiński, a German from Hanover, a denationalized ancestor of some Polish miner from Westphalia. A tall man with a charming look, he speaks beautifully classic German, his voice is endearing. His profession: meeting women on the street and then stealing their purses. He becomes the second *Lagerältester*. He is to take care of the field, while Hessel, who is supposedly overworked, will limit himself to managing the office. Despite this Hessel butts into Lipiński's job and schemes against him with Gosberg, Albrecht, and Tempel.

Another scoundrel came over with Lipiński from Field 5, kapo No. 2, Schommer. He is a communist that has been in concentration camps since 1933, a cook by trade. Since he happens to be No. 2 and was in the Revier, and the *Revierkapo* Benden is No. 1, Schommer still pompously highlights that he is second in line of responsibility for prisoners' health. He was shot alongside Tomaschek on Christmas Eve, but his wound healed quickly. He has a few screws loose. He is very hostile toward Poles and on the evening of the first day he slaps Tetych from the *Arbeitseinsatz* when he didn't immediately carry out some personal instruction given while he was typing a work document. Who was Tetych supposed to complain to? Hessel? He would slap him too.

Tetych has been doubly oppressed by the Germans. His entire family in Zamość declared themselves *Volksdeutsche*, adjusting the spelling of their last name to "Tätig." He was the only one to oppose the Germanization and that's why he was arrested. Here in the *Politische Abteilung*, they kept encouraging him to sign the *Volksliste*,[52] the guy finally broke down

---

52. A list of people in a German-occupied country who declared themselves as German.

and signed it six months ago, since they swore to him that he would be released. Nothing doing: he's still sitting here, and it gnaws at him that they fooled him like that. He likes to drink and he's never low on vodka, since everyone who comes with a request to change a work assignment pulls a half-liter out from under their shirt. He's a lightweight and after two or three shots he loosens up and sings the refrain of the song "*Tylko we Lwowie*."[53]

Zelent asks me to deliver various reports for the organization, death rates from previous years, the current makeup of the camp according to nationality, lists of the sick transports, and other details which I can't provide immediately, but only when I have the opportunity to access the old files that Hessel keeps in his bedroom. Though I look very hard, I can't find the *Stärkemeldung* from that day in February 1943 when eighty Poles from Warsaw were gassed, despite being asked several times to supply the list.

The camp and our field is regularly visited by Engineer Klaudiusz Jeliński, who wears the white armband of a free laborer, making measurements with a theodolite around the camp. These measurements are just a false pretense, of course, and are intended to justify his presence. Jeliński works in a branch of the organization and has two civilian worker assistants, but when he needs to communicate with a certain prisoner, he sends the assistants away on some errand like getting poles or pins. He calls over passing acquaintances to help, and while pretending to note measurements, he writes down addresses of family members with whom he makes contact . . . Worth remembering for his contribution is the civilian worker Józef Duda, working in the camp headquarters. Duda cooperated with Jeliński and facilitated contacts for many prisoners.

Only now do I witness what an all-powerful figure Hessel is. The head count by nationality in the *Politische Abteilung* card files doesn't match what is in the *Stärkemeldung*. It's not appropriate for the *Politische Abteilung* to send a correction to Oranienburg noting that there are three Germans less and one Czech and two Russians more.

53. Polish: "Only in Lwów."

The *Stärkemeldung* prepared by Hessel, or under his direction, is considered "off-limits." So life is bent to match the rolls and with the stroke of a pen, one Russian is transformed into a German homosexual (RD Homo §175), another Russian into a German bandit (RD BV), and a Czech into a German Jehovah's Witness (RD Bifo). Depending on the need, hostages (*Geiseln*) are changed to Sch (*Schutzhäftlinge*). It's the greatest villainy and injustice. Every so often, the Gestapo asks to see the lists of the hostages kept in the camp, and depending on the time they've spent there, they get released. But when someone is removed from the card index and placed with the *Schutzhäftlinge*, they no longer appear on the list of hostages awaiting release. Someone like this will stay in the camp until they die or God shines his mercy upon them.

One of the hostages just went through such a tragedy. His release was imminent, but the doctor held him because he looked compromisingly thin, and he had to improve his condition. While he was waiting to get better and gain weight, he got typhus and died.

They caught a wagon driver, the father of the one who took secret messages for me and Kleniewski to his sister. They found vodka under his seat. The camp commandant personally sentences him to four weeks in the camp. They shave his head and send him to a barracks, I tried to get him assigned as a block custodian, to repay his son for the free delivery of letters and packages. But as luck would have it, the old man catches typhus and dies. Smuggling vodka wasn't worth it.

The Jehovah's Witnesses, the so-called Bifo, are martyrs for their faith. The only reason they are here is because their interpretation of Holy Scripture clashes with the National-Socialist system. Every six months they are called to the camp office and presented with a declaration to sign, renouncing their faith. From what Hessel and the kapos have said, not a single Bifo in any of the concentration camps has signed the declaration which would have instantly given them their freedom. Several times I witness Hessel trying to convince individual Bifo to sign the declaration. He explains to each one:

"Sign it, it doesn't obligate you to anything. You're doing it under duress after all. In your spirit you will remain true to your faith—but you'll be free again, you'll save your life and return to your family."

Each of them replies without a second thought, with all firmness and seriousness, that they won't sign such a declaration. Their reply to the coaxing question "Who does it hurt, if you sign it?" is:

"God sees that I'm lying, and I don't want to owe my freedom to a lie."

Standing by your faith like this is probably only comparable to the martyrs who died for their Christian faith in the first century after Christ. I'm convinced that if freedom were simply a matter of signing such a declaration, without exception, all of the Catholics, Protestants, and Jews would sign it. Because of this the Bifo enjoy the respect of the SS men and they are assigned to work groups that depend on trusting the prisoner, so that they won't "organize."

Sunday brings a sensation. Two Russians escaped, a Soviet captain and a civilian. They had been working at a coal depot for the SS. None of the *Kommando* left for work because of fog and only the little *Postenkette* stood guard. The SS man escorting them went into the depot where both of them were working. The Russians overpowered him, gagged him, stripped him to his underwear, and tied him up with a rope. One of them put on the SS uniform, slung the rifle over his shoulder, and escorted his friend toward the forest where they disappeared. A nice, clean job.

A few days later, another escape. A block overseer and a clerk, both Poles and purportedly officers, escape from Field 4 in the most brazen fashion.[54] At night they made it through the wires near the gate in between the *Blockführer* gatehouse and the tower. No one saw them. When camp commandant Weiß visited the site of the escape the next morning, he declared: these were heroes. He ordered the roll call to end before waiting to see if they would be found and had them immediately stricken from the rolls. Normally, it's customary not to take escapees off the rolls right away, but rather to list them as *"Beurlaubt,"*[55] and only after two or three

54. The escape of three Polish prisoners took place on March 16, 1944.
55. On leave.

weeks, once the searches fail, do they get taken off. Some escapees even thumb their noses at the camp command, sending greetings from the outside. This was done, for example, by two Slovak Jews in 1942 who sent a postcard to the commandant from Budapest after their escape. In the past when this happened, the entire camp was kept on the roll call square up to thirty-six hours nonstop. The kapos from Buchenwald tell me that a prisoner working in a factory allowed himself to be packed into a cage along with a machine that was being shipped. It was loaded onto an open freight car. Through confidential channels the camp command found out about the prisoner's escape route and the entire camp stood for a day and a half until the freight car was located at some station, and the prisoner was pulled out of the crate and off the train.

They bring a prisoner from the DAW to us in a striped uniform, without a coat. He must stay in the office all night and sew on a *Fluchtpunkt*, so it's some kind of isolation. He's a prosecutor from Wilno[56] named Fiedorov, I ask whether he is a Pole and he swears that he is a Polish reserve officer. I let Pietroniec know and get him a striped jacket, and once Hessel goes to sleep we clear off one table for him to sleep on and give him a blanket, since it's hellishly cold in the office at night. I can't speak with him much, but he manages to whisper that he was caught while trying to escape. In the morning they take him for interrogation to Thumann and he returns with a battered face, but still relatively intact, not like the escapee whose wounds they painted with a red and white *Fluchpunkt*. In the evening, Fiedorov tells me that he and his friends at the DAW had dug a tunnel toward the cemetery and on the last night, when it was finished and they were about to escape, someone ratted them out and he was the only one arrested. He is pissed that he was so close to escaping and now it's all lost.

Executions by gunfire keep happening. Since January, not a week has gone by with less than five to ten people being stricken from the rolls as "*exekutiert.*" Just the same, around fifteen women from Field 1 have been shot, mostly Polish women, and two or three Russians. The gray buses from the

---

56. Today Vilnius, Lithuania.

Castle keep delivering their offerings to Moloch in the crematorium non-stop. One person passes on the short message to another: "Today there were five buses," we all know the rest.

Gosberg is designated the *Feldführer* of Field 4; however, he still comes to eat at Hessel's, which strengthens his unique position. Our new *Feldführer* is a fire brigade commandant, Corporal Villain, a young whelp who is unable to write two sentences in German. When he has some report to complete, he calls me and orders that I compose it for him. He can't even express in words what he wants written down. He brings a blasphemous poem for me to copy, denying the Mother of God, praising a mother to whom the author refers with veneration, denying the Church, and glorifying the old, spiry forest.

Laurich is under some kind of inquiry from the *Politische Abteilung*. He comes to Hessel and they lock themselves away, consulting in whispers, and then Hessel takes the typewriter into his room and types some kind of letters for Laurich, probably explanations.

Villain often comes to the office around noon with his submachine gun. He comes back from the direction of the crematorium and orders a sumptuous breakfast. Whenever I see his *Empi*, I know that soon I will find out that buses came to the crematorium that day.

The evening roll calls have been moved to 3:00 p.m. The prisoners get dinner afterward and supper two hours later. In the morning it's just black coffee. All eating for twenty-four hours is condensed into a two-to-three-hour period. When I suggested to my friends in the kitchen back in December that we change the order of meals and serve the evening soups in the morning—and in exchange to give just coffee for supper—they tell me that the order of meals is set in stone.

I am unexpectedly told that I have been assigned to the *Politische Abteilung*, hence to the department where all of the prisoner files are kept, the department which initiates releases and gets the documents for incoming transports, where interrogations are carried out by the visiting Gestapo officers, and where death sentences are sent. Hessel protests to Kostial against taking his "best" worker (a dubious honor that I inherited from Knips) and asserts that after I leave he can't guarantee the proper functioning of the card files and whatnot. As a result of this complaint, Noak and Węglarz get transferred there instead of me. I'm satisfied, since some people say that in other camps, prisoners working in the *Politische Abteilung* are finished off from time to time, like in the gas chamber and crematorium, because they know too much.

The bookbinder, a Pole who came on the transport from Sierpc several weeks ago, has died. He worked with us in the office, but he did jobs for the SS men. Even though he had comparatively better work conditions here, he couldn't adjust to the sudden change in his lifestyle and developed edema—a young, thirty-year-old man. He ignored our cautions to not drink too much coffee nor eat several bowls of soup, and to limit himself to dry food, which we have plenty of. A few days after he left to the hospital, I got the *Totenmeldung* of his passing.

The Revier

I have a problem with Field 5. Their office is a mess and my colleagues there aren't too concerned with the accuracy of reports. It's understandable to a degree, since thousands of sick evacuees from all of the camps were dumped on them in January and early February. Even though the sick are divided between Fields 3 and 4, they are on the books of the Revier. They do have interpreters, but it's rare that someone can communicate with an Albanian or a Greek. First names are written down as last names, and so on. Then reports come about the death of people who aren't even in the card files, and if the number is missing, it's even harder to identify the dead. I have a list of over a dozen dead people who I can't find in my card index and only by laboriously comparing the transport lists, and sometimes asking acquaintances from those transports can the reports be rectified. I happen to find several people alive on Fields 3 and 4 who are actually registered as dead. Others die after a few days, they die again in the paper reports. So you remove one person from the head count—but where is the body? Various discrepancies crop up, which in theory shouldn't happen since every prisoner has neck tags, and besides, the moment they are admitted to the Revier they should have their number written in large digits on their leg and chest with an aniline pencil. But the sick lose their numbers or come to the Revier without them and accidentally provide false numbers or the orderlies write down the wrong ones.

The *Politische Abteilung* summons loads of prisoners, fifteen to twenty times a day from the new arrivals, for various interrogations. I made a deal with Grudowski that if he can't locate someone, he doesn't reply that they are gone, but notifies the *Politische Abteilung* that they are bedridden and can't be interrogated. Then he sends his assistant, Jan Zakrzewski (a technician from Lwów), called "Mickey Mouse," to me to help figure out what's happening with this guy, when he arrived, and whether he is on another field. Sometimes we find him, sometimes we don't. They can't find someone with the last name Krüger, who the *Politische Abteilung* summoned twice in a week, my skin crawls and so does theirs, they can't find a trace of him. Finally the news arrives that he died. They christened some extra dead body with the last name Krüger.

Medical care deteriorated since the elimination of the Jewish doctors, after November 3, 1943, when one Polish doctor had about one hundred patients. This state of affairs worsened even more after the arrival of the sick transports. Then the total number of sick rose from seven hundred to about three thousand. Indeed, around three thousand sick people arrived, but they came at intervals, and mortality among them was between fifty and seventy daily, and their numbers quickly shrank. There is currently one doctor for every four hundred sick people. The care of the sick that arrived on Field 5 is substandard. While those who were directed to the empty barracks on Fields 3 and 4 are slowly dying without even nominal medical care. They lie two to a bed with one blanket. They supply each barracks with twelve kilograms of coal for every twenty-four hours, just enough for the orderlies to fry their potatoes.

While the treatment itself is deficient, the bureaucratic part and the paper manipulation is very well-developed. When admitted to the Revier, they create a file for the sick person in the admitting room and the hospital office. The sick person is sent with their card to the relevant department and here, the entire history of his disease is written down, and later, during the course of treatment, annotations are made based on which it can be determined at what stage of treatment the sick person finds himself in. This history of the disease is kept for possible use in case the prisoner gets sick again. After they die, a death report is created. The listed causes of death are: *Lungenentzündung* (pneumonia), *Kreislaufstörungen* (blood circulation disorder), enteritis (diarrhea), TBC (tuberculosis), or phlegmon. Other causes of death from beatings or hunger are not in their vocabulary. Even the hour and minute of death is noted. They balance it by proportionately distributing the overall number of deaths for a given day over the course of twenty-four hours. So there were days when someone died every ten to fifteen minutes. The *Totenmeldung* (also called the *Totenschein*) is sent to the *Politische Abteilung*—the reply goes to the camp office, and the former notifies the family (after a long delay) about the prisoner's death, on redacted pages and in very guarded language. There is a statement that all available medical techniques were used to keep the dearly departed alive, that he was given the best care available, and that he didn't reveal any last will and testament. The pharisaical document ends with expressions of sympathy. The hypocrisy goes so far that the hospital forms have a space to mark: "A salt-free diet has been prescribed." While in 1943 everyone got rutabaga or cabbage soup. And the newest treatment methods took the form of removing the mattress and blanket of someone sick with dysentery and leaving them on the bare boards to speed their demise; those with a fever had to give the Jewish nurses their portion of bread to get a bowl of "coffee," i.e., brewed herbs. The disease histories and treatment descriptions written down in the Revier are also fictions.

After Weiß took over as camp commandant, the Revier started to officially receive ready dishes for Polish prisoners in the form of dietetic soups, cocoa, milk, and soups for the convalescents (an intense pea soup with bacon and meat dumplings), as well as white rolls with butter, apples, and compotes. So the Poles in the Revier get nearly three thousand calories daily. The sick of other nationalities receive just over one thousand calories.

They whisper to each other that certain functionaries from Field 5 have enriched themselves tremendously from searching clothing left behind by the seventeen thousand executed Jews.

Dr. Sztaba maintains constant contact with the world beyond the wires and sends reports on what is going on in the camp as well as information collected from the sick transported from other camps. He pilfers various data from the camp doctor's office and sometimes he sends the original documents. Dr. Wielczański has earned a name for himself among the prisoners as a Good Samaritan. He goes above and beyond his responsibilities, he keeps people alive with smuggled injections, and he even gets admonished by certain doctor-colleagues who are jealous of the sympathies he has engendered among the prisoners. In the Field 5 pharmacy a priest is active who is hiding under the alias Witold Kołodko.

The Jews are still listed in the camp register; evidently the entire liquidation operation was carried out at the personal initiative of the camp
command, and now they want to hide it, or keep it under wraps for other
reasons. Those thousands of Jews still live in the card files. Only at the end
of February do I get the order from the *Rapportführer* to cross out all of
the Jewish names with a blue pencil and insert two mysterious letters "SB"
(*Sonderbehandlung*—separate treatment). My work lasts over a week, I do
it in my spare time. And again Hessel hassles me for doing it too slowly.
They hadn't been crossed out for nearly four months, now there's a rush. At
the same time the Jews are removed from the count on the *Stärkemeldung*.

The Daily Pensum

My daily work goes as follows: in the morning, notices come from individual fields about prisoners sent to the Revier. I have to check in the card index whether the spelling of the names on the notices match what's in the files, since the prisoner's name in the camp is what the Gestapo officer named him on the transport list when he was handed over to the camp. That's how he passes through all of the card files and that's the last name he dies under. At the same time I have to check the date of birth, prisoner category, and nationality. Based on this data the Revier admits the sick into their rolls. It's also irrelevant whether a prisoner considers himself a Pole; what matters is only what the Gestapo classified him as. Białystok doesn't belong to the General Government, so the Gestapo classifies these nationals as "SU" (*Sowjetunion*). After the sick person is examined, the notice returns to the camp office with the annotation of the Revier office, as to which prisoners were kept and which were insufficiently sick and sent back. So then I have to pull out the same card files again to note a transfer to Field 5. In the meantime, Hessel notes in the roll call plan how many left Field 3 or 4 and how many were added to Field 5. Besides this, special forms are used to note how many Sch, BV, and Aso left our field and were added to Field 5; furthermore, the number of Poles, RD, SU, and so on. I've barely finished this work and notices come for those released from the Revier and returned to their old fields. Again I have to check the last name, category, nationality, and whether they are returning to the right field, since a sick person from Field 4 is not allowed to go to Field 3 after being sick. For the sick returning to Field 3, I also have to note which barracks they are going to. I look at the block head counts and place the appropriate amounts to the less populated barracks. I send the Poles to the better ones, the Russians to others, and I try to send the Germans to settle in with their old allies, the Russians. I create a breakdown of how many Sch, BV, SV, Aso, AZA, etc. and how many of each nationality we have received, and I send a copy to Grudowski, so that if a mistake is made—it will be identical on both fields and this way we'll avoid a complaint from the *Rapportführer*. The sick come only after I check the list; I read their last names, check the numbers, a messenger brings the barracks clerks, and a certain number of prisoners are handed over to each of them so that they know how many new people have come to their blocks so that they can account for this change in the evening roll call. I haven't yet divided everyone up yet and Hessel is already shouting for the card files with names of those who were registered on the general list as deceased. The cards have to be pulled and checked again: prisoner category, nationality, number, and birth date. A black cross is penciled in for now and that's all. The last names are included in the *Stärkemeldung* among the dead and taken off the camp rolls. The next day, Olszański returns the cards of the deceased to be filed in the main card file. After two or three days, the death reports arrive, an original for the *Politische Abteilung* and a copy for us. Again I have to check the name, category, nationality, birth date, and number. A messenger waits and takes the originals, and the copy is used to note the date of death and the last name is crossed out, and the death report is filed alphabetically in the deceased files. Releases come in, as do transfers to other camps; the files have to be pulled out once more and sent away so that names can be added to the *Stärkemeldung*, which serves as the basis for appropriate annotations the next day. Around 3:00 p.m., we receive summons for interrogations for the next day, or, God forbid, executions. Sometimes only the numbers are given without names. So you have to determine the name, field, and barracks where these people are, send a written notice to the correct field to have those summoned appear in our office after roll call, and notify the barracks clerks on our own field who they need to send over the next day. The work starts with checking whether those who have been called in are all present and use a messenger to remind those offices that haven't sent people yet. Those summoned are escorted to the *Politische Abteilung* by Corporal Albrecht.

Besides this, mail for Field 3 arrives every day, which has to be distributed to the barracks, and furthermore, letters that are undelivered because of the sloppily organized post office card file. To be precise, the post office doesn't maintain its own card index *à jour*[57] and it doesn't have visibly noted changes and transfers. I get around one hundred undeliverable letters a day, and my ambition is to get every letter delivered. The name file renders a huge service with this, but only up to a point, since it's arranged according to the Gestapo's official spelling of last names. Some people are registered under their first names, like Trofim, and their last names are considered their first names. I can find certain people only thanks to the number provided. After several days of work, I got to know the files and last names so well that all letters get to their intended recipients—except for those who died or left. It's sad to read the letters of loved ones to those who are no longer alive.

What's interesting is reading the letters of Germans in the Reich, and how openly the authors describe the losses suffered during bombardments and how draining the air raids have been. It's just as interesting to read letters from eastern Małopolska, especially from simple people who don't realize that censorship exists and don't mince words. They describe terrible, bloody raids by Ukrainian gangs on Polish villages, forcing many Poles to relocate to towns.

Of course I only look at the letters of Poles whom I don't know and share the contents with my friends, since it's a sui generis newspaper with reports from particular provinces. The least interesting letters are from the intelligentsia, since they steer clear of general news and only bring up family matters. The letters of our *Volksdeutsche* are interesting. Reich's sisters write to him in Polish. Knips's wife writes in Polish and his brother Leon, a senior official in the Lublin province, in German.

That's not all. I also get a statement of undeliverable packages twice a week. Again, up to 120 items. Packages regularly arrive for some people who have been dead for four or five months, which is a gauge of how late the *Politische Abteilung* sends death notices. Various attempts are made by block overseers to claim the packages, even though the addressee doesn't match the name of anyone living in a given barracks. And there are six or seven Marciniaks, Wójciks, and Wiśniewskis like this in the camp. I oppose their designs without mincing words, condemning every try. The

57. French: here, updated.

namesake with the correct name is on another field and he's surprised that he doesn't get packages. Actually, there are only three or four packages per transport that are undeliverable because the last name is totally unknown. The rest are undeliverable because of death, departure, or the most pleasant, release. The fate of these packages doesn't concern me, the Revier is supposed to get them, but it seems to me that most are taken by the SS men. If I can, I reassign the packages of the deceased to people with the same last name, though they have a different first name.

This is my daily work pensum, mostly carried out while standing at three card files. I don't allow anyone else to make entries in the card files, or to remove or refile them, since I am personally responsible for each missing card, and Hessel, the "master" at work, has filed returned cards in the wrong place several times and I only found them after two or three weeks. It's not possible to search through twenty thousand files while you wait!

Hessel doesn't have the slightest idea about office work, it's plain to see that he never did it before, he demands that we hurry but working peacefully is precisely what guarantees precision and less mistakes. He keeps telling the *Feldführer* and the *Rapportführer* that any company that operated at our level of productivity would go bankrupt, since we would be overpaid employees and our work is of such low value—according to Hessel—that it shouldn't even cover our room and board. Not to brag, but I have to say that Hessel had good taste in choosing experienced workers and if it were a bank or in industry, our labor would have to be carried out by twice as many clerks.

My cooperation with the barracks clerks is going well; every once in a while I inspect the barracks files. My only conflicts are with the clerk for Block 14, Piotrowski, an old bookkeeper, who doesn't appreciate the importance of the camp files. He received verbal instructions from me to bring people from his barracks for interrogations and he forgot, they left for work. Hessel gets a reminder from the *Politische Abteilung* asking why they aren't there, and he takes all of his anger out on me. Luckily, I don't get knocked in the head, but he doesn't quite believe my assurances that I told Piotrowski. When he is called to Hessel, Piotrowski has the gall to deny that I notified him. From then on, I ask the clerks to confirm receipt of the notices in writing. A week later, Piotrowski forgets to bring people over again, I "get my ass handed to me," in Majdanek speak, and show Hessel Piotrowski's signature.

And he has pulled even better stunts. He got a written instruction to move the entire squad of bricklayers, twenty-one people, to Block 8. Sometime later, the *Politische Abteilung* calls one of the bricklayers, and Block 8 replies that he isn't there. It's a very unpleasant situation for me, I can see that my card file is wrong and apparently I mistakenly moved this person to Block 8. The next question is whether I didn't account for the entirety of some list. A few days later I can't locate someone in Block 8 again, who, according to my annotations, was recently moved there. A light bulb comes on in my head. I reach for the list of bricklayers who were moved and I ask Piotrowski who is in his barracks. He admits that he kept fourteen of them in his barracks without permission, and sent the other fourteen to the new barracks, so overall twenty-eight people in my card file were listed in the wrong barracks. "What's the problem?" someone who doesn't know about camp life might wonder. Thumann or Kostial will come to the office, they will give me the number of a prisoner who broke some rule, and they'll order me to immediately bring him over. I'll check the files for where the person is and will send a messenger to the barracks, Thumann is waiting, and just imagine the moment that the messenger returns and says that no such prisoner was there. Hessel would kill me on the spot for such carelessness with the records. Piotrowski had a rough evening that time, since I run a psychoanalysis on him without mincing words.

The letters from my brother are increasingly enigmatic. He doesn't mention my release, I've noted his silence on this issue for weeks and deliberately don't ask about it; I want to check if he legitimately doesn't have anything to say or if his replies to my questions are meant to pacify me. Unfortunately, he writes infrequently, and when reporting specific matters, like the administration of my houses and the course of work in the factory, he's brief: "It's fine on Chocimska Street, it's fine in the factory." I write to him, since he obviously doesn't appreciate the significance of frequent correspondence and doesn't realize how much strength and moral support it gives me. It's not enough that I get very regular, well-stocked packages every Friday, though even they have stopped being an attraction, since their contents have been the same since last July and I know how they're packed by memory. My requests to leave the arrangement and composition of the packages to Ninka or Mary have no effect, even though they are both ready and willing. Evidently this would wound his pride. I do, however, get frequent and detailed letters from Mary and Ninka, who inform me about all the minor events in Warsaw and friendly gossip. With all the charm of the women's letters, full of sentimentality and emotion, I miss even a few prosaic words from my brother. I see that on the outside they can't empathize with the mindset and spiritual needs of prisoners.

All of us are plagued by a mycotic infection on our faces. It spreads very quickly since there are only a few razors and brushes in each barracks and no disinfectant. It looks like a mosquito bite at first and then expands into the size of a large blemish. None of the ointments from the Revier help. Only by accident does someone discover that iodine or its substitutes can burn through and eliminate the fungus within two or three days.

Hessel tells me to draw up a list of everyone with a *Fluchtpunkt*. Every one of them has a red point with a white circle painted on their card. There are over eighty of us. The *Politische Abteilung* is to decide which points can be removed, since, as it turns out, the camp commandant doesn't have the authority to assign them.

Noak divulges the goings-on in the *Politische Abteilung* to me. Above all, they had to swear an oath of strict secrecy about everything they learn while working there, otherwise—you know. Noak has access to all of the personal files and tells me that in mine the reason for arrest is noted as membership in the WB (*Widerstandsbewegung*[58]) and that I am classified as *Lagerstufe* I. No one knows what this designation means. He speaks of

58. Resistance activity.

the remarkably pleasant working conditions. Müsch, from on the Rhine, who rebukes Hessel for the brutality with which he treats us, is an ideal boss. Węglarz wrote something up incorrectly, so Müsch came to Noak and asked him to rewrite the document in the other room so that Węglarz wouldn't notice and feel bad about it. They both have golden lives now, they go back to the roll call and then it's back to heaven. They still live with us. This offends Hessel and he tries to corral them into evening work, but Müsch intervenes and reminds him that those two aren't subject to his authority.

During the morning or evening roll calls, Hessel often sends me to locate or summon a prisoner. It has to be done "*schnell, schnell,*" so he doesn't even let me take my cap, not to mention a cloak. With freezing temperatures lower than −10 degrees, the change from inside to outside is about 30 degrees. I caught cold and got such an inflammation of my vocal cords that I could only speak in a whisper. I report to Professor Michałowicz who prescribes me some kind of tablets.

Our *Fluchtpunkte* list returns from the *Politische Abteilung*. Of the eighty-three, seventy-two were crossed out, leaving eleven. Mankiewicz and I are among the eleven. All of those who were sent from the Castle to Majdanek in anticipation of a hearing in the *Sondergericht*—Lipski, Kaszubski, Serafin, Szwajcer, etc.—had their points removed. Could I be such a big fish that I am counted among the most dangerous eleven prisoners subject to special security by the camp command? I start to get arrogant and begin feeling self-important. The list of the eleven *Fluchpunkte* goes to the *Blockführer* offices on Fields 3 and 4, and they are to make sure that these prisoners don't leave their fields. I type the notice myself.

A message arrives from the DAW that the tunnel prepared by Fiedorov and company was used by eleven prisoners to escape.[59] We find out that the SS men didn't order the tunnel filled, but only had the entrance bricked up. It exits into the cemetery, and that's where the brotherhood

59. On the night of March 22–23, 1944, twelve prisoners escaped from the camp on Lipowa Street in Lublin.

split from. Not one was caught. Fiedorov is in despair for getting nailed too soon and he admits that all of the escapees were his accomplices who helped with the digging.

At practically the same time there is another escape attempt. A Ukrainian working in the hospital kitchen asks to be buried under the potato peels on a wagon which belongs to a local peasant. The peasant apparently noticed something and reported his suspicion to the *Blockführer* who pulled the Ukrainian out from under the peels. They bring him to the office where Hessel, Kostial, and Villain beat and kick him bloody. He is handcuffed.

The police hand over a prisoner to the camp, Klewar, a Pole, who had escaped three weeks earlier and had already been taken off the rolls. He already escaped from a concentration camp once, Buchenwald. A young, twentysomething, handsome lad. He's held in the office pending Thumann's instructions. We ask him how he escaped. He says that he was working on the road by the entrances to the sewers. When no one was looking, he crawled into one of these openings and sat underground for two days until he assumed that the *Postenkette* had been withdrawn at night, then he came out and ran away. Indeed, the *Postenkette* was active for forty-eight hours nonstop and they searched for him in vain on the camp grounds. He walked toward Kraków by foot, in the region where his parents live, and he slept in huts and forests. Just outside of Kraków, an officer of the "Polish" Blue Police[60] stopped him, and despite pleading and cursing, he led him to a German military police post, who sent him to a work camp in Płaszów, nearby, and then back to Majdanek. He praises the conditions in Płaszów, the living quarters are better, so is the food, and more. No surprise: it's only a labor camp. They take him for an interrogation to Thumann, he gets whipped, he has to describe the method of escape, and he comes back to us on the field.

When I enter the *Blockführer* gatehouse on official business, I often see the truck that brings the RGO soups. It's escorted by a pretty, tall brunette with nice legs, dressed in a sporty fur. The *Blockführer* surround her and

---

60. The Polish police force tasked with keeping public order in the German-occupied General Government.

joke around, she flashes them a bright smile. In the meantime, the unloading of full cauldrons and the loading of empty ones takes place. The prisoners are not allowed to bow to female prisoners, and especially "civilians." I would gladly take my cap off for her in gratitude for her work, for coming on the open truck every day to Majdanek in the frost and rain. I know from Kaszubski, who knows her, that she is a bachelorette, a landowner, and while the cauldrons are being loaded, other shipments, packages, and messages come for us, and in empty cauldrons under screwed-down tops, our secret messages are sent off into the world. Her role is to charm the SS men, to draw their attention away from what is happening.

Trips to the Laundry

We—I mean my fellow prisoners without *Fluchtpunkte*—have an excellent rallying point to meet with our families. In Lublin, the striped *Häftlinge* uniforms are taken to a big laundry.[61] A truck brings these uniforms, along with several prisoners from the *Bekleidungskammer*. Anyone in the world outside can just go to the laundry in Lublin, of course. The meetings are prearranged and relatives wait at the laundry, disguised as staff. Naturally, you have to give the unit's kapo a bottle of vodka to allow a prisoner who doesn't work in the clothing warehouse unit to take a trip to the laundry. Like everyone who works outside the camp, you have to wear stripes. You also have to provide the attendant SS men with liquor, and then you can peacefully spend a few hours talking with your loved ones. Unfortunately, this road is closed to me, Hessel won't let me go, and even if he did—my *Fluchtpunkte* bar me from exiting the camp. I'm jealous to hear my friends talking about meeting their wives, fiancées, and mothers. My friends in the clothing warehouse—Krupski, Rode, and others—bring underground publications hidden under the laundered underwear and uniforms: above all the *Biuletyn Informacyjny*.[62] The laundry workers slip the weeklies into sleeves which are folded in a special way. The bundles of uniforms that contain the publications are handled with great care. The materials are disseminated among trusted people in the camp; Władysław Dębski is one of the distributors, among others.

The other primary mailbox for secret messages is the bookkeeper of the brewery where prisoners from the SS canteen *Kommando* go to get beer and lemonade. More important letters to Warsaw are collected and sent by a courier to avoid censorship, which is especially severe in Lublin because of Majdanek's being there. We get replies the same way.

---

61. A reference to the Łabędzki laundry on Farbiarska Street.
62. Polish: "Information Bulletin."

The air-raid sirens are increasingly frequent. Sometimes you can hear squadrons of Soviet planes flying overhead, but there is no antiaircraft fire nor the sound of any air battles. You also don't hear the sounds of any bombs being dropped. We don't get any reports from Warsaw, Kraków, or other places about bombings, so we assume that airdrops for partisan units are being carried out. Each alarm fills us with bliss and we sleep even more soundly.

Thumann introduced some variety for us on Sunday afternoons. After the roll call at noon, lunch is unexpectedly served outside, no one is allowed into the barracks as searches take place there. Several hundred SS men come and flip over all of the mattresses, taking away any clothing, underwear, shoes, scarves, etc. that they find. The search lasts three or four hours—the SS men curse because they lose their day off. The loot is always abundant, some two or three wagons full of confiscated items leave the field. We're anxious that a search could also happen in the office, so I keep my spare underwear in a box hidden with Pietroniec at the clothing warehouse. These searches are irregular, taking place every second or third Sunday, once on Field 3 and then on Field 4.

The mortality rate in the camp is very high. There are seventy to ninety new corpses each day. The main contingent is supplied by the prisoners evacuated from hospitals in other camps.

We are generally *au courant* with world events and the situation on the fronts. The *Głos Lubelski*[63] comes every day for the kapos, as well as thirty copies of the *Warschauer Zeitung*,[64] a copy of which we surreptitiously receive. The news is corrected or gaps are filled in by the broadcasts from London on the radio in the camp commandant's eight-cylinder Tatra at the auto shops, and local messages from Lublin.

63. Polish: "Lublin Voice."
64. German: "Warsaw Newspaper."

———————

At the beginning of March 1944, Zelent is glad to inform me that all the military organizations of the most diverse political persuasions (except for the communists) have combined into one Home Army.

A transport of several hundred Polish Jews arrives from the labor camp in Budzyń.[65] These are largely Jewish engineers from Warsaw and Łódź, who were told in Budzyń that technical specialists were needed. They volunteered and are presently terrified that they are now in Majdanek, where they find out from us that there is absolutely no industry where they would be needed as specialists. Another transport also comes from Bliżyn with Jews marked with the letter A. The Gestapo sends a special name register for these Jews, they must be placed together in one barracks on Field 4 and they aren't allowed to leave the field. Kostial and Hessel talk about them in whispers. It looks suspicious to me.

My sore throat doesn't go away, even after two weeks of swallowing the tablets prescribed to me by Professor Michałowicz. So I go to him again but I can't see him since he's with some commission. I report to Dr. Pawłowski, who gives me a different medicine. While there I learn that they've opened a dentist's office. I have been suffering for three months since I chewed down my gold bridgework in such a way that a sharp edge has formed that cuts my tongue every time I move it. The entire left side is inflamed. The dentist, a Frenchman, freshly transported from Buchenwald, made one pass with his drill over the sharp edge and gives me immediate relief.

Cases of insubordination and drunkenness among the green bandits are becoming increasingly flagrant. Hardly a day goes by that one or two greens aren't brought to the office on orders from the *Feldführer* and whipped twenty to fifty times by Hessel. They demonstrate a defiant attitude toward the SS men, which leaves me puzzled. If a Pole or a Russian displayed the same behavior, they would crush him underfoot on the spot.

65. The transport from Budzyń reached Majdanek on March 19, 1944.

I don't deny that our folks drink, but they do it in a way where they don't stagger through the field gate. The Germans haven't mastered the ability to drink—they do it on an empty stomach and "chase" it with a cigarette and they're finished after three shots, going out into the cold. Our people munch on some bacon as a foundation, and they mainly drink in the evening, after the roll call. There's so much vodka on the field that it becomes repulsive to me.

The official punishment of lashing is itself a circus act. When a prisoner does something wrong, a report is drawn up which goes, along with Thumann's dispatch, to the Camps Inspectorate in Oranienburg. They decide the sentence, which can be meted out after the camp SS doctor's examination. The maximum penalty is twenty-five lashes. The sentence is recorded on a large form that includes not only the punishment carried out, but even the names of the kapos doing the whipping, and of course the doctor's certification. That's the ideal. These sentences take about eight weeks to be handed down. In reality, a prisoner gets his first whipping as soon as the kapo nabs him; then, after he is taken to the SS officer, he gets more lashes and kicks; the *Feldführer* whips him while the report is being written; and Hessel doesn't want to be left out either. Once he receives the report, Thumann calls him in for interrogation and uses his heavy whip to give him fifty to seventy lashes, so altogether the prisoner will collect up to 120 extra lashes and then, once everything is healed and forgotten— after the "doctor's examination"—he'll get whipped twenty-five times and sometimes only ten or fifteen. The doctor's exam consists of him observing the whipping. The farce with sending the reports to Oranienburg has been going on for several months; before, Thumann would give a sentence of seventy-five lashes, for example—but the prisoner would get double that, counting what the *Blockführer* also delivered.

It was a terrible sight to see one such sentence, which came from Oranienburg for a Polish woman. Called over to us on Field 3, she was a short, thin blonde, maybe twenty-five or thirty years old (everyone looks older here). They stretch her out on the rack in front of the office, some bandit is holding her by the arms, the sadomasochist Thumann is leering and smiling, listening to her moans, and the scumbag Hessel whips her with such force that he comes back sweating, even though it's maybe −10 degrees [14°F] outside. Oh you sons of bitches, you'll pay a heavy price for this horror!

The investigation into the matter of Birzer and Marmorstein is apparently still going on. The *Lagerarzt* comes to Hessel and they pull out Marmorstein's death report; he died of "pneumonia" according to this document. The next day, the *Lagerarzt* brings a different one to replace it, listing the cause of death as "suicide." I hear Hessel sarcastically comment to Corporal Albrecht that Marmorstein's files keep shrinking instead of expanding. Everyone who has access to the documents tries to whittle them away one page at a time.

The concentration camp in Radom has been subordinated to Majdanek.[66] Again, more work for Olszański. We're pleased that the camp has been brought under "our" management, since according to the rumors of the necessity of evacuating Majdanek to the west, beyond the Vistula, Majdanek would transfer over as the superior authority and we wouldn't have to start camp life from the beginning in Radom, but would continue our work in our current assignments. The head counts of the subordinated camps make their way to Zelent. Both Poles and Jews are interned at Radom.

On the morning of March 7, a transport of the entire women's camp left for Ravensbrück.[67] Fifteen hundred women left, mostly Polish, and not one woman remains. Andrzej, Olszański, Gröner, and dozens of others are separated from their sweethearts. I can see through the windows of our bedroom as the women, all dressed in stripes and with white handkerchiefs on their heads, march alongside our field, and turn left near the auto shops, through the *Gärtnerei*, and toward Dziesiąta. They're taking the short road through the city to the train station. They're escorted by SS men with dogs on leashes. The women are going to Ravensbrück in

66. The labor camp in Radom was subordinated to Majdanek in January 1944.
67. Only some of the women were actually taken to Ravensbrück in March 1944. The rest were deported to Auschwitz, Płaszów, and Ravensbrück on April 13–19.

Mecklenburg. It's a world away. How many nights they'll spend in cattle cars, on bare wooden boards, with temperatures below zero. Our office gets the women's card files to send to Ravensbrück. I look through them and I determine that among those that have left Majdanek are Irena Pannenkow, the social activist Prauss, Iłłakowicz, Kurcyusz, the daughter of the executed mayor of Warsaw Słomiński, and others.

Scześniewski is taking care of the juvenile *Kommando* and is working in counterintelligence. He sends comprehensive, coded reports to Lublin. He is exceptionally creative in how he hides and sends the reports. He makes clay figurines from cement: elephants, dogs, and other toys for the kids, and inside these he conceals the reports. He almost got caught. The *Rapportführer* stopped him on the field, since his number was half torn off his shirt, and led him to the office. A panic arose on the field, since just a moment earlier, Zelent had handed him about a dozen secret messages with incriminating contents to forward. We know that the first thing they'll do is search him and pat him down. That'll give it all away! Szcześniewski enters the office with a bewildered look on his face. The *Rapportführer* begins slapping him. In his zeal, Hessel jumps in, calling him the obligatory "*Scheisspolacken*," and . . . they order him to leave. After the evening roll call, over at Zelent's, Szcześniewski confides in me about the material that he was loaded with and what a threat he and the senders faced.

I am surprised by the huge sums that the German kapos have at their disposal. None of them receive packages, but they eat much better than we, who receive packages, do. Poultry, fish, cakes, vodka, liqueurs are all on their daily menu. It has all been looted from prisoners, Jews above all. They often get into arguments, and sometimes into fistfights. A particular antagonism develops between Schommer and Lipiński, the German. Schommer weighs fifty kilograms while Lipiński is over one hundred kilograms, everyone knows who dominates over whom. Despite this, Schommer goes to Field 5 and brags that he flattened Lipiński in wrestling. Finding out about this, Lipiński goes into a rage and the following evening, Schommer catches hell again for his boasting.

Transports

They start saying that some transport is supposed to depart. Admittedly, the Bolsheviks haven't advanced in the Łuck-Dubno region, but we read that as a result of their attacks, the Germans are constantly "depriving" the Russians of exploiting their successes, shortening their own front. The skeptics ponder whether this isn't also shortening the Russian front line. How the occupiers' propaganda manages to seep through even the barbed wire. The former *Lagerältester* Ott, a teacher, so, you would think, an intelligent person, explains to me with all conviction that the German armies are preparing the most enormous trap for the Russians. They are retreating from the far reaches of Russia, destroying the countryside and rail network, and drawing near to their own supply bases. So the Russians are going to have colossal problems in supplying their front, which is constantly moving to the west. And therein lies—as Ott assures me—the brilliant trap. I see that although both of us are victims of Hitlerism and we hate it, he is still a German patriot and I am a Polish one, and he believes in and yearns for a German victory. On the other hand, the German communists, comprising the majority of the German prisoners, behave differently. When the *Warschauer Zeitung* brings news of some breakthrough at the front by the Russians or a massive bombardment of German cities, we know that in the evening there will be a great drinking binge, a joyful celebration of the successes achieved by the enemy against the German nation. I am glad with them through the wall, but their joy fills me with contempt.

A transport of seven hundred prisoners is announced, where to—nobody knows; as always the destination is kept secret until the last moment. Hessel and the *Feldführer* choose people for the transport and bring me seven hundred numbers, warning me, however, that there should be no Russian prisoners among them, for which I am responsible. I have to pull out the card files of those chosen for the transport in order to compile an alphabetical transport manifest. Hessel authorizes me to cross off all of the essential people who are in permanent work units. That's fine with me. I take off all of the Poles I know, and all of the intelligentsia Poles that I don't know personally. I consult with Zelent about which Poles should be kept.

In the evening, Hessel comes to me and orders that Professor Karabanik's card be added to the transport list. He is a Pole who has been in Majdanek from the moment it was founded, along with Hessel, and whom we all value as a patriot who raises our spirits. "What's going on here?" I think to myself. He also orders that another Pole be added, but he can't remember his last name, he knows that his nickname is *"Kuchenblech."*[68] I pretend that I don't know who he's talking about, even though I do, it's the *Vorarbeiter* of the SS barbers, Żurawski, a civil servant in the National Engineering Works, who also came to Majdanek with Hessel. So Hessel is sending away his two Polish colleagues with the most seniority.

Hessel goes to sleep. I return Karabanik's card to its place in the files. I look through the cards again to see if any of my people are there. Tomorrow I will trick Hessel into thinking that Karabanik's card was mislaid by accident and that he wasn't added. Three typewriters are waiting to work, there are forty names for each sheet, so eighteen sheets to write. Each writer has six sheets to type, name and surname, number, birth date, prisoner category, nationality, and profession. At 1:00 a.m. I go to sleep. I have seven hundred people ready. I saved Karabanik.

In the morning, before the roll call, Karabanik rushes into the office. In a whisper I tell him:

"Get away, don't attract Hessel's attention."

"But I'm slated for the transport," he replies anxiously.

"No way, make tracks."

Hessel is already approaching and says:

"Ja, mein lieber Karabanik. Du gehst in Transport."[69]

I reply that his name didn't make it into the seven hundred.

"How so?" says Hessel. "He's right here," and he points under the letter K: Karabanik!

---

68. Baking tray.
69. "Yes, my dear Karabanik. You're going on the transport."

I can't believe my eyes. What happened? Who pulled Karabanik's card out at night and put him in the place of someone else who was withdrawn? I read the list and find the name of Engineer Eustacy Gorecki, a co-creator of the Zamość Castle miniature, the one who plays chess by memory. Some miracles must have happened at night, but none of the writers admit to knowing anything. Is this someone's revenge, or did a bribe remove some big shot, or I should say two of them, and replaced them with Karabanik and Gorecki? Who knows. Unfortunately the list is written and so I can't save Gorecki. Karabanik negotiates with Hessel, and in exchange for some bribe (since that's what Hessel was after) he takes him off the list and replaces him with some Russian instead. Only now can I finally explain to Karabanik what happened. He's livid at Hessel for squeezing a bribe out of him, and he adds that this dirty trick will cost him a two-carat diamond that he has stashed with one of our acquaintants.

I get instructions from Zelent to provide the nationality breakdown of the transport of the seven hundred and the approximate departure date, since a possible rescue of the transport needs to be planned by the organization. The transport is split fifty-fifty between Poles and Russians, and I tell Stach the expected date of departure.

The transport passengers are assigned to two separate barracks. Before the departure the transport manifest needs to be read out loud, to see if anyone else has wiggled their way in. People get in formation on the roll call square. A cold wind blows. Jabłoński comes out and starts reading the list. Those whose names are read have to go to the other side of the field. Discipline has become lax among the prisoners slated for the transport, since they think that nothing will happen to them, given that the worst punishment, i.e., getting assigned to the transport, has already been meted out. They are talking to one another and no one really cares whether their name is read out by the clerk. Check marks are made next to the names that are read out, a lot of names are left over to which no one responds. Seven hundred people continue conversing, a hubbub of voices, the wind carries away the sound of names being read. The wind tears two pages of the list out of Jabłoński's numb fingers and they fall into a puddle. Jabłoński picks them up and runs to the office to dry them off with blotting paper. Hessel runs after him and starts hitting and kicking him in the office, throws a stool at him, and knocks him (a guy who's almost two meters tall) onto the ground. Now he orders me to go outside and keep the work going. I see that the matter is hopeless, so I order everyone to form up into one group, to walk past my table single file, and to state their last name. It seems to take longer to find the names, but with so many people not responding to their name being read out, who knows how long it would have lasted otherwise? Despite being in alphabetical order, finding the last names is not as easy as you would think, since the official spelling differs from their actual pronunciation. Besides this, there are two lists: Russians on one, and all the other nationalities on the other. More than one Pole from the Borderlands—mistakenly counted as Russians by the Gestapo—finds himself on the Russian list. Another group forms of those whose names can't be found on the list; they wait until the end, the rest get to go back to the transport barracks. Reading the seven hundred names lasts longer than everyone who wasn't there would think. Finding a surname lasts an average of fifteen seconds. Even though I loudly announce that each person should state their last name without prompting, the same dialogue repeats with each simple person. He comes to the table and is silent, I ask him:

"What is your name?"

Each of them is puzzled by this and asks:

"Who, me?"

I streamline the search by telling the block overseers to group people alphabetically, A, B, C, etc. But here, the Russians are confused. Within an hour we have over two hundred people checked off and overall, along with locating all of the mangled last names, it takes up four hours. Only now can we say that the transport is alright. Leaving the transport barracks is forbidden, since if someone from the transport hid at the last minute, it would have to depart incomplete, and reading all the names again in order to figure out who is missing would take another four hours.

Arbeitseinsatzführer Staff Sergeant Troll, assisted by Thumann, conducts a sorting of the permanent *Kommando* which serve the camp's administrative departments: the *Poststelle, Bekleidungskammer, Effektenkammer,*

Bad,[70] SS-*Küche,* SS-*Kantine,* etc. Basically, each work squad is to be halved. Everyone lines up on the square. *Feldführer* Villain and Hessel are assisting Troll, they call me over to write down the numbers. It's maybe −8 degrees. Troll dictates the numbers to me of those who are to stay with their units. I stand with a bare head, without gloves, and write. Writing down numbers according to German dictation is very burdensome for a non-German, since the language is perhaps the only one on earth where digits aren't stated in the order they are written, but you always say the single-digit number before multiples of ten. Eighty-seven is pronounced: seven and eighty. For four-digit numbers, the person dictating doesn't say the thousands, hundreds, or tens, and only says "48-87." You have to write with tremendous concentration in order to not note down the digits in sequence when you hear them phonetically. Since last names aren't stated, fixing mistakes is very hard; and sometimes, after taking out the card files, you see that you pulled out a number that died long ago or left on a transport. Writing down numbers isn't actually my responsibility, but Tetych's from the *Arbeitseinsatz.* But he, Olaszański, and others don't know German as well and they regularly rearrange digits—so Hessel pulls me away from the card file for this strenuous work.

I am now eye to eye with my colleagues from the *Bekleidungskammer,* who didn't have pants for me. There are twelve of them, including Kapo Marciniak. Troll dictates only six numbers to me and goes to the next group, I walk by the six who were passed over, I hear pleading whispers: "Please sign me up, sir"—I know them all by last name. But Troll is already dictating the next numbers. Everywhere there are whispers and winks in my direction. After the segregation, Troll comes back and adds one or two people to certain groups. Now, no one will remember how many from each unit were set aside. My fingers are blue and swollen, I can barely hold on to the pencil. When I return to the office, Hessel is already calling for the list, I tell him that I have to copy it, but that my hands are numb at the moment. Hessel goes for dinner, meanwhile, Corporal Müller runs over to me to have his protégé (i.e., the kapo who snitches about hidden vodka

---

70. Bathhouse.

and jewelry) put on the list. I tell him that I already handed it over to Hessel for him to take care of. Now I have to quickly search the card index for the last names and numbers of these bigwigs from the *Bekleidungskammer*. I add three Poles, the same for the other units, one or two depending if I remember their names. Hessel comes back from dinner, the list is already finished and ready.

The transport of the seven hundred departs, and afterward I get the instruction to note in the card file that the transport went to Natzweiler.[71] A lousy camp, stone quarries on the border of Lorraine and Germany. I feel so sorry for Gorecki, that someone deceitfully packed him into the transport.

I get a practically new pair of military bootees from Pietroniec. Finally, after a year's torment, decent footwear.

The new concentration camp in Warsaw has been subordinated to Majdanek.[72] It is to be established in the Ghetto on Stawki Street, completely isolated from Polish Warsaw. Our field commandant, Villain, leaves for the concentration camp in Warsaw and is replaced by Corporal Groffmann, the one who was the field commandant a year ago and who was demoted by Thumann for not nailing shut the doors of the barracks where the Buchenwald transport was spending the night.

In the second half of March 1944, a general segregation of prisoners begins. The work squads don't leave Field 3 to go to work, everyone stays in the barracks. An order comes down that two or three blocks have to group into one barracks and strip naked there. The prisoners wait unclothed for hours until Thumann shows up. He comes in the company of Dr. Rindfleisch, *Feldführer* Groffmann, and Hessel. They call me over as an expert in writing down numbers dictated in German. When Thumann enters the barracks, the overseer calls out "*Achtung*," and one prisoner after another marches past the commission. Thumann instructs that everyone who he qualifies

---

71. The transport left Majdanek on April 2, 1944.
72. KL Warschau, as the *Arbeitslager Warschau*, was subordinated to KL Lublin in May 1944.

as a "*Schuster*"[73] should be written down. Whenever he mutters "*Schuster*" to someone, Hessel reads out his number. I see that Thumann is choosing "shoemakers" from the lame, disabled, sickly, and so-called *gamel*. He rips the holy medallions and scapulars off the necks of anyone wearing them and throws them on the ground, hits that person twice in the head with a reed, and asks, ironically, "*Kommunist?*" One of the Poles is wearing a *Sodalis Marianus* breastplate. Hessel angrily tears it from his neck, throws it to the ground, and stomps on it with his heel several times.

Thumann tells me to separately write down everyone with scabies, sores, and various skin conditions. I'm horrified by the tremendous proportion of diseases caused by dirt, poor metabolism, and vitamin deficiency.

After the entire field is segregated, Thumann goes to the kitchen where the cooks and the entire office staff also have to parade naked in front of him. Those classified as shoemakers are to be moved to Field 4 on the same day. What work they're going to be used for—no one knows. The work begins for me now. I have to pull out the card files of several hundred people, draw up a *Verlegungsliste*[74] with numbers, names, and prisoner categories. Among the card files pulled out are several who couldn't be added because they are already on Field 4, or they have already died. So either Hessel read out the wrong numbers, or I wrote them down incorrectly. Luckily, Thumann didn't ask me for the exact number of people written down as shoemakers. I skip the incorrect numbers of course. I arrange the cards according to barracks and I inform the gathered clerks which numbers are leaving for Field 4 and how this changes their roll call head count for each of them. The transfer to Field 4 has to be noted in all of the files. I hand over this repetitive, mechanical operation of writing in the Roman numeral "IV" on the cards to my assistant. I still have to send all of the sick to Field 5.

Two days later Hessel takes me to Field 4 and an identical segregation takes place there. Everyone strips naked, they wait two or three hours in the unheated barracks until the commission arrives, medallions and scapulars are ripped off, they are hit in the head with a reed, and the taunt "*Kommunist*" is added.

73. Shoemaker.
74. Transfer list.

Groffmann recognized me, and he is surprised that a gardener is the driving force in the office behind dispatching transports. I hear him murmur a question to Hessel, the word *"Gärtner"* reaches my ears, to which Hessel proudly replies—as if he were the one being referred to:

"Yes, he's an industrialist, who just had an estate as a pastime (*Zeitvertreib*)."

What an upstart Hessel is, to boast about who he has as a subordinate. Once, when I was still a gardener, he interrogated me about where I learned so much theoretical knowledge about botany and farming. I replied that I studied several semesters at the Warsaw University of Life Sciences. This information that he had managed to wheedle out of me later gave him a basis at every incident to scornfully call me a *"Doppeldoktor,"*[75] who wasn't able to handle the simplest matter.

Again, several hundred shoemakers are separated out, I have to go through the same process, but I've learned from experience; when Thumann asks me, I tell him a number that's five people less than what I have written down, thereby making a buffer against incorrect numbers. We still don't know what's supposed to happen with the shoemakers, those from Field 3 weren't moved separately to Field 4, but instead distributed among various barracks. An indication of how arbitrarily this "medical segregation" is being carried out is the fact that around a dozen of those who Thumann counted with the shoemakers two days ago on Field 3 are people he now considers healthy and strong. I remember some of them by their faces. Among them is a Russian, Ivan, the caretaker of the latrine on Field 3, who managed to profit from even that position, allowing after-hours access to the latrines only for those who gave him cigarettes. With diarrhea and dysentery being widespread, many prisoners had "urgent business" for Ivan. I remember him because he wears the letter *P*, meaning that he was categorized as a Pole by the Gestapo since he arrived with a transport of prisoners from Lwów, even though he comes from the Urals and doesn't know a word of Polish.

---

75. Here, a double PhD.

Thumann Leads Me to the Crematorium

On the next day, Thumann selects some people on Field 3 again, but Hessel doesn't dictate numbers anymore, he just sends them to a separate group where I can calmly note the numbers down that are sewn on their chest. There are about one hundred people. I've written down the numbers of about eighty of them when Hessel calls out and tells me to stop and go with Thumann. I tell him that I haven't finished writing down the numbers.

"It's nothing," he says, "I'll take care of it, go catch up with the *Schutzhaftlagerführer*."

He's waiting by the camp gate with *Arbeitseinsatzführer* Troll. So I run after them and call out, as I pass the *Blockführer*:

"8830 *aus dem Lager*."[76]

I assume that we're going for an identical selection onto Field 4. No, Thumann keeps going. Aha, we're going to the Revier on Field 5. But Thumann and Troll pass that gate as well and continue on. I'm breathless. "Jesus and Mary"—they're leading me to the crematorium. I remember the Polish girl who realized that she was being led to her death in the same spot and "took refuge" in the *Blockführer* gatehouse, refusing to take another step. I feel the blood drain from my brain, it becomes cold inside my skull . . . And so my turn has come, did I know too much, and now I have to be rubbed out? I keep going as if hypnotized, trying to escape is useless, since there is a guard tower with a machine gun right at the turn of Field 5 toward the crematorium, and running toward the field would take me right into the *Postenkette*. I stare at Thumann's back and I try to gather something from the gesticulations of his conversation with Troll, it seems immaterial, but since Thumann takes his four-year-old daughter to look at prisoner executions in the crematorium, why should he betray any emotion as he's leading one culprit with him? We near the crematorium, with

76. "Number 8830 from the camp."

every step the contours of the chimney grow larger and taller. We walk on the left side of the road, alongside the barbed wire of Field 5. The crematorium is on the right side of the road. We're twenty paces from the gate to the crematorium. Thumann stops his conversation with Troll. I also stop behind them. Every second feels like an eternity. Thumann leaves Troll and crosses the road to the gate of the crematorium alone, there he turns around, and . . . motions with his finger at me. And so I'm finished, I run up to him. With his cold, green eyes he stares at me, as if relishing the sight. A pause—stillness—I hear the blood pulsing in my ears—silence; finally he says:

"You'll go to Field 6 and wait for me in front of the gate."

I breathe a sigh of relief, as if he had read a not-guilty verdict. I leave, and at the same time Troll crosses over, having observed our conversation from across the street, and together with Thumann they enter the crematorium. Once I've recovered from my initial scare, I start to wonder why Thumann sent me to Field 6.

I know that the barracks were finished recently, but no one lives there. There is no SS guard post by the gate to Field 6, but I see that a dozen people or so are moving about the field. I wait around fifteen minutes and Thumann finally draws near.

We enter the field and go to one of the barracks. There are storerooms of old shoes, which prisoners from Field 4 are busy sorting. I didn't know that some of the warehouses had already been set up here. Again, undressing, writing down numbers, done calmly for the first time, since Hessel isn't here wanting to document his exceptional competence by rushing everything. People already know about the medallions being torn off, so they remove them when they undress and leave them with their clothes. After the segregation, Thumann orders me to return to Field 3 and pull out the card files of those written down.

I return after the lunch bell. I haven't even taken off my cloak before Hessel runs out and starts demanding that I give him the list of the names I had begun writing down from Field 3. I remind him that he told me to stop the work and run after Thumann, and that he said he would take care of it himself. He becomes furious and says that he knows nothing of it and that I have to immediately give him a list of the numbers—if I don't do it within half an hour he will kill me. Typical Hessel and the typical way that matters are presented in the camp. I'm speechless; what would I say anyway? I mechanically button up my jacket, take paper, and ask Olszański to help me find these people! We know that they were from Field 4, and not from ours. But where should we look for them there among twenty-two barracks? The *Blockführer* at the gate doesn't want to let us in, asking us where we plan to roam about during lunch. Besides this, I am not allowed to leave the field alone, thanks to my *Fluchtpunkte*. I explain what's going on to him. Finally, he lets us in. On the way, Olszański tells me that the group of one hundred was sent to Field 6, but they probably didn't stay there for the lunch break. But we have to pass Field 4 in order to look for them on Field 6. We see a group heading in our direction. I ask them where they are coming from, and what work they were doing: they are coming back from Field 6 to Field 4. After exchanging a few words, I realize that these are precisely the people who were on Field 3 whom I had begun writing down. I call out a few numbers from the list I started—they reply. We divide them into two groups and each of us writes down half of their names. What a lucky break! If they had managed to enter Field 4 and had spread throughout the twenty-two barracks, Thumann himself would not have been able to reconstruct the group. What good fortune! When we return after fifteen minutes and I tell Hessel that we have the numbers, he is dumbstruck, but despite his insolence, he's too embarrassed to ask where I conjured up the numbers from.

The "shoemaker" files, collected over the course of three segregations, are arranged separately and Hessel warns me several times that if even one of them is removed, I will be personally responsible. I tell him that I can't be responsible for what happens at night. The open boxes with the card files have no lock. German kapos come in the evening and rifle through the files, and besides, various prisoners, newly sent from jails, or *Häftlinge* are isolated overnight in the office for various reasons. Hessel kicks up a big fuss about it. Kostial orders a large sign to be drawn up on cardboard banning strangers from approaching the files. I give Hessel a draft of the text. It consists of six words. Hessel replies: "*Quatsch*,"[77] he'll

---

77. "Nonsense."

write it himself. He has one idea, a moment later he discards it, then he has another, he changes it four times, and in the end, he tells the draftsman to use what I wrote in the first place.

Another transport is supposed to depart. Thumann orders all the healthy people from Field 4 to come to Field 3 for segregation. This time he only chooses healthy people for the transport, but he orders extra numbers that he qualifies as shoemakers to be listed separately. For some, he doesn't order them written down at all. The Russian, Ivan, the latrine chief, is again listed as a "shoemaker," so he has now had three different categorizations. The segregation lasts all day, and none of the prisoners know which group they were put into. The permanent, recently reduced work units aren't called to the segregation. Some of our jobless people hid from the segregation with Zelent, Pietroniec, etc. Over the course of the day, about 1,800 people are selected. I have to locate these files, no one knows how many numbers I wrote down. I see the haggling and taking of bribes beginning. Through Lang, the Russians propose ten gold rubles to Hessel to cross them off the transport. Hessel takes from everyone and asks me if this or that name is on the list. If it is, he orders it removed. On my own, without notifying them, I remove all of the Polish intelligentsia, so the most biologically valuable part of society. They are all political prisoners. Each of them has some influence here, with underground contacts and the ability to get packages delivered, while in a new camp in a foreign land they would have to start all over. I settle on this tactic with Zelent.

Several days later, Thumann selects the next batch to get to three thousand, he chooses a little more to have a reserve in case there are any complaints. And official complaints start coming in from the horse stables, the SS kitchen, and the SS canteen, as well as objections from the top, requesting that particular prisoners not be sent on the transport. I begin to compile the materials for the transport from the card files.

Wacek Lipski asks me to take care of the lawyer Mieczysław Pruszyński (from the National Radical Camp "ABC" grouping), who was moved from Field 4 to Field 3, and shield him from the transport. Hessel qualifies him for the transport; I see Pruszyński's haggard, emaciated face, and I write his number on the side. He has no idea that his situation was taken care of—and I don't have time to search for him throughout the barracks and let him know that I did what Wacek asked me to.

Today is March 26, 1944. It has been a full year since I came to Majdanek. I was so helpless and mistreated then—an anonymous number. Today, a large portion of significant work is in my hands: I can now change (even improve, who knows) the fate of my friends, crossing out certain names during the selections for the work groups and the transport lists. I wonder if I will get help when I am in need. There were so many times when I was supposed to be on the verge of release—and it came to nothing. My brother doesn't mention the matter in his letters, and Mary asked me outright to tell her what she should do to gain my release. I see that it's a hopeless case.

Rumors have circulated that the transport to Natzweiler escaped around Tarnobrzeg in two groups of around sixty to seventy prisoners each.[78] And indeed, they bring in thirteen Russians in handcuffs, captured in the vicinity of Tarnobrzeg. They have all been badly beaten. They are sitting in our office and the *Feldführer* makes it known that they will be shot. One of them is wounded in the leg. They call them in for the traditional interrogation to Thumann with lashes. The wounded man has to be carried to the whipping by his friends. Everyone gets a *Fluchtpunkt* and a list of their names goes to the *Blockführer* gatehouse as a supplement to the register which already bears my name as someone who can't leave the field without an escort. I ask *Feldführer* Groffmann if we can send the wounded man to the hospital. He replies with a curt "No." The next day I remind him about the wounded man again, and he repeats the reply: "No, let him die."

Skin is stripped off the prisoner's leg, it's swollen, surgery is required. The makeshift bandage that we fashion for his foot won't stop the gangrene.

A message arrives from Natzweiler that the transport has arrived, but that sixty-seven prisoners are missing. Only once the new camp accepts the

---

78. The escape took place on February 27, 1944, on the transport from Majdanek to Flossenbürg.

transport can those prisoners be stricken from our rolls and the date of transfer noted in our records. Escapes are counted against the camp of origin. So I can't finalize who was transferred, since we are waiting for Natzweiler to reply by telegraph to provide the names of the missing. So there was no rescue of the transport.

In connection with the escapes from the last transport, the carpentry workshops were instructed to build a large number of wooden frames, as wide as a railcar and surrounded with barbed-wire braiding. I am told to put twelve of the thirteen Russian escapees from the Natzweiler transport onto the new transport of three thousand; the thirteenth, who has gangrene, went to the hospital with a fever. They don't tell me where the new transport is going, but I did overhear Kostial telling Hessel that it's heading to Auschwitz. I send a runner to get Zelent, since it's hard for me to leave the office now to tell him the news immediately.

The alphabetical transport list is ready, with the Russians separate from everyone else. Now the list has to be read out. Naturally, there's no way that three thousand people can be assembled on the square and have their names read out loud. So it's established that each block will be led, one after the other, to the office and they'll walk past me, single file, and names will be checked off. The reading of the list begins on March 29 at 7:00 p.m. Around 9:00 p.m. the alarm from the *Blockführer* gatehouse sounds: Thumann is coming. Hessel runs in from the kapos' dining room, pulls out a random bunch of files, grabs the old *Totenmeldung*, a binder with old *Stärkemeldung*, surrounds himself with them, and pretends that he is working so hard that he can't see what's going on around him. Only at my yell, "*Achtung!*" does he jump to his feet as Thumann walks in. Has Hessel no shame, doesn't he realize how foolish he's making himself look? Or does he just completely disregard us, like a bunch of animals?

Thumann closely observes the checking of the list for half an hour and then leaves. I see that two Russians are led in past the line and taken behind the banister between our desks; there are two SS men seated there, including Gosberg, the current Field 4 commandant.

A block overseer reports that the Russians are hiding steel handsaws. Indeed, as they are searched, Gosberg finds a pair of saws sewn into their jackets. He starts to beat them in the face with his fist, then he beats them with his cane, finally he grabs one by the head, then the other, and pounds them against the wall. A big bloody stain forms on the wall, everything within a two-meter radius is splashed with blood. The Russians are groaning terribly, their faces are massacred, covered in blood. Gosberg orders them led away, and without any self-restraint and out of breath, he tells the seated Groffmann:

"Ah, what a pleasure it was!"

His eyes are gleaming as brightly as if he just had an orgasm. A messenger washes the blood off of the floor, the spattered cabinet, and the table nearby. The reading continues. Hessel goes to bed at 11:00 p.m. and tells me to wake him up at 2:00 a.m. to relieve me. I work until 5:00 a.m.; I prefer to do everything myself, since Hessel will probably screw something up. If he forgets just one check mark they'll say that someone is missing. But then when they count everyone it will turn out that everyone is actually there, so then the question will come up about who managed to squeeze into the place of the person whose name wasn't checked off. Hessel wakes up at 5:30 a.m. and asks me, without anger, why I didn't wake him up. I knew that he wouldn't beat me up for disobeying this order.

The prisoners know that a general search will take place before they leave the camp, so they won't be able to bring along money or jewelry, which means drinking binges have been taking place in the transport barracks for the last few days. Money has no more value; if you're going to have to give it up, it's better to buy vodka. A half-liter bottle costs close to 1,500 zlotys. The suppliers are various operators, among them the workers in the baths, who are on very friendly terms with the SS men. Corporal Müller delivers vodka from morning till evening, he rides to Lublin on a bicycle and supplies his trusted associates in the baths, like Voropayov, with twenty bottles at a time at three hundred zlotys each, directly onto Field 3—they buy as many as they can.

The transport leaves on March 30 in the morning. The RGO sends food packages for the transport. Directly after they are distributed, an "*Antreten*" is ordered on the square. Swarms of SS men appear and a detailed search commences, every seam of clothing is felt down, and the

RGO packages are taken away at the same time, most of them unopened. Even bread is taken away. The *Feldführer* orders that the crates used to carry the bread for the barracks be brought over to gather the confiscated food. Several dozen crates are filled up and taken as feed for the SS pigsty, next to the SS kitchen, where pigs are raised. It wouldn't have been appropriate to send the RGO packages directly to the pigpen; they had to be distributed first, and only then confiscated as contraband. The groups that have been searched are standing at the front of the square, and no one is allowed to approach them, so nothing can be given to them to take. Everyone has wooden Dutch clogs that clumsily drag along the ground. They are supposed to hamper escape during the transport. Prisoners with *Fluchtpunkte* are handcuffed together in pairs by the SS men. They look like bracelets and have the feature that if you tug at them, they tighten by several notches and don't loosen again. Reckless movements can increasingly tighten them around your hand. A nice thing to look forward to—a trip like that for a few days. The same journey in handcuffs awaits me! Mankiewicz and I look at each other with pity.

I provided Zelent with another breakdown of the nationalities on the transport and Lublin was informed about the approximate departure date forty-eight hours earlier. They also know the direction that it's headed. Maybe they'll rescue the entire transport this time.

As they are leaving through the gate, Thumann carries out another random search and throws toothbrushes, soap, and other items irrelevant to transport safety into the mud. The prisoners leave through the gate and they are counted for the last time in Majdanek. Companies of SS men are waiting in front of the gate with submachine guns and an entire pack of around fifty or sixty dogs, specially trained to recognize striped uniforms. It's empty on the field.

Right after the transport leaves, Hessel hurries us to work. Then, the *Feldführer* enters the office and orders all of us to stop working and go to sleep immediately. Is it a recognition of our work—or just a human gesture? In any case it's a sensible approach to give us a break, since more difficult work awaits us in the coming days.

All of the carpenters and metalworkers are called up to the train station in Lublin to send off the transport. After they return, they say that twenty-five prisoners were placed on each side of a freight car, separated from the middle by a barbed-wire net mounted to a frame. The frame was nailed to the walls of the car. The middle of the wagon, the width of the sliding doors, is meant for the armed escort. All of the prisoners have to sit and they are told that if any of them get up, the guards will shoot. Several prisoners were already shot at the station for ignoring this order and moving around.

I overhear Kostial saying to Hessel that soon the entire camp will be liquidated and all that will remain in Majdanek will be a small contingent of prisoners to evacuate the warehouses and run the office.

The departure of all of the Jews is being organized. An easy transport, several hundred people. Lippmann isn't supposed to go with the transport, but Hessel convinces Kostial that since Lippmann is mixed, he belongs with the Jews. I put him on the list, and the next day an instruction comes from the top to cross him off. I also write down the numbers of the fifty Polish Jews with the letter A from Field 4, but they order these numbers listed separately, not on the transport list.

After I leave the barracks of those Jews, the doors are locked. The next day the transport leaves. As a result of Hessel's efforts, they change Lippmann into stripes and clogs at the last moment. The *Feldführer* gives him a loaf of bread and a hundred zlotys, but Hessel got his way. The transport leaves to the labor camp in Płaszów, near Kraków. Płaszów and Radom are the two locales being considered as places to evacuate the rest of the camp to.

In the *Stärkemeldung*, Hessel orders the fifty Jews with the letter A (probably "*Aktion*") to be listed as "*exekutiert*." Who they were, why they were killed, we don't know. They took their secret to the grave.

A death report arrives, the Russian with gangrene on his leg has died. The *Feldführer* has tallied another human life.

I get another death report. A Jehovah's Witness who Hessel presented with a declaration to sign a few weeks ago has died of typhus. A rare example of a martyr for his faith in the 20th century.

Eighty kapos and eighty Polish intelligentsia are to remain in Majdanek as the staff of particular offices. The rest are to leave in two transports. The healthy in one, and the Revier, "shoemakers," and feeble in the other. The transport of the healthy is being prepared. There are around seven hundred of them. Mostly Polish intelligentsia, since I tried to exclude the most valuable element from previous transports, now everyone will go together: is it good that everyone has been consolidated?

The Best Depart

Thumann conducts a selection among the doctors on Field 5. Professor Michałowicz has to strip alongside Soviet savages and march naked. I've gotten used to this sight, but while looking at a naked academic, I become explicitly aware of how the Polish nation is being humiliated and disgraced. They take most of the doctors to the transport, including Professor Michałowicz, Hanusz, and Dr. Sztaba, also Engineer Witold Sopoćko, Prince Krzysztof Radziwiłł from Field 2, Professor Poniatowski, and the lawyer Gacki. Part of the Revier office leaves, including Captain Wolf, Gregorowicz, the entire Field 4 office, including the economics reporter Garczyński, and from Field 3 almost all of my friends, including: Zelent, Szcześniewski, Dębski, Stamper, Kaszubski, Malanowski, Wszelaki, all three Polish block overseers—each worse than the next: Skiba, Olczyk, Meller (who has yet to be taken into the army, apparently Hitler expects to win the war without him). The transport is consolidated into Blocks 5, 6, and 7. I have a lot of work to do associated with this transport, but I go to the barracks whenever I can to say goodbye to everyone I know, even though I only know some by sight and not by name. Michałowicz and Sopoćko gave their packages to me in the office to protect them from searches and theft. They are lying down, two to a bed, Zelent is nearby, he's listless. I feel sorry for him. I ask:

"Stach, would you like to stay?"

He hesitates with his answer; we all know that no one goes willingly. I go to Hessel and explain to him that if so many people are going to remain, we of course need a technician to maintain the waterworks. Hessel ponders this, and finally he says:

"Cross him off the list."

I run to Stach and tell him that he has been taken off the transport. He looks at me, extends his hand through the slats of the headboard, and shakes my hand in silence. The grip of his handshake is more meaningful than profuse thank-yous. I consider it a success that our chief, who holds all the contacts with the outside world in his hands, is staying in Majdanek.

On the way to the train, someone whispered to the prisoners that their transport will be rescued; indeed, only Poles were in it—and the mood among them was elevated. Mieczysław Pruszyński, the lawyer, also left with the transport. My modest protection was only able to extend his stay in Majdanek by seven days.

A message comes from Auschwitz that the transport from March 30, 1944, arrived within thirty-six hours. The intention to free the transport went unfulfilled again; it was determined that the transport wasn't carrying enough Poles.

Good Friday, April 6, 1944. A precise search of the transport takes place on the roll call square. Thumann calls me over as an interpreter. So I have access to the transport and the opportunity to discreetly shake the hands of my friends. At the last moment, Professor Michałowicz asks me to tell a certain lady in the Polish Red Cross in Lublin to buy his grandson a scout's dagger. This learned man over sixty, known throughout Europe, who has been in Majdanek for a year and who now faces an uncertain road, remembers to do something to make his grandson in Warsaw happy. Maybe the grandson will be able to avenge his grandfather's suffering with that dagger. At the last moment at the gate, Engineer Sopoćko has his toothbrush taken away. The clerk from Field 4, Gregorowicz, hands Pietroniec 130,000 zlotys before the search, asking him to send it to his fiancée.

It's a drizzly day, everyone is hunched over, at least there is no frost. The transport leaves for Gross-Rosen. Maybe it's better than Auschwitz, since we haven't heard as much about this camp. The real "Majdanek" is leaving now, Poland's best sons, those who suffered for their convictions in the camp, who are proud of their stripes, the elite of Majdanek. Those that left before: the dregs, smugglers, criminals, schemers, asocials, and some individuals tangled in with them by chance, like Engineer Gorecki. They will spend Resurrection Sunday in barbed-wire cages.

Shipping Corpses

Last year I spent Easter Sunday laying sod, this time I'm with Hessel listing part of the numbers from the Revier. It's a gorgeous spring day. I come back late for dinner, after everyone has shared the egg. I got my holiday package on time, ham, a delicious cake, eggs. The RGO and PCK also sent us cured meats, honey, apples, gingerbread, butter, and white rolls.

Engineer Merta is sitting in our room, he is a Czech from the *Politische Abteilung*. He was a forester in the Soviet Union for more than a decade. He can't speak any language properly. He forgot how to speak Czech, he didn't learn Russian correctly, his German is full of mistakes. A man older than sixty, very polite and kind. He's sitting sadly, he didn't get a package from his sister in Vienna. I'm glad that I could invite him for the blessed food and we eat the contents of the package.

Wet Monday[79] begins with writing down the transport in the Revier. I imagine that it won't create a lot of work for me, since Hessel arranged with Captain Grudowski that he would make the list of the sick according to the hospital's files, to which the "shoemakers" and some of the feeble eliminated from the Gross-Rosen transport will be added. Thumann is not present since there is no segregation to carry out: all of the sick are going. Hessel enters one hall, this one is for tuberculosis sufferers. He only looks through the door of another since it's the typhus ward. A decision is made on the spot. He orders *Revierkapo* Benden to organize all of the nurses, he sends some of them to the auto shops to get auto trailers. What's this? He stands by the first barracks and orders all of the sick to get out of bed. None of them have clothing, since theirs is sent away to the clothing warehouse once they are admitted to the hospital. The mud begins to melt where the sun is shining, but everything in the shade is

---

79. Easter Monday, known as *Śmigus Dyngus* in Poland, where people traditionally soak each other with water.

frozen. The sick emerge barefoot, in shirts, covered in a blanket. We stand by the doors, Hessel dictates numbers to me, the sick form up by the gate in groups of one or two hundred and are led to Field 4, which is empty (except for the office staff). Those who can't walk are carried by the nurses to the trailers. They take a sick person on piggyback, or two of them will carry one in a blanket. Once twenty-five are gathered into a trailer, the nurses push them onto Field 4 and unload the sick into empty barracks. The Revier is emptied systematically, one barracks after another. This is all being done because the monster in human form, Hessel, wants to make writing down the numbers easier for himself and to avoid walking into foul-smelling rooms, rubbing against densely packed, lice-filled beds, and breathing in tuberculosis or dysentery bacteria. Taking care of his valuable person, he orders 1,800 sick people to move in just their shirts from one field to another, to half-vandalized barracks, partially without mattresses and blankets, which is their condition after every departing transport.

Even after having been in Majdanek for a year, I didn't realize how terrible conditions were in the Revier. Admittedly, these are foreigners, not Poles, who are deprived of RGO care, and were recently evacuated from the hospitals of other camps in order to die in Majdanek, and they haven't complied yet. Hessel reads the numbers off the necks of the sick who can walk under their own strength. But he's afraid to touch those who are carried on backs or in blankets and I have to dig around under the shirts of the unconscious or totally emaciated to pull out the number and read it. Sometimes I think that this light bundle contains a ten-year-old child, and here the gray-haired head emerges of a person so scrawny that they might weigh thirty-five or forty kilograms. I had never imagined such heavy lice infestations. The strings that contain the numbers around their necks are covered in nits, and some of the heads of the sick who are lying motionless are so covered in lice, that where the hair has grown back behind their ears or on the nape of their necks, there are entire clusters of nits, not of hundreds but thousands, piled one on top of the other. The lice have eaten away wounds on their bodies. Most of the sick are caked with feces, and not only those from the enteritis ward with the sweetly nauseating smell that makes you want to vomit.

There are several bodies lying by the entrance to the barracks. Even their crap-covered shirts were torn off and the waxen-purple corpses are each so emaciated that the contours of the pelvis and spine are visible through the skin of their stomachs. Their hands and feet are shockingly black with dirt, their torso plastered with excrement down to their calves. This death looks different in reality than the doctor's description included with the prisoner's death notice and the condolences from the camp commandant.

Thumann came to the field for fifteen minutes, accepted Hessel's idea to move all of the sick prisoners to Field 4, and left. The mud is starting to freeze again. It's 5:00 p.m., we have to go back to Field 3 for the roll call. Hessel stops writing down any more numbers. My count of the numbers doesn't match with what was counted at the gate of Field 5. Field 4 provides different numbers still. Obviously, with the dying and unconscious stacked like cordwood one on top of the other in the auto trailers, the *Blockführer* must have made a mistake while counting. The roll call doesn't add up, but Kostial waves it off, since it's clear that none of these gravely sick people ran away.

I spend the entire evening pulling out card files, and my assistants arrange them alphabetically, getting them ready to draw up the list.

On Tuesday, the move to Field 4 continues. The sight of these human marionettes is macabre, they are counted and arranged like sacks; even *Revierkapo* Benden, who was a permanent member of the selection commission for the gas chamber, shakes his head in pity and emotion while watching Hessel's "efficient" method of inventorying the sick. "Is it sincere?"—I think to myself. "Or maybe, my dear, you're trying to absolve yourself in the presence of us Poles?"

Field 5 has been completely emptied, since Field 1 is also empty, the guard posts are only active at night around Fields 2, 3, and 4.

We work all night to finalize an alphabetized list of all the last names. Overall, everyone on the transport, including the "shoemakers," adds up to around 2,700 people. We write all night, in the morning the transport manifest is checked and ready.

The railways hadn't prepared the cattle cars by Wednesday, so Hessel sets the reading of the list for Thursday. Thumann comes for this. Hessel wants to show off his creativity again. He takes the entire office staff and a few passing prisoners, ten total, and divides the transport list into ten parts, so that the first person gets the letters A, B, and part of C, the second person C, all of D, and E—however the pages end. The ten of us are seated at two tables in the dining room, the sick are roused out of their beds to the dining room and one at a time they are able to return to the sleeping area. The person entering has to state their name and it is then checked off. Hessel divided the list into ten parts so that locating the names would be faster. It is going so-so at first, then one of us won't hear the name or the first letter or someone will zone out and the sick person is left standing and waiting. Hessel hurries us along, looking for the last names himself, slapping those who haven't found it fast enough. I see that nothing is going to come of this work. It's enough for one distracted assistant to forget a check mark by a name after getting slapped—then, after the reading, I will be responsible for entering incorrect names onto the transport list. About fifteen people are already set aside in the first barracks since their names can't be found. It's not surprising: they are Dutchmen, Frenchmen, and Albanians who pronounce their names differently than what the Gestapo officially christened them. All of them are taken to Block 11. After reading and checking off all of the names, it's easier to find the distorted names among those few that haven't yet been checked off. In the second barracks, Hessel convinces himself that this collective reading doesn't expedite the work at all. He sends away all of the clerks to Field 3, and he tells me to read the names by myself. Most of the barracks aren't divided into sleeping and dining areas. In those, the sick have to leave or are carried outside. They are laid down in the mud, wrapped in a blanket. Above all, I try to check off those who are lying in the mud first, and then those who are standing on their own two feet. Unfortunately, the ones in the mud are often unconscious and they can't state their names. Who should I check off? These poor fellows are carried away to Block 11. I send the numbers that I read off from their neck tags to the Field 3 office to have them check the names of the prisoners, and only then do I know whether to check off the name.

Thumann has introduced the principle that whoever is placed on the transport list is considered alive even if they already died on Field 4. The dead are to be loaded onto the transport and they'll be considered dead only on the way.

What scenes I see now! Sick, unconscious people with high fevers, spasms convulsing their bodies in the mud. A Frenchman crying out in delirium:

"Kill me, finish me off!"

You would have to be a polyglot to understand these moans in Serbian, Hungarian, Dutch, Albanian, and Italian.

It has begun to drizzle. Two Soviet generals are lying in the mud and a colonel of the general staff, one of them is named Novikov, and one is a director of the military academy in Moscow. I remember when they were transferred to the camp six weeks ago. While drinking vodka one evening, Hessel was boasting about the transport that had come in, and around 10:00 p.m., they summoned the three officers from their beds to the kapos' dining room and stared and made fun of them as if they were some kind of freaks. One of the generals addresses me and asks to translate his request to the "gentleman officers." Next to me are all noncommissioned officers: fat Gosberg, the corporal from the hospital with the buckteeth, and a few other SS crumb crunchers. The general says:

"I am very sick, I will probably die, let me go peacefully here, and if my health improves then send me with the transport in a few days."

I translate this. Gosberg laughs out loud and says to those around him:

"And that's what Russian generals are like!"

The obliging Hessel adds:

"*Das sollte die Welt regieren!*"[80]

I'm standing next to Dr. Hett, a prisoner from Field 2, where there are only Soviet invalids. He's here on assignment today. He was an old National Socialist who got cured of his passion for Hitler by the concentration camp. He looks at Hessel with contempt. Several times he witnessed the insults Hessel aimed at me and in a calm voice he told me not to let it get to me. I turn to Hett now and tell him:

"I wonder what a German general would look like if he had been starved for months, unable to wash, dressed in rags, and deprived of medical care."

80. "This was supposed to rule the world!"

Hett nods his head in silence.

Marching past me are phlegmons, enteritis, tuberculosis, surgical patients, skin conditions, and what remains is typhus fever. No one has the courage to enter this barracks, they send me in alone. The sick are grouped in the dining area, I deliberately don't sit down or lean against the table where the transport list is. Among the typhus sufferers is the freshly transferred legal trainee from Lwów, Meinhardt, my gardener in the fall of 1943. At the end, I bid farewell to Dr. Metera and Dr. Tomaszewski, who are leaving with the transport.

The "shoemakers" are spread across three barracks. The reading of the names is going efficiently. Among them is Kapo Bolesław Reich, who at the last moment asks the *Feldführer* in my presence to be excluded from the transport, since he is a *Reichsdeutsch*. I protest that he's not a *Reichsdeutsch* but a *Volksdeutsch*. The *Feldführer* says in that case there's nothing to talk about. Reich stares daggers at me. I think to myself that I've paid you back in small part for your villainy against Poles. Why should you always be the better passenger in second class? Among the convalescents I see the second pearl of Majdanek, the *Volksdeutsch* Knips, who asks me to intervene with Hessel to keep him in Majdanek. I nod my head and think to myself: "Right, you're exactly the type we need here. Godspeed!" Among the convalescents leaving with the transport is Wacek Lipski. I embrace him warmly. Will we see each other again? Our beautiful plan to free the camp has come to nothing!

Block 11 is all that's left, where those whose names we couldn't find on the list were sent. This is the hardest work. There are over 120 of them. When I enter the barracks I see that some of them couldn't wait for my arrival. One corpse is seated, leaning against the table as if asleep, and several more are lying in the corners. It's dark already. The guessing of names begins and pondering how they were twisted around. I discover a Rudkowski here who arrived six weeks ago, but he isn't in the files of our office or of the hospital, and he doesn't have a number. Finally all of the names are sorted out, I go with Hessel to the hospital office and I look through the list, several names weren't checked off; it means that these people aren't real, they only appear in the files. But both of us remember and Hett confirms that in the morning before the collective reading of the list, one of the names was called out, and after it was repeated several times, one of the clerks found the person, so the "assistant" forgot to check off the name. What should be done? Check it all again? It's impossible at night, and the transport has to be loaded onto trucks in the morning. So there's no other option: tomorrow, while they are being loaded, we will count how many people leave. They bring several trucks with clothing and throughout the night they will be dressing the sick.

I return to Field 3, obliterated by the intense stress and the nightmarish impression that all of those devastated people made on me. I wash my hands and then the first thing I do is check my underwear. I find a large louse in my long johns. Damn . . . Does it have typhus or not? Did it bite me yet? We'll see. Today was the last chance for me to catch typhus!

The following day is April 13, the transport is loaded. The trucks drive in and loading and counting begins. The SS men count when prisoners are carried and led out of the barracks, others count during the loading onto trucks, a third counts when they leave the field, another at the station while the trucks are unloaded, and finally another when they are loaded into the freight cars. The cars are also divided into two cages enclosed with frames nailed with barbed wire. The loading of the dying, unconscious, and sick, since they are all going together, is a gruesome sight. These shadows of humanity are piled up in several layers like logs in the trucks and that's how they depart. Over eighty corpses, counted as alive, left this way. I'll admit that I don't know Dante's *Inferno*, but I suppose that a director of the caliber of Reinhardt[81] would have to have seen the last three days of putting together the transport of the sick in Majdanek in order to realistically stage Dante.

At the last moment, I have to create a name list of the sixteen Russians staffing the crematorium. It will be attached to the transport list. The purpose is clear: they will be the first to go to the gas chamber in Auschwitz.

---

81. Max Reinhardt (1873–1943) was a Jewish Austrian theater director, head of the *Deutsches Theater* in Berlin, famous for its naturalistic performances.

The fivefold counting of the sick by the SS men doesn't bring results. Each one gives a different number, some are off by as many as six people. In the end we don't know how many people left.

Now we have to prepare the entire documentation related to the transport. *Arbeitseinsatzkarte*, files including the prisoner's profession and the work squads they were members of, have to be sent to the correct camps. The *Politische Abteilung* sends the prisoners' personnel records. Instead of sending sacks with personal clothing to the appropriate camps, the *Effektenkammer* sends all the clothing to Germany as bombardment relief.

Guards are now only posted to Field 2, where all of the 1,500 or so Soviet prisoners are,[82] and Field 3, where there are 185 of us. At the same time as the transport, all of the hostages were released. I was personally responsible for making sure that none of them happened to get onto the transport. At the last second, Hessel packed in the sick former *Lagerkapo*, Krause from our field, one of the most solid kapos who always rose to the defense of prisoners. Hessel found out that he had a fever and ordered him brought by force to Field 4, telling Kostial about this, who accepted it, after the fact, as with everything Hessel does. Krause has the beginnings of typhus. He'll surely be finished off on the way without injections or medical care.

The survivors of Majdanek remain, four Polish hostages and one tubercular German, slated for release but they have to gain weight, since the doctor doesn't want to release them in their emaciated state. The SS doctor determined that the health conditions of the camp are such that the RGO no longer needs to send soup.

With 99 percent of the camp having been evacuated (not counting Soviet invalids), the post office in Majdanek was ordered closed. The post offices in the General Government won't accept packages, and those in transit will be automatically returned by the Lublin post office. So we are switching over exclusively to camp fare.

---

82. After the April evacuation of prisoners, 2,500 men remained in the Field 2 hospital for Soviet war invalids.

Now an inventory needs to take place to see if the balance sheet adds up. There are 180 of us plus the five sick people to be released. All the files of those who left have been removed—I also separated the 185, now I've been instructed to determine whether anyone living remains in the files. In theory, the numerical file should only contain the numbers of the dead or prisoners who were transported away earlier. The Soviet invalid hospital on Field 2 has autonomy and their patients don't figure into our files, since they don't have camp numbers. After a two-day review, I have the cards of seven people who, on paper, are still in the camp. Where did they go?

The Soviet invalids are cleaning up Fields 4 and 5. They bring over the card files from the hospital, which Grudowski is supposed to compile, as well as medicines, instruments, etc. While organizing the barracks on Field 5, the Russians find two corpses in beds under mattresses. At the same time, they find three living people on Field 4, also buried between mattresses. They are so starved that they can't stand up. They are Russians, they've already been sleeping outside the *Postenkette* for two days, since Field 4 is no longer under guard, they might have escaped if they wanted to and if they could. They went unnoticed during the hurried loading and they didn't have the strength to move; if they had laid there for another day or two they would have died of hunger. Hessel tells them that they have to die, since officially, they don't exist in the camp. They are sent to the near-empty Block 15, where the five convalescents waiting to be released already are. The corpses are "christened" with names from seven of the files, which means three people were found. The remainder from the seven weren't located, nor was their status clarified, so they probably left with the transport.

While rummaging through various old papers, I find a letter from the Lublin municipal council to the Majdanek camp command, from July 1943, where they give notice that there will be a renovation of the waterworks and filters over a two-week period and ask that the camp reduce its water consumption by 50 percent. Thumann simplified it for himself—he shut off all of the water (there were so many mothers and small children on the field then!), and the only water he allowed to be taken was for the flowers.

———

Our office staff has been reduced. Jabłoński and Laskowski went to the SS kitchen, Serafin to the SS lodgings, and the rest of us will have to process a vast amount of material for the bimonthly report to Oranienburg.

One of the kapos bursts into the office with an inhuman yell. Thumann has been moved to Neuengamme as the camp commandant. This produces universal enthusiasm, and the evening brings an occasion for a huge drinking binge among the kapos. Now life in Majdanek might be a little more pleasant.

Kostial becomes the *Schutzhaftlagerführer*; Mußfeld, the crematorium chief, becomes the *Rapportführer*. The *Arbeitseinsatz* is taken over by Corporal Kostoj. An even greater schemer than Laurich. He orders ten pairs of pants and five suits at a time from Pietroniec, sells them in Lublin, and pockets thousands. In exchange he buys large hunks of pork fat, and orders them packed up in the office, and addressed to the *Vaterland*.

The Last of the Mohicans

Besides our contingent of 180 prisoners, and the 1,500 Soviet invalids on Field 2, over 350 prisoners remain in the DAW in Lublin,[83] where Enders is the *Lagerältester*. They are all specialist woodworkers: Germans, Dutchmen, Frenchmen, Norwegians. They produce tables, cabinets, and other furniture for the *Wehrmacht*.[84] The atmosphere is sublimely friendly there. Enders takes care of his subordinates and when some SS man hits a prisoner, he reports him and gets him transferred. It's no wonder that Hessel took twenty gold rubles apiece from the Russians to get themselves transferred to the DAW.

Majdanek is supposedly going to become an *"Auffanglager,"*[85] where the newly arrested will be sent and from which transports will leave for other camps after they've been registered here. Poles have remained as the intellectual workers in all of the vital *Kommando*. Each unit has a German kapo assigned to it to keep an eye on the Poles, and the rest of the Germans, near-illiterates, loiter around the camp. I am under the impression that they are to play the role of security guards so that the Poles don't gain the upper hand. They assign Soviet invalids as assistants and laborers. We've been reduced to the point that all of us can be evacuated at any time.

My colleagues in the *Bekleidungskammer* remind themselves that I don't have pants. Pietroniec brings me a pair. In light of such an *embarras de richesse*,[86] when the civilian clothes of so many thousands of prisoners were taken away, it would have been hard to assert that there still aren't any pants.

83. Nearly five hundred prisoners were held in the camp on Lipowa Street at the time.
84. Here, the German Armed Forces.
85. Transit camp.
86. French: an embarrassment of riches, a confusing abundance.

———

Hessel orders me to plant the seeds gathered last year. The weather is beautiful and sunny. I gladly take a spade and dig around in the soil. I imagine myself in my garden in Komorów, or at least in my farmstead. A year ago these flower beds were created under my direction—I planted flowers—collected seeds—now I'm planting again! While I was collecting the seeds my friends were bantering, wondering why I was collecting them, and whether I intended to be in Majdanek next spring. I didn't believe it myself, spring came and I remained, but I know for sure that I won't be gathering the flowers from the seeds I am planting.

The field is empty, Hessel isn't hovering over my shoulder so I can truly delight in the gardening and my thoughts. The achievements of monasteries in the Middle Ages in elevating farming and gardening culture come to mind. How exaggerated were our laypeople's imaginings about monastic orders with their severe rules, such as the Trappists sleeping in coffins, fasting, silence, waking at 2:00 a.m. to say prayers, self-flagellation. I would gladly change places with the Trappists, their rules would feel like a stay in a luxury resort. We prisoners don't need to greet each other with *memento mori*—we see death every day. I remember Certosa di Pavia, the monastery of the Carthusians some thirty kilometers from Milan. Each monk had a small apartment, with a bedroom, a workroom, and their own garden and toilet. What comfort! In their free time, outside of prayer, they produced the famous Chartreuse in two flavors and colors. Such a lifestyle is described as an offering to God—is our sacrifice for our homeland not incommensurably greater?

Pohlmann is hounding poor Zelent. He has to relocate the stools, tables, blankets, brooms, and other movable property from all of the barracks to Block 8. That's where he has situated himself and where he lives. He walks around covered in dust like a wild animal. His friend, Kazimierz Mliczewski from Wąbrzeźno, is bedridden there with typhus. Hessel has decreed that we're not allowed to be sick now since there is no hospital, whoever gets sick will be sent to another camp on a special transport.

———————

Camp Commandant Weiß leaves for another camp, supposedly back to Dachau. Some new commandant has arrived. Hessel is disparaging toward him, apparently he isn't a scum sucker, since those are the only types he respects.

While clearing things out, Zelent finds a gold watch and two rings. He sends them to the RGO right away for social-welfare purposes, scrupulously asking for a receipt. A friend of Olszański's gave him four thousand zlotys as he was leaving, since he wouldn't have been able to take the money anyway. He asks my advice about what to do with it; he's living well here and his wife, who is working as a teacher, is suffering in poverty. I reply that if he had earned the money honestly, he would have the right to send it to his wife. But if he came to possess it by chance, as was the case, then he should send the money to the RGO, to which he owes a lot for their help. If he tries to send the money back home, he'll be under suspicion that he was engaged in shady business at someone else's expense, obviously—and this won't bring him any honor.

"Thank you very much," Olszański says, "I wanted to confirm my thinking with you."

A fire breaks out on our field at night. According to the rules, prisoners are not allowed to leave their barracks, except for those called to help. I hear them summoning the German kapos—let it burn, I turn over and fall asleep. In the morning I find out that half the kitchen burned down. An investigation is taking place. The fire started in the addition that included the private laundry for the cooks. All eleven cooks are arrested right after the roll call and taken to Kostial. An SS officer comes over—he's an engineer by trade and he looks into the cause of the fire. He brought the head cook, Siwiński, with him and calls me as an interpreter. A large amount of scorched linens are lying in the burned-down laundry. There's a suspicion that the head cook forgot to unplug the electric iron after he finished ironing and after it overheated there was a short circuit that sparked the fire. The SS officer orders the rubble to be picked through, especially in the spot where the outlet and table used for ironing were. At a certain moment the officer bends over, picks up a cord with a plug like those used with irons, and in the blink of an eye he hides it behind his back. He asks Siwiński what color the cord was; he replies that it was black.

"Are you sure?" asks the officer.

Siwiński confirms it again, he didn't notice that the officer already found a cord and I can't whisper it to him. Then the officer orders the digging to continue, and after a while the Russians pull out a tangle of wires and a charred plug—another cord, burnt to a crisp. I see the investigation is being carried out by a professional. Now he pulls the other cord out from behind his back and says:

"You were right, this one is reddish, but a black one was burned, and so you forgot to unplug the iron!"

It's obvious that he forgot, but it would have been so easy to blame it on sabotage.

I get a message from home that a telegram came from Hańka in Lwów that I will be released within a week. I'm dragged out of my apathy again, the mirages of my discharge appear once more.

A speakeasy forms over at Zelent's. We go there after the roll call to chat. He got a package from Elżunia, of whom he speaks with a playful wink, which contained a bottle of *krupnik*.[87] For two days in a row the two of us pass the bottle of vodka. I sense that Elżunia is one of the ladies from the organization who works in the RGO or the PCK. Stach tells me about his son Marek and his older foster daughter. Captain Kowalski spends time there, hiding under the alias Orpisz, a landowner from the Borderlands, Captain of Horse Jan Wolski, Noak, Żurawski ("*Kuchenblech*"), and later, the permanently plastered Kapo "Adam" Marciniak, No. 33 from the *Bekleidungskammer*. He brings with him a company of other German kapos who come with vodka, which prompts our Polish group to leave that barracks.

---

87. A honey-spiced liqueur based on grain spirit, usually vodka.

My Typhus

My name day is coming up as well as my twentieth wedding anniversary. Maybe my release will fall on that day? We get a surprise as a result of the fire in the kitchen.

We find out that the new camp commandant, Liebehenschel, who came to us from Auschwitz, had all of the cooks fired and wrote a report to Oranienburg where he advised that the fire was contained only thanks to the devoted help of the prisoners and that its cause had not been determined. Indeed, an SS dog like Hessel can only scorn such a commandant.

Gosberg, the Field 4 commandant, leaves to become the commandant of the Jewish camp in Budzyń.

Since such a small handful of prisoners remains, on April 18, 1944, they mandate the wearing of uniforms, and we all get stripes. I didn't enjoy my civilian pants for long. Only Hessel has the right to wear civilian clothing.

The PCK obtained permission from the camp commandant to record the names of the Polish prisoners remaining in Majdanek and the addresses of their relatives to be notified that we remain here. I can't wait for my name day. On April 23 I get a gift package from my brother, who came to Lublin and left it with the RGO. I have chills and I lie down right after roll call. I take two aspirin. I was sweating all night.

On my name day I wake up without a fever. I invite my friends for supper. I got a thick Kraków sausage from my brother, nearly half a meter long. Olszański asks if there will be vodka (which would set me back six hundred zlotys per bottle), I don't have that much money so I tell him there won't be. In the afternoon I have the chills again and a fever. I lie down and ask my friend, Henryk Zalewski, to open the package, cut the sausage, and treat my friends. There are also sweets. I don't eat anything.

Olszański's and Tetych's portions are untouched, they don't return until about 10:00 p.m. and Olszański jokingly says:

"We didn't come to your gathering since we were invited to another, where there was vodka."

Tough luck, apparently vodka is more of an attraction than I am. I check my temperature, it is 38.4 degrees [101°F]. The flu. I toss back more aspirin to lower my fever. I sweat all night. On the morning of April 25, it's 36.8 degrees [98°F]; at noon, 38 degrees. But I'm still sitting at my desk. In the evening, 39 degrees. I down more aspirin. April 26 in the morning, 37 degrees; at noon, over 38 degrees.

I sneak out of the office and lie down in bed. If Hessel calls for me my friends are supposed to give me a heads-up. Laskowski, my former colleague from the office, who recently started working in the SS kitchen, is sick. His temperature is 39 degrees. He has reported as sick to the office. Hessel forces him to work for two days. An SS man, the head of the kitchen, allows him to sit out both days in the potato warehouse. Only on the third day does he get into the improvised hospital with definite typhus. In the afternoon I go to Dr. Gabriel, a Pole from Wrocław and a German citizen, locked up because he was the doctor of the Polish middle school in Olsztyn. I show him the notes of my temperatures, and tell him that I was there when the transport of the sick was being sent off and I found a louse. Gabriel counts on his fingers and says:

"Right, the incubation period for typhus is nine to twelve days. It perfectly lines up with the date of the transport's departure. You have to keep monitoring it, don't take any more aspirin, it weakens the heart and won't get rid of the fever."

Typhus or the flu—to be, or not to be? Hessel is still threatening that all of the sick will be sent away somewhere on a transport. So I am not allowed to be sick. Luckily, there isn't much work, I sit in the office for an hour, lie in bed for two, and then make an appearance in the office again. If my release were to happen now, they wouldn't let me go, I would have to suffer through my sickness here. In the evening my temperature is 39.4 degrees. On April 27 in the morning, a shade over 37 degrees; at noon it's 38.4 degrees. I'm tormented by terrible cramps in my arms and legs, they are extraordinarily painful. Besides this I have no symptoms, pain or rashes. In the evening, 39.8 degrees. On the evening of April 28, over 40 degrees. It's getting better. I'm totally lucid—but listless. The transport of the sick is supposed to leave in two days, so I have to hold on through then.

Our field is supposed to move to Field 1 due to our kitchen burning down. Since then, we have gotten our food from Field 2. They are terrible cooks, they can't even make coffee. Our Polish cooks had been preparing food for 180 people splendidly. Right now, as we are deprived of packages, Russian cooking hits us doubly hard.

I tell everyone that I'm having heart problems, so that Hessel doesn't add me to the transport like Krause, who we learn has died en route. I have started to discreetly review the number of death reports to check how many deaths the camp is officially admitting to. I want to send this number out into the world through Zelent. I counted through the first letters, but my fever got the better of me, and I can't delegate the work to anyone else. On April 29, they start packing up the entire office. I ask Zalewski to watch the files as they are being loaded. Everyone helps with moving out the tables and chairs while I am lying down and I arrange with my friends that I'll go with the last wagon. I'm in bed when *Feldführer* Groffmann walks in and asks what's wrong with me, I tell him that I had a heart attack last night.

"OK, then, stay in bed," he says and leaves.

My bundle of blankets has already been taken. I'm lying down on a bare mattress in my stripes. I haven't had time to sew my number and *Flucht-punkte* to my jacket. They take the rest of the furniture. I have to get up, I can't put on my jacket, I toss it onto the wagon and walk alongside it. My knees are buckling under me. *Lagerkapo* Pohlmann walks up to me and asks:

"Why aren't you pushing?"

I reply that I had a heart attack.

"You're lying," he replies, "your eyes are glistening like you've just gotten a shot of atropine, naturally, a big shot from the *Schreibstube*, now pull, otherwise you'll get a beating."

I take a wire hanging down from the side of the wagon and pull. On Field 1, I go to the hall where our tables have been dumped and sit down by the card files to pretend that I'm arranging the cards in the compartments. Hessel comes over and calls everyone to work. I sit.

"*Willst du nicht mithelfen?*"[88]

But he has already taken off. I tramp outside after him. "*Los, los,*" yells Hessel, carry the beds.

"*Lagerältester* Sir, I wanted to tell you . . ."

"I don't want to hear anything, now you carry, you'll tell me in the evening!"

I have to carry the beds from barracks to barracks. The entire SS cast is standing there: Kostial, Mußfeld, Groffmann, so I can't just carry one board, but the regulation four sideboards or one headboard. I take long breaks and I hide. There is a bedroom by the office where I lie down immediately after the roll call. Only then does Hessel take an interest and ask me what I wanted. I reply. He sends for *Revierkapo* Benden (the waiter), to examine me. He looks over my body, takes my temperature, fortunately it's low, 38.6 degrees, and he says that the condition needs to be observed. On April 30 I stay in bed, I don't rise for the roll call. Groffmann let me stay in bed. Hessel bursts into my room.

"Are you sick or healthy? Because if you're healthy you can't be in here."

I tell him that the *Feldführer* let me.

"I don't care about that, I'm the decider!"

In the morning I find out that the sick transport, which they were frightening us with, isn't leaving. Oranienburg didn't authorize it. And so I am sick. I know that in Block 3 the sick are lying in one room, there are about ten of them. Around 4:00 p.m. they're supposed to be moved to Block 15, which is being scrubbed. So I want to stay in bed until noon, in order to move to the new barracks. Hessel forces me out to go to Block 3 immediately. There's a small room there with ten beds, all of them occupied. Mliczewski is already convalescing, he gets up and makes room for me. Kapo No. 2, Schommer, comes and insults us, saying that all of the Poles

---

88. "Don't you want to help?"

are thieves, that we've stolen some blanket of his. I make an ironic reply confirming that only Poles steal, that Schommer is right, and that others don't need anything. This infuriates him and he threatens to slap me:

"*Du Scheisspolacke*," if I don't shut up.

Unfortunately I don't have the strength to haul myself up and face him. I have to stay silent. But you son of a bitch, you'll still get yours. I see that other Germans are nodding their assent, so he confidently adds:

"You Poles allow yourselves too much around here."

I lie like a log until noon. After 4:00 p.m. they order us to move to Block 15. Someone is leading me by the arm, I don't know who. As I enter the block, the terror of Majdanek, Mußfeld, the former head of the crematorium, is standing there. In a humane voice he asks:

"What's wrong with you?"

I say that I have a fever.

"I see that you are sick."

That's how one of the executioners of Majdanek spoke to me. In that case, what rung in the hierarchy does the prisoner Hessel occupy in relation to Mußfeld?

In Block 15 the floor is wet, the hay and mattresses are dirty, I get two worn-out blankets, I'm shivering. I'm officially sick. After situating all of the sick a few hours later, Dr. Gabriel gives me a third blanket. It's so dirty here— what a gem my Block 15 on Field 3 was in comparison. Now Dr. Gabriel is taking my temperature, I don't care what it is anymore. I get a shot, I don't care what it is. I hear Dr. Gabriel's deep voice, seeing his gentle eyes I know that I am in good hands.

The next day, Pietroniec brings me two throw pillows, a quilt, and apples. I have no appetite, just thirst. I only have a hundred zlotys and I send it to Krupski in the clothing warehouse, from which there are daily trips to Lublin, and ask that he buy some dried apples so I can have compote made for me. I realize that I won't get much, so I call Serafin to me and hand him a postcard to my brother. In it I ask him to give Serafin's sister (through whom my correspondence comes) one thousand zlotys, and also ask Serafin if she could front me some money to buy the apples. He says that it will be hard for her financially. When the money comes from Warsaw she'll gladly take care of it though. So I have to wait at least ten days, and by that time I'll either recover or I won't need it at all.

Zelent comes and brings me apples. Pietroniec brings me two hand-fuls of dried fruit, the orderly makes me compote, it's enough for one day. Krupski doesn't bring any fruit. I have a huge craving for lemons, for hours I can see the yellow lemon skin, I smell them and my mouth waters. I have to satisfy myself with bitter coffee made with beet slices by Soviet invalids. I have an entire bowl next to me and I take a few spoonfuls from time to time at night. Noak brings me a few eggs.

The biggest surprise came from Jabłoński, who brings me a bottle of vegetable juice from the SS canteen. It's unexpected because we were indifferent toward one another, and at odds during the first days of his work in the office, when I reprimanded him quite sharply since the "power" went to his head. He didn't go through the stage of shoveling in the rain and cold, in the dirt and hunger like the rest of us, he came straight to the clean, warm room, to a desk job with sufficient food. He couldn't recognize his lucky break and he was flippant about the work assigned to him. And he's the one who came to help me, while Olszański, who empha-sized his friendship so often, hasn't shown up.

My temperature is stable at around 38 degrees in the afternoon, it's lower in the morning. My condition is bearable. Laskowski is lying next to me, he has a very high fever, he's babbling and doesn't recognize me, he drinks and drinks the black swill.

A few beds away, Papst is sick with typhoid fever, and nearby, the last *Lagerältester* of Field 4 also has typhus. There are perhaps fifteen of us, I don't know the others. Someone dies every night, one wheezes for hours, a second groans melodiously, a third is gasping, no one is moved by it, in the morning the orderlies carry out the naked body to the washroom and lay it on the concrete floor until the corpse is taken to the crematorium. The moans and sighs of the dying don't make any impression on me, I calmly sleep onward. I guard my bowls to make sure they aren't swapped, I have to be careful not to get a bowl or spoon that Papst was using to avoid getting typhoid fever on top of it. Gabriel keeps filling Papst and Laskowski with coffee and soup.

Just like healthy prisoners, we get black coffee twice per day and cabbage or rutabaga soup for lunch. Not really a healthy diet for typhoid fever. But it's written so nicely into the hospital files.

Papst is raving about a car, about going back home, he yells at night and issues commands, he's growing thinner by the day. My requests sent by Pietroniec to have Olszański, Tetych, Zalewski, and Mankiewicz visit me and bring me newspapers—has no effect. The kindhearted Gabriel and Zelent bring me books.

The former cook Zalewski, hailing from Kolomyya, has pneumonia. Next to me is the young Jarmołowicz from Wilno (he works in the DAW) with a wounded leg. He brought a thick book with him, which he doesn't read. It's the *Antologia poezji religijnej*,[89] edited by Stanisław and Wanda Miłoszewski, with a preface by Archbishop Teodorowicz. How many memories those names bring back. Teodorowicz, a personal friend of my father's, cooperated with him politically and came to our home when I was still in middle school. I remember the Battle of Grunwald anniversary celebration in 1910, his blessing the Falcons' sports field in Czerniowce,[90] and his visiting my ailing father in my home in Warsaw a few weeks before he died in 1925. I remember Wanda Miłaszewska offering *Czarna Hańcza*[91] with a dedication to my deceased wife. A positive aura emanates from this volume, which was published with refined graphical taste. The poems of Kochanowski, Kasprowicz, Słowacki, Krasiński, Norwid, *et tutti quanti*.[92] I read the first printed Polish words since my arrest. What a fortunate coincidence to have received such a pearl of literature into my hands. Every poem read with feeling—at least as much as I can muster—is a prayer, and I am so thirsty for it. I read several pages each day in order to properly imbibe the beauty of the poetry.

The good Zelent visits me every day. He brings me *Pan Tadeusz* with commentary by Pigoń. I revel in the beautiful descriptions. How much depth

89. Polish: "Anthology of Religious Poetry."
90. Today Chernivtsi, Ukraine.
91. The title of the book is the Polish name of the river that runs through northeastern Poland and northwestern Belarus (Belarusian: *Chornaya Hancha*).
92. Italian: and all of them.

and timely substance do the words of the bard gain, which a person was not able to truly feel the spirit of before:

> Lithuania, my country, thou art like health;
> how much thou shouldst be prized only he can learn
> who has lost thee. Today thy beauty in all its splendour
> I see and describe, for I yearn for thee.

> Holy Virgin, who protectest bright Częstochowa
> and shinest above the Ostra Gate in Wilno! [...]
> so by miracle thou wilt return us to the bosom of our country.
> Meanwhile bear my grief-stricken soul
> to those wooded hills, to those green meadows ...[93]

I also get a collection of poems by Kazimierz Wierzyński, whose brother Hieronim (editor of *Wieczór Warszawski*) died here a year ago. How wealthy I am.

I ask Gabriel what exactly is the matter with me, to which he replies:
"You went through typhus."
And so it was! Is it possible that it ran such a mild course, after all I "walked through" the heaviest period, and after lying down my temperature did not exceed 38.5 degrees. Gabriel reminds me that I was vaccinated against typhus twice, in 1942 and 1943, and there are mild cases of typhus known to medicine. I was one of these lucky ones. I am so happy to have gone through this disease and to be immunized from lice once and for all. I notify my brother and Mary that I made it through typhus.

The anthology made such a deep impression on me that I ask my brother to buy a copy and give it to Mary on the feast day of Anthony of Padua, a memorable day for us. Certain poems by Wierzyński so masterfully reflect the state of my soul, full of longing, anxiety, hesitation, and desire, that I

93. From *Pan Tadeusz* by Adam Mickiewicz, translation by George Rapall Noyes (1917).

specify the titles of the poems that she should read—she'll know the rest. I believe that my release is imminent, and while writing to Mary I even make detailed plans for where I will go to recuperate after I am let out.

But how many times has this illusion of release appeared before me? Will I live to see the moment when I can, with deep gratitude, kiss your hand, Mary? This is no pathos or platitude to say today, after five quarters staying in Majdanek: Mary, with your visits in April and May of last year, you gave me the incentive and strength to survive behind the wires—even if you had gone silent after that. Let these words committed to this diary, which is after all just a long letter to you, record my feelings of thanks and debt!

Olszański comes to our hospital barracks to the doctor for some head-ache powder. I call him over to my bed and ask him why he hasn't visited me. He replies that he is extremely busy. I know all too well after half a year's work in the office that there can't be too much to do, since there's no movement in the camp. Krupski still hasn't bought my dried fruit.

The Air Raid of the Camp

On May 11, around 11:00 p.m., we get another air-raid alarm. We don't make much of it. The planes fly low, there's a flash, a second, then a third, it becomes as bright as day. Suddenly there's one explosion, another, the crash of broken windows, the medicine cabinet fastened to the wall falls to the floor, the bombs are falling one after the other, all of them nearby, there is no defense, dozens of bombs drop, new waves of planes are flying over and keep pounding the area. It lasts maybe thirty or forty minutes. I lie in bed since there's nowhere to shelter anyway. I rack my brain for why the Bolsheviks would bomb the camp since they must know very well that so many Russians are kept here. Finally it quiets down. The last whir of a plane engine fades away.

The next day we find out that the Bolsheviks dropped eighty-three bombs onto the camp in the shape of a horseshoe on about five of the residential fields. Bombs fell on the camp command barracks (empty offices at night), on the transformer, on the SS detention center (the bunker), in the vegetable gardens, and on the crematorium. Two SS men were killed. Not one bomb fell in the center of the camp, where the barracks for prisoners are located. So their aim was very accurate, with an excellent understanding of the camp's layout. On Field 1, where we are now located, an entire handbarrow of shrapnel was collected. In Lublin, the bombs hit two houses that were occupied solely by Germans; supposedly several dozen people were killed. The bombing raid stirred up great excitement and joy in the camp.

My stay in the hospital is the most pleasant period of my time in Majdanek, my temperature holds steady at a shade below 37 degrees, I sleep long and devour books. Gabriel gives me shots to strengthen me and is painstaking in his care. For several days, Engineer Merta is lying next to me and goes on for hours about conditions in Soviet Russia.

Pietroniec brings the news that a court-martial against SS men has taken place. They shot some staff sergeant, and Laurich, the arrogant demigod from the *Politische Abteilung,* was sentenced to ten years in prison; another got three years. Now I understand that when Hessel met with Laurich behind closed doors, he was preparing some defense documents for him against the charges. They found him guilty of theft and embezzlement. The scoundrels are finishing each other off.

Zelent comes in sick, he has a fever, it's either the flu or pneumonia, he already had typhus a year ago.

In the afternoon, Pietroniec rushes in, terrified—there's been a huge bust. Rode and his friend from the SS canteen picked up thirteen secret messages from the cashier in the brewery, where they had gone with a new SS man who looked innocent on the surface. After returning to Majdanek, he searched them and took away the messages. He did it before arriving back at the canteen, however, so that the rest of their friends didn't know about the bust. Both of them were placed between the wires and the SS man took two other Poles from the canteen who weren't aware of the development, and went again with them to the brewery, probably so that they would pick up the next batch of messages. Who were the messages meant for? Both of us get goose bumps, because none of us has a "clean" conscience. I haven't used the "brewery" route, but my backup mailbox is W. Szyszko on Kapucyńska Street, and in case he was not contacted, he took the letters to the cashier in the brewery. So a message for me could also be there.

After 9:00 p.m. they bring Rode to us in the hospital, he is supposed to spend the night here, but he is not allowed to talk to us. Gabriel, who spends the night here, is responsible for it. After the lights go out, Rode goes to Zelent and shares the details. He can't answer the questions that are nagging us the most. He doesn't know who the messages were intended for, since he hid them in his pocket and he couldn't look at them on the way. So the terrible uncertainty continues. The contents of the messages could have been varied. It's not such a big problem if they were purely personal in nature, but if they were organizational or related to trade, for example the confirmation of receipt of jewelry or money—then it's worse. The messages are sitting in the *Politische Abteilung* and even the regular translator, Albrecht, didn't get them for translation. The matter is shrouded in great mystery. Noak can't penetrate any further. The cashier split from the brewery at the behest of the organization; officially he left on vacation. I experience a moment of great depression, since I've been expecting messages to arrive for some time, so it's likely that there was some message for me.

Mußfeld, the executioner, visits our camp. He asks each person what he is suffering from, when Gabriel explains that I went through typhus he says:
"Don't let him get up too early, he needs to regain his strength."
The next day, Hessel comes over and asks when I will be getting up. Why does he care about me leaving the hospital quickly? After all, there is no mountain of work.

Zelent and I talk for hours about the future political system in Poland. He has a radical streak, but he speaks very persuasively. I'm especially convinced by his projects for education reform. Although I support a nationalist course, I have to admit to myself that Stach could be entrusted with the highest positions in government, since he combines the virtues of idealism, exceptional intelligence, and a crystal-clear, and simultaneously strong, character.

Papst is lying there in agony. It takes him nearly twenty-four hours to die. At 4:00 a.m. he stops wheezing. Only now does everyone start to take an interest in him. Hessel comes and orders him washed, shaved, and placed on a bed with sheets; he orders flowers from the gardens to decorate the bed. Kostial comes to make sure that the body is neatly arranged. The *Lagerarzt* comes and checks Gabriel's notes about the course of the disease and the treatment given. He instructs Gabriel to add much more detail and rephrase the description of certain medical procedures. He announces that Camp Commandant Liebehenschel will come soon to see the corpse. Gabriel is seething under his breath:
"What hypocrisy, suddenly they've taken an interest in him. If they'd provided him with a liter of milk and a few eggs every day starting two weeks ago, he would be alive. Now they'll start writing down fairy tales about treatment that wasn't carried out."

In the afternoon, Dr. Hett returns the description of the care that Papst received and says that the *Lagerarzt* is not happy with Gabriel's account. He says that the account of what measures were taken to keep him alive have to be expanded upon, since it is to be expected that due to Papst's high rank in the SS and SA, the leadership will be interested in his fate. This is the true face of the Germans—the main thing is to keep up appearances on paper; later, they'll demand that these fictitious inventions be recognized by everyone as credible and authentic evidence and documents. The orderlies find a photograph of a woman and several letters written from Kraków in Papst's wallet. It's probably the picture and correspondence from that Polish aristocrat whom he had a romance with, because of which—according to Papst's revelations—he was locked in the camp.

Hessel comes again to ask me brusquely when I'm coming back. Gabriel replies for me, saying that I have to stay for another week. During the week Hessel comes several more times and asks when I'll be discharged—and Mußfeld tells me and others again while he's visiting that we shouldn't leave the hospital too soon. What a maggot that Hessel is. I feel OK, it's just that my legs are very weak, they feel like cotton and bend under my weight.

I get sad news from home. Ninka informs me that my cousin, Stefan, who sent me the anti-typhus shots, has died. He was the head of a ward at St. Lazarus Hospital, he had an abscess in his lung and despite the best medical care, he died. God truly works in mysterious ways. We both got sick at practically the same time. I had to pull a wagon and carry beds with a fever of 40 degrees, while he had the best professors, the most expensive pharmaceuticals, medicines, equipment, and nurses at his disposal. Despite this, his judgment came and God didn't call me to him!

On the name day of my dearly departed mother, Julia, May 22, I leave the hospital. As I depart I hand Dr. Gabriel the most valuable thing that I own, as a thank-you for his care: the *Antologia*, to raise his own spirits and for the patients who are able to take this tome into their hands, comprehend it, and draw strength from it.

Convalescence

I enter the office before the evening roll call and report to Hessel. I ask where I should stand for the assembly, at the office or by my barracks, which houses all of the office staff who are just detailed to the office. He replies that I am to stand by my barracks and that I won't be "detailed" during the roll call. I still sleep in the hospital, and the next day Pietroniec takes my blankets for disinfection. Hessel declares to me that I won't be working in the office and that I'll be doing various jobs on the field. Two isolation wards are to be created for typhus and tuberculosis patients in the hospital barracks. In Block 3, Mankiewicz and I are supposed to disassemble the partitions and move them to the hospital barracks. Various parts of these walls weigh fifty or sixty kilograms and are very unwieldy to carry, since they are very wide and long flat pieces. My legs are buckling underneath me, I feel an enormous weakening of my heart after carrying in a piece like this; Gabriel gives me drops to support my heart.

Hessel is hanging around the square all day and yelling that we're working too slowly. He's seconded by *Lagerkapo* Pohlmann, who is also haranguing me. Unfortunately, I am now under his command. I reply that he himself was sick with typhus in February after all and then, when he didn't believe that I was sick and claimed that my eyes were glistening from atropine, I was admitted to the hospital with typhus. Pohlmann tells me that I am insolent. Olszański doesn't notice me. For three days I heave walls around; we're supposed to do the work with four people, the other two are Germans with *Fluchtpunkte*. They do nothing and sit in the barracks. I tell them that each of us should carry our part. They say that they'll set up the walls and we Poles should do the moving. When I refuse to agree to this, the German, Bubi Ilke, threatens that he'll slap me. Who will I go complain to? To Hessel or to Pohlmann, who they are on a first-name basis with and drink with every day?

Jewish women are expected at the camp. Beds have to be set up in two barracks on Field 1, and again our foursome has to carry them. The

Germans force us to do the heavy lifting once more, and they assemble the beds.

I'm ravenously hungry. Packages from my brother aren't arriving because the post office still isn't accepting any for Majdanek. And after typhus you have a wolf's appetite. My friends with relatives in Lublin get packages through the RGO—or their families are more creative in their shipping methods. Almost everyone has something to eat while I am stuck with camp food. Rutabaga doesn't give you much strength. I see them frying potatoes every day for supper, they get them from the mounds in the gardens, they're delivered by the office messenger, Miron Klisz. I go to Olszański and ask him if I can get potatoes from them, since Miron can bring an unlimited amount and since the RGO started sending us Poles packages every week with a loaf of bread and a quarter-kilo of bacon with a few onions, I'd gladly hand it over to season the potatoes. Olszański replies with the expression of a bank president:

"My dear, you know that I never dealt with the kitchen—talk to Panasiewicz about it."

Of course I didn't talk to him, and I considered our relationship to have been sufficiently clarified. I've lost my utility to him, so he set me aside just like Hessel did. I speak about this new life experience—another letdown—to Pietroniec. He invites me over for supper. The next day around 2:00 p.m. he brings me an excellent soup from the SS kitchen.

Something happened to Andrzej Stanisławski. He was removed from the position of messenger for the *Schutzhaftlagerführer* and assigned to penal work with the bunker builders, which are led by Fritsche. Only Kostial and Hessel know the reasons, and Andrzej doesn't want to reveal them; he makes allusions to having been falsely accused of something in relation to the affair with Laurich in the *Politische Abteilung*, who was sentenced to a decade in prison. The bunker builders construct concrete shelters for the SS men. Fritsche drives them hard during the work and beats them mercilessly.

A siren starts blaring at 8:00 a.m. Someone ran away, all of the work squads return to the field. It turns out that our former messenger in the office, Gaweł, the son of a civil servant in the National Development Bank in Warsaw, ran off.[1] After all the transports left he was assigned to the SS kitchen. That work squad, consisting of several prisoners, is "*kommandiert*,"[2] so they leave for work before the roll call in the morning. They're escorted by one "*Post*."[3] Gaweł had a military cap prepared in the kitchen, a canvas cover used by soldiers as a rain cloak, and a belt. He walked around in boots and greenish pants. The striped uniforms had since been eliminated, and they gave out civilian clothes again. Only the four of us *Fluchtpunkte* stayed in stripes. When the prisoners entered the kitchen in the morning—before dawn—and the guards waited in front of the barracks, he threw on the canvas cloak, grabbed the cap and belt, and left through the back door. It was still dark so the *Postenkette* wasn't yet active. He had just a few hundred steps to the road, and someone was likely waiting for him there. The search doesn't yield any results, of course. Two hours later, the *Kommando* leave for work again. We're all happy about this elegant and stylish method of escape.

I meet with Pietroniec, and he swears at me for not coming over to his place for supper. But I wasn't invited, I tell him. This drives him mad. He says that it was always understood. This gives a good description of his teddy-bear kindness. Irritated, he declares with a furious face that once and for all I have to come to him for dinner and supper until I start getting packages. He takes care of me like a woman does a lover. I'm outright embarrassed by his thoughtfulness.

After preparing the barracks for the Jewish women, a barbed-wire fence needs to be installed around it, which we have to dismantle first from around Block 12, the current office. Mankiewicz, Zalewski, and I tear off the barbed wire and dig out the posts, and each of us carries one; the beams are over three meters long and as thick as a telegraph pole. Being disabled, Zalewski can't carry the posts. Hessel tells us that the fence has to be ready in two days. It's a job for twenty workers over the course of

1. Czesław Gaweł escaped from the camp on July 12, 1944.
2. Here, sent outside of the camp.
3. Guard post.

three or four days. I don't worry about Hessel's orders, that idiot has no clue what one person is capable of in a day.

We've barely moved a few posts when the *Lagerkapo* calls us and tells us to stop our work and carry sacks from Block 2, where *Revierkapo* Benden lives. Hundred-kilo sacks with kasha and peas are sitting there. Apparently these are RGO gifts for the sick that were "saved" by Benden. We have to carry these sacks to Block 5. We grab handbarrows and carry them with Mankiewicz. I have absolutely no strength in my arms and knees. Every ten steps we stop and put the barrow on the ground, looking around to see whether Hessel or Pohlmann is nearing. Such a light case of typhus, but it burned me out so much. Thank God that no post-typhus complications have cropped up—the most common being reduced hearing, which fades after several months, and mental dullness. Of course a crazy person always says that they are sane, but since Hessel calls me the same thing now as he did before the typhus, "*Kretiner*,"[4] I rest assured that no unsettling changes have taken place in my mental faculties.

Benden allows me to take kasha *à discretion*[5] from the sacks set up in his room if I need any. I take some to Pietroniec as my contribution in kind to our shared kitchen and I'm proud to be able to introduce some variety into the menu. Rudek brings lettuce, radishes, and strawberries from the *Gärtnerei*. I rinse the lettuce, he boils vinegar with sugar, fries some pork rinds, and uses a large bowl to pour the vinegar over the heaping lettuce leaves. I eat myself full of just lettuce—what a delicacy these fresh vegetables are.

A surprise awaits us after the roll call. Hessel orders all of us to grab some tools and he hurries us to work, some of us to put up the fence around the barracks for Jewish women, others to dig up the cultivable land. Hessel is supervising by the fence and Pohlmann is at the digging site with about 140 people. He's such a mental primitive that he can't give the instruction for prisoners to form up in groups of five and dig up a long strip of the

---

4. Literally, "Cretan"; here, likely "cretin."
5. French: at your own discretion.

field. He beats prisoners with a rake handle, unable to verbalize what he means. I also get several whacks. The work lasts until dusk.

The next day they bring over ten Soviet invalids without legs, walking on stilts or self-made wooden legs. They are put under my supervision and ordered to pull weeds from the limestone rubble spread across the area between the barbed wires. They even have to crawl, since one can't weed while sitting down. I separated the Bolsheviks into groups and went back to my work loading beds from the barracks onto military trucks.

Mankiewicz and I act as the "yard service," as it's called in factories, in other words as caretakers, porters, handymen, gardeners, etc. We keep being torn away from one job and sent to another. Every day I have to carry away empty coffee buckets from the barracks, each weighing up to thirty-five kilograms, and line them up by the gate where they are taken to Field 2. Pohlmann doesn't allow me to move them on the small, two-wheeled cart, I have to carry them. It's terribly exhausting for my heart. The good-hearted Gabriel saves me with the drops. Kostial—who calls me by my last name—doesn't return my bow of course, but during the daily work he politely chats with me, smiling at Mankiewicz and me. Hessel, on the other hand, bellows from the window of his room every few days:

"Natürlich der K. geht ganz pomalu."[6]

Today, Kostial orders me to fill in the potholes that have cropped up throughout the barbed-wire area after the downpours as the ground settled. Hessel is standing by his window twenty paces away and hears this instruction. It's a custom in the camp that such an order from your boss isn't just a guideline, but rather something for which you should drop everything and immediately get started on. So I take the invalids from weeding and have them fill in holes up to fifty centimeters deep with rocks on the other end of the field, behind the kitchen.

Today is my birthday, June 8, I'm fifty years old, my brother forgot about it. I'm celebrating my second birthday in the camp. Today I'm also marking the twenty-fifth anniversary of obtaining my doctorate. Back then I was the

6. "Naturally, K. is walking very slowly."

recruiting officer in the Fourth Rifle Division under General Żeligowski, which was marching from Odessa through Bessarabia to Poland, and at the same time I was a liaison officer to the Fourth Romanian Corps in Bukovina. My headquarters was in Czerniowce (Chernivtsi). That's where I passed my final *rigorosum*.[7] Several days later, Żeligowski entered Czerniowce with his division. I invited him and his staff to my promotion ceremony. I gave my oath in Latin on the old Austrian baton with the two-headed eagle wrapped in the Romanian *tricolore*. Present were General Żeligowski, General Albinowski, Lieutenant Colonel Małachowski, Lieutenant Colonel Bobicki, Major Thommée, First Lieutenant Jan Kowalewski, Stanisław Strzetelski from the Ministry of Foreign Affairs, the commander of the Fourth Romanian Corps, General Costea, the commander of the Eighth Romanian Division General Zadik . . . Today, Żeligowski is a member of the National Council in London; Małachowski and Thommée, the defender of Modlin, are in German captivity; Bobicki was shot by the Gestapo in his Warsaw apartment; and Kowalewski, the head of OZON,[8] is abroad somewhere. Strzetelski, the editor of *ABC* and *Wieczór Warszawski*, edits some publication in America, Albinowski's son is trying to use his contacts to secure my release, and I am walking around in camp stripes today with *Fluchtpunkte* . . .

Pohlmann is standing at the gate and calls me over. He asks me why I stopped the invalids from pulling weeds. I say that Kostial told me to. In reply I get two tremendous whacks to the face. Pohlmann lurches forward and squeezes his groin. I see Hessel standing in the window watching. I repeat that Kostial ordered me to send my people to a different job. Hessel is silent. Pohlmann silences me again, grabs his groin, and says:

"You got that because you talk back." He straightens up and strikes me two more times, saying:

"And that's for the pain in my hernia that I feel every time I hit you."

The maggot Hessel knows that Pohlmann is wrong, and that I was speaking the truth, and the sadist just watches as this green bandit pimp

7. Latin: oral doctoral examination.
8. The informal term for the *Obóz Zjednoczenia Narodowego* (Camp of National Unity), a political organization of the interwar *Sanacja* movement in Poland.

beats me. I go to Hessel in the afternoon and ask him how I should have carried out Kostial's order, since Pohlmann is going after me for it. He gives a weasel-like reply, as if he didn't see what Kostial had instructed me to do. Just you wait, you bandit, it'll be your turn soon!

They order Mankiewicz and I to clean up the barracks. I scrub the floor in Block 17. It's the barracks where the *Aufnahme* were filled out after our arrival on March 26, 1943. Our old stomping ground; I try to find the place where we stood together with Rector Drewnowski and Professor Michałowicz. But the barracks has been "refurnished" and the beds are set up differently.

After a lengthy absence, Corporal Müller reappears on the field. He was arrested at the end of April because he shot a Pole that he found at the home of a Polish female acquaintance he was courting. Müller was sentenced to six weeks' arrest which he spent in the bunker, where he also sat out the bombing. It's probably a sufficient punishment for shooting "*eines Polacken*"[9] who dared to visit a Polish woman.

A new sensation. Three prisoners from the auto shops escaped.[10] They got a hold of SS uniforms, got into a passenger car, and left through the *Gärtnerei*, via a rarely used gate where there is naturally still a guard post. The guards saluted and approached the car as if they wanted to give a report, but its occupants just waved patronizingly, making it known that they would come right back this way. Of course, they didn't actually come back, and the car vanished.

I write to my brother to send his messages in the food package, hidden in cellophane at the bottom, where he arranges roasted meat covered in butter so it won't spoil. Having seen the method of package inspection over recent months, I have become convinced that this method of sending messages is safer than others. The civilian workers don't come onto

9. A Pole.
10. The escape took place on May 15, 1944.

the fields any longer. The brewery fell through. The RGO doesn't bring in soups anymore. Admittedly, there is a new route, namely a spot in the gardens where we place letters in a sewer ditch and people from the organization pick them up at night, and when the *Postenkette* is off duty, incoming letters are left for us there. I get a letter from my brother that Szyszko came to Warsaw for several months and he told him about the bust with the messages. So apparently Szyszko was mixed up in it then. The investigation has gone silent. The cashier returned from his vacation, he paid off the Gestapo, and they buried the matter. Supposedly a review of the messages didn't turn up any compromising information and Commandant Liebehenschel ended it, declining to make a mess of it with Oranienburg.

A transport of two hundred Jewish women from Bliżyn arrives. Praise God! Hessel's attention is focused on Block 1 where they are housed. He makes the prettiest one the block overseer and at the same time his mistress. He sits there for hours at a time—but always with an eye out the window onto the gate, ready to slip out the moment Kostial approaches. All of the kapos make trips to the women at night. It doesn't matter that the barracks is surrounded by barbed wire and the gate is padlocked, because the key is with . . . Hessel.

Every day we all work after the roll call until twilight, Hessel keeps thinking up some new beautification for the camp, which, one way or another, we'll have to abandon in the face of the advancing Russians: the sodding of the sewage ditches, the cleaning of sedimentation tanks in the unoccupied barracks, the movement of the fence around the women's barracks a few meters toward the roll call field. We've finally started cooking our own food on Field 1. However, we are divided into four groups and every fourth day we have to go peel potatoes for two hours after the evening roll call. The work is quite laborious since the potatoes are heavily rotted by this time.

The women stand behind the barbed wire during roll call, while we are on the other side. The German green bandits are up to unbelievable things during the assembly: they throw the Jewish women sweets through the wires as well as packages of food. There is one Viennese *"Pülcher,"*[11] Peer, who, while standing on the right side, pulls out his genitals and flashes the women.

The office stops being exempted from the roll call. Olszański stands next to me sometimes, remains silent, and looks into the sky. He doesn't see me, though there was no conflict between us. But today I am *non valeur*,[12] and he's not such a hypocrite that after the help I gave him over the course of half a year, that he would want to engage in even a casual conversation with me. I stopped speaking to him first, since several times when I asked him what was new, he replied:

"Nothing important, nothing worth mentioning," or in reply to specific questions he would say: "My dear, do you think I'm interested in such details?"

In our Block 13, where everyone besides the kapos and the office staff lives, bacchanals take place among the Germans every night. Leading the way are: Lipiński, Kursch, Ihle, Peer, Gabriel (a different one, called *"Poczekaj,"*[13]—including prison time, he has been locked up for eighteen years), and Bubi Ilke. They pull out a guitar and accordion and they sing and scream until midnight each day, while the wake-up call is at 4:30 a.m. They are of course on friendly terms with Pohlmann, Hessel, and other kapos from Block 12. We Poles don't get to complain about being deprived of sleep. And the Krauts sleep during the day afterward with lookouts spread around.

Schommer has a falling out with Hessel who kicks him out of the kapos' sleeping quarters and into our barracks. There he falls into the clutches of Lipiński, who is the block overseer. He harbors a grudge against Schommer for the wintertime boasting that he flattened him while wrestling. In the presence of *Feldführer* Groffmann, I hear Schommer accuse Hessel of shady business smuggling jewelry out of the camp. Hessel is terrified by this and convinces the field commandant to order Schommer to tell *Schutzhaftlagerführer* Kostial what he wants. They happen to find a secret

11. Scoundrel.
12. French: here, unneeded, superfluous.
13. Polish: "Wait for it."

message from Schommer to someone in Lublin in which he asks them to send him food. Hessel makes a big deal out of this and suggests giving Schommer a *Fluchtpunkt*. He doesn't want to sew one on and demands to speak to Commandant Liebehenschel. He warns that if he isn't let out of the field (he got the *Fluchtpunkt* to prevent him from leaving) he'll crawl through the wires to get to the commandant.

There is a terrible downpour. Hessel puts on an oilcloth cloak and rubber boots and goes out onto the roll call square. He calls me and Mankiewicz; he tells him to fix the barbed wire on the fence and me to shovel mud from the square and throw it on top of the antiaircraft shelter which is being built. Once the rain becomes unbearable, he goes into the closest barracks and stands by an open window to supervise my idiotic work. He can't even see Mankiewicz from his observation post. It's cold, the wind is biting, I am soaked to the bone, this work doesn't make any sense at all. After three hours, once the rain has stopped and the sun starts to peek through the clouds, he orders Mankiewicz and I to stop working and go to the shed. We are supposed to chop wood to make stakes for a short fence around a patch of ground. What wickedness!

  The moment the rain stops he sends me to a job under a roof. I stop to see Pietroniec on the way, who gives me a shirt, long johns, and a sweater. I have to put my wet stripes on top of this since I can't walk around without my uniform and *Fluchtpunkte*. At night I feel a sharp pain in my kidneys, the next day the entire area around them hurts terribly, I can't bend down. What did I ever do wrong to that guy? Not to brag, but he always had the files in excellent order, I never made any mistakes that made him look bad to his superiors, transports of people numbering in the thousands, tables drawn up as needed, there were no mistakes in the letters—and now, when his helper is redundant, he humiliates and persecutes him.

We have another escape. At the evening roll call, eleven people are missing, they worked in the *Gärtnerei*.[14] The entire area is searched, among those who disappeared was the Jew, Henio Silberspitz. I find out that they

---

14. On March 28, 1944, nine prisoners escaped through the sewers.

crawled into the sewer pipe and came out beyond the *Postenkette*, obviously someone was already waiting for them.

The Germans that engaged in unruly behavior are assigned penal labor on Sunday afternoon. They have to dismantle the villa in the gardens that was being used as a bunker and was hit during the air raid.

They introduce strict inspections at the gate in order to make the bringing of vodka onto the field more difficult. But the Germans find a way around this. Next to us is the *Zwischenfeld* with the laundry, between Fields 1 and 2. There is no gate or *Blockführer* there. So that's where they take the vodka, pour it into aluminum flasks, and throw the flasks across the wires to Ihle, who transfers the vodka again and throws back the flasks. The flasks travel back and forth like this a dozen times a day. The conflict with Schommer heats up—by the way, he's a creep.

While he's drunk, Kapo Peer provokes the Poles in the barracks by insulting us. Unfortunately, I wasn't there when it happened. A short, stocky Pole, a mechanic from the auto shops, jumped up to Peer and knocked him down with a few punches, to the point Peer was begging and pleading for mercy. No one who was watching intervened; even the kapos were afraid to come help since they sensed that a brawl could start. From that time on, the Germans are more careful with their words.

Judgment Day

I had another confrontation with Pohlmann. He hit me in the face and aimed at my head with a spade.

I visit Zelent in the evenings, he's still in bed—Gabriel is waiting for the exudate in his lungs to resorb. I advise Stach to not leave the hospital early since Hessel and Pohlmann are pulverizing our spirits. Andrzej Stanisławski has thinned out terribly. Fritsche is driving them mercilessly. I hear that Hessel is scheming some intrigue against Fritsche, generating reports or information from other SS men. They send Fritsche to Schommer's room that he cobbled together in the washroom barracks. He confiscates all of the ample clothing and underwear that he has collected for himself...

One of the larger drinking binges takes place in our barracks again. Singing and then more partying. The bandits borrow assault helmets from the kapos in the *Luftschutz*[15] (OPL) and have fun by smashing empty bottles against them. Half asleep, I hear Schommer singing a lengthier song—they invited him specially to this party—and I'm still awake enough to appreciate the musicality and authenticity with which he sings this sentimental tune. Tired from this constant sleep deprivation, I drift off.

In the morning I hear in the washroom that Schommer hung himself on the gate leading to the hospital. I step out and Schommer is hanging on a belt, but the back of his skull is smashed in. The fiction is clear. An investigation begins, but no one knows anything—and whoever does is afraid to say anything. It looks like the affair won't have any epilogue. A day goes by without incident. The next day, the *Feldführer* takes all three prisoners who had guard duty that night to be interrogated to determine when the murder took place. The Viennese Czech Sedláček, a tailor—and communist, who along with the Czech Pejsar, keeps close contact with

---

15. Antiaircraft defense.

the Poles and keeps his distance from the German kapos—steps forward and tells us the whole story.

It turns out that the previous day a secret crime-scene investigation took place in our barracks, which led to the discovery of bloodstains and spots on the beds and the entryway spattered with blood, as well as the lost watch crystal and its gold rim. The watch wasn't found with the corpse. Schommer was killed with a blow to the head and his body was dragged out of the barracks. Lipiński and Bubi are the perpetrators and they hung the corpse by the belt.

Both are arrested, as well as Kursch, whom they suspect of having hidden cash. They put all of them in handcuffs between the wires, but about one hundred meters apart from one another so they can't communicate. During the day, rumors circulate that Pohlmann took part in the drinking, not to mention the murder and robbery of Schommer. Pohlmann isn't interested in my work anymore; he's busy with his bunny rabbits all day. Ah, if only this villain could find himself between the wires as well. In the afternoon, Pietroniec rushes over to me and happily reports:

"Jerzy, do you know, Pohlmann is already standing between the wires."

I go right away to feast my eyes on the sight. Hessel walks up to the wires and even though it's forbidden, he talks with Pohlmann for half an hour. It's obvious that he's giving him tips for how to get out of it, or he's pleading with him not to finger him as the moral perpetrator of the murder. It's unquestionable to me that Hessel is behind the scenes of everything, but he has been so meticulous in his performance that he can plausibly deny anything.

In the evening after the roll call, the *Feldführer* calls me over and orders me to prepare nails and short boards. Around 9:00 p.m., he leads each of these bandits into small rooms in the former hospital barracks—each into a separate barracks—and they lay down on prepared mattresses with their handcuffs on. I nail the doors and windows shut with boards and scrap wood. It's symbolically significant, it doesn't so much prevent escape as much as it makes communication between other possible accomplices and the arrested more difficult. What satisfaction it was when Pohlmann saw me and lowered his head and looked at the floor. They stand between the wires for several days and are taken for interrogation in the daytime. Finally a prison van arrives and takes them to the Castle. There's a lot of

wisdom to the Chinese proverb that you should sit and wait at the door-
step of your enemy until they carry him out in a coffin! Over the course
of six weeks, the long arm of justice touched three Germans who insulted
me: Pohlmann, Schommer, and Bubi Ilke; they kept Kursch in handcuffs
for a few more days—but they're letting him out.

A transport of several hundred Jews from Budzyń arrives. Hessel makes a
speech to them with instructions on the lifestyle here, and he ends with
the saying: "Anyway, you'll all go to the gas," and he laughs sneeringly,
showing his twenty-four teeth. *Lasciate ogni speranza, voi ch'entrate.*[16]

Polish organizations are taking care of us Poles: on Tuesdays and Fridays
the RGO gives us bags, each containing one loaf of white bread, a quarter-
kilo of bacon, several onions, ten cigarettes, and two hundred grams of
sugar. Once a week, the PCK hands out one loaf of black bread, an onion,
a little sugar, and 150 grams of bacon. Packages have started arriving regularly. So we have first-rate provisioning. All we take from the cauldrons
is black coffee and potatoes, which we fry for ourselves. We don't touch
the beet marmalade, horsemeat sausage, or rutabaga soup. The *Herrenvolk*
wolf down our portions of sausage.

The *Wehrmacht* has taken over Field 5. They haul in peasants from around
Chełm, transports of several hundred people arrive every day. They are
supposed to build field fortifications around Lublin. They are driven to
work by truck at 7:00 a.m., they come back at 5:00 p.m., they get excellent
military food, they even get an allocation of vodka. They receive health
care from Dr. Maria from Lublin and Miss Ewa, who come every day to
make sure the blankets are deloused and to provide medical care. The
peasants aren't considered prisoners of the concentration camp.

At the same time, the women from the organization keep contact with
our camp. The meeting point is in the washroom barracks where the blan-

16. Italian: "Abandon all hope, ye who enter here." Words inscribed above the entrance gate
to hell in Dante Alighieri's *Divine Comedy*.

kets are gassed. Kapo Benden leads Zelent out of the hospital under the pretext of taking a sick person to wash in order to meet the women. They deliver letters and take new ones. The word spreads that Ms. Maria was arrested; indeed, she doesn't show up for several days, and once again there are concerns about whether messages from us were discovered on her person. After some time she reappears—it turns out she left on purpose since she was forewarned of the possibility that she would get arrested.

Noak says that after Thumann's departure, the SS men in the *Politische Abteilung* are talking about how nearly every prisoner-release application sent in by the Gestapo was formally rejected by Thumann, which included his annotation "his behavior is unsatisfactory, the stay in the camp has not yet favorably influenced his worldview." Panasiewicz is one of these victims: the Post Office Management in Warsaw had managed to secure his release, and a full year ago they showed his wife the Gestapo notice that the application for his release had been sent to Majdanek.

I keep having dinners and suppers with Pietroniec, he brings: strawberries, cherries, kohlrabi, and cauliflower. He is overjoyed, since he received confirmation that money which one of his friends asked him to hand over to the organization made it to the woman it was intended for. His friend pestered him for two months about where the money had ended up and Pietroniec had been cast under the unfortunate cloud of suspicion. After a pause, he adds:

"You know, Olszański sent it, but he asked me specifically to make sure that you didn't find out about it."

I reply: "That's fine," and I explain where the money came from and the conversation that I had had with Olszański about it.

Hessel takes advantage of the fact that Jewish craftsmen are in the camp and he orders shoes, a full set of clothes, and a cloak to be made for him. Out of three old pairs of shoes, they make one new pair and out of a gabardine cloak they make breeches. He's so impatient that he orders the Jews to work all night so that everything is ready in the morning, within twenty-four hours. Of course he pays the Jews nothing for the work, and he doesn't even allow them to make up for lost sleep during the day and sends them to their regular work.

Charlie Popowski becomes the new *Lagerkapo* after Pohlmann, he's also a German with a green triangle. He seems to be an improvement; in any case he's polite to us. They set up several antiaircraft batteries around the camp. They are dug into a plowed field that lays fallow and that's surrounded by a large embankment laid with sod, so that a green ring jumps out at you from a distance. I presume that these positions are visible on every aerial reconnaissance photograph. One of the guns is placed between the *Bauhof* and the *Weisses Haus*, the commandant's home; others are situated in the back of Field 1 toward the *Lagergut*. On the slopes among the green fields you can see yellow strips that grow larger by the day: our peasants are digging positions there "to shorten the front."

We've heard through the grapevine that the Anglo-Saxon Allies have begun an invasion of France, but we don't get any confirmation of these rumors in the incoming newspapers in the nearest days. In the evenings after the bell, when the field falls silent, and especially at night, you can hear artillery fire from the direction of Chełm; the SS men tell us that heavy live-fire exercises are taking place there. It's funny that after five years of the war the Germans would still need to practice, and you don't train fresh recruits in live fire just ten kilometers behind the front.

I've gotten very close to Orpisz, a landowner from the Borderlands, we have mutual friends, he worked in the Copper-Roof Palace[17] while I was with the general staff on Saski Square in Warsaw. He tells me about various improvements that he introduced on his property from orcharding, preserving fruit, making cheese, and so on. All our friends have set themselves up well, only Mankiewicz and I are suffering since we can't leave the field because of our *Fluchtpunkte* and there's only custodial work there. It's

---

17. A Baroque palace adjacent to the Royal Castle in Warsaw.

also irksome that we're the only two who walk around in stripes, so we can be seen from far away and stand out from everyone else.

Hessel brought a Jew into the office who paid him a bribe.

Rumors circulate that an entire sick transport was gassed as soon as they arrived at Auschwitz. A female SS soldier visits the SS men in our camp and denies this information. We find out that Thumann became the *Schutzhaftlagerführer* in Auschwitz and he's showing off his tricks there, while also bringing in the crematorium chief Mußfeld to help.

By all reasonable accounts, our camp should be totally eliminated, but as a result of things left unsaid, I figure out that our camp leaders are holding on tight to their positions. They know that after the Majdanek apparatus is eliminated, around 1,500 SS officers and rank-and-file soldiers will be left without assignments. They'll be sent to reinforce some SS division at the front—and it's dangerous there, since those Muscovites, as opposed to the Soviet *Häftlinge*, shoot back.

Hunting for Home Army Soldiers

In spite of our predictions, a new transport arrives. At the end of June 1944 they bring in several hundred peasants from the regions of Grabowiec, Hrubieszów, and Biłgoraj. The army came to their villages and ordered them to take their horses and cattle to be registered in nearby towns. Their livestock was taken away there and they were put in cattle cars and sent to Majdanek. I find out that the Home Army (AK) has become very active in that area.

The next day, a batch of a few hundred more peasants arrive. Within ten days we have around 1,500 peasants on the field; a few hundred women with children also came. Once again, Blocks 2 and 3 are surrounded with barbed wire for Polish women. Every day the highest rung of the Gestapo, the SD, arrives and carries out a registration of the people in a very innocent manner. Everyone gets to say whatever they want about themselves. Everything is naively documented—the stupid SD believes the people 100 percent. These examinations last for over two weeks.

We discover two boys from the AK. Janek Średnicki and Jędrzejewski, who was shot in the leg, both of them from Warsaw. I suggest to Średnicki that he write a letter to his parents in Warsaw, but that he'd better address it to a third party. He writes to the owner of the "House of Stockings" at 8 Zgoda Street. Pietroniec sends the letter. Średnicki is a medic, he was sent to the AK with twelve thousand zlotys in his suitcase and a large amount of medicines, he was arrested during a manhunt in the forest. Jędrzejewski, the son of a dentist from Warsaw who died in Auschwitz in 1943, is friends with the family of a dental surgeon I know, Dr. Franciszek Stempniewicz, who died in an *Oflag*[18] in 1942. Jędrzejewski got injured, he was laid up with a peasant who was caring for him, a Ukrainian neighbor, who ratted him out. We advise both boys to deny involvement in the AK. Średnicki

18. A German POW camp for officers.

comes back pleased from the interrogation. The Germans treated him with a cigarette, they said that they know the AK is fighting against the communists, so that this way they are cooperating with the Germans, and they are interested in capturing communist partisans. Średnicki decides thus that he had nothing to hide and with a smile he admitted to being in the AK, which is the moment the interrogation ended.

Jędrzejewski goes to be interrogated the next day, and again we warn him—he comes back and says he told them he was proud to be part of the AK, that's what they wrote down. Hessel calls Pietroniec and warns him not to get involved with the new transport too much, since everything is being observed. They call in Średnicki to the office. A messenger says that an SS man came with some kind of package. Pietroniec says to me:

"Look, a package came for him, now they'll open an investigation into how his family found out that he was here, they're not allowed to write letters after all. A nice piece of work—the truthfulness and straightforwardness of these youths."

Minutes turn into hours for both of us. Średnicki comes back beaming with a huge package. His mother brought a package for him all the way from Warsaw just forty-eight hours after he sent the letter, she left it and a letter at the guard post near the main road. The letter was evaluated on the spot and handed over to him, and no one asked how his mother knew his address. His mother writes that his father was very angry at her for giving her son a gold watch to sell to buy things. Surprised, Średnicki tells me:

"But my mother didn't give me any watch."

"Ah," I said (I wanted to say "You moron"), "your mom just wrote an alibi for you."

He understood, lowered his head, and said:

"Too late, I already confessed yesterday."

Kapo Kursch, a German who's decent toward us, a safecracker by trade, comes to Pietroniec, takes him to Block 21, and discreetly points out a "Blue" policeman who is tall with a grizzled beard and long hair combed back, and says:

"That's an SD informant who rats out everyone."

I've observed this policeman myself, he works as a barracks orderly, he pretends to be in terrible despair, sitting for hours with his face buried in his hands. He's from a police station in Grabowiec. Kursch found out about this informant from chats with Hessel. Obviously Hessel has contact with the SD. The information Kursch provides is confirmed when the SD is seen taking this policeman to the Castle several times in their limousine.

A transport is supposed to leave with about a dozen prisoners that got on Hessel's bad side—that's how much influence he has. The ones whose names are read out laugh it off, asserting that it's impossible, this is the group of German kapos who beat up Hessel a year and a half ago. He didn't accept their invitation to a concert on a Sunday afternoon, he ordered the musicians to come to him—and when the kapos refused, it came to blows and Hessel got a beating as a result. He hasn't forgotten it to this day.

The evacuation of the camp has begun, they're taking away hundreds of rudimentary stools—could these be the most valuable items, or are there still six months left to evacuate?

The SD interrogates everyone again, but this time they compare previous testimonies with their other notes, and they fish out ten to fifteen people from each barracks; these people are put between the wires and ordered to take their bundles. These peasants weren't admitted into the camp rolls as *Häftlinge*, so they remained in their clothes, their hair is uncut, and they have all of their things with them. These groups go to the *Politische Abteilung* where they are ordered to strip naked and other men from the SD in the Castle beat them unmercifully and interrogate them again, then take them to the Castle. A new batch leaves every day. My predictions are coming true. They take Jędrzejewski and Średnicki without a follow-up interrogation.

After the evening roll call, they call Kursch, Gröner, Gabriel (the German), Ihle, Peer, and seven other Germans into the office. They are all hell-raisers and drunkards who didn't let us sleep, and unfortunately, a Pole, Kapo Adam Marciniak, goes as well. They handcuff them in pairs, and Gröner, as the fifteenth, doesn't get handcuffs. They tell them that the following day they will be sent on a transport to Mauthausen.[19] Hessel rules the camp! The day before yesterday Kursch was mocking me when I told him that a transport was imminent.

The 1,500 peasants need to be put to work and they can't go outside the wires, so Hessel comes up with the idea to level the roll call square. Since the difference from one side of the square to the other is maybe two meters, there's plenty to carry on the handbarrows. Hessel even mobilizes wagons to carry the dirt.

The women go to work in the gardens. We give all of our RGO and PCK packages to them and the children. The barbed wire around the women's barracks is torn every night, or dug under, and the guard posts in the towers get special orders to shoot at anybody approaching the wires surrounding those barracks. I recall the saying of some German sexologist: "*Sexualnot.*" That drive is stronger, and doesn't even mind rifle fire. The males go in blind to a strange barracks, to unknown women, and randomly pick one in the dark. During the early-morning haze, fifteen to twenty people return to our barracks. Such animalistic rutting is incomprehensible to me; admittedly, it seems like none of my closer friends have been there at night, crawling under the wires. One night "the gang" bribed the *Blockführer* with a certain amount of vodka and they turned the lights on from 11:00 p.m. to 4:00 a.m.—so shooting was not allowed. Apparently the turnout was like at a premiere in Warsaw's Cyrulik cabaret.

Pietroniec tells me in a roundabout way that a trip is being prepared for us. Soon after, he's incensed because something has happened in the gardens. They bring in Orpisz and Wolski and isolate them. They mutter something about an escape attempt. Reportedly, some wagon showed up there with straw, or to get straw, and the two of them tried to hide under it, but the Soviet invalids squealed on them. It was preplanned of course and a woman from the organization was involved in it. Both of them deny it, but it seems to me like they must have greased some palms heavily, since

19. Nineteen prisoners from KL Lublin were registered at Mauthausen on July 7, 1944.

it ends with them getting *Fluchtpunkte* without any beating. This route is now lost to us. Orpisz brings Pietroniec two half-liter bottles of vodka as a gift. One goes under the mattress, the other is opened, we keep it under the bed and the three of us drink from it on Sunday afternoon. Olszański shows up unexpectedly. He sees that there is vodka so he takes a seat. We drink modestly—just one cup each. Pietroniec goes to the kitchen to brew tea, I hide the half-full bottle in the bed since we aren't in the mood to drink with Olszański. After tea we go our separate ways. In the evening during supper, Pietroniec is indignant and tells me that right after we all left, Olszański came back to him and asked for the rest of the bottle of vodka. Rudek says:

"I was surprised that he knew that there was one more bottle of vodka, but I gave it to him since you always have to be on good terms with the office."

I laugh:

"Man, you got duped, Olszański made money off of it, he saw that I hid the half-finished bottle and he came back for it, I pull it out from under the mattress—and you gave him the full bottle!"

"Dammit!" Rudek hisses through his teeth and pounds his fist on the table.

Hessel has a brilliant idea. In order to prevent grass from growing among the rubble between the wires, he orders the rubble moved to have the entire area laid out with roofing paper, which will then be covered with the rubble again. The belt of ground is about two and a half meters wide, and the entire stretch around the field is around eight hundred meters long. So we need two thousand square meters of roofing paper. Since there isn't enough of the old paper, Hessel sends people to the empty Field 3 to tear paper off the roofs there. The thing is that water is pouring into our currently occupied barracks, but the thought doesn't occur to him to plug those holes. What difference does it make if water pours into the bed of a *Häftlinge*? The main thing is to prevent grass from growing between the wires. I tell him that because of the windstorms here, in a matter of a month, a lot of sand will be blown onto the rubble, that the paper will soak up all the moisture, and then vegetation will begin to grow again. After all, water flowing down from the elevated areas of the *Lagergut* constantly fills the field with silt. But Hessel wants to show Kostial that he has his own ideas! The work doesn't cost anything after all.

We have several more air raids with impressive antiaircraft tracer fire at the Soviet planes. Several bombs fall on Lublin, but our camp is untouched. Hessel continues the building of shelters—but not to protect prisoners, just to show Kostial how quickly he can build shelters. Trenches two and a half meters deep and one meter wide are dug in the sand, without any bracing of the walls: half-charred beams from the burned-down kitchen barracks on Field 3 are laid across the top. Hessel checks the endurance of this ceiling by standing on top of it, and if the boards don't bend under his feet, he orders that part covered over with dirt. God forbid that a bomb hits a few hundred meters away, then the sand walls will collapse and bury everyone inside the shelter up over their heads. It's terribly stuffy in there after just fifteen minutes. They are so jammed that one prisoner is smashed against another.

Hessel's next idea: he orders covers made for the entrances to the shelters. They are panels made out of boards that are each two or three meters long. They are so heavy and unwieldy that at least five or six people are needed to move them. The covers prevent air from circulating in the shelters, and if there were to be a panic and crush from all sides, there would be no way to open them. They were cobbled together so quickly (the "*schnell, schnell*" principle) that the nails sticking out from the back aren't bent and some people have already been seriously injured at night when moving the covers, not knowing the nails were there. But it's not about our safety, rather about keeping up appearances—just like the composing of the description of the exceptional medical treatment after the death of SA General Papst.

They make me the commander of a unit of several hundred peasants. One group under the direction of one of the few intelligentsia, the merchant Gorczyński, lays out the roofing paper and then covers it with rubble; another group pulverizes rock into rubble; and a third group brings the rubble to the barbed wire. There aren't many hammers, so they use pickaxes and pieces of iron. This group is led by the blacksmith Jaśkiewicz from Grabowiec, a lesser nobility type, a person who unknowingly gives me strength. I admire his natural, honest sense of humor, which he uses to accept his new life circumstances, and how his jokes hearten his companions in misery, whose faces are resigned. He continues leading them like he did until recently as their technical adviser for the repair of all sorts of agricultural machinery. I see the authority he commands among them. They don't listen to me, but the blacksmith is still their chief.

Hessel sets my daily pensum of work with the sacramental clause that if my group doesn't get it done, I will get my "*Arsch voll.*" I establish these things with Jaśkiewicz in a relaxed way and he uses his persuasions to encourage people to work who have no clue that they are in a concentration camp and what threatens them if they don't carry it out. Another group levels the ground on the hill by the kitchen. Mankiewicz is overseeing the spreading and pressing, while the technical part, i.e., the marking out of levels, is done by Zalewski. The division of work does not stop Hessel from calling me over to Mankiewicz's area and cursing me for the work going too slowly there, or him sending Mankiewicz to my workers and thus causing only mess and confusion.

Lang, the former interpreter and *Lagerkapo*, has fled. He was a kapo in the work group that goes to the electric power plant to unload coal. They only work for eight hours every day, they get a nourishing lunch in the plant, the work isn't much of a strain, and every day after work they get to shower. He probably had clothes prepared in the gatehouse at the plant, or he was wearing them under his stripes. He went into the gatehouse through one entrance and left through the other door and wasn't seen again. The last camp millionaire has departed. Although he boasted about being a legionary officer, apparently his marriage to a German influenced him to the point that he didn't seek the company of Poles; his close friend was Victor, the Soviet agronomist engineer (Hessel's lackey), and he only gambled with Germans.

Shortening the Front

We see columns of peasants' wagons on the main road going from Chełm to Lublin. Sometimes they wait on the road for hours, evidently there is a traffic jam on the way into the city. We learn that these are *Volksdeutsche* running away with all of their belongings, the men are mostly in party uniforms with a swastika on their shoulder, but some of them are barefoot, since that's what they're used to at home. The Ukrainians, who so loyally cooperated with the Germans, are also running away, preferring to continue sharing their fate with the *Herrenvolk*.

You can hear the boom of heavy guns in the daytime now. During the air raids at night, only one or two batteries fire, while two weeks ago maybe fifteen of them were firing, apparently the guns have also been redeployed to "shorten the front."

There is no sign of impending evacuation here in the camp. They aren't taking away the dozens of expensive cauldrons for cooking with a capacity of three hundred liters each. They aren't emptying the warehouses of underwear, clothing, and shoes. They pull me away from my work and instruct me to disassemble all of the beds on Field 3 and prepare them for transport. I have to put together sets of one hundred beds each. It's not such a simple task, since each set must consist of one type of bed, and there are four types in the camp. The only difference is the way in which the sideboards connect to the headboards, namely: with hooks, buttons, knobs, or removable pegs. A hundred beds fit in one railcar; I have a group of two hundred people. The barracks that have been empty since the middle of April are thoroughly infested with fleas. They cluster around your legs by the hundreds and crawl upward. People strip naked since it's easier to wipe the swarms of fleas off your legs which come back after three seconds. Our clothes are lying on the grass in the middle of the square. The field has been surrounded by guard posts just for us, but otherwise we are alone. Only at noon and in the evening does some corporal come, a different one each day, to take us back to Field 1. During the day, a sergeant with gray hair comes over to me and mutters something as he approaches. I stand at attention with my cap in hand and say that I did not understand.

"*Guten Tag—habe ich gesagt.*"[20]

Well, well, we must be in good stead if you are the ones saying "good day" to us first.

I am walking around Field 3 like someone who came back from a trip to his old stomping grounds. Here in Block 5, I spent the first freezing nights on the bare floor, without a blanket; I lived in Block 9 with the overseer Zygmunt, then in 15 with Janusz, then in 12 at the end with the office from which I left with a 40-degree fever, pulling a wagon of tables during the move. The flowers I planted have bloomed, they are thickly overgrown with weeds, and right now I have nothing else to do so I start weeding my flowers. My pansies sown last year are blooming beautifully. Then Mankiewicz comes over with several handbarrows to get flowers, since Hessel ordered flower beds placed along the length of the trench running from Block 1 to Block 11. Help yourself—the Muscovites will enjoy it, he's probably only doing it for them.

Some of the peasants that the SD sifted through that aren't under suspicion were sent to Lublin to the *Arbeitseinsatz* to be shipped to Germany. Among those that left was Jaśkiewicz, the blacksmith full of humor and spirit. After a week, all of them come back to the camp, supposedly there weren't enough railcars available.

The SD continues to extract AK soldiers from our camp. Another young guy was taken—his father is in despair, realizing that he'll never see him again. There's a bell after the lunch break, he's sitting and crying convulsively and not moving. *Lagerkapo* Charlie Popowski lunges at him and beats him over the head with a stick, breaking the skin and covering him in blood, he shoves him toward the work squad that is moving out behind me to Field 3, two people lead the staggering father who is pouring out tears over his son. I sit him with people who are tying bundles of fifty wooden bed slats together with wire and excuse him from work.

20. "I said—good day."

————

We see the gray buses going to the crematorium again. Every day there are eight to ten of them, so around two hundred to two hundred fifty prisoners from the Castle are being shot every day. Those working in the crematorium say that there are young, attractive, elegantly dressed women among them, meaning they were newly arrested, without the telltale signs of lengthy imprisonment.

I finished sorting the beds on Field 3, and they send me to Field 4 with the same order. At the gate to Field 1 they are laying brick on the entry road and the SS men are still calling out, "*Los, los*"; in the washroom they are building a new oven and chimney. At noon and in the evening, when coming back to Field 1, each of my workers has to take a concrete slab for lining the sewer channel under construction there.

Meanwhile, the main road is crammed with refugees—you can see groups of people with bundles on their backs making their way toward Lublin. I can see through the wires on Field 4 that trucks have arrived on Field 3 and are loading the beds. Five stacks are taken, so enough for five railcars. The next day the trucks return with the beds and dump them out. The army requisitioned the railcars that the SS had ordered. It's clear that they probably have more important things to transport than flea-infested wooden beds. On the other hand, I think it would be a good thing if they were able to send away the beds, since evacuated prisoners in one of the camps would have something to sleep on. The fleas are a bit weaker on Field 4, since it was emptied earlier. I wonder what these fleas have been living off of for the last three and a half months, not having had any contact with living beings. The washroom barracks on the field contains a store of pillows taken away from the Jews. They are piled up to a height of two meters, mixed in with empty suitcases, sweaters, and shoes. The roof is full of holes, the pillows are rotting and emitting a terrible stench. They cover an area of about seven hundred square meters, you could probably supply an entire city with those pillows. Rats are nesting there.

The kitchen across the way is being cleaned out by the Soviet invalids. A truck pulls up and about ten well-dressed German women get out, they've brought provisions with them. A moment later several gleaming limousines drive up and Germans get out in brown party uniforms with gold badges, medals, and armbands. They are dressed like for a *Parteitag* in Nuremberg. The German women look at us like Egyptian princesses looking at slaves. They are in high spirits, they are cooking soup for escaping *Volksdeutsche*, which is taken in cauldrons to the road. There's something to be delighted about! After two days the cooking ends, the wave on the road ebbs, apparently the front is so close that no one is left to escape.

A very strict selection of Soviet invalids took place on Field 2. Almost 90 percent were sent to Mauthausen, leaving only those without arms or legs in the camp. The rock quarries in Mauthausen will take care of them.[21]

The beds were taken again and put onto three railcars, and this time they were sent, what a success for the evacuation of the camp! My *Kommandoführer*, some corporal I don't know, graces me with a conversation and says that he is a fellow countryman from Poznań, where he has lived since 1939:

"But '*nieprawdaż*'[22] you understand that I had to become a *Volksdeutsch* and join the SS."

I stay silent and don't reply, but it's looking good if you bastards are starting to explain yourselves.

The evacuation plans are very wide-ranging. Civilian workers come and start dismantling the roofs of several barracks on Field 3. A drop in the bucket; how many trains will you need to take all of the barracks from Majdanek, and aren't there more valuable things to take away?

Hessel is running wild on Field 1. The closer the front moves the more he increases the tempo of the work. He's having a concrete footbridge built by the kitchen. He slapped Zalewski for preparing wooden molds; he wanted to pour the concrete and form it in stages, as technical experience dictates. He hits him in front of Kostial and says:

"I'll show you that it can be done within a day!"

21. In early July, 1,250 Soviet POWs were sent to KL Mauthausen and registered there on July 14, 1944.
22. Polish (broken): "really."

After Hessel leaves, Kostial comes up to Zalewski and pats him on the shoulder, cheering him up saying: *"Gut, gut."*[23] What a mess. The *Schutzhaftlagerführer* comforts one prisoner after being struck by another prisoner, and at the same time he doesn't have the courage to chasten the first one for unfairly beating his fellow prisoner.

Every day before we return to Field 1, Bargielski comes to Field 4 with his disinfection unit which sprays our naked bodies with a Kuprex solution—as well as our clothing, from both the outside and inside—to kill all the fleas.

July 24 is set as the date for the trial in the Castle against Lipiński, Pohlmann, and Bubi—Schommer's murderers.

We see military vehicles on the road, columns of cars, artillery units, spotlights, etc. extending to Lublin—so it's a full-blown retreat.

On July 21, they tell me that Hessel let it slip in secret that there will be some fireworks tonight, and he added, "Things look bleak for the Jews." So, likely they'll be gassing or shooting the Jewish survivors. I keep this information to myself—since what would it matter if I warned one or another Jew? They can't escape their fate, why should they anxiously await this awful moment for hours in advance. The night passed peacefully, thank God nothing happened. The order was evidently withdrawn, since I don't think that Hessel was misinformed. Probably there isn't enough time to cover their tracks after such a massive execution.

---

23. "Good, good."

Camp Evacuation under Soviet Fire

On July 22, I am still taking apart the beds and I get a new order to sort out the new mattresses from the old. You can hear explosions in Lublin, as if some structures are being destroyed, and you can see fires in several places. We go back for lunch—while we're eating word spreads that we won't go back to work in the afternoon and that no one can leave the field. Hessel is burning all of the main files and records from the office. At 1:00 p.m. they bring in trucks with striped uniforms, bread, and sausage. They announce that the camp will be evacuated in an hour. Everyone has to put on the stripes, and take a blanket and as much food as you want. *"Ausländer"*[24] are not allowed to have backpacks, only Germans. Pietroniec gives me a Polish military rucksack and I make a deal with the German Kapo Knipp, the head of the *Dachdecker*[25] and my neighbor in the sleeping quarters: he'll carry the rucksack and I'll share the food with him that's packed inside. Now I have thirty minutes to decide what to take and what to leave. I bid farewell to my skiing gloves lined with fur and my rabbit-fur slippers which can be worn inside shoes. I got them in the fall from Mary, but sitting in the office through the winter I didn't wear them once. I take one change of underwear, a red sweater from my brother, toiletries, a chain of sausages, and a one-kilo can of meat, all of which I wrap in a blanket and tie with a thick paper rope. I put the remainder of the food from the Warsaw packages into the rucksack: lard, bacon, cake, a Haag coffee can (sent to me from my apartment) filled with sugar, coramine, Cardiosol, iodine, Vaseline, and a piece of gauze. I take all of my official correspondence which made it through the censorship, two boxes of kola tablets, and one loaf of bread. From the washroom I take a rounded handle from a short

24. Foreigners.
25. Roofers.

broom to use as a walking stick during the march. By 2:00 p.m. we are packed.

The peasants ask me what will happen with them, and I say that they will probably stay since they weren't instructed to pack up. I tell them that we left a ton of things and they should take all of it for themselves. The thunder of artillery fire keeps getting closer. We are standing in fives, friends grouped together. Lublin is burning in more or less ten places. Black curls of smoke are rising and intensifying.

The fires must have been set intentionally by the Germans, since otherwise the fire brigade would have been able to put out at least one of them during all these hours. A small passenger bus, kind of an auto ambulance, drives onto our field. It's supposed to take those who are unable to march. Tomaschek, whose leg still hasn't healed, gets in; Zakrzewski (Mickey Mouse), with an ulcer on his leg; a few other bedridden sick people; and, a surprise, two Jews with small children. We stand on the roll call square and wait. All of the *Unter-* and *Oberscharführer* are gathered with bicycles loaded with packages and suitcases. Hessel speaks at Kostial's instruction and calls for discipline during the march and warns against escape, since everyone remaining will be held collectively accountable if someone gets away. Captain Grudowski, who had most recently been working in the *Politische Abteilung*, translates all of this into Polish.

Feldführer Groffmann goes into Block 12 and breaks all the windows and mirrors in the sleeping quarters and in the kapos' and barbers' dining rooms, I hear chairs being broken. He wants to diminish the Soviets' spoils of war. We stand and wait—I recall the refrain from the recitation— "And here it's burning like hell." What are we waiting for? Probably for the Bolsheviks. Not until 5:00 p.m. do SS companies line up in front of the Field 1 gate. You can hear dogs barking. The crematorium *Kommando* enters the square running. They are ordered to immediately change into stripes. The reason for the wait has been cleared up: they tell me that they were burning the bodies of the slaughtered prisoners from the Castle all day, but that several hundred more remain in a shallow grave. So the Bolsheviks will have their first *corpus delicti*.

At last, at 5:50 p.m., we hear the order: "*Im Gleichschritt marsch.*"[26] The Jew-ish women go in front, then the Aryans, and the Jewish men at the back. One of the jokers chants "*Links, links, links*" as we march through the gate, but no one stays in step, and they count us for the last time in Majdanek. There is almost an entire regiment of SS men standing outside the gate. On the side road leading past the transformer, upward along Field 1, wag-ons are harnessed with horses. There are ten of them, and they are loaded with all of the files of the *Politische Abteilung, Arbeitseinsatz*, the camp com-mand, Revier, etc. The head of our procession has reached the *Bauhof* and the barrier by the road. There's a traffic jam on the main road, heavy guns, pontoon trucks, ambulances, peasant wagons loaded with suitcases, and soldiers on foot. So we're waiting for a gap for our procession to ease onto the road. SS men are standing on both sides of our column, all strange faces; many of them have dogs on leashes, German shepherds, Dobermans, Great Danes, bulldogs, most of them the size of calves, well-fed and tug-ging on their leashes toward us. Airplanes fly low overhead, we don't pay attention to them, then suddenly machine-gun fire rains down from above. These are Soviet planes which are shooting up the bottleneck on the road, now they are turning around and circling above our column, everything is thrown to the ground, bullets whiz nearby. The planes return several times, flying at an elevation of three hundred meters. It lasts for five to eight min-utes; finally they fly away. One SS man has been killed, one Jewish pris-oner is heavily wounded. After the planes leave we don't wait for space to clear on the main road. Tearing myself off the ground I forget to take the handle lying in the dust—I really miss having it during the march. They order us to walk along the wide embankment and ditch alongside the road. The groups of five have dissolved. Passing our barrier and coming onto the main road, which runs on top of an embankment on this segment, on the right side of the field, five hundred meters away, German artillery pieces are positioned out in the open in the middle of the field and shooting, and German tanks are cutting across the field in the direction of the enemy. Walking along the ditch, I look at the tangle on the road, and as an old

---

26. "An even-paced march."

soldier from the First World War, I can tell this isn't an army in retreat: these are the shattered remnants of units and marauders lifelessly escaping ahead. Women are sitting with soldiers on all of the wagons.

We march like this for a kilometer and then they lead us in between the fences to the side streets of Lublin. We reach the gasworks near Dziesiąta. We could have shortened our way by going straight through the *Gärtnerei*, through Dzięsiąta and the bridge, and we would have totally bypassed the main road. The person leading us is obviously not a great strategist.

A shed is burning; it's probably full of lubricants since black plumes of smoke are rising up. "Hawk" unshoulders his rifle and is beating everyone with its butt who doesn't stay in line. It's very difficult since military columns, covered wagons, and trucks are standing on all of the streets and you have to go around them.

The front of our column has stopped. Długa Street. An older woman is sitting at a high first-floor window and looks at us with tears in her eyes, her gaze meets mine. She sorrowfully nods her head and then, encouraged, she says in a half-whisper:

"They shot my son at the Castle yesterday."

"*Los, los!*" We move onward under the rail overpass, freight trains are standing there, their wagons full of military equipment, but none of the trains are moving. The DAW command joins up with us along with three hundred prisoners,[27] of course under escort as well. We pass the square in front of the passenger station. All of the exits are closed, the square is totally empty—the trains have stopped running. We go further, we pass the gate of the freight station through which they led us at 6:00 a.m. on March 26, 1943. The crows were circling over our heads then. How many of us from that transport are still alive, what's next?

I'm thinking about where we are marching to now. The Bolsheviks broke through around Chełm in a westerly direction, so they'll lead us west, probably to Puławy, to get to the left bank of the Vistula there and further on to Radom, where the camp that's subordinate to "us" is located. We pass factory buildings, I think it's a sugar factory, then we turn left onto a side street but it's also jammed with fragments from the *Wehrmacht*; we

27. On the day of the final evacuation, 229 prisoners were in the camp on Lipowa Street.

cross over the train tracks and pass a park with what look like industrial buildings, there's a German artillery gun firing somewhere in the park. "*Aufschliessen, aufschliessen,*"[28] yell our SS man escorts, terrified by the awareness that the Russians are hot on their heels. The street turns into a sandy, country road, and we pass heavy, eight-ton trucks, wagons with pontoons, antiaircraft guns, all of it sitting idly.

Twilight descends. We are distancing ourselves from Lublin but not from the front. Soviet shrapnel hits near us and explodes about a hundred to a hundred and fifty meters away. "*Los, los!*" scream the hoarse SS men. In their agitation they speak with one another in Romanian and Croatian. We keep moving past stationary German columns, are they not in a rush? It's dark now—you can only see silhouettes. A huge, red glow rises above Lublin, which grows in strength as it gets darker. I hear the order: "*Deutsche austreten.*"[29] I go to the group of "*Ausländer.*" They march the group of Germans forward separately, while they order us to turn off to the side and downhill. We are standing at the edge of a stream and they command us to cross it; I want to take off my shoes. "*Los,*" and I get a rifle butt to my back. So I just pull up my pant legs up to my knees. The water isn't deep, half a meter at most, but my feet sink deep into the mud. After we are out of the water, again "*Los,*" and you can't take off your shoes to pour out the sloshing water. Suddenly, I hear German voices—they are our kapos. It turns out that the bridge was damaged, but it was still serviceable to cross on foot, so the Germans took the bridge, while we, the "*verfluchte*[30] Ausländer,*" were hurried through the water. Now I understand why that kilometers-long *Wehrmacht* column is standing helplessly. Let's hope that the damaged bridge was the work of our underground soldiers. Crossing through the warm water wasn't bad, but I realize that the water and mud in our shoes will chafe and rub our skin during the long march.

The glow above Lublin reaches halfway up the sky. The SS men say that the *Vernichtungskommando*[31] stayed at Majdanek to burn down the entire

28. Here, "Catch up, catch up."
29. "Germans, step out."
30. Damned.
31. Extermination squad tasked with liquidating a camp.

camp and blow up the crematorium. I hear from my friends who worked in the warehouses that thousands of bottles of vodka remain in the SS canteen, thousands of articles of clothing, and railcars full of food supplies, and none of it was taken out (actually it's an exaggeration, since three cars of flea-infested beds did get shipped out). Admittedly, we don't know if they are still stacked at the station in Lublin. We keep walking along the side roads. Remnants of military units, individual trucks, and marauders on peasant wagons are everywhere. I assume that they are leading us along the back roads so as not to jam up the main highway to Puławy-Dęblin, and to avoid an ambush by underground units who might try to rescue us. I find out that there are 1,300 SS men for seven hundred prisoners (including the DAW). Since we are marching in fives, there are 140 rows, so for each row there are nearly ten SS men, five on each side. Escape is out of the question.

Rain starts to fall, it begins pouring. We are soaked to the skin, but thanks to the forced march we don't feel cold. Slowly, our clothes dry out in the warm air. Around midnight we stop in an open field, it's totally wet, I sit on my rolled-up blanket; fifteen minutes later they hurry us onward. Only now do I feel fatigue in the legs. I'm in better shape than others though, most of them used to work seated, while I was on my feet and walking around for twelve to fourteen hours a day after leaving the hospital, so I'm in good shape. It's so dark that I only see the contours of the five people marching in front of me and I hear the constant yelling of the SS men. I recall how Corporal Müller and Albrecht only spoke in Polish today on the roll call square before the march. During the march I learn that all of the bandits accused of murder being kept in the Castle were executed yesterday next to the crematorium, so Schommer's murderers also found themselves there.

I have the opportunity to make an accounting of my sixteen-month stay in Majdanek. Who caused me direct harm? With the exception of Sieberer, not one SS man laid a finger on me, and even when meeting with such a terror as Thumann, I didn't feel any of the fear that showed itself on the face of Hessel, for example. My own fellow inmates beat and insulted me: the *Lagerjüngster*, the little Jew Bubi, Rockinger, Pohlmann, Schommer, Bubi Ilke, and the scum of all scumbags, Hessel. Four of them are dead. Rockinger didn't enjoy his freedom for long and returned to the penal unit in Buchenwald—but God be with him; what really interests me will be the rest of the existence of that wretch Hessel. In any case, I have his private address, he lives on Gartenstrasse in Frankfurt an der Oder, his wife lives there, I saw the address on mail that came for him and I imprinted it deeply in my memory. I'm curious if the sentence of an underground court was carried out on Sobczak, that Gestapo dog who hounded me and put me away. The German saying goes: "God's mills grind slowly, but surely." Actually, I can't say that they are grinding that slowly at all.

My reflections aren't to suggest that the SS men are angels and only fellow prisoners are villains, but that the perfidy and hypocrisy of the camp system rests upon the infrequent involvement of the SS men in the daily dirty work. The brutalization and life's torment is left to the various creatures among the prisoners, who do this to "elevate themselves" on the backs of other prisoners.

There is thunder and lightning, after a hot day a storm is coming, it starts pouring buckets again. The bread I keep under my arm is soaked like a sponge and is slipping out. My bundle falls out of my hands, I'm left holding the rope. Someone is already on my heels. I grab my bundle under my arm rubbing my hands over it, the paper rope dissolved. What should I do? I can't carry it under my arm for long. I undo my belt, tighten it around my bundle, and I carry the pack over my shoulder, alternating from left to right. It's tiring.

We keep moving along country roads like this, we pass villages and settlements. There are army columns everywhere. Dawn is breaking. Around 3:00 a.m., once there's daylight, we come out of the forest onto the highway. There's a meadow next to it where we stop on the wet grass and spread out. I eat a piece of bread, I take off my shoes, and I scrape the mud off of my feet. They are totally black up past the ankles, I don't see any blisters for now. The German, Knipp, comes to me with my rucksack and says he can't carry it anymore, he suggests taking turns. I repack my bundle so that I can carry it easily with my hand; I sling the rucksack onto my back, and after a half-hour break, we get going. We're walking along the highway. After a few hundred meters I see a road sign: "12 km to Lublin." So we've been zigzagging all night and we've only gone twelve kilometers! Why? Where we're going—we don't know. We pass the same columns again—or maybe I'm just imagining it—which we passed before that demolished bridge yesterday. We will get to the crossroads soon, all of the army columns are turning to the right, as if to the west, we are going due south, I look at a road sign "42 km to Kraśnik." What—to Kraśnik? And so a parade along the length of the Soviet front? Instead of going as far as we can to the west! All the better if the Bolsheviks rescue us, then we'll disperse throughout the area. Back in the camp we questioned intelligent Russians about what fate might await us if the Bolsheviks liberated Majdanek. Their horoscopes weren't very reassuring: they presumed that the Bolsheviks would not free the camp, but they would start looking into each individual case to find out the reasons for why people were locked up. The fact of being locked up by the Nazis, and so a sign of an anti-fascist attitude, isn't a strong enough legitimization as far as the Bolsheviks are concerned. They can't stand anyone involved in politics, even communists from abroad. I'm reminded of the various Polish communists: Dąbala, Wieczorkiewicz, Bagiński,[32] who either ran away to Russia or got there through a prisoner exchange. After receiving honors initially they went silent, and then they disappeared without a trace. But if the Soviet armies ran into us while we were marching, we could quickly hide on our Polish home soil. There aren't many of us. Eighty Poles total.

The day is cloudy, a light rain falls every now and then. The highway turns into sloppy mud, gunk two or three centimeters thick. Herds of horses pass us, three to four hundred each, driven by Russians in German uniforms riding bareback. Two squadrons of Vlasov's army pass us, all Kalmucks with Kalmuck officers, they are patrolling near our column. We

---

32. Tomasz Dąbal was indeed killed during the Great Purge in 1937, but the other two were shot by a Polish guard in 1925.

aren't marching in tight fives anymore. I made a round of our column and I see that Wolski disappeared at night, and my friends confirm this. I learn from the German kapos that the Lublin SS and SD ran away back on Friday, July 21, 1944, with their boss, *Brigadeführer*[33] Globocnik,[34] they left no instructions as far as the peasants who remained at Majdanek. Since they were at the disposal of the SD and weren't formally registered into the camp, Commandant Liebehenschel took the formal position and washed his hands of them at the moment of evacuation.

---

33. Brigade leader.

34. Jacob Sporrenberg was the head of the SS and police force in the Lublin District at this time.

A Brickyard in Kraśnik

Around noon we have a stopover on a field during a drizzling rain. I repack my things, tying everything into my shirt, and I take my blanket as a covering. It gets soaked during the march and becomes terribly heavy, but it still protects me from the rain and wind. All of us are thirsty. The stops are made outside of villages and when we do pass them, SS guards are standing with their submachine guns at the ready next to wells and shoot in the air if prisoners get close. Sometimes a woman will bring out a bucket of water, but what's that to seven hundred people? I'm never lucky enough to get to a full bucket. Half the water is spilled out anyway since everyone is pushing and crowding around the bucket. I don't feel any hunger, I swallow kola tablets and sugar mixed with a phosphate preparation. The SS men rush us forward. Poor Zelent can barely drag himself along, no wonder, he was laid up for over two months and he hit the road straight out of bed. The road leads through the forest. We walk along its edge, since an army column is taking up the middle of the road. I tear leaves from trees and lick the raindrops off to moisten my tongue a little—sometimes I'll pick a blackberry that I happen to see, my palate is completely dry.

SS men from Lublin ride up on bicycles. They say that the Bolsheviks occupied Majdanek at 9:00 p.m., so three hours after we left; furthermore, Corporal Müller, who stopped in some bar in Lublin, was murdered. They must have been keeping an eye on him, judging that a six-week arrest wasn't a sufficient punishment for shooting a Pole. Hessel has set himself up ingeniously. He is wearing a raincoat and twirling a cane, he divided his luggage between the cook Kaźmierczak and his lackey Victor. Miron the messenger is lugging the box with his violin, and he orders Pietroniec to carry three loaves of bread in a backpack, so four and a half kilograms.

Our road is never ending. Thirty kilometers—twenty-five—fifteen—ten to Kraśnik. The mud is getting worse, the road is almost empty, we haven't seen one peasant wagon this whole time. In the afternoon we don't see any more German army remnants. We walk up a hill and the signpost

shows the road to the Kraśnik train station to the left and the road into
town to the right. The road leads downhill where Kraśnik lies in a valley. I
know since there was a labor camp there and that's probably where they'll
quarter us. They lead us through the entire city, the people have come out
into the streets, guards are watching to make sure no one says anything
to us. One of the townspeople standing by the gate of a house called out
to a friend of mine. An SS man yelled at him, and he backed into the gate.
The SS man followed him and I heard two shots ring out. We go uphill, it
seems like we're nearing the other end of the city. We turn left and we're
standing in a yard.

There is a brickyard at the back, a Hoffmann kiln, and next to it are
three sheds with piles of raw bricks; there's a house in front.

It's 7:00 p.m. We assumed that there would be a roll call, but they
order us into the brickyard, each of us looks for a spot, most people
crowd upstairs while Pietroniec and I situate ourselves on the outside of
the brickyard in an alcove that's still warm from a recently extinguished
oven. I go to the well outside and after drinking myself full, I wash my
feet so they can rest after the forced march. On top of the actual distance
between Lublin and Kraśnik, which we added to at night (marching rap-
idly from 6:00 p.m. until 3:00 a.m.), we moved about sixty kilometers.
We marched for twenty-two hours, the stopovers lasted maybe another
three hours. I'm conservatively estimating three kilometers per hour—the
distance covered should add up to sixty-six kilometers. No small achievement, even for the army, not to mention out of shape and malnourished
prisoners (such as Jews and foreigners). When I return to our sleeping
place after washing, I find Kapo Wyderka with Pietroniec. He says that
the Bolsheviks are near and that an order came down for the German,
Dutch, and French prisoners to go west; for the Poles to be released; and
the Jews—shot. There is indescribable joy among us Poles.

I go to the well to drink water again, my thirst is tremendous. One of
the residents of Kraśnik is standing there with a briefcase, he takes out
bread sandwiches with cold cuts and cheese, he gives it to me to eat, as
well as one hundred zlotys. He tells me he's prepared to lead me out to
freedom. I thank him cheerily, but tell him that it's not necessary anymore
since we are all going our separate ways soon and I will go with my friends,

and I hope that I'll meet him for a vodka as soon as today. Kapo Knipp, who split the carrying of the rucksack with me, approaches; I share my supplies with him and since he has a long road ahead, I give him more than half. He says with envy:

"You'll have food galore when you are free."

A wagon rides onto our yard with white bread, rolls, hard-boiled eggs, and thousands of cigarettes. It's being pushed by the people of Kraśnik. A group of ladies comes with the wagon and they start passing out food. All of a sudden I see Andrzej Stanisławski dressed in civilian clothes. The women discreetly hand out bottles of vodka, I get half a liter. I sit down in our alcove to stretch my legs, a woman comes up and hands me a warm coffee with milk, we're glad that we'll be free soon. The conversation lasts for half an hour before I hear calls to step away from the wagon. The SS men order the civilians to take the wagon and leave, whereas they tell us to leave the brickyard building, there will be a roll call. We stand and wait, for now they aren't ordering us to form up in fives. They call the Germans to the side, some kind of consultations are being held. *Rottenführer* Eberle comes, takes me to the side, and says:

"I know that some of you are getting ready to escape, but I warn you, sir, that the brickyard is tightly guarded from every direction, and if you try to run away you could be shot."

I believe Eberle's candor, he's probably the only SS man that I do believe. In March, before his vacation to Bavaria on the Swiss border, he revealed to Pietroniec that he likely wouldn't be coming back. And indeed, he didn't come back for a long time, until the news came that he was shot on the Swiss border and he was laid up in a hospital. Apparently his escape attempt was unsuccessful, but he was still able to weasel out of it. I didn't broach the subject with Pietroniec again after his return.

Pietroniec comes over and says that the lady brought about a dozen sets of clothing which were laid out in the shed, between the heaps of bricks, and that a number of our friends already changed and left with the ladies. Leaving were: Stanisławski, Orpisz, Krupski, Rode, and Serafin's very own father, who lives in Kraśnik, took him. But two SS men are now standing by the shed. One of the Germans comes over and says that there's either supposed to be a general execution at night, or that the brickyard will be set on fire. I see Zelent and I momentarily pass on that information. I go to the well and I think that I can get through the orchard to the yard of the neighboring house, but Corporal Kostoj comes running with a pistol in his hand and orders us to back away. I go back to our alcove and I want to lie down there, maybe in the twilight I'll manage to bolt across the yard. Kostoj approaches with his gun again and, aiming at me, he orders both Pietroniec and I to move away and go to the interior of the brickyard. They're hurrying everyone inside.

Jesus and Mary! My skill crawls. We're trapped. Upstairs it's so packed that even if you're careful you always step on someone's hand or foot. It's almost completely dark there. It's well past 9:00 p.m. I find Captain Grudowski deep in the crowd, I lost Pietroniec in the jam. I deliberate with Grudowski, what should we do, is it possible that they would finish us off? Having experienced the events of November 3, 1943, and the execution of the seventeen thousand Jews, we know that the SS men would have no scruples about eliminating seven hundred prisoners. The SS men place all of the Germans downstairs in a hallway, and around six hundred prisoners sleep upstairs. I decide to wake up at night and try my luck, maybe there will be kapos that I know by the door and they'll let me out. I fall asleep like a rock. I wake up after a few hours and I try to walk over these hundreds of people nestled together. In the dark I step on hands, legs, faces, even though I probe the area with my foot before each step, and I lose my balance a few times. People swear at me, I get kicks and shoves, finally I reach the stairs. They are covered in people sleeping in a sitting position. At last I get to the bottom. The Germans lying on the ground start questioning me, they pinch my legs, I maneuver my way forward. Several kapos are on duty at the door, they cuss me out in the coarsest terms and command me to turn around, again I step on human bodies on my way back. I finally feel my way to my spot which my neighbors have spilled into, folded up like herring in a barrel. I lie down and sigh, my attempt to get out failed, now I entrust my fate to your hands Merciful Lord, and I fall asleep.

I'm woken by cries of "*Auf, auf!*" It's gray, I see an SS man hitting people lying on the floor and driving them out. My first thought is that they didn't set it on fire, but maybe the execution will happen now. I walk down the stairs, SS men are standing in a row outside the doors and yelling: "*Los, los!*" I see those in front of me running toward the main road, an SS man in the yard kills his dog with a shot from his revolver. "Execution . . . so the dogs won't be needed anymore"—shoots through my mind.

Another row of SS men on the road, it leads uphill, around the cemetery, the procession is already marching. As we pass the cemetery, prisoners are still catching up, since only one person at a time could come down the narrow stairs.

The SS men hurry us at a much faster tempo than yesterday. Fatigue sets in. My feet are sore, bruised, blistered, and rubbed raw; we feel like we've just come down from a cross. Dr. Gabriel and R. Hett are barely dragging along, one supporting the other, I give them several kola tablets. While we are moving I learn that the Bolsheviks seized our rolling stock this morning, ten wagons of files; the SS men barely managed to unharness four horses, the rest became Soviet plunder. Ah, what a good thing, the world will learn what they locked us up for and what the secret memos say about the treatment of prisoners. So the Bolsheviks really are hot on our heels.

The two Kalmuck *sotnya*[35] in German uniforms are riding near us again. They are searching the forests, thickets, and wheat fields for runaways. I see that Zelent, Olszański, and Panasiewicz are gone. Someone says that Panasiewicz was planning to hide under the stairs in the brickyard; someone else says that an SS man claimed that after we abandoned the brickyard, they let dogs loose there which tore apart one, some say three, prisoners. I've been left completely alone. My closest friend, Zelent, the confidant who listened to my most deeply held thoughts, disappeared. God willing he finds his way to freedom and can proceed to carry out his lofty ambitions. The future Poland needs a lot of Zelents. In April I already lost my partner for serious conversations about society and politics— Wacek Lipowski. With my other friends, talk is limited to more earthly matters.

Kaźmierczak and Victor bring me some murky water to drink; this is my breakfast. The weather clears up and it gets warm. People are so tired

---

35. Russian: here, a troop of one hundred Cossacks.

and burned out, and the SS men keep hounding them to speed up, so they start to slowly throw things out, sweaters, blankets, bread, even untouched canned goods. Some are moving along without a backpack and with both hands empty. I don't part with any of my possessions. I grit my teeth, I know they will still come in handy. The worn out and weakened begin staying behind on the road, mostly Jewish men and women. At first the SS men push them forward with their rifle butts to keep them moving, and they also sic their dogs on people lagging behind the column. But seeing that some people only take two or three steps and then drop to the ground again, they let them sit. They stay behind. We hear from the SS men that the *Vernichtungskommando* is bringing up the rear and is killing anyone unable to march. They are shot behind the ear (*"Genickschuss"*[36]). Men and women are all mixed together now. The Germans carry packages for their Jewish lovers and support them. The Jews carry young girls and other Jewish children on their backs. One person drags along the other to prevent them from sitting down on the edge of the road, because that means death.

We have to cross the Vistula today, we are marching toward Annopol. One of the SS men tells us that Corporal "Hawk" was taken prisoner by Poles in Kraśnik when he went to some little restaurant at night, or maybe they killed him. That one had lived it up enough already, they don't need his assistance in Auschwitz or Mauthausen. We keep hearing shots fired, it's our SS men shooting whenever one of the prisoners approaches a well in a village we are walking past, or when someone is relieving themselves and then tries to crawl away into the rye. I've walked a long ways with Noak. Pietroniec is sore at me that we believed what Wyderka said and that we didn't immediately take advantage of the help offered us to escape. Along the way we find out that we weren't the only ones to miss out. Jabłoński's skin is split in between his eyebrows from getting hit with the barrel of a gun. He was in the middle of changing when they chased him out of the shed. Kostial stopped Miron Klisz, who was already dressed

---

36. Neck shot.

in civilian clothes at the gate, but he didn't say anything. Kostial caught Engineer Krygowski in civilian clothes, he recognized him by his close-cropped hair, he ordered him to lie on the ground while he loaded his revolver, he aimed at him, but then he holstered the weapon. Many others were turned back at the last moment. Pietroniec wants to make up for it today. He knows how greedy Kostoj is for money. He takes up a collection among us: I give five hundred zlotys that was hidden in the visor of my cap; Engineer Pilarz, a Czech, gives a gold wristwatch, and Kazimierz Gałczyński gives two hundred zlotys (both are from the Field 2 office); Pietroniec doesn't have anything himself. He takes all of this to Kostoj, hands it to him, and discusses the matter, and at the right moment he is supposed to lead us somewhere on the yard of a farmstead, ostensibly to get water from the well.

Those who threw out their bread are already tearing off ears of wheat and rye and are chewing the grain to satiate their hunger. Many prisoners are walking barefoot, because they've gotten their feet so badly chafed. Hessel is also parading barefoot. A few hours pass and Kostoj still hasn't come. Just outside of Annopol, Pietroniec asks him if he remembers about the deal. "That's right," he replies, and hands him a canteen to drink from. It's filled with vodka. Pietroniec looks surprised, Kostoj laughs and says:

"You wanted vodka after all."

"*Jawohl, Herr Unterscharführer*,"[37] replies the devastated Pietroniec.

The way into Annopol is thick with escaping German units. All of them remnants. There are no commanders to be seen. These crowds have to be formed into companies and batteries again, but that's for deep behind the front; here, facing the enemy, they are good for only one thing: to be taken prisoner. The waves of the armies escaping through Annopol must have been immense, wide tracks have been carved through the wheat on both sides of the road. An interesting sign—I keep an eye out on purpose—over the past two days we haven't come across a single squad, not one company or column moving in the direction of the enemy. Everyone

37. "Yes sir, Mr. Corporal."

is hightailing it across the Vistula. The SS men reply to groups that are passing us that we are bandits, criminals, and Jews. Some of the soldiers respond with puzzlement:

"Why are you transporting them? You should kill them all on the spot."

We reach Annopol. It's a scorching-hot day. They stop us on the street. Three buckets of water are brought from a house. Everyone lunges at the water. The SS men shoot into the air, others point their guns straight at us. I back away and give up on the water, I'd rather be thirsty. Three buckets handed out to seven hundred people and they order us onward. The SS men tell us that it's not good to drink while marching, but they refill their canteens in each village. We pass by a small town, there's no possibility of escape here. I see that we have a *Stabsfeldwebel*[38] from the *Wehrmacht* in command of our column, he bosses around all of the SS men. It puzzles us. Some of the SS men have torn the skull and crossbones emblem from the black flaps on their collars and hats. This is how they look "*Einsatzbereit*"[39] when facing the enemy. Now they're fleeing from the Bolsheviks, while in the camp they were terrified of fleas, it was enough to whisper the warning "typhus," and they were instantly afraid to enter a barracks. They are only brave when facing starved, sickly waifs. That's when they are ready to give the last drop of blood to the *Führer*—the tortured prisoner's blood that is.

We pass a town and approach a bridge. Feverish preparations to defend the bridgehead are being made. Old trees have been cut down, they're starting to dig trenches, I see two or three antiaircraft batteries. This is supposed to be a defense?

We walk down to a meadow next to the main road to make way for a jumble of soldiers tumbling by. The front is no longer behind us, we can't hear any firing.

The bridge stirs up memories in me. I marched over it—"recently," in 1915, as an Imperial-Royal cadet in the Third Dragoon Regiment in Archduke Ferdinand's Fourth Army. I was riding a beautiful chestnut then. The Eleventh Dragoon Regiment marching with us still had red pants

38. First sergeant.
39. Ready for action.

and stern, gilded helmets. We were chasing the Russian Army which was retreating in good order toward Dęblin-Lublin. Several weeks earlier I had been decorated with the silver medal of bravery; photos of me were in the *Wiener Bilder*[40] and *Interessantes Blatt*.[41] Today I'm sitting in a ditch by the road in camp stripes with a shaved head, driven forward by the rifle butts of SS men frantically running from the Russians. *Fortuna variabilis—Deus mirabilis*.[42]

"*Auf, auf, los, los.*" My legs are as heavy as logs, they're barely moving. My feet are rubbed raw and starting to blister. You don't feel it while you're walking, but after you rest, every little touch hurts. The heels of my socks are worn through and all of my toes have crept out. Taking my shoes off when we stop and rubbing Vaseline into my feet doesn't help much. After crossing the Vistula we are in the Opatów District. We've gone maybe two or three kilometers before we enter a ravine; the highway is filled with rolling stock, cars, and the fleeing *Wehrmacht* which no longer has the letter "V" painted on its vehicles. I feast my eyes on the sight. I am reminded of scenes from our roads in the second half of September 1939 after the Polish Army was defeated by the Germans.

We walk off the highway and wait, since we can't move forward along the sides. After an hour the order comes down that we will spend the night in the grove that's on a slope. The SS allows us to take sheaves of grain from the neighboring field. A group of our people went under escort to get water. I get in line and wait until that group returns. Unfortunately, for some unknown reason they don't let us go get water right away. My thirst is terrible, worse than hunger. We find out that Hessel's cook Kaźmierczak and the Russian, Victor, were shot while attempting to escape, and that one of the SS men who knew them brought Hessel the backpack with his underwear that Victor had been carrying. Others are saying that Noak was shot. In any case he's not here. Dr. Gabriel and Dr. Hett have also vanished.

40. "Vienna Pictures."
41. "The Interesting Sheet."
42. Latin: the expression is actually *Deus mirabilis, fortuna variabilis*, or "God works miracles, and fate is fickle."

Pietroniec, Pilarz, Gałczyński, and I all settle in for the night. It's cool, even cold in the morning. The grove is surrounded from all sides. Guards are standing in the adjacent fields.

At 4:00 a.m. we get the wake-up call. I'm well rested after a good night's sleep, there was no nightmare like last night's "would they light us on fire or shoot us?" I slept beautifully; the tumult, hubbub, shouting, swearing, and rattling coming from the road four hundred meters away was music to my ears. An ant colony of escaping armies was tripping over itself all night. The road is jammed in the morning as well. We are walking in pairs in the ditch, then the ravine widens and we are marching through the fields. I eat a piece of bread and bacon, but I'm terribly thirsty. Dr. Klonowski gives me a sip from his canteen. The rumor spreads that Himmler has been killed. The German kapos tell us in secret that the brickyard was indeed supposed to have been set on fire. The SS men wanted to do it, but the commandant of the transport, the *Stabsfeldwebel* from the *Wehrmacht*, categorically refused, asserting that his orders were to lead the transport to the next camp and he will carry it out no matter what. The question is why the *Wehrmacht* is leading the transport when there are 1,300 SS men here, on the way I hadn't seen a single SS officer, not even Kostial, I only see *Feldführer* Groffmann. Certain SS men, like Kostoj, are riding horses bareback and barefoot, making themselves comfortable.

Supposedly we're going to get to a train station today where railcars are waiting for us. But they were saying this before we even arrived in Kraśnik. The thirst is grueling. For the first two days I pitied those that couldn't contain themselves and scooped up water to drink from roadside ditches or puddles. Today I can't stand it any longer. I myself drink water from a puddle in the forest, assuming that it's less contaminated with bacteria than those by the road. Tough, in fourteen days we'll know whether there were any typhus bugs in the puddle. At noon, they stop us by a train track. The SS men separate out the German prisoners and sit them down by the railway gatekeeper's house next to a well. They seat the rest of us a kilometer away. All we have is a swampy puddle running along the greenery by the tracks. At first we drink water from it and fill our bottles, then we wash ourselves and soak our feet. Today we saw the first two companies of infantry marching toward the Annopol bridgehead. Could it be that the OKW[43] doesn't have any more reserves to hold the Vistula line?

We march onward. Around 3:00 p.m. we reach Ćmielów. We pass by a porcelain factory and make a turn after the train station onto an empty square. Stopover time. We're supposed to take a train from here. Where to—no idea, maybe Płaszów, maybe Auschwitz, Radom is already out of the question since it's reportedly under threat from the Dęblin side. We wash ourselves again in a pond by the station. I spread my blanket on the ground and rest. The ambulance in which Tomaschek, Zakrzewski, and others went didn't make it across the Vistula. It got stuck in the columns on the highway and was probably nabbed by the Bolsheviks.

Around 6:00 p.m. a freight train arrives with flatcars loaded with rails. They command us to sit in the middle of these cars, the SS men sit on the edges. What a comfort to ride like this. It's a little breezy but I cover myself with the blanket. We pass little stations that I do not know, I can't figure out what direction we are headed in. At night we hear an air-raid siren while we are pulling into some large station. I hear a German conductor in the next train over saying that transports to Auschwitz are standing on the line for ten days at a time because the tracks are overwhelmed. Nice prospects.

We stay like this until morning. They order us to get off and we walk for half a kilometer, we are near the steam engine depot in Skarżysko-Kamienna. Another stopover.

---

43. *Oberkommando der Wehrmacht* (High Command of the Wehrmacht).

A Shed in Skarżysko

We camp on the square near the depot. There's a carpenter's workshop next to us. They bring us warm coffee in big pots. True, "our" camp Bliżyn is here, which is subordinate to Majdanek, and provides labor for the Hasag company from Lipsk, which took over the state munitions factory in Skarżysko. There is a marsh nearby which they let us go to. I wash myself and borrow a dull razor to shave with. An SS man I know takes me as an interpreter to the depot to ask the trainmen to buy him something to eat and smoke. I anticipated the possibility of contact with civilians and I already had a postcard written to my brother telling him that I'm alive and on the road—probably headed toward Kraków-Auschwitz. I hand it to a trainman to drop in a mailbox. Pietroniec has also made contact. He got a card from another railroader with the following message: "There are four sets of clothing hidden in the plank warehouse. Climb up the boards to the attic, wait until nightfall, we'll help you escape." Pietroniec discreetly shows me the card and the door to the warehouse. We're lying down close by. We move right next to the door. The railroaders are going in and taking out planks from time to time and locking the door with a key. As luck would have it, Kapo Naumann from the *Arbeitseinsatz* and several other kapos sit down beside the door. There's shade on this side. The guards are standing maybe one hundred meters away, alongside the train tracks, facing us. A trainman comes again, he looks into the storehouse, and then I see him turning the key in one direction and then quickly back in the other, pretending that he locked the door. They bring soup from Bliżyn. Everyone diverts their attention to the food and lines up. After I get in line I observe Pietroniec. He gets up, opens the door, throws his backpack inside and closes the door behind him. I sit by the door with my soup, it's noisy again. I'm waiting until Naumann and the others get out of here. I'm thinking about whether to take my rucksack or to leave it, taking it in with me will be suspicious, but leaving it on the square will also draw attention to the fact that someone escaped when they march off. Pilarz and Kazio

Gałczyński, who know what's up and are also supposed to slip away, are sitting next to me. A trainman goes in and comes out after a moment, locking the door behind him. I wanted to call out: "What are you doing, leave the door unlocked!" but I can't, the Germans are sitting steps away from me, and I also don't know whether he is in on the plan. But it's nothing, in a moment the right guy will come and unlock it again. The SS men set up tents, it'll be easier to disappear at night. It feels like all of the guards have their eyes glued on me. We sit like this for maybe an hour, the doors are locked. Suddenly I hear the command: "*Fertig machen,*"[44] the SS men take down the tents. We are leaving. Pietroniec is staying, we have to go onward. Seconds were all that separated me from freedom. They lead us to open freight cars on a side track behind the depot. They pack us in, sixty to a car. The SS men place planks crosswise in the cars to sit on and tower over us like from a loft. It's extremely cramped. During a stop in a field, we grab a few sheaves of grain so as not to have to sit on coal dust. It's so tight that you can't stretch your legs. We agree among ourselves that one group will lie down, while the other will sit. The Dutchmen are exceptionally unfriendly, they're selfish people who want to lie down all the time. The night is cold, my legs are like wooden blocks, I can't move at all.

In the morning we start counting to figure out what day it is. We left the camp on July 22; from the 23rd to the 24th we spent the night in Kraśnik; from the 24th to the 25th we camped in the grove beyond Annopol; from the 25th to the 26th we were riding to Skarżysko, which we left at noon; so today is the 27th.

Around noon we pass Kielce. We eat the rest of our food reserves. They didn't give us anything along the way, even though it would have been easy to order a few cauldrons of coffee in Kielce. There's a German Red Cross station there and we can see German soldiers with our own eyes getting coffee. We keep going, but we are mostly stopped at small stations. The line ahead of us is backed up. No trains are going in the opposite direction, individual locomotives are all that pass us. I've counted around thirty so far. They are moving at breakneck speed to pick up more evacuation trains from Warsaw or Radom. Only once we are on the train do we see how

44. Here, "Get ready for the road."

injured our feet are from the march. Both of my small toes have water-filled blisters the size of plums. Three toenails are seeped with blood. All of us are sitting barefoot, some of my friends are developing inflammation and infections on their feet.

Night falls. We are stopped and then we go a few stations further. On July 28, we crawl along haltingly again. At the stations we see piles of suitcases, trunks, and chests being brought by civilians with swastika armbands. Run away, run away to the *Vaterland*! A train is standing next to us with a hospital unit on flatcars, including ambulances and soldiers. We talk to them. They find out that we are from a concentration camp. Without holding back they tell us that the war and everything else is lost. During the stops we collect heads of cabbage from the fields and stuff ourselves. I've already eaten all my perishable food. All that's left is my canned meat, and Gałczyński has one piece of bread. We share with each other, but in homeopathic doses, since we still have a long way to go. The rain starts to fall. We are helpless against it, all we can do is cover ourselves with blankets. We've reached Olkusz. I give a trainman a postcard to send to my brother. I learn that we are already on the territory of the Reich, but the railway worker will toss the card into the mailbox at the next station over, which is still in the General Government. I can toss out the rest of the postcards that I took from Majdanek with GG stamps. Here they are worthless. He tells me that the Bolsheviks are supposedly in Tarnów already. All of the stations have German names now.

Night falls. With every turn of the wheel I am further and further away from home and my loved ones. The secret messages and possibility of frequent contact with home have ended, and so have the packages. Now I'm all on my own. Admittedly, the interventions for my release have had no effect for seventeen months, but my family knew where to find me and my living conditions were more or less settled.

While talking to Dr. Klonowski, I learn that he spent an entire summer on my former property in Józefat in Pomerania, which the Fourth Infantry Division from Toruń purchased as a training camp. He tells me about the changes made to the manor house and distillery by the army. It's an odd turn of events that I haven't run into any of my prewar acquaintances besides Rector Drewnowski. It's a great pleasure to talk to Klonowski at least about my old stomping grounds in Józefat.

Tetych is terribly upset that Olszański left him without saying anything about his plan for escape or taking him with him. He pours out all of his grief, saying that he fed Olszański the whole time (in truth, Tetych received about ten to fifteen kilograms of food every week), that he supported him financially, and that Olszański acted like a big shot on his dime—like when he paid Corporal Albrecht twenty dollars for a bottle of liqueur.

Supposedly we are about a dozen kilometers from Auschwitz. Twilight again. I try to take a nap, since I know how knew *Zugang* are admitted into the camp. My nerves are frayed, I can't sleep, all of Majdanek passes before my eyes in a kaleidoscope of images. The camp will be different, but the SS men and their attitude will be the same, and all the more so if we are to meet Thumann again. There is the same tendency everywhere to ruin and break our spirits. Atheism, the negation of God, depriving us of spiritual solace, the opportunity to hear Mass. The chapel in Pawiak Prison was used for torture and beatings. The commandant of Pawiak put on a cassock and engaged in farcical performances to disgrace the religious vestments. Medallions and scapulars are ripped off and trampled underfoot. The clergy has their official nomenclature in concentration camps: "*Pfaffen.*" The hatred is also directed against intelligent people in general; those with academic qualifications are deliberately and consistently ridiculed. Even having glasses in the camp is a liability to their owner. Women are forced to show themselves naked in front of men in order to deaden their sense of modesty. Everyone is taught to steal, which in the camp jargon goes by the euphemism "organizing," and whoever is a better organizer, the more respect they gain. Our youth are the ones who imbibe this destructive influence the most, who absorb the basest, vulgar expressions, demonstrate the most cunning for "organizing," and are the most proud that they can taunt and ridicule senior, and even older, prisoners, whom they address as "you" with impunity.

Zugang 190 513 in Auschwitz

I can't sleep, I'm anxiously anticipating the new events that will decide my fate. I'm ready to get off; once the train reaches the station it'll be too late to gather up my things in the dark.

Around 3:00 a.m. on July 29, our wagons roll into the camp. We didn't see the name of the station, the tracks are brightly lit by arc lamps. Without waiting for encouragement, we jump down nimbly. They form us up in fives and we march through some inner gate onto a road that is fenced off from the rest of the area. Beyond the wires on the right side I see wooden barracks surrounded in mud. I hear a woman's voice, "*Kaffee holen.*"[45] The women come out, lift their dresses, sit down on crates next to the barracks, and relieve themselves. Life in the camp is waking up. It's totally dark, so the schedule is the same as in Majdanek. We pass by a large camp, we go through some inner gate again, we pass by a tower, crow's nests with guards. An empty, dark landscape. At a distance of five hundred meters the contours of a grove appear. Where are they taking us? We've passed the camp already. As we near the grove, chimneys poke out from the tree-tops. A crematorium. The roots of my close-cropped hair stand on end. We know where they are leading us. But we don't turn to the crematorium, they take us further; it's silent and empty everywhere. Are they leading us to getting shot? Again the silhouettes of trees, the outline of a large building—also with a chimney, they lead us into a large hall, we are in a bathhouse.

The local *Lagerältester* comes over, elegantly dressed, and tells us that the women will bathe first, and then the men. We learn from the local prisoners that we are in Rajsko (Birkenau), a branch camp of Auschwitz. Five crematoria are operating nonstop here, processing ten thousand people per day. I sit on the concrete floor, finally I can stretch out after several days of riding—how long I am. I fall asleep despite the light and commotion.

45. "Get your coffee."

My friends wake me up, it's time to go to the shower. We have to undress and leave everything, taking only our personal toiletries, food, and shoes. I leave and bid farewell with a warm glance to my talisman, the silk handkerchief from Mary, and the red sweater from my brother. We stand naked in a long corridor and wait for an inspection of our things. The entire bathhouse staff consists of Jews of various nationalities, mostly Czechs, Poles, and Germans. We stand and wait for several hours, they don't let us move since it has gotten crowded in the next room where barbers are cutting all the hair off of people's bodies. The windows in the hallway are covered with black curtains, even though you can see daylight through the gaps. One of the prisoners pulls back the curtain—I see women standing outside, naked, covered only with blankets. An SS man jumps forward and slaps the overcurious prisoner and threatens to shoot anyone who looks through the window. Panic sets in among us again. We know that they send people to the gas chamber naked with blankets over their shoulders, so it's clear why they don't want us to look. The same fate likely awaits us too. I am overwhelmed with resignation, I am completely defenseless and powerless.

The line to the barbers gets moving again. At the inspection at the door, they take away almost everything. They take away my golden, clip-on lenses for my glasses to shield my eyes from intense sunlight; they take my kola pills, even though I tell them that they are chocolate tablets; they throw out my thermometer and all of my letters, the last link and contact with my loved ones. Luckily, I hid coramine and Cardiosol under the sugar in my Haag coffee can. They also took my spoon and towel. I lost my toothbrush along the way. I go to the barber with only my shoes, soap, belt, glasses, and a can of sugar. This scratched-up tin can has become very valuable to me, it's the only thing that I have from my apartment on Żurawia Street. I let the barber do his work, injuring me several times with the clippers. I enter the showers, finally I can satiate my thirst, I gulp the warm water streaming over me. In the changing room they toss a shirt, pants, jacket, cap, and "socks" sewn from different-colored woolen scraps, onto my wet shoulder. I put the wet shirt onto my body, the same kind of rag as in Majdanek, they didn't give any long underwear. The clothing is dirty and greasy, the Jewish star has been cut out of the back of the jacket and resewn with a contrasting material. We go out onto the square and wait for the rest to shower. I look how I did when they dressed me up in Majdanek in March of last year.

I start camp life all over again—from the beginning. I sit down on a square covered in gravel and dirt. I'm so tired that I stretch out on the bare earth and fall asleep. After a few hours I wake up, things are moving since they are giving out soup. They hand out enameled bowls of a different shape than in Majdanek; they serve cabbage soup seasoned with flour. Not bad, but not enough. Again we wait. The kapos, block overseers, and local big shots are eyeing up our transport. Everyone is walking around in form-fitting linen stripes, narrowed at the waist, freshly laundered, and in pants with ironed creases, silk underwear, and ties—something that would be unbelievable in Majdanek. The shoes are the same—Warsaw-style.

They are supposed to register us. We go into a hall in groups, I take a spot in the line. I go to the bathroom every fifteen minutes to drink water, that's how thirsty I am, my body is resorbing all of the liquid that I consume and dissolving my thickened blood. A quarter of an hour later, I'm thirsty again. While I'm being registered I state my profession as "*Maschinenschreiber-Dolmetscher*"[46] and I get number 190 513. It would seem that everything is taken care of—I have to take the card with my number to the neighboring table. What else is there to write down? As an experienced professional from Majdanek, I'm puzzled by it. They order me to present my left arm . . . they're tattooing numbers! Every fiber in my body rebels. Am I supposed to be marked for life? The tattooing is done by Jewish prisoners. They order me to flex my muscles tightly by squeezing my fist. An instrument like a fountain pen is used by someone to perforate my number onto my arm. I am so livid that I hardly feel any pain. They don't allow us to rinse the pierced spot—I go to the bathroom immediately to suck out the ink, but it doesn't help, the number stays. I see that one of my friends has the wrong number tattooed, it has been crossed out and the correct one added next to it. The Germans (*Herrenvolk*) are exempted from the tattoos. I go outside. I watch some work squads occu-

46. Typist-translator.

pied with digging or clearing out a ditch. More of them are leaning on their shovels than working, and seeing this raises my spirits.

Around 6:00 p.m. they order us to line up. We are to march to Auschwitz. We pass sewage sedimentation tanks, reeking of excrement; one, then another crematorium, next to it are hundreds of cords of firewood, the crematoria are surrounded with a barbed-wire fence with leafy branches woven in to block the view of what's going on inside. SS guards stand by the gates to the crematoria with submachine guns. We leave through a gate under a tall tower made of red brick, train tracks where transports enter the camp run through it. We are outside the camp—fields and meadows all around. After a march of two kilometers, we reach an overpass above the train tracks of the Auschwitz O/S[47] station. We pass some freshly built factory buildings, large complexes, some of them are still unfinished, I see the signs: *Fahrbereitschaft, Schutzhaftlagerführer*, so we are nearing the camp. Suddenly, past the turn, I see a brightly lit gate with a raised barrier.

We are in Auschwitz, *that* Auschwitz O/S, whose name filled so many hundreds of thousands of mothers and wives with fear and terror!

"*Mützen ab!*"

The *Blockführer* are counting the new *Zugang*. As the old guard, we know how to march. "*Links . . . links . . . links . . .*" The barrier slowly drops behind the last five with the sign: "*ARBEIT MACHT FREI.*"[48]

Bordesholm—Maczków, Christmas Day, 1945

47. "O/S" here stands for *Oberschlesien* (Upper Silesia).
48. "Work makes you free."

Glossary

Unless otherwise noted, all terms here are from the German.

abtreten: march out.

Achtung: careful, at attention.

antreten: line up.

Arbeitsdienst: labor service; see *Arbeitseinsatz*.

Arbeitsdienstführer: see *Arbeitseinsatzführer*.

Arbeitsdienstzettel: a report on the number of prisoners employed in a *Kommando*.

Arbeitseinsatz: labor section, a group of SS men responsible for organizing prisoner work.

Arbeitseinsatzführer: the SS man directly responsible for organizing prisoner work.

Arbeitskommando: see *Kommando*.

arsch voll (bekommen): (to get) your ass kicked.

Asoziale (Aso): antisocial, a prisoner category.

Aufnahme: admission, registration, here: prisoner questionnaire.

Aufseherin: female prisoners' supervisor.

Ausländer: foreigners.

Ausländische Zivilarbeiter (AZA): foreign civilian worker.

Aussenkommando: external *Kommando*, working outside the camp.

AZA: see *Ausländische Zivilarbeiter*.

Bad: bathhouse.

Bauhof: construction warehouse.

Befauer: see *Berufsverbrecher*.

Bekleidungskammer: clothing warehouse.

Berufsverbrecher: professional criminal, a prisoner category.

Bettenbau: making beds.

Bibelforscher (Bifo): Jehovah's Witness, a prisoner category.

Blockältester: block overseer, a prisoner functionary, senior prisoner responsible for maintaining order inside the barracks.

Blockführer: SS supervisor of a prisoner barracks or group of barracks.

Blockführerstube: a room for SS barracks supervisors, office of the SS man on duty.

Blockschreiber: barracks clerk/block secretary, a prisoner functionary.

Blok: Polish, from German *Block*; barracks.

Blokhaus: see *Blok*.

bück dich: bend over.

BV: see *Berufsverbrecher*.

DAW (*Deutsche Ausrüstungswerke*): German Equipment Works, an SS defense contractor.

Effektenkammer: prisoner property warehouse.

Entlausung: delousing.

Esfauer: see *Sicherungsverwahrte*.

exekutiert: executed.

Feldführer: an SS man, head of a prisoner field.

filc: from German, *filzen*; body search.

Fluchtpunkt: here, a red dot on a white background, a mark on prisoners who attempted to escape or are suspected of planning escape.

Fluchtverdacht: flight risk.

Führer: leader, commander.

gamel: in Majdanek camp slang, an extremely emaciated prisoner.

Gärtner: gardener.

Gärtnerei: the part of the camp designated for vegetable gardening.

Gestapo (*Geheime Staatspolizei*): German secret state police.

grosse Postenkette: see *Postenkette*.

Gruppenführer: rank in the SA and SS, equivalent to lieutenant general in the German Army.

gut: good.

Häftling: prisoner.

Häftlingskrankenbau (HKB): see *Revier*.

Hauptscharführer: SS rank equivalent to staff sergeant in the German Army.

Herrenvolk: master race.

Innenkommando: a *Kommando* working on a prisoner field.

Jude: Jew.

kapo: prisoner functionary responsible for a prisoner work squad.

kleine Postenkette: see *Postenkette*.

kommandiert: to command, here: sent outside of the camp.

Kommando: prisoner work squad.

Kommandoführer: SS man, supervisor of a work squad sent outside of the camp.

Konzentrationslager (KL or KZ): concentration camp.

Kriminalsekretär: dectective sergeant, a rank in the Gestapo, equivalent to second lieutenant in the German Army.

Kuchenblech: baking tray.

Lagerältester: most senior camp prisoner, the highest prisoner functionary rank. At Majdanek they were responsible for keeping order on a given prisoner field.

Lagerarzt: SS man, camp doctor.

Lagerführer: see *Schutzhaftlagerführer*.

Lagergut: camp farmstead.

Lagerjüngster: the unofficial name for the most junior prisoner functionary, facetiously: the opposite of "camp senior."

Lagerkapo: prisoner functionary, deputy to the *Lagerältester*.

Lagerschreiber, Lagerschreiberin: the main (male and female, respectively) camp clerk; a prisoner functionary.

Lagerschreibstube: camp administrative office.

Lagersperre: quarantine.

Lagerstufe: a concentration camp regime severity ranking.

Läufer: messenger.

Läusekontrolle: lice check.

links: left.

los: forward, or let's go.

Luftschutz (OPL): antiaircraft defense.

Mützen ab: hats off.

Mützen auf: hats on.

NSV (*Nationalsozialistische Volkswohlfahrt*): The National Socialist People's Welfare, a Nazi welfare organization.

Oberaufseherin: a female member of the camp staff, head supervisor of female prisoners.

Oberkommando der Wehrmacht (OKW): High Command of the Armed Forces.

Oberscharführer: rank in the SS, equivalent of sergeant in the German Army.

Obersturmbannführer: rank in the SS, equivalent to lieutenant-colonel in the German Army.

Parteitag: party convention.

Pfaffe: derogatory, clergyman.

Politische Abteilung: Political Department.

Postenkette: chain of guard posts; at Majdanek, there is the *grosse Postenkette*, the large chain of guard posts within the borders of the entire camp, active between the morning and evening roll calls, and the *kleine Postenkette*, the small chain of guard posts right next to the camp's barbed wire fence, active between the evening and morning roll calls.

Poststelle: post office.

Rapportführer: SS man, the report officer or noncommissioned officer responsible for the prisoner count.

Reichsdeutsch (RD): German citizen living in the Reich.

Reichssicherheitshauptamt: Reich Main Security Office, the central SS organization responsible for the policies of terror.

repeta: Polish; second helping.

Revier: camp hospital.

Revierkapo: prisoner functionary serving the role of kapo at the camp hospital.

Rottenführer: rank in the SS, equivalent to private first class in the German Army.

Russische Kriegsgefangene: Russian POWs.

SA: abbreviation of *die Sturmabteilungen der NSDAP*, the assault detachments of the NSDAP, the paramilitary arm of the Nazi Party.

Sämtliche: everyone, all.

Sanitätsdienstgrad (SDG): SS man paramedic.

SAW: see *Sonderaktion der Wehrmacht*.

Scharführer: rank in the SS, equivalent to junior sergeant in the German Army.

Scheisspolacken: shitty Poles.

Schlauch: at Majdanek, the double barbed wire fence surrounding the prisoner fields.

schnell: fast.

Schreiber: clerk, a prisoner functionary in a barracks or in the camp office.

Schreibstube: the clerk's room, office.

Schuster: shoemaker.

Schutzhaftbefehl: protective custody arrest warrant.

Schutzhaftlagerführer or *Lagerführer*: SS man, chief of the prisoner department.

Schutzhäftling: literally protective prisoner, a category referring to political prisoners.

SD: see *Sicherheitsdienst*.

Sexualnot: "sexual emergency," or insatiable sexual drive.

Sicherheitsdienst (SD): Security Service of the SS.

Sicherungsverwahrte (SV): recidivist under preventive arrest, a prisoner category.

Sonderaktion der Wehrmacht: expelled from the German Army, a prisoner category.

Sonderdienst: see *Sicherheitsdienst*.

Sondergericht: Nazi special court.

Splittergraben: antiaircraft trenches, here: execution trenches.

SS: abbreviation of *die Schutzstaffel der NSDAP*, Protection Squadron of the NSDAP, an armed and uniformed structure of the Nazi Party, their main instrument of terror and extermination.

SS-*Kantine*: canteen for members of the SS.

SS-*Küche*: kitchen for members of the SS.

SS man: member of the *Schutzstaffeln der NSDAP* (SS).

SS-*Panzerjägerdivision*: SS antitank division.

SS-*Sonderkommando*: here, SS men expelled from Waffen-SS, a prisoner category.

Stabsfeldwebel: senior platoon sergeant in the German Army.

Standarte: guard companies.

Standortverwaltung: here, the camp administration and supply department.

Stärkemeldung: report on prisoner numbers.

Stubendienst: member of the barracks maintenance crew, a prisoner functionary.

Sturmführer: rank in the SA, equivalent to second lieutenant in the German Army.

Tableau: French; an event putting someone in an embarrassing situation.

Totenmeldung (or *Totenschein*): report on the death of a prisoner.

Unterkunft: accommodation.

Untermensch: subhuman.

Unterscharführer: rank in the SS, equivalent to corporal in the German Army.

Untersturmführer: rank in the SS, equivalent to second lieutenant in the German Army.

Vaterland: fatherland.

verflucht: damned.

Vernichtungskommando: extermination *Kommando*, or unit tasked with liquidating a camp.

Volksdeutsch: a person of German descent living outside the Reich, who declared themselves a member of the German nation.

Volksempfinden: national feeling.

Vorarbeiter: prisoner functionary, leader of a work squad.

Wagenkolonne: transport column.

Waldkommando: forest *Kommando*.

Waschbaracke: washroom barracks.

Wehrmacht: German Armed Forces.

Winkel: literally angle, a triangle indicating a prisoner category.

Zigeuner: gypsies.

Zugang: entry, or here: a transport of newly arrived prisoners.

Zwischenfeld: here, the area in between the barbed wire of two camp fields.

Index of Names

Note: Photo insert images are identified by the letter of the alphabet for their respective pages.

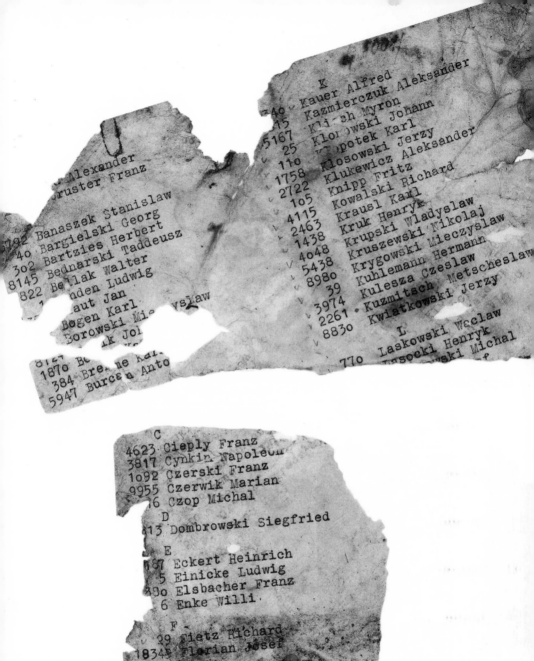

Alexander
ruster Franz

792 Banaszek Stanislaw
40 Bargielski Georg
302 Bartzies Herbert
8145 Bednarski Taddeusz
822 Be lak Walter
nden Ludwig
aut Jan
Bogen Karl   yslaw
Borowski Mie
k Jo
1870 Be   ne Ka
384 Bre   e Ka
5947 Burc n Anto

K
40 Kauer Alfred
15 Kazmierczuk Aleksander
5167 Kli ch Myron
25 Klo owski Johann
110 K potek Karl
1758 Klosowski Jerzy
2722 Klukewicz Aleksander
105 Knipp Fritz
4115 Kowalski Richard
2463 Krausl Karl
1438 Kruk Henryk
4048 Krupski Wladyslaw
5438 Kruszewski Nikolaj
8980 Krygowski Mieczyslaw
39 Kuhlemann Hermann
3974 Kulesza Czeslaw
2261 Kuzmitsch Metscheslaw
8830 Kwiatkowski Jerzy

L
770 Laskowski Weclaw
Lasocki Henryk
wski Michal

C
4623 Cieply Franz
3817 Cynkin Napoleon
1092 Czerski Franz
9955 Czerwik Marian
6 Czop Michal

D
13 Dombrowski Siegfried

E
7 Eckert Heinrich
5 Einicke Ludwig
0 Elsbacher Franz
6 Enke Willi

F
39 ietz Richard
1834 Florian Josef

G
l Fra
ar c